T5-AGB-051

ANGLICAN CLIMATE IN CONNECTICUT

HISTORICAL PERSPECTIVES FROM IMPRINTS OF THE LATE COLONIAL AND EARLY NATIONAL YEARS

Edited by

KENNETH WALTER CAMERON

TRANSCENDENTAL BOOKS—DRAWER 1080—HARTFORD 06101

TO

J. WARREN HUTCHENS

IN

SEABURY'S APOSTOLIC LINE

WITH THE SAME

CATHOLIC COMMISSION

INTRODUCTION

Largely because of their scarcity or rarity (they often appear only in restricted, special collections) or because they are too fragile to xerox, or because they are passed over by American bibliographers—even by cataloguers in the Library of Congress—Anglican pamphlets from the sixteenth century to the present have been little valued by Church historians, who have preferred books and manuscripts to the blurred printing and cheap paper of ephemeral broadsides and stitched booklets. The remarkable accumulations of tracts both in the Trinity College Library and in the Diocesan Archives remain unexplored notwithstanding the fact that certain valuable evidence can be obtained from no better sources.

Besides taking the reader into the midst of heated debate and theological battles of our forefathers, tracts explain the relevance of the sacred to the secular (e.g., why American Masonry found ceremonial Anglicanism more congenial than spartan Congregationalism); throw light on polity and church government and the conflict between religious and secular jurisdictions; reveal the strategy of Anglican convocations of clergy in an age of persecution; outline the apologetic of a Church on the defensive to protect its heritage of creed, code and cult; illuminate its quest for a protective episcopate; establish homiletical patterns, distinguishing between Anglican and Dissenter in the use of the pulpit; answer questions about liturgical practice (frequency of services, use of the Prayer Book, projected revisions thereof, ceremonial norms, and the ethos of Catholic worship); give insight into pastoral procedures and discipline; reveal the place of the arts in Anglican churches (music, bells, stained glass, architecture and color); and offer biographical information (obituaries and details concerning authorship) not to be found elsewhere. All in all, tracts offer one God's plenty!

The present sampling—chronologically arranged—is meant to stimulate serious researchers to examine resources long neglected but near at hand.

K. W. C.

COMPANION

STUDIES IN AMERICAN HISTORY

American Episcopal Clergy: Registers of Ordinations in the Episcopal Church in the United States from 1785 through 1904--with Indexes. Edited by Kenneth Walter Cameron.

The Anglican Episcopate in Connecticut (1784-1899): A Sheaf of Biographical and Institutional Studies for Churchmen and Historians with Early Ecclesiastical Documents. Edited by Kenneth Walter Cameron.

The Catholic Revival in Episcopal Connecticut (1850-1925). By Kenneth Walter Cameron.

Centennial History of Trinity Episcopal Church, Bridgeport, Connecticut, Missionary of the Catholic Faith 1863-1963. By Kenneth Walter Cameron.

The Church of England in Pre-Revolutionary Connecticut: New Documents and Letters, with a Detailed Index. By Kenneth Walter Cameron. [In progress.]

Connecticut Churchmanship: Records and Historical Papers concerning the Anglican Church in Connecticut in the Eighteenth and Early Nineteenth Centuries. Edited by Kenneth Walter Cameron.

Documentary History of the Protestant Episcopal Church in Connecticut, 1704-1789. Edited by Francis L. Hawks and William Stevens Perry. [Originally published in 1863.] (Re-edited by Kenneth Walter Cameron, 2 vols. in 1.)

Early Anglicanism in Connecticut: Materials on the Missionary Career of Roger Viets, Samuel Seabury's Communion Office, and Aids for Scholarly Research. Edited by Kenneth Walter Cameron.

Facsimiles of Early Episcopal Church Documents (1759-1789). Edited by Kenneth Walter Cameron.

The Genesis of Christ Church, Stratford, Connecticut: Pre-Revolutionary Church of England; Background and Earliest Annals... With a Detailed Index. By Kenneth Walter Cameron. An Appendix by Carolyn Hutchens.

Historical Resources of the Episcopal Diocese of Connecticut. Edited by Kenneth Walter Cameron. Index by Carolyn Hutchens.

Index of the Pamphlet Collection of the Diocese of Connecticut. By Kenneth Walter Cameron.

Letter-Book of the Rev. Henry Caner, S.P.G. Missionary in Colonial Connecticut and Massachusetts until the Revolution. A Review of his Correspondence from 1728 through 1778. By Kenneth Walter Cameron.

The Life of Eben Edwards Beardsley, Connecticut Churchman and Ecclesiastical Historian (1808-1891). By William Agur Beardsley. (Edited by Kenneth Walter Cameron.)

The Works of Samuel Peters of Hebron, Connecticut, New-England Historian, Satirist, Folklorist, Anti-Patriot, and Anglican Clergyman (1735-1826). With Historical Indexes. Edited by Kenneth Walter Cameron.

TRANSCENDENTAL BOOKS—DRAWER 1080—HARTFORD 06101

AN

ATTEMPT

TO VINDICATE

SCRIPTURE MYSTERIES,

PARTICULARLY,

The Doctrine of the HOLY TRINITY, the ATONEMENT of CHRIST, and the RENOVATION of the HOLY GHOST: Also, of the ETERNITY of the *Future Punishments*:

WITH

Some STRICTURES upon what Mr. *J. Taylor* hath advanced upon those Points.

IN A

SERMON,

Preached before the Clergy of the *Church of England*, in *Connecticut*, at their Annual Convention, at *New-Haven*, *June* 4th, 1760.

By J. BEACH, A. M. *and a Missionary from the Venerable Society for Propagation of the Gospel in foreign Parts.*

St. MATT. xiii. 25. *While Men slept, his Enemy came and sowed Tares among the Wheat.*

Printed by JAMES PARKER, *and* COMPANY,
MDCCLX.

PREFACE

IT cannot be denied that Arian, Socinian, Pelagian, *and* Latitudinarian *Errors, are gaining Ground in this Country; which, though rise and rampant in these evil Days, were in the ancient Times condemned by the Universal Church in its purest Ages: And it is a Thing of melancholy Consideration, that such an innocent young Country as this, should be debauched by them.----It seems therefore highly expedient, that the Church of* England *should bear her Testimony against them; which, as she hath always been the chief Bulwark of the Reformation, seems providentially to have been propagated in this Land, for that End; that, against those and all other Errors, she might support the Cause of pure primitive Christianity; preserving (as indeed she does) the golden Mean against all Extremes:---And that, like the Ark, the ancient Type, she might be a Refuge, amidst the boisterous Waves of this contending World, to which every honest Dove may resort, that can no where else find any Rest for the Soles of his Feet.--I am therefore glad the reverend Author hath been prevailed upon to publish this Discourse, which is very well calculated to obviate these Errors; and I pray* GOD *to attend it with his Blessing.*

S. JOHNSON.

Advertisement.

IT *is with Pleasure, we the Subscribers, having heard the following Discourse delivered, take this Occasion to testify our Approbation and Esteem thereof; as being agreeable to the sacred Scriptures, to the Doctrine of the first and purest Ages of Christianity, and to the Articles and Liturgy of the Church of* England: *And think we can do no less, than recommend it to the serious Perusal of our respective Missions uniting our Prayers that the Divine Blessing may attend it.*

New-Haven,
4th of June, 1760.

EBENEZER PUNDERSON,
JOSEPH LAMSON,
EBENEZER DIBBLE,
JEREMIAH LEAMING,
RICHARD MANSFIELD,
ICHABOD CAMP,
EDWARD WINSLOW,
CHRISTOPHER NEWTON,
JAMES SCOVIL,
SAMUEL PETERS.

St. JOHN, iii. 9.

----- *How can these Things be?*

T often happens, that the less the real Difference is, between two Parties contending about some Points of Religion, the higher the Contention arises: And by how much, of less Importance the Thing in Controversy is, by so much the more fierce and outrageous our Anger and Hatred grows against those who happen to differ from us; which may, in Part, be owing to this, that in order to justify our unhallowed Wrath and bitter Zeal, we strive to magnify the Errors of those who differ from us, and convert Mole-Hills into Mountains: Whereas, if the Difference was but fairly stated, it would appear too small to be a sufficient Ground for Alienation, much less of Rage and Persecution. Whatever may be the Cause of this unreasonable Conduct, it is certain, that at the first publishing of the Gospel to the World, the Rage of the Jews against it, was vastly more fierce than that of the Gentiles; although Christianity was infinitely nearer akin to to the Religion of the Former, than to that of the Latter; and had exactly the same Sort of Evidence of its divine Original. Indeed Christianity was nothing else but the Religion which God, immediately after the Fall revealed to *Adam*, republished in Types by *Moses*, and explained in its utmost Perfection by Jesus Christ. Yet, when St. *Paul* preached

to

to the Gentiles, all Orders of Men heard him without any Fear or Shame; but when he was at *Jerusalem*, he was obliged to preach *privately* to those of *Reputation* and *Character*, lest they should be exposed to the Malice of their Country-men; and yet these Zealots, sometimes joined in strict Friendship with the Saducees against Christianity, who denied the Resurrection, and were but little better than Atheists. So *Nicodemus*, who was a Man of Quality, in a high Station and Authority among the Jews, tho' he had conceived a most venerable Idea of our Lord, and ardently desired to converse with him, yet dared he not discover his Sentiments to the World, lest he should expose himself to much Obliquy and Reproach, and perhaps entirely ruin his own Character. He therefore paid Christ a Visit *incog.* in the Night, and when he was come into his Presence, he complimented him in this Manner; "Sir, I am fully convinced, that you are no ordinary Teacher, but a Messenger sent from Heaven to instruct Men in Matters of the greatest Moment; for the miraculous Facts which you constantly perform, are a full Attestation of your divine Legation."

Nicodemus's Faith, Self-Denial, and Fortitude, were but very imperfect. He doth not acknowledge Jesus to be the *Messiah:* Nor had he so much Courage and Resolution, as to prefer known Truth and Duty to his Reputation and Honour in the World. He was too fond of that Honour which he received from Men: Whereas, he should have been contented with that Honour which cometh from God alone. And seeing he was convinced that Jesus was a Teacher sent from God, he should have glorified God by openly acknowledging his Messenger; and not have

been

been aſhamed or afraid to learn God's Will of him. However, Christ treats him tenderly, and doth not upbraid him with his Cowardice and Inconſiſtency, but ſuits his Inſtruction ſo as to rectify the dangerous Miſtakes of his *Pupil*. And he lets him know, tho' he had begun well, yet he muſt go a great deal further, if he meant to obtain eternal Life, *v.* 3. Jesus *anſwered and ſaid unto him, Verily verily I ſay unto thee, except a Man be born again, he cannot ſee the Kingdom of* God. The Meaning I take to be to this Purpoſe; "You are dangerouſly miſtaken in thinking that your entertaining a good Opinion of me in private, and ſo maintaining your worldly Reputation, will recommend you to the Favour of God. So much will not ſerve your Turn. But if you are in good Earneſt to obtain Salvation; you muſt become an entire Proſelyte to that ſpiritual Religion which I came to publiſh to the World. You muſt renounce all worldly Conſiderations, and openly eſpouſe my Cauſe; you muſt by Baptiſm receive my Spirit, and begin a new and ſpiritual Life---Christ's ſaying to *Nicodemus*, that he muſt be born again, if he meant to ſee the Kingdom of God, is parallel to his ſaying to another great Man, *Luke* 18, 22. *Yet lackeſt thou one Thing, ſell all that thou haſt, and diſtribute unto the Poor, and thou ſhalt have Treaſure in Heaven; and come and follow me. To be born again*, certainly denotes the beginning of a new Life: *And to be born of the Spirit*, denotes the beginning of a ſpiritual and divine Life by the Operation of God's holy Spirit. It was the Cuſtom of the Jews when they admitted Proſelytes from the Heathen Nations into their Church and ſacred Polity, they not only circumciſed the Males, but alſo waſhed or baptiſed

tiſed all, both Adults and Infants; and then ſtiled them *regenerate*, or *new-born:* Becauſe they had now changed their Religion, their Nation, and all their Relations; and were entered into a new State, and become as natural Jews.

This was a very proper Metaphor to denote ſo great a Change: Therefore it was ſtrange that *Nicodemus*, a *Maſter of Iſrael*, ſhould ſtumble at a Phraſe in common Uſe among them. But ſeeing that he miſtook Christ's Meaning, and underſtood him in the moſt groſs Senſe, to make his Leſſon the more intelligible, our Lord repeats it a little more explicitly, *Aſ.* v. 5. Jesus *anſwered, Verily verily I ſay unto thee, except a Man be born of Water and of the Spirit, he cannot enter into the Kingdom of* God.---To be *born of Water*, or, as St. *Paul* calls it, *The Waſhing of Regeneration*, denotes the outward relative Change made by Baptiſm. And to be *born of the Spirit*, is to receive the Spirit of God for the Purpoſe of Sanctification, for the beginning and maintaining of that ſpiritual and divine Life in the Soul of Man, whereby the Foundation is laid for an everlaſting bleſſed Life with God, in the World to come. Christ obſerveth to *Nicodemus*, that tho' we do not know how this Life of God in the Soul of Man is produced, and how it is maintained until it endeth in eternal Glory, yet that is no valid Argument againſt its Exiſtence: For we know not the Nature of the Wind, how it riſes, how it overturneth Trees and Buildings, and how it ceaſeth; yet we are ſure of its Exiſtence by its Effects. So tho' we know not how the Holy Ghoſt (whoſe Operations upon our Minds, generally cannot be diſtinguiſhed from the Motions of our own Thoughts and Affections) doth produce in us that holy Temper and Diſpoſition

Disposition which terminates in the everlasting Vision and Enjoyment of GOD; yet that so it is, is very certain. For natural Generation can produce no nobler Effect than the animal or natural Life. The spiritual Nature, the divine Life which alone can qualify us for a blessed Immortality, must descend from Heaven, and be the Product of the Holy Ghost; who is the Author of all Holiness in the Creation. Our LORD's Argument from the Wind seems to import thus much; that a Thing is not therefore to be pronounced incredible, because its Essence or formal Nature surpasses our Comprehension. We may be absolutely certain that such a Thing is, altho' we know not how it is, or why it is. We may know, that such a Being existeth and produceth real Effects, tho' the Manner of its Existence and Operation, we can by no Means explain, but it seemeth an unscrutable Mystery. We know very well that we are the same Persons we were some Years past, but what it is that constitutes personal Indentity, we cannot discover; or what makes us the same, we know nothing at all. We are sure there is such a Thing as Power, Force and Causality, and that there be Causes and Effects in the World; for we see it every Moment; yet we have no *Idea* or Conception of the hidden Nature or Essence of Power and Force. Nor can any Mortal tell what that is in the Cause, which produceth the Effect, and so necessarily connecteth them together. Shall we then doubt whether there be any such Thing, because it is mysterious and inexplicable, altho' we experience the Truth and Reality of it every Moment? Yet after all, *Nicodemus* was dissatisfied, and would not yield his Assent to what CHRIST had taught, but asketh, *How can these Things be?* The Spirituality and Mysteriousness

Mysteriousness of the Doctrine made it seem improbable, and caused him to doubt the Truth of it. His Fault lay in this, because the Doctrine was mysterious and surpassed his Understanding to comprehend the *Modus* or Manner of it, and to know how it must be; (tho' he was convinced of the Capacity and Veracity of him who taught it,) yet he doubted of the Truth of it. And he was inconsistent with himself; for he had acknowledged that JESUS was a Teacher come from GOD, and that Men ought to apply to GOD's Messengers for Instruction in divine Matters. And after so much was admitted, he ought to have given entire Credit to his Doctrine: And if in some Respects it appeared unintelligible, yet he ought not for that Reason to have cavilled against it; but to have ascribed its Obscurity to his own Incapacity and weak Sightedness, as Beginners in all Arts and Sciences do, believing with an implicit Faith at first, until at length they come to see the Truth in the same Light as their Teachers do. But *Nicodemus* had not so much Modesty and Sense of his own Weakness and Ignorance, nor so much Confidence in his divine Instructor who sealed his Doctrine by innumerable uncontestable Miracles, as to acquiesce as a Learner in the Veracity and Ability of his Teacher, concerning those Points which he came to him to be instructed in. And a great many *Nicodemuses* there be in the World, who are much more disposed to doubt of, and call in Question, such Truths as GOD of his condescending Goodness hath been pleased to teach us by his standing Revelation, than to suspect their own Blindness and Incapacity. We all acknowledge the Bible to be the Word of GOD. The Proofs of its divine Original, tho' not so irresistible but that a Person of a captious Temper, whose

whose Humour prompts him towards Infidelity, may find some Thing in it to cavil, and to wrangle against; yet it is so evident and clear, that no honest Mind and Lover of Truth, can fail of Conviction. The Doctrines and Laws contained in the Holy Bible, are worthy of God; plainly calculated to promote the Glory of God and the Good of Men, and to raise us to the highest Pitch of Virtue and Happiness that human Nature is capable of. The miraculous Facts and innumerable Prophecies recorded throughout the sacred Volume, evidently fulfilled, and now fulfilling, prove the Doctrines and Laws to be divine. That the Bible hath not been forged nor adulterated, we have at this Day the same Proofs, but much stronger, than we have for the Genuineness of any the most creditable History, public Record, or Book of standing Laws, now in Use in any Nation.

Now this Revelation containeth many Discoveries of an extraordinary Nature, relating to the invisible and spiritual World, which lie quite out of the Road of common Experience. When therefore we apply ourselves to the Study and Contemplation of these heavenly Doctrines, we presently find our Intellects *nonplussed* as to the Manner of them; many Mysteries start up which we cannot fathom, many Knots appear, which we cannot untie, and Difficulties which we cannot surmount. Now what shall we do in this Perplexity? Shall we conclude that there is no Truth in such Doctrines as are clearly and repeatedly taught in the holy Bible, because there is a Difficulty attending them? Then for the same Reason we must part with all religious Truths, both natural and revealed;† for natural Religion

B

† Tho' I use the common Distinction of *natural and revealed* Religion, yet I do not think, that there ever hath been any true Religion discovered by the meer Light of Nature: But for all the fine Schemes of Morality, called *natural* Religion, we are indebted to the Father of Lights, for his Revelations afforded to Mankind from the very Beginning; without which, I believe, Men would have had no Religion at all, or that which would have been worse than none. For demonstratively to discern the evident Connection of Truths and Duties, when by the Help of Revelation we are brought to the Knowledge of those Truths and Duties; and to discover the same, with the divine Authority enjoining them upon us, by our own Sagacity; are two very different Things: And it doth by no Means follow, that Men are capable of the *Latter*, because they are of the *Former*. The right Notion of *natural Religion* is, not those divine Truths and Duties which meer uninstructed Nature would ever have discovered of itself, (for they, as appears by undeniable Fact, would have been very few, if any,) but those which having been discovered by Teaching, either Divine or Traditional, do, upon due Consideration, evidently appear to be founded in the Nature of the Things themselves. Whereas, *revealed Religion*, properly so called, relates to Matters above our Reason, and Matters of meer Institution.

ligion hath its Mysteries as well as revealed. And if we are too arrogant to believe Mysteries, we must turn Atheists, and even deny our Senses. And yet even that will not mend the Matter; for then we shall be haunted with the most palpable and shocking Absurdities of all.

Is it not then more reasonable to suppose, that in the holy Bible, the Wonders of the Spiritual World are discovered to us; not indeed, as they really are in themselves, but in such a Light, as our weak Eyes can best bear the Sight of them? And that since heavenly Things must be revealed to us in earthly Language, and to our low Capacities, or not at all; this must unavoidably make them appear to us unaccountable? And tho' God revealeth them to us in such a Manner as best suiteth our present Capacity, yet when we cease to think and speak as Children, and enter into the *Inheritance of the Saints in Light*, we shall then see them as they are, and all Obscurity and Mystery will vanish in a Moment?

Perhaps,

Perhaps, you will ſay, we muſt follow Reaſon, as our Guide, and not believe what we have no good Reaſon for.

This I readily grant: Reaſon muſt be our Guide in Religion: We muſt embrace nothing as true, but what we have good Reaſon to believe is ſo. But then, we muſt know when we have good Reaſon for our Belief, and not reject that Evidence which it is no Diſparagement to the ſtrongeſt Reaſon to yield to. When once a Propoſition is proved to be true by many concurring Paſſages of God's Word, let the Manner of it remain ever ſo unaccountable, yet we have good Reaſon to aſſent to it. For we certainly do not underſtand the Eſſence of any Thing in this World. We cannot conceive how Graſs and Trees can grow as they do; how our Blood can circulate, or how our Souls can think, will, remember, or move our Bodies. The whole World is a Myſtery to us, and we are a Myſtery to ourſelves. Shall a Myſtery then ſtartle us, and cauſe us to withhold our Aſſent to a Doctrine proved to be true by God's Teſtimony? Human Reaſon hath its Province and Sphere to act in; but when it goeth beyond its proper Bounds, it becomes Folly and Arrogancy; then the Wiſdom of Man is Fooliſhneſs with God: By our Reaſon we muſt try a Revelation, whether it be of God, by Reaſon we muſt judge of the Meaning of any Paſſage in holy Writ.

But then it is contrary to Reaſon and to that Modeſty which becometh Man, *who is born like the wild Aſſes Colt*, to conclude, that a Doctrine which is plainly taught by the holy Spirit, is abſurd and to be exploded, merely becauſe of the Obſcurity which attendeth it; when that Obſcurity doth not ariſe from the imperfection of the Revelation, but from the Weakneſs

and

and Darkneſs of our own Underſtandings. Is it not the moſt unreaſonable Thing in the World, and next to Madneſs, when an Article of Religion of the higheſt Importance is proved by a great Number of concurring Texts of holy Scripture, for us to ſlight and redicule it, merely becauſe we are not capable of diſtinctly explaining it, and of clearing up all the Difficulties which belong to it? For when God is pleaſed to reveal to us his Nature, and the wonderful Things of the ſpiritual World, common Reaſon and a very ſmall Portion of Modeſty muſt teach us in that Caſe, to expect and to prepare ourſelves to meet with many unaccountable and incomprehenſible Things in ſuch a Revelation, As our Lord obſerved to *Nicodemus*, *John* iii.. 12. *If I have told you earthly Things, and ye believe not, how ſhall ye believe if I tell you of heavenly Things?* If Nature and Providence abound with Myſteries, is it a ſtrange Thing if we meet with the like in Revelation?

But, to come to Particulars: (Beſides what I have already ſpoken of, *viz.* Our Renovation by the Holy Ghoſt) among many Inſtances which might be given of Doctrines plainly taught in holy Writ, which yet have been cavilled at, and exploded, upon the Score of Difficulties attending our underſtanding them, I ſhall name three more. *Firſt*, The Doctrine of the ſacred Trinity: *Second*, The Expiation or Atonement of Christ: *Third*, The Eternity of the Puniſhments of ſuch as die impenitent. Theſe I chooſe to conſider diſtinctly, becauſe they are fiercely attacked by that Spirit of Innovation, which is growing very much into Faſhion.

Firſt, As to the Doctrine of the bleſſed Trinity, if it had been intimated only once or twice in the Holy

Bible

Bible, in that Caſe we might have been at a Loſs to know what to make of it. But as the Matter now ſtands, from the Beginning of *Geneſis* to the End of the *Revelations* there ſeems to be a plain Declaration of this Propoſition, *viz.* That altho' the Godhead is but one, yet in this Godhead there are three diſtinct Perſons or Subſiſtences. The very firſt Sentence in the holy Book ſeems plainly to reveal the bleſſed Trinity. *In the Beginning God created the Heaven and the Earth.* In the Original the Word is plural, GODS, or the divine Perſons *created the Heaven and the Earth.* And we know, that the Hebrew Language is very exact, ſo that one Letter added to a Word, augments its Meaning: As when GOD changed the Names of *Abram* and *Sarai*, for *Abraham* and *Sarah*, it denoted a great Alteration in their State. And the ſame Word is always tranſlated GODS, when it is applied to the Heathen Deities. And agreeable to this, it is remarkable, *Eccl.* xii. 1. In the Original it is plural, *Remember now thy CREATORS, in the Days of thy Youth.* So *Gen.* i. 26. *And God ſaid let US make Man in OUR Image, after OUR Likeneſs.* Here is certainly the Appearance of more Perſons than one in the Godhead: For if GOD be but one Perſon, where is the Propriety of ſuch plural Expreſſions? So, *Gen.* iii. 22. *And the Lord God ſaid, behold, the Man is become as ONE of US.* *Gen.* ii. 7. GOD ſaid, *Go to let US go down.* When the Deity ſaith, *US, OUR,* and ONE of US, how can we expect any clearer Intimations of a Plurality of Perſons in the divine Nature than theſe be? But to evade this a twofold Anſwer is invented: *Firſt*, It is pretended that GOD here ſpeaketh in the Stile of Princes, who ſay, *We*, inſtead of *I*. But I would obſerve this is but a late Cuſtom:

Cuſtom: No Inſtance of it is to be found in *Moſes's* Writings, or in any Writings for ſome Thouſands of Years after his Time. And the Foundation of that modern Mode of Speech, is becauſe Kings repreſent many, *i. e.* all their People; but this can not be the Reaſon of the Almighty's uſing that Stile.

Secondly, They aſſume, that GOD here ſpeaketh to the Angels.

But there is not the leaſt Foundation for ſuch a Suppoſition. Nor is here the leaſt Intimation of the infinite Being's putting himſelf upon a Level with his Angels. And when there is no warning given of any Creatures being taken into Council with GOD, and yet GOD ſaith, *Let US go down, let US make Man in OUR Image and after OUR Likeneſs, and Man is become as ONE of US*, ſuch Expreſſions neceſſarily induce us to think, that there are more Perſons than one in GOD. How can we avoid ſuch an Opinion, when we are ſo naturally led into it, unleſs we willfully ſhut our Eyes againſt the Light, and reſolve to pervert the plaineſt Declarations, and to put off the cleareſt Aſſertions, with any Kind of Evaſions? Which Method would defeat the Deſign of the cleareſt Writings in the World. If we indulge ſuch a Liberty, no Book can teach us any certain Truths: For evidently there is as much Difference between *I, Me*, and *Mine*, and *US, ONE of US*, and *OUR*, as there is between a ſingle Perſon and a Plurality of Perſons. Again, we read, *Gen.* iv. 1. That when *Eve* had born her firſt Son, ſhe called his Name *Cain*, becauſe, ſaid ſhe, *I have gotten a Man from the Lord.* Which in the original Hebrew, is Word for Word thus, I have gained a Man the JEHOVAH. From hence it evidently appeareth, that our firſt Parents knew that the

the SEED of the Woman, who was to redeem them from all the Miſchief which the Devil had brought upon them, was to be JEHOVAH, or the eternal GOD incarnate; tho' through their eager Deſire and Expectation of his ſoon appearing, they miſtook their firſt Child, for IMMANUEL. I would obſerve once for all, that whenever we meet with the Name *Jehovah*, which is generally tranſlated the LORD, it always denotes the one eternal ſelf-exiſting GOD; and never is applied to any meer Creature. *Pſ.* lxxxiii. 18. *Thou whoſe Name alone is JEHOVAH.* We read, *Gen.* xviii, that the LORD JEHOVAH appeared unto *Abraham* in this Form, three Travellers came to him and eat and drank with him, and one of them is called the LORD JEHOVAH; and when the two Angels departed towards *Sodom*, ſtill that divine Perſon continued and talked with *Abraham.* Who could this be but the ſecond Perſon in the holy Trinity, who before his Incarnation appeared in Human Form; whilſt the Father *no Man hath ſeen or can ſee?* This adorable Myſtery, is in a Multitude of Places in the Old Teſtament intimated, altho' not ſo clearly revealed as in the New. Thus, *Num.* vi. 24, 25, 26. *The Lord* (Jehovah) *bleſs thee and keep thee. The Lord* (Jehovah) *make his Face to ſhine upon thee, and be gracious unto thee. The Lord* (Jehovah) *lift up his Countenance upon thee, and give thee Peace:* Which Benediction of the holy Trinity in the Language of the New Teſtament, runs thus, *The Grace of our Lord Jeſus-Chriſt, the Love of God, and the Communion of the Holy Ghoſt, be with you.* All Happineſs floweth from the Father's Bleſſing, the Son's Grace, and the Spirit's Peace.

Again, *Deut.* vi. 4. *Hear O Iſrael, the Lord, our God,*

God, is one Lord; from whence, the modern Jews argue againſt the holy Trinity. But when it is rightly underſtood, it is a very full Proof of it: For, the LORD (*Jehovah*) denoteth the divine Eſſence, or Godhead; and the Word GOD, is plural, and denotes the three Perſons, our Creator, Redeemer and Sanctifier: And the Text may be thus paraphraſed. Hear O *Iſrael*, JEHOVAH (the divine Nature and Eſſence) who is our GOD, our Creator, Redeemer and Comforter; is but one *Jehovah*, (one divine Nature, Eſſence or Subſtance.) Or thus, the Father is *Jehovah*, the Son *Jehovah*, and the Spirit *Jehovah*; and yet they are but one *Jehovah.* This Sentence is introduced with a Note of Attention, *Hear O Iſrael*; but is it any Thing ſurpriſing, to hear that One is One, or that the LORD is one LORD? Therefore I cannot avoid thinking that the Word GOD, here imports a different Senſe from the Word LORD, or JEHOVAH; that is, it denotes the bleſſed Trinity, who are coeſſential.

Thoſe Things which in the Old Teſtament are appropriated to the one true GOD, in the New Teſtament are expreſsly aſcribed to JESUS-CHRIST, thus, *Pſ.* xlv. 6. *Thy Throne O God, is for ever and ever. Pſ.* cii. 25. *Of old haſt thou laid the Foundation of the Earth, &c.* Now, we find by *Hebr.* i. 10. that theſe Things were ſpoken to, and of CHRIST; which implies, that he is the true GOD. So, *Iſa.* vi. 1, 7, 8, 9, 10. There the Prophet tells us, that he ſaw the Glory of the LORD, and heard the Angels crying and ſaying one to another, *Holy, holy, holy, Lord God of Hoſts. And he ſaid, go and tell this People, hear ye indeed, but underſtand not, &c.* Now St. *John*, when he citeth this Paſſage, acquainteth us, that this Glory

ſaw, was the Glory of CHRIST. *John* xii. 41. *Theſe Things ſaid Eſaias, when he ſaw his Glory and ſpake of him.* Again, *Jere.* xxiii. 6. The Name of CHRIST is the LORD JEHOVAH, (our Righteouſneſs). Another clear Declaration of CHRIST's divine Nature we find, *Micah*, v. 2. *Thou Bethlehem Ephratah, though thou be little among the Thouſands of Judah, yet cut of thee ſhall be come forth unto me, that is to be Ruler in Iſrael, whoſe Goings forth have been from of old, from everlaſting.* So, *Zacha.* ii. 8, 11, *For thus ſaith the Lord of Hoſts, The Lord of Hoſts hath ſent me unto thee.* Here is one JEHOVAH of Hoſts ſent by another JEHOVAH of Hoſts, to dwell amongſt them. *Zacha.* xii. 10. GOD ſays, *They ſhall look upon me, whom they have pierced*, which in the New Teſtament is ſaid to be fulfilled in CHRIST; who muſt therefore be GOD. Indeed GOD could not be pierced by them, unleſs he were incarnate.

As the Knowledge of the holy Trinity, and of the Atonement which the Son of GOD in our Nature was to make for the Sins of the World, became neceſſary to Mankind after the Fall, as a Foundation of religious Hope, and a proper Encouragement to Repentance: So it is reaſonable to think, that the Method of offering bloody Sacrifices by Way of Expiation, was then inſtituted by GOD himſelf; in order to preſerve among Men the Belief and Expectation of the Coming of the *Lamb of God, who was to take away the Sins of the World:* And who was therefore called *the Lamb ſlain from the Foundation of the World*, being ſo exhibited in thoſe Types: As the LORD's Supper was inſtituted to keep up the Remembrance of that great Sacrifice afterwards, until the End of the World. For as this Cuſtom did prevail early and univerſally,

 not

not only among Idolaters, but among the moſt religious Worſhippers of the true GOD, ſuch as *Abel* and *Noah*; ſo Reaſon alone would never have led Men ſo univerſally into ſuch a Practice to placate the Deity. And as the Knowledge of theſe Myſteries and Inſtitutions, were preſerved by oral Tradition, ſo in Proceſs of Time they were corrupted, but yet not entirely loſt, even among the Gentiles: For when *Nebuchadnezzer* and the *Roman* Centurion ſpeak of the Son of GOD, I cannot think, but that it was owing to the Remains of the primitive Revelation: Or at leaſt they had learned it from the Jews. For the Jews in their moſt degenerate State, knew that GOD had one Son, and that this Son of GOD was of the ſame Nature with the Father. And they condemned CHRIST for Blaſphemy, becauſe he anſwered affirmatively to their Queſtion, *Art thou the Son of God?* So, *John* v. 18. *Therefore the Jews ſought to kill him, becauſe he ſaid that God was his Father, making himſelf equal with God.* Which implieth, that they knew the Son to be of the ſame Nature and equal with the Father. Therefore the Writers of the New Teſtament make no Kind of Apology for their teaching the Doctrine of the Trinity; which might have been expected, if it had been entirely new and unheard of before. Thus St. *John* beginneth his Goſpel, *In the Beginning was the WORD*; which might appear very ſtrange and unintelligible, if we do not conſider, that the WORD of GOD, was a Term in Uſe at that Time to denote a Perſon in the Deity, or the only Son of GOD. Tho' the modern Jews, merely in Spight to Chriſtianity, are Enemies to the Doctrine of the Trinity, yet in the Ages which preceded CHRIST Advent it was not ſo. But the *Word* of GOD, and the

Word

12

Word of the LORD, is a common Term in the moſt ancient Jewiſh Writings now extant, to denote a divine Perſon.

* And when the Text hath only JEHOVAH, they they paraphraſe it, *The Word of the Lord*; for which no Reaſon can be given, if they did not believe that there are more Perſons than one in JEHOVAH. Thus, *Gen.* xxviii, 20, 21. *Jacob vowed a Vow, if God will be with me, then ſhall the Lord be my God*; which they tranſlate thus, *Jacob* vowed a Vow, ſaying, if the WORD of the LORD will be with me and keep me, *&c.* then ſhall the WORD of the LORD be my GOD. In which they plainly acknowledge the WORD of the LORD to be a divine Perſon; and ſuppoſe that *Jacob* dedicated himſelf to him, as to his GOD. So, on *Gen.* iii. 22. they uſe theſe Words; the WORD of the LORD ſaid, *Behold Adam whom I have created, is my only begotten in the World, as I am the only begotten in the Heavens above.*

Indeed the Chriſtian Religion, which teacheth the Doctrine of the con-ſubſtantial Trinity, and Satisfacton for Sin by the Blood of the *Meſſiah*, is as old as the Fall, being then preached to our guilty Firſt Parents, to encourage their Repentance with the Hopes of Pardon and eternal Salvation upon their new Obedience; which Myſteries before CHRIST's coming were vailed with Types and Figures, but now appear with open Face in the Goſpel. And there never hath been but this one true Religion. All other Religions which have ever appeared in the World, have been only Corruptions of, or Excreſcences from this divine Syſtem. And *Mehometiſm* is nothing but a corrupt Branch of the Hereſy of *Arius*: So that we have the

* See Biſhop *Patrick*'s Comment, upon *Levit.*v. 19.

the Conſolation to know, that we live by the ſame Faith, and venture in the ſame Bottom with all true Believers from the Beginning.

Having cited a few out of many Teſtimonies in the Old-Teſtament, let us now come to the New. Here, it appeareth in ſo full and ſtrong a Light, that one would think, that no honeſt Mind could fail of Conviction; For throughout the New-Teſtament there is a conſtant and clear recognizing of three divine Perſons by the Name of the Father, the Son, and the Holy-Spirit. Thus, *Matt.* xxviii. 19.---*Baptizing them in the Name of the Father, and of the Son, and of the Holy-Ghoſt.* *Luke* i. 35. *The Holy-Ghoſt ſhall come upon thee, and the Power of the higheſt ſhall overſhadow thee: therefore that holy Thing which ſhall be born of thee, ſhall be called the Son of God.* Here each divine Perſon is diſtinctly named, the Holy-Ghoſt, the Higheſt, *i. e.* The Father, and the Son of GOD. *John* xv. 26. *When the Comforter is come, whom I will ſend unto you from the Father, even the Spirit of Truth, which proceedeth from the Father, he ſhall teſtify of me.* Here is the Son who ſends, the Spirit who is ſent, and the Father from whom he proceedeth. 1 *Cor.* vi. 11. *But ye are waſhed, but ye are ſanctified, but ye are juſtified in the Name of our Lord Jeſus Chriſt, and by the Spirit of our God.* Here the three bleſſed Authors of our Salvation are diſtinguiſhed from each other. The LORD JESUS, and GOD. *i. e.* The Father, and his Spirit, *Eph.* ii. 18. *Through him we both have an Acceſs by one Spirit to the Father.* Here is the Son thro' whom, the Spirit by whom, and the Father to whom we are reconciled, and have Acceſs. 2 *Cor.* xiii. 14. *The Grace of our Lord Jeſus Chriſt, and the Love of God, and the Communion of the Holy Ghoſt, be with you all.*

all. Now, why should we in Baptism be dedicated to the Son and Holy Ghost, equally and exactly in the same Manner as to the Father, and why blessed in their Names just as in his, and why should all be commanded to worship and honour the Son, as they do the Father, if the Son and Holy Spirit be not divine Persons? If they are not equal Co-partners in the Godhead, why should they have an equal Share of our Adorations? It is certainly one great Design of the Christian Religion to banish Idolatry and Creature-Worship out of the World, and our Lord JESUS hath taught us to worship one GOD alone. Would it not then be a strange Inconsistency, if this same Gospel set up two meer Creatures to be worshipped and adored together with the Father? That the Rite of our entering into the Church should be performed by an Act Creature-Worship, and our Dismission from our solemn public Assemblies should be an Act of Idolatry?

Our LORD saith, *John*, x. 30. *I and my Father are ONE.* Not one Person, (as *Sabellius* dreamt) but one Thing, one Being, one Essence. For ONE, in the Original is not of the masculine, but of the neuter Gender. So it is, 1 *John*, v. 7. *There are three that bear Record in Heaven, the Father, the Word, and the Holy Ghost; and these three are one.* † *i. e.* One Nature and Substance. So, *Phil.* ii, 6. *Christ Jesus, who being in the Form of God, thought it not Robbery to be equal with God.* *John* x. 38. *The Father is in me, and I in him.* How can the Father and the Son be reciprocally in each other, unless they are consubstantial?

† Some doubt of the Genuineness of this Text, because not found in some ancient Copies; but it cannot reasonably be doubted, when it was quoted and alluded to by St. *Cyprian* and *Tertullian*, within about 150 Years of the Time of St. *John*.

CHRIST saith, *John* xii. 45. *He that seeth me, seeth him that sent me.* How can this be true, if he were not the same Substance with the Father?

If there be no Perfection or Attribute belonging to the Deity, but what is in holy Writ ascribed to CHRIST; if there be no Honour or Service due to the true GOD, but what is likewise due to CHRIST; if no Works performed by the Father, but what likewise are performed by CHRIST, except personal Acts and Properties, such as begetting the Son, and communicating the Godhead to him by eternal Generation: If this be really the Case, I would fain know, how we can deny CHRIST's real and eternal Godhead, without renouncing the Bible. And that the Former is true, will easily appear; *e. g.* Is the Father the true GOD? So is CHRIST. 1 *John* v. 20. *We are in him that is true, even in his Son Jesus Christ. This is the true God.* Is the Father the Great GOD? So is CHRIST. *Titus* ii. 13. *The Great God and our Saviour Jesus Christ.* Is the Father the Supreme GOD, and blessed for ever? So is CHRIST. *Rom.* ix. 5. Is the Father the mighty GOD? So is CHRIST. *Isaiah* ix. 6, 7. *For unto us a Child is born, unto us a Son is given---his Name shall be called Wonderful, Counsellor, the mighty God, the everlasting Father.* Is GOD eternal, without Beginning or Ending? So is CHRIST. *Rev.* i. 8, 11. *I am Alpha and Omega, the Beginning and the Ending, saith the Lord; which is and which was, and which is to come, the Almighty. I am Alpha and Omega, the First and the Last.* These are the Words of the Son of Man. Is our GOD, the living GOD, or he who *liveth?* So is CHRIST. *Rev.* i. 18. *I am he who liveth, and was dead, and behold I am alive for ever more.* None but the true GOD can say in this Sense, I am he who

who *liveth.* Is our God alone the Jehovah? So is Christ; as hath been largely proved already. Is God the neceſſary and ſelf-exiſting Being, and therefore ſaith, *I AM?* Is God unchangeable? So is Christ. *Hebr* xiii. 8. *Jeſus Chriſt, the ſame Yeſterday, To-day, and for ever.* When God would diſtinguiſh himſelf from all other Beings, and take to himſelf his peculiar Titles, he ſaith, *Iſa.* xliv. 6. *I am the Firſt, and I am the Laſt, and beſide me there is no God.* Yet theſe Perfections our Lord aſſumes to himſelf. Is the true God the Almighty Creator of all Things? So is Christ. *John* i. 3. *All Things were made by him; and without him was not any Thing made, that was made.* *Coll.* i. 16. *By him were all Things created that are in Heaven, and that are in Earth, viſible and inviſible, whether they be Thrones or Dominions, or Principalities, or Powers: All Things were created by him, and for him; and he is before all Things, and by him all Things conſiſt.* Doth God preſerve and uphold all Things? So doth Christ. *Heb.* i. 13. *Who being the Brightneſs of his Glory, and the expreſs Image of his Perſon, and upholding all Things by the Word of his Power.* *John* v. 17. *My Father worketh hitherto, and I work.* Is God omnipreſent? So is Christ. *Matt.* xviii. 20. *Where two or three are gathered together in my Name, there am I in the Midſt of them.* *John* iii. 13. *No Man hath aſcended up to Heaven, but he that came down from Heaven, even the Son of Man which is in Heaven.* He was in Heaven at that Inſtant, when being upon Earth, he ſpake theſe Words. Is God omniſcient, and doth he know all Things? So doth Christ. *John* xxi. 17. Saith *Peter* to him, *Lord thou knoweſt all Things.* Doth God alone know the Hearts of Men? 1 *Kings* viii. 39.

39. *Thou, even thou only knoweſt the Hearts of all the Children of Men.* So doth Christ. *John* ii. 24, 25. *But Jeſus did not commit himſelf unto them, becauſe he knew all Men, and needed not that any ſhould teſtify of Man; for he knew what was in Man.* Is God the holy and peerleſs Being? So is Christ. *Rev.* iii. 7. *Theſe Things ſaith he that is holy, he that is true.* Is God the Lord and Owner of the Univerſe? So is Christ. *Acts* x. 36. *He is Lord of all.* Is all religious Honour, Adoration and Worſhip due to God alone? So it is to Christ. *John* v. 23. *That all Men ſhould honour the Son, even as they honour the Father.* *Heb.* i. 6. *When he bringeth in the firſt begotten into the World, he ſaith, and let all the Angels of God worſhip him.* Is God alone to be loved with all our Heart and ſerved with all our Strength? So is Christ. *Phil.* i. 21. *For to me to live is Chriſt.* Is an abſolute Truſt and Affiance due to God alone? So it is to Christ. *Pſ.* ii. 12. *Bleſſed are all they who put their Truſt in him.* Laſtly, Is God alone the proper Object of Prayer, being able to hear and help at all Times? So is Christ. *Acts* vii. 59. *And they ſtoned Stephen, calling upon God, ſaying, Lord Jeſus receive my Spirit.* Chriſtians are ſtiled, ſuch as call upon the *Name of Chriſt.* 1 *Cor.* i. 2. *All that in every Place call upon the Name of Jeſus Chriſt our Lord.* Seeing then, every Thing peculiar to the one true God, is ſo fully, frequently and clearly in holy Writ aſſumed of Christ, how ſhall we know by the Bible, that there is any true God, at all, if we deny Christ to be ſuch?

If Self-Exiſtence, if Eternity, if Omnipotence, if Omnipreſence, if Omniſcience, &c. do not prove Christ's natural Divinity, pray, how can we poſſibly diſtinguiſh between the true God, and a meer Creature?

ture? For my Part, if I could once think, that the Son was not co-essential and con-substantial with the Father, I should immediately conceive a very low Opinion of the Scriptures: For tho' I should esteem the Doctrine false, yet I could not possibly persuade myself, that it is not a Scripture Doctrine.

And as the Father and the Son, are Omnipresent, so is the Holy Ghost. *Ps.* cxxxix. 7. *Whither shall I go from thy Spirit?* Are the Father and Son omniscient? So is the Spirit, 1 *Cor.* ii, 10. *The Spirit searcheth all Things, yea, the deep Things of God.* May we swear only by GOD? *Deut.* vi. 13. *Thou shalt fear the Lord thy God, and serve him, and shalt swear by his Name.* So may we swear by the Holy Ghost. *Rom.* ix. 1. *I say the Truth in Christ, I lie not, my Conscience also bearing me Witness in the Holy Ghost.* Are our Bodies the Temples of GOD? So are they the Temples of the Holy Ghost. 1 *Cor,* iii. 16. *Know ye not that ye are the Temple of God, and that the Spirit of God dwelleth within you?* Are the Father and Son Almighty? So is the Holy Ghost. The Creation of the World is ascribed to him. *Gen.* i. 2. *The Spirit of God moved upon the Face of the Waters.* *Job* xxvi. 13. *By his Spirit he garnished the Heavens.* The miraculous Works of CHRIST, which none but GOD could perform, were the Works of the Father and of the Spirit. *John* x. 37. *If I do not the Works of my Father, believe me not.* *Matt.* xii. 28.---*If I cast out Devils by the Spirit of God.* And as the Son and Holy Spirit are GOD, so they are represented, as being as distinct from the Father, and from each other, as any three Persons whatsoever. The Father *did beget,* the Son *is begotten,* the holy Spirit *proceedeth,* and *is sent.* He who begetteth, is a distinct Person from him who is begotten

 of

of him. So the holy Spirit must be a distinct Person from the Father and the Son, from whom he *proceedeth.* The Father and the Spirit, were not made Flesh; but the Son was. The Blood of CHRIST was the Blood of GOD, *Acts* xx. 28, But it was not the Blood of the Father, nor of the Spirit. And as the Holy Ghost is distinct from the Father and Son, whose Spirit he is; so he is a real Person, and that divine. 1 *Cor.* xii. 11, *But all these worketh that one and the self-same Spirit; dividing to every Man severally as he will.* The Spirit and his Gifts are plainly distinguished. Will and Choice belong only to a Person. *Acts* xiii. 2. *The Holy Ghost said, separate me Barnabas and Saul for the Work whereunto I have called them.* He is *the Comforter, the Spirit of Truth, he convinceth the World of Sin, &c.* These are all personal Actions. And to lie unto the Holy Ghost, is to lie unto GOD. *Acts* v. 3, 5.

Thus, we see, that the Doctrine of a co-essential Trinity is not built upon a few obscure Expressions in holy Writ, but it is most clearly and repeatedly taught in innumerable Passages throughout the holy Bible. It is now Time to inquire what there may be to outvie and weigh down all this Scripture Evidence? The most weighty Objection that ever I could hear of, is to this Purpose: Three Persons denote three distinct and separate Beings. And it is impossible that there should be three real Persons of Men, without being three Men; therefore it is impossible that there should be three Persons in the Godhead, unless there be three GODS; and three GODS, altho' we should suppose them to exist in ever so great an Harmony or Tritheism, is abhorrent to Christian Ears. They therefore, rather choose to think that CHRIST's *Supreme Godhead,*

is

16

is no more, than, *as he is by the Father appointed Lord, King, and Governor of all.* This Appointment and Commission, *is our Lord's Supreme Godhead.*†

But I would observe, That the Word Person, (tho' Scriptural) when applied to this Mystery, doth not convey altogether the same Idea, as when it is applied to the Creatures. But it is used in this Case, because we have no properer Term in Human Language to express it by. We mean no more, than that the Father is God, the Son is God, and the Holy Ghost is God; all subsisting in one Godhead, or divine Essence; and yet the Father is not the Son, nor the Father or Son the Holy Spirit. And where is the Absurdity, or Contradiction in this Representation which is made in the holy Scripture? We do not say that three Persons are but one Person, or that but one God is three Gods; nor any Thing equivalent.

All the Difficulty ariseth from our not comprehending the divine Nature, which admitteth of a Plurality of Persons in one and the same Essence; while our Nature doth not so. And we ought not to measure the divine Nature by our own: For that is true when ascribed to God, which is false and contradictious when applied to Men. To say that a Thousand Years are as one Day, and one Day as a Thousand Years, is false when affirmed of Men, but true with Regard to the Deity: He is no older now, than when he created the World. God's Manner of existing is so infinitely different from ours, that we should be very cautious of judging of his Nature by our own. And, do those Men get rid of all Difficulties, who deny the Son's eternal Generation? They are compelled to acknowledge that Christ is Supreme God: But then they say

† See Mr. *John Tarlor*'s Notes on *Rom.* xi. 5.

say, his Supreme Godhead is only by Appointment or Commission. If so, then any Man that ever lived on Earth, might have been the Supreme God; if the Father had been pleased to appoint him to it. They deny him to be by Nature God; yet they give him the Honour and Worship which is due only to the living and true God, If they say that God's Command obligeth us to adore the Son, equally with the Father; they say true: But then, while they think the Son a meer Creature, and the Object of our Adoration only by Appointment, they must think, that God's Laws are not founded in the Nature of Things, and are inconsistent with themselves; and that they oblige us to Creature-Worship, and Idolatry; when at the same Time he hath most expresly forbidden it: And hath declared himself a *jealous God*; and that he *will not give his Glory to another.*

They allow Christ to be Omniscient and Almighty; for he created the World, and will judge Mankind; which requireth infinite Knowledge and Power. But then they deny his Eternity, and say he is but a temporary *Supreme God*; an Almighty God, who once was nothing, and may be reduced to nothing again; and can you form even in your Imagination, greater Absurdities? Thus some Men *strain at a Gnat, and swallow a Camel.*

Secondly. I come now to the second Article abovementioned, *viz.* Christ's Satisfaction. When once Men have robbed Christ of his divine Nature, it is not so great a Wonder to see them attempting to degrade his Atonement, and to hear them saying, ‖ *That it is no Disparagement to the Dignity of our blessed Lord, or the glorious Work of Redemption, that among Men are found*

‖ Mr. *J. Taylor*'s Paraphrase on *Rom.* p. 48. 51. 2d Edit.

found Actions similar to his, both in Nature and Effect. And that he cannot better explain himself, when he says Christ's Love and Obedience, is a just Foundation of the divine Grace, than by the following Instance. There have been Masters willing, now and then, to grant a Relaxation from Study, or even to remit deserved Punishment, in Case any one Boy, in Behalf of the whole School, or of the Offender, would compose and present a Distitch or Copy of Latin Verses. This at once shewed the Master's Love and Lenity; and was a very proper Expedient for promoting Learning and Benevolence in the Society of little Men training up for future Usefulness, and, under due Regulations, very becoming a good and wise Tutor. And one may say, that the kind Verse-Maker purchased the Favour in both Cases; or that the Learning, Ingenuity, Industry, Goodness, and Compliance with the Governor's Will and Pleasure, was a just Ground, or Foundation of the Pardon and Refreshment, or a proper Reason of granting them.

So then, the great Mystery of Man's Redemption, which nonplusseth the Intellects of Angels, 1 *Pet.* i. 12. is become a very plain, easy, and familiar Thing: So far from being worthy of the Study of Cherubims, that every Child at the first Glance, may understand the *Ground* and *Foundation* of it. But alas this Representation is as distant from Truth, as it is from Mystery: For,

First, It is built upon the Popish Doctrine of Works of Supererogation; or voluntary Works, besides, over and above God's Commandments, which is absolutely false, arrogant and impious.

Had Christ been a meer Creature, tho' the most innocent and virtuous in the Universe, and had he died a violent Death a Thousand Times, and in every Death

Death had he endured a Thousand Times as much Shame and Pain as he did upon the Cross; tho' his Obedience and Sufferings might have rendered him inconceivably dear to God, yet would they not have merited Salvation for any other Creature. For all this would be no more than paying a Debt. Every Creature oweth this to his Maker, to do, and to suffer all that he layeth upon them. When we love God with all our Heart, and serve him with all our Strength, (which, to be sure, is the Utmost we can do) we only discharge our Debts to him; we are unprofitable Servants, and have done no more than was our Duty. Tho' the School-Boy may do more than his Task, and so merit Pardon and Relaxation for his Fellow Scholars; yet no Creature can do any more than the Task which God hath set him. That which makes Christ's Obedience productive of Effects more noble, not only in Degree, but in Nature or Kind, is, that it is not only eminent and perfect, but it is the Obedience of God, and not of a meer Creature. And tho' Christ did his Father's Will in undertaking the Work of our Redemption, yet was it not a Task which he was obliged to, as all that we can do for God, is.

Secondly, So far is it from being true, that we can *purchase* God's Favours for others by our Obedience, and buy off their deserved Punishments by our eminent Worth, as the School-Boy is supposed to do, that we cannot obtain Pardon for our own Sins, nor Acceptance for the best Works we ever performed, without an Interest in the Blood of Christ. The holiest Man that ever lived, is a Sinner, under Guilt, and stands in Need of Mercy. The Law affordeth no Mercy. The best Work that ever such an eminent

nent Saint as *Abraham* did, is defective, sinful, and exposeth to Punishment when tried by the perfect Law. The only Foundation of our Pardon and Acceptance, is the Blood of that *immaculate Lamb which taketh away the Sins of the World.* Good Men it is true, work out their own Salvation: Nay, in some Sense they *save* others; but not in that Sense as CHRIST *saveth* us; not by meriting, nor by *purchasing*; but by qualifying themselves for that Salvation which CHRIST alone hath purchased. And even this is not of themselves, but is owing to the Influences of the holy Spirit, which CHRIST has purchased; and is the Gift of GOD.

What this Author calls eminent *Worth* in such Men as *Abraham*, which, he says, is *similar*, or like in its *Nature* and in *its Effects* to that Obedience and Merits of CHRIST, by which he redeemed the World, because it did procure Blessings for others; is so far from being *similar in its Nature and Effects*, that it is for CHRIST's Righteousness alone, as the meritorious Cause, that GOD doth at all accept, or is pleased with their imperfect Obedience.

Our Obedience, if perfect, would be only paying a Debt; but as it is very imperfect, and doth not quadrate with GOD's perfect Law, it would be sinful Disobedience and Unworthiness, were it not for CHRIST's invaluable Merits; which have procured for us the Covenant of Grace. So that all the Blessings and Rewards which ever have been bestowed upon good Men for their moral Worth, or upon others for their Sakes, are really and truly, the blessed Effects and Fruits of CHRIST's Blood; in *whom God is reconciling the World unto himself, not imputing their Trespasses unto them.* The Law requireth perfect Obedience:

Whether GOD can consistently with his Wisdom and Justice dispense with the Law, is not the Question. That he hath not done so, is out of Question. The best Man's Obedience, when compared with the Law, hath the Nature of Sin. Now as it is the Blood of CHRIST that cleanseth from all Sin, so the sinful Imperfections of good Men's Obedience, are forgiven upon his Account, and the Rewardableness of their imperfect good Works, ariseth from his infinite Worthiness.

Where was there ever a more eminent Instance of moral Worth than St. *Paul?* Yet he said truly, I am *Nothing*. All his Worth was derived from CHRIST. It is very true, good Men have, and must have a personal Righteousness in Respect to the Law of Grace. But they have no Righteousness, no Worthiness at all, in Respect to that perfect Law which CHRIST fulfilled. Our Obedience is a subordinate not a co-ordinate Cause with CHRIST's in our Salvation: Or rather it is only a necessary Qualification in us, requisite to render us capable of an Interest in the Merits of his Obedience. And tho' we must imitate CHRIST, yet we can no more imitate him in redeeming, than in creating the World. To what Purpose doth this Author argue from its being our Duty to die for CHRIST, and to lay down our Lives for the Brethren, that therefore we must merit in the same Manner as CHRIST did; unless he means to prove, that we must redeem one another; nay, redeem CHRIST; as he hath redeemed us?

In a Word, if our Obedience, which hath in it the Nature of Sin, be of the same Nature with spotless Innocence and perfect Obedience; if Law and Gospel be one and the same Thing; if to believe, repent,

pent, and accept of Pardon; be the ſame Thing as never to need Repentance or Forgiveneſs; if Grace and Works be the ſame; then may CHRIST's Obedience and our's be the ſame in Kind, and Produce the ſame, or ſimilar Effects; but not otherwiſe. Nay,

Thirdly. Let us ſuppoſe that CHRIST, being a meer Creature, did a great deal more than he needed, or than GOD required, and that his overplus Merits were imputed to us, and ſet to our Account: Yet, how could this redeem us? Our ſad Caſe was thus: *Adam* had forfeited *his* Right to Immortality, and had communicated to us a corrupt and mortal Nature, without a Poſſibility of eſcaping Death, or a Power of riſing again. So that we were loſt, dead, and under the Dominion of the Devil, *who had the Power of Death.* Now GOD *ſent his Son into the World, that we might live through him.* He ſatisfied the Law by dying, He died not as a Debt, not by Compulſion, as other Men do, but at his own Election, *John*, x, 18. *No Man taketh my Life from me, but I lay it down of myſelf. I have Power to lay it down, and I have Power to take it again.* His human Nature being vitally united to the Divine, and the Law being ſatisfied, it was impoſſible for him to be detained by Death. And now being raiſed to Life again, he is become the Fountain and Source of eternal Life to all Mankind in a future State. As our Life in this World is derived from *Adam*, ſo our Life in the World to come, is from CHRIST. *Our Life is* now *hid with* CHRIST *in* GOD, *Coll.* iii, 3, As the Life of the Tree in Winter is hid in the Root. *As in Adam all die, ſo in* CHRIST *ſhall all be made alive.* CHRIST *is the Reſurrection and the Life.* CHRIST's human Nature being united to the Divine, is that *Bread of* GOD *which cometh down from Heaven, and giveth Life to the World.*

John, vi. 33, Hence St. *Paul* aſcribes our Juſtification and Victory over Death, rather to CHRIST's Reſurrection, than to his Death, *Rom.* viii. 34. *It is* CHRIST *that died, yea, rather that is riſen from the Dead.* Yet, after all, to pretend to explain the Myſtery of Redemption, or to pretend to ſay, from whence the Neceſſity ariſeth of an Atonement for Sin; why without ſhedding of Blood there can be no Remiſſion of Sin; why no Blood but that moſt precious Blood of the Son of GOD can take away Sin, I dare not, becauſe I don't find that it is revealed. And perhaps, the Reaſon why it is not revealed, is, becauſe we are not at preſent capable of underſtanding it. But that the Thing is ſo, though we cannot ſay, why it is ſo, is as certain as Words can make it: Nay, it is the Grand Point in which all the Rays of Revelation, from one End of the Bible to the other, do unite and centre. And, is it not then, very ſurpriſing, when Men, who have a great Veneration for the holy Bible, aſſume, that the Blood of any Martyrs in Kind though not in Degree, is as expiatory for Sin, and doth in the ſame Manner make an Atonement and Satisfaction for the Tranſgreſſions of other Men, as the Blood of CHRIST did? Is this the Language of the holy Scriptures? The Blood of *Abel*, and of all the Martyrs *crieth* for Vengeance; whilſt the Blood of CHRIST crieth for Mercy, *and cleanſeth from all Sin.* Was it in their own Blood, or in the Blood of the Lamb, that the Martyrs *waſhed their Robes and made them white*? *Rev.* vii, 14. Tho' I do not pretend to underſtand the Secrets of the Divine Councils, or what Satisfaction for Sin, the eſſential or governing Juſtice of GOD doth require: Yet if I can underſtand the plaineſt Declarations concerning our Redemption, which are obvious to the moſt curſory

cursory Reader, throughout the whole Bible; not all the Worthiness and Righteousness active and passive, of every Saint and Martyr, from the Beginning to the End of the World, is sufficient to deliver one single Soul from Hell, and advance him to the Glories of God's Kingdom, *Ps.* xlix, 7, 8. *None of them can by any Means redeem his Brother, nor give to God a Ransom for him. For the Redemption of their Soul is precious, and it ceaseth forever.*

Indeed, this Author found himself under a Necessity to pull down with his own Hands, all that he had built upon this false Foundation. For thus, he says,* *Nor is our Faith and Dependence in Revelation directed to any other Worthiness,---but that of our blessed Lord and Saviour Jesus Christ.* This, in Effect, is to give up the Point: For if Revelation directeth us according to the Truth of Things, there certainly cannot be any other Worthiness in the Universe besides that of our blessed Redeemer; *i. e.* none of a similar Nature, none of which produceth similar Effects; but all Worthiness and of the most eminent Saints (tho' for Christ's Sake they are well pleasing to God) yet in Point of *Merit, and for Dependence of others,* they are no better than than *filthy Rags and broken Reeds.*

To hide the Deformity of this monstrous Doctrine of Supererogation, *he is obliged to put in a* Caveat, viz. † *That it cannot belong to us to set a Value upon the Obedience and Goodness of supposed Saints, and then determine how much it shall redound to the Benefit of ourselves or others.* But this Cover is too thin; for if it be true, that other good Men have a Worthiness and Righteousness altogether like Christ's, and productive of the same salutary Effects for other Men, as our Lord's is

* Page 52. † ibid.

is, altho' not in so high a Degree: Why may we not then, have *some* Dependence on the Merits of these Saints; tho' we cannot tell how to set an *exact* Value on them? Where there is *something* to be had, tho' we are at a Loss to know justly how *much* it is, yet surely we may have *some* Expectations and Dependence; tho' not *so great* as if we knew the exact Sum of their Merits.

And if this Doctrine be sound, I should be loath to lose the Comfort and Advantage of it. And tho' some of their Saints in the *Romish* Church are *suppostititicus*, yet the Scripture Saints, are Saints indeed, Why then may we not pray to God in their Names, as well as in the Name of our Lord Jesus Chist? if this Doctrine be true, why may we not beg God's Mercy by the Worthiness of St. *Peter*, or by the Merits and Sufferings of St. *Paul*? He says, because God hath not appointed it. But still the Question returneth, If it be true, that many Saints have done and suffered more than they needed for themselves, in like Manner as Christ did, and if their Obedience and Righteousness, like his availeth others for Pardon and Salvation; why doth not Revelation direct us to look to, and depend in some Measure upon their Merits? The only Answer which can with Truth be returned is this: Because there is no such Thing in Nature; but it is a mere Fiction and Chimera. Thus, you see, how one Extreme begetteth another, and Socinianism sinks into Popery,* But, then there is an extreme

* Mr. *Taylor* carries the Doctrine of Merits and Supererogation, as high as any Romanist whatever, but differeth from some of them, in denying the Pope's Infallibility, or Skill to set a Value upon the Surplussage of Merits that remain in the Church Treasury, and his Right to keep the Key, and to grant Indulgences and Pardons upon, or out of this common Stock of Merits. In which Opinion, many, otherwise good *Catholicks*, do concur with him.

extreme on the other Hand, which we muſt beware of. For while this Author maketh our good Works to be as meritorious in Kind, as CHRIST's: There are ſome, who will not allow our Repentance and Goſpel Obedience to bear any Part at all in our Salvation, no, not as a Condition or neceſſary Qualification. Whereas, nothing is more evident, than, that tho' CHRIST did fulfil the Law of Perfection for us, and freed us from it's Condemnation: Yet CHRIST himſelf hath enjoined his own Laws upon us in the Goſpel. He hath commanded us to believe in him, to repent, to mortify our Luſts, &c, Which Things CHRIST never performed for us. If by his Grace we perform theſe Things, through his Merits we ſhall be finally juſtified and ſaved. But if we neglect them, in the Day of Judgment CHRIST's Righteouſneſs will be a uſeleſs Plea to prevent our Condemnation. And to reproach this Doctrine, as teaching *Self-righteouſneſs*, *Salvation by our own Works, and as joining our own Righteouſneſs with* CHRIST'*s, and as falling from Grace to Works*, IS VERY UNJUST; for it is only a truſting to CHRIST alone to ſave us in his own Way; who is the Author of eternal Salvation to them that obey him, and to none elſe,

Fourthly. One Thing more I deſire to Name, becauſe it is much ſpoken againſt by the ſame Sett of Divines, that is the everlaſting Puniſhment of thoſe who die impenitent.

They ſay it would argue Revenge in GOD, and cannot conſiſt with his infinite Goodneſs, &c.†

I will not abuſe your Patience by entering into Particulars. But let me a little inquire. How do we know, but that the vicious Habits contracted in this Life,

† See *J. Nicoll Scott*'s Sermons,

Life, may render bad Men utterly incapable of the Happineſs of the Next; and that their being excluded out of the Kingdom of Heaven, and left in utte Darkneſs, may not be the natural Effect and neceſſary Conſequence of their paſt Wickedneſs? How know we, that the bad Habits and helliſh Tempers acquired in this World, can be put off and exchanged, when we feel the dreadful Effects of them in the World to come? How do we know, but that the everlaſting Flames of Hell are kindled and upheld by the voluntarity Pravity and Malice of the Damned? How do we know, that if GOD had informed us, that our Wickedneſs ſhould expoſe us to none but temporary Inconveniencies and Evils, that this would have been ſufficient to bring Sinners to Repentance; eſpecially, if they knew at the ſame Time, that they ſhould outlive their Puniſhments, and enjoy an Eternity of Bliſs and Glory?

Though we know that GOD is infinitely good, yet we may conſtantly obſerve in this World, that Perſons by neglecting Self-government, and indulging a perverſe Humour for a While, may ruin a good Conſtitution, and deprave their Minds paſt Recovery: Nay, by one preſumptuous Action, may in a Moment undo themſelves; ſo, that even Repentance, tho' ever ſo ſincere, will not retrieve the Miſchief. And why Wickedneſs perſiſted in, ſhould not have as fatal Effects with Regard to the next World, who can tell?

Who can tell, but that the Sight of the ſad and amazing Fruits of Diſobedience in the Devils and wicked Men's eternal Miſery, may be the Means of preſerving innumerable Worlds of intellectual Beings, in their Integrity? Who knoweth, whether the Hell of Devils and bad Men, may bear any greater Proportion

portion to the Reſt of God's inconceivably vaſt Creation, than one ſmall Priſon to a great and flouriſhing Kingdom; in which all the Reſt of the Inhabitants are very happy? Who in that Caſe would reproach the King with Cruelty; when theſe miſerable Priſoners came into it by their own Choice, after ſufficient Warning; and would be a Nuſance to the Reſt of the Inhabitants, if they were releaſed? Sure I am, that the Scripture Declarations, that the Puniſhments of the Damned ſhall be perpetual and endleſs, are full as clear, as that the Rewards of the Saints ſhall be ſo. And it giveth no Intimation, that there ſhall be any future Probations or Trials after Death. And I would not be he that ſhould encourage Sinners to make the Experiment, for more than the Devil offered our bleſſed Saviour; For in that Caſe I ſhould only act the Part which the old Serpent did with *Eve*, who flattered her that God was too good to put his Threatenings into Execution: And ſaid, *Ye ſhall not ſurely die.* For the Devil to pretend to more Mercy than God, is no new Thing.

God is good, ſay ſome, therefore an everlaſting Hell is impoſſible. And they might as well ſay, God is good, and therefore there can be no Hell at all; nay, no Evil, no Sin, no Sorrow and Miſery in this World. Tho' God maketh no Creature for Miſery, yet he certainly hath made Men and Angels ſuch free Agents, and put them in ſuch a Condition, that through their own Perverſeneſs and abuſe of their Powers, they may, and many actually do make a wrong Choice, and make themſelves miſerable. Our Lord, not merely as a Law-giver, but as a Prophet and Teacher declaring Facts and Events, hath ſaid, *Matt.* xxv, 46 *Theſe ſhall go away into everlaſting Puniſhment: But the Righteous*

Righteous into Life eternal. Did Christ intend that we ſhould regard this Doctrine as a Reality, or only as a Scare-crow? *Numb.* xxiii, 19. *God is not a Man that he ſhould lie, neither the Son of Man that he ſhould repent: Hath he ſaid, and ſhall he not do it? Or hath he ſpoken, and ſhall he not make it good?* As we judge of other Men's Hearts by our own, and all Men have pretty near the ſame Affection, ſo my own Experience teaches me, that Fear is the King of all our Paſſions, and we have no Appetite ſo violent, but that ſtrong Fears will check and controul it. And there is nothing that can enter into the Imagination of Man, more dreadful and amazing, than that *Fire which ſhall never be quenched, and that Worm which ſhall never die.* He therefore, who in any Shape, goes about to abate Sinner's Fears, and to make this Matter doubtful, doth in Proportion weaken the moſt powerful Argument in Nature to awaken them to Repentance: And whether he knoweth it or not, is the Dupe of Satan to harden unhappy Wretches in their Courſe to eternal Ruin. It's very true, God is good, infinitely good: But then his Goodneſs is a holy, wiſe, and juſt Goodneſs. We, ſhort ſighted Creatures, are not competent Judges of what it becometh the Wiſdom and Goodneſs of the Governor of the Univerſe to do. We know too little of his Counſels to determine, what the ruling ſo many Millions of Millions of intelligent Creatures requireth. It may well ſatisfy us, that tho' we know not how, yet we ſhall know hereafter, the Reaſons of the divine Diſpenſations; and being tranſported with the Contemplation of divine Wiſdom and Goodneſs, we ſhall join with Angels in that Acknowledgment, *Rev.* xvi, 5. *Thou art righteous O Lord, which art, and waſt, and ſhalt be, becauſe thou haſt judged thus.*

Upon

Upon the whole, *Let us earnestly contend for that Faith, which was once delivered to the Saints.* That the eternal Son of God should become Man, and deliver us from Death and all Evil, was that reviving Doctrine, which God of his infinite Pity taught our first Parents, immediately after their Fall: And hath been the strong Consolation of all good Men in every Generation. *Abraham* rejoiced to see Christ's Day, he saw it and was glad. *Jacob* went out of the World longing for this *Salvation of GOD.* This was *Job's* Support under his dreadful Calamities, that *he knew that his Redeemer liveth.* With *David* it *was all his Salvation, and all his Desire.* But what need I name Particulars? This *was the Desire of all Nations.* And that with good Reason; for it openeth to our View a most ravishing and transporting Scene; the eternal and only begotten Son of God is become our Brother, Bone of our Bone, and Flesh of our Flesh. By this Union of God and Man, by this Conjunction of Heaven and Earth, we, Worms of the Dust, are higher advanced, and are become nearer a-kin to the Deity, than any Order of the Angels. By this Pledge we are secured of God's everlasting Love, in Consequence of his Promise and Oath. Christ being the Son of God by Nature, we his Brethren thereby become the Sons of God by Adoption; and so Heirs of God, and Co-heirs with Christ. God is his Father, and therefore our Father: And *because he liveth, we shall live also.* This stupendous Event is the Admiration of the Angels, and the Envy of the Devils. Therefore have they always been attempting to corrupt and undermine this inestimable Truth, and transcendent *Mystery of Godliness, God manifest in the Flesh.* But my Brethren, let not

Satan have the Satisfaction of beguiling and cheating you out of it. If you once let go your Hold, you will become like a Stone rolling down a steep Hill; and perhaps never stop till you settle in Infidelity, Scepticism, or no Principles at all: Which hath been the Case of a great many. Men may know, when they begin to make too free with divine Revelation, by twisting it to what Sense their wanton Humour pleaseth; but God knoweth, where such Arrogancy will end. I must own, I am so far from conceiving a meaner Opinion of the Bible, because I find Mysteries in it, that I look upon them as a strong Proof of it's divine Original; for human Sagacity never could have invented them. And they are all *Mysteries of Godliness*: That is, revealed in such a Manner, as to have the strongest Tendency to make Mankind Godly, righteous, charitable, pure, and in every Respect virtuous, happy and excellent Creatures. Those Expressions are very pertinent to this Case, *Job*, xxviii, 28. *And unto Man he said, Behold, the Fear of the Lord that is Wisdom, and to depart from Evil is Understanding.* God hath limited our Knowledge in this World, and confined it to the Bounds of Practice. He hath revealed the Things of the spiritual World to us, so far, as is sufficient to make us wise unto Salvation: And we can know enough of God, so as to love, fear, and obey him. And that will lay the Foundation for our everlasting Happiness in the next State, which will be a World of Light and Knowledge. And methinks, Men do not shew their Wisdom, but their Weakness, when they attempt to explain the Mysteries of God's Word by Hypotheses of their own Invention, however ingenious: For the Effect always must be, that either they explain them away to

nothing, as the Socinians have done; or elſe after all their Pains, they remain inexplicable ſtill; for it is not in Man's Power to mend the Word of God.* I ſhall now conclude with a few Words to you my reverend Brethren, which, it is like, will be the laſt that I ſhall ever addreſs to you. I beſeech you, for the Glory of the great God, which doth in a ſpecial Manner depend upon your Conduct; for the Honour of our bleſſed Lord Jesus Christ, who hath betruſted you with his glorious Goſpel, his Authority and his Church, which is the purchaſe of his own Blood; for your own eternal Intereſt, which is nearly connected with that of your People; and for the Love of your Hearers' Souls, which in a ſhort Time muſt all be inexpreſſibly happy, or undone to Eternity; *Take heed unto yourſelves, and unto your Doctrine.*

Let us ſtudy carefully to acquire and propagate ſuch Ideas and Conceptions of divine Things, as the holy Spirit in the Bible teaches, without any Bias towards human Schemes, whether ancient or modern; which like *Wood, Hay, and Stubble, will be burnt.* And tho' the Authors and Propagators of them may be ſaved, ſo as by Fire, yet will they ſuffer Loſs.

But if you faithfully preach the true Senſe of the holy Scripture, which lies open and fair to the View of honeſt and inquiſitive Minds: And if you adorn, this ſound Doctrine with an exemplary Life; if you both teach and do God's Will, your Reward will be great in the Kingdom of Heaven. *Yet a little While, and*

* The Athanaſian Creed is not an attempt to explain; but to bring into one View, what in divers Places of holy Writ is revealed concerning the holy Trinity and the Incarnation. Nor is there one Propoſition in it, which being conſidered with common Candour, may not be eaſily and certainly proved to be true by the Word of God. And even that damnatory Sentence meaneth no more, than our Saviour's Words, *Mark*, xvi, 16. *He that believeth not ſhall be damned.*

and he that ſhall come, will come, and will not tarry. And when the great Shepherd and Biſhop of our Souls ſhall appear, he will applaud and reward your Fidelity; and ſay, *Well done thou good and faithful Servant, enter thou into the Joy of thy Lord.* O happy End of a Chriſtian Courſe! What Applauſe! What Shouts and Acclamations of Millions of the heavenly Courtiers will welcome you into your eternal Preferments! The Riches and Honours of this World are childiſh Trifles; nay, the triumphs of the *Roman* Generals after their Victories, and all the Grandeurs of mortal Men, are not to be named with the Magnificence of that bleſſed Day. The Bliſs is too big, too noble and divine, for the Idea of it to enter into the human Mind: All the Languages on Earth do not afford any Words to expreſs it; and you never can know what true Pleaſure Means, until you obtain the *Euge* and Approbation of our eternal Judge.

Foreſeeing then, *the Joy ſet before us*, let us put on the Reſolution of bleſſed *Paul*, Acts, xx, 24. *I count not my Life dear unto myſelf, ſo that I might finiſh my Courſe with Joy, and the Miniſtry which I have received of the Lord Jeſus, to teſtify the Goſpel of the Grace of God.* With which heavenly Zeal, O Holy Ghost, inſpire all our Hearts, through the Merits of the bleſſed Mediator, that we may bring forth much Fruit to the Glory of the Father.

A M E N.

APPENDIX.

The Controversy about Creeds and explanatory Articles beginning to obtain in this Country, which may perhaps be attended with ill Effects, it is thought expedient to subjoin the following Extract from Mr. GEORGE HARVEST'*s Defence of requiring* SUBSCRIPTION *to Explanatory Articles, against Mr.* SAMUEL CHANDLER'*s Case of Subscription, &c.*

BY Explanatory Articles of Faith, I presume, we both mean the same Thing; *viz.* certain Human Explications of the Words of Scripture; those Words which are supposed to contain The Principles of the Christian Religion; which Explanations are proposed to be subscribed, or assented to by the Candidates for the Christian Ministry. Let the one be called, for Brevity-sake, *Explanatory Articles*; the other, *Scripture-Creeds.* At present we will use the Words ASSENT, and SUBSCRIPTION, *indifferently*; for the Debate is, not about the *Manner* of expressing, or giving Assent; but about the *Thing* to which Assent or Subscription is required. *Your* Language, that Subscription is *a Qualification* for Admission into the Christian Ministry, shall be complied with, to avoid Contention about Words; though, in truth, the Subscription

tion is not *itself the Qualification*, but the TEST, or *Evidence* of the Qualification for the Ministry.---The Case then is as follows: You contend for Subscription to a *Scripture-Creed* only, as such Qualification: I, on the contrary, maintain the Reasonableness of Subscription to Explanatory Articles. The Question is, *not* about the Articles of the *Church of England*, or about any other Explanatory Articles in particular; but it is, in *general*, concerning *Explanatory* Articles, *as Explanatory*. Thus stands the Question.

Now, to be decisive, I will not put the Debate with you upon the Foot of *Expediency*, or *Inexpediency*, of your, or my, Method of framing Articles for Subscribers: The Question shall not be, which Method, that of *Explanatory Articles*, or of a *Scripture-Creed*, is preferable? But I will try the Point with you, upon the Foot of *Necessity*; and, if I shew that 'tis *necessary*, indispensably necessary, that Candidates for the Ministry should subscribe to *Explanatory Articles*, there will be an End of the Question; for such *Necessity* does at once put an End to all Disputes about *Expediency* and *Inexpediency*.

First then, Sir, you allow that 'tis necessary there should be *Pastors* or *Teachers* in the *Church of Christ*, to instruct the People in the *Christian Faith*: That they, whose Office it is to instruct others in the Christian Faith, must *themselves* hold the Christian Faith: That, therefore, the *Pastors*, or *Teachers*, of the Christian Faith, must be duly *qualified* for such their Office, by their holding the *Christian Faith*. i. e. the Faith of the Gospel: That, therefore, certain Persons must have a Right, or be appointed to judge, to examine and determine, concerning the *Qualification*, the *Fitness* of those who are Candidates for the Christian Ministry: That the

Rule

Rule of their Judgment, or Determination concerning ſuch *Qualification* of Teachers, is the holy Scripture,--Thus far, I think, we are both agreed; at leaſt, I ſee no Reaſon why it may be ſuppoſed you ſhould deny any of theſe Propoſitions. Indeed, as to the two Propoſitions, the *Quaker* will deny the former, and the *Papiſt* or *Roman Catholick* the latter; but I am ſure that the Practice of all Proteſtant Churches (as they are uſually called) will juſtify my laying down theſe Principles, as *Poſtulata*, or common Principles in this Debate.

Well then, the *Holy Scripture* is *the Rule*, by which the Perſons, who are to examine the Candidates for the Chriſtian Miniſtry, are to be guided, in order to determine whether they be *qualified*, or not *qualified*, for Admiſſion to it.---Now, I doubt, we are going to differ: *You* think 'tis ſufficient to anſwer the End of Examination (which is, that they who are to teach the Truths of the Goſpel, ſhould be duly *qualified* for their Office, by their *Belief* of the Truths of the Goſpel,) if a *Scipture-Creed*, i. e. a Formulary conſiſting of the Words of Scripture, *without any Explication*, containing the *Principles*, and perhaps ſome Doctrines of Chriſtianity, be ſubſcribed by the Candidates. On the contrary, I aſſert the *Neceſſity* of Subſcription to *Explanatory Articles*: And my Reaſon for aſſerting the *Neceſſity* of this Subſcription, is drawn from the *abſolute Inſufficiency* of the other Method propoſed, for the Examination of Candidates for the Chriſtian Miniſtry, *viz.* that of ſubſcribing to the *Scripture-Creed* only, to anſwer the End of Subſcription; which is, that the Miniſters, the Teachers of the Goſpel do *themſelves* hold the *Faith of the Goſpel*.

'Tis ſcarce worth while to take notice, that though I every-where ſpeak of the *Qualification* of Candidates for

for the Miniſtry, which is their Belief of the Truths of the Goſpel, I do not mean that *That* is the *only Qualification* for the Miniſtry: No, ſurely; Morals and Learning are alſo required in this Caſe. But theſe have nothing to do in the preſent Queſtion. We are talking about the *Qualification* of FAITH, to which *Articles* and *Subſcription* are relative, and not about the other Qualifications of Morals and Learning; about which (except indeed with the *ſinleſs Elect*, whoſe *Morals* need not to be inquired into; the *gifted Brethren*, who look upon *Letter-Learning* as *carnal* and *unprofitable*) there can be no Diſpute.

To ſhew then, as plainly as poſſible, the *Inſufficiency* of Subſcription to the *Scripture-Creed only*, I would lay down the following Obſervations.

I. The *Faith of the Goſpel* is that *one Senſe* of the *Words of the Scripture* which was affixed to them, or *intended* by the ſacred Writers.

II. The *Words of Scripture* having been uſed or taken in ſeveral *different Senſes* and *Interpretations*; it is thereby become *ambiguous* and *indeterminate*, what Senſe any Perſon affixes to the Words of Scripture.

III. An Aſſent, or Subſcription, therefore, to the *Words of Scripture*, or to a *Scripture-Creed only*, can be *no Proof*, *Teſt*, or *Evidence* of any Perſon's holding *the Faith of the Goſpel*.

Firſt, The Faith of the Goſpel is that *one Senſe of the Words of Scripture*, which was affixed to them, or *intended*, by the ſacred Writers.

This is ſelf-evident. The ſenſe of Scripture can be but

but *one*, and that one Sense can undoubtedly be that only, which was *intended* by the sacred Writers. *How* we are to judge, and to determine *what* this Sense is, is *another* Question, to be considered hereafter.

Secondly, The *Words of Scripture* having been used or taken in several *different* Senses and Interpretations; it is thereby become *ambiguous* and *indeterminate*, *what Sense* any Person affixes to the Words of Scripture.

'Tis extremely difficult to guard sufficiently against being misunderstood, or misrepresented, by those who cannot, or will not, understand a plain Distinction. But, to express myself as clearly as possible upon this Head, my Meaning is This; that Words being used in *different Senses*, by different Persons, is the Foundation of *Ambiguity*; and therefore, the Words being used by one Person in one Sense, by another Person in another Sense, it will be *doubtful*, *uncertain*, or *ambiguous*, *what particular Sense* any Person affixes to them, or *how* He understands them, till he has *explained* and *declared*, *what Sense it is* that he does affix to them. When different Persons affix different Meanings to the *same* Words, then these Words become, in Language or Discourse, so far *ambiguous*, or *indeterminate*. Neither you, nor I can know how others understand them, without *Explanation*. As to the Thing itself, that the Words of Scripture are thus differently understood by different Persons, 'tis Fact, and undeniable: And 'tis equally certain, that it cannot be known from the Use of the Scripture-Words only, what it is that any one means by them; and that therefore Explanation is become necessary.

Take this Proposition, for Instance, *The Word was God:* Can I tell merely from another Person's repeating these Words to me, what he *means* by them? Is

he an *Athanasian*? Is he a *Sabellian*? Is he an *Arian*? or, a *Socinian*? In a Word, does he mean *something* by it; or, does he mean *nothing*; for there is plainly as great, the same infinite Difference, between what the one means, and what the other means, in this Case, as there is between *necessary Existence*, and *not being*. How is it possible that I should know what you *mean*, what *Sense* you affix to this Proposition, unless you *explain* it to me, since the Words are used in many different Senses?

Again; *This is my Body:* The *absolute* Meaning of this Proposition is *plain* to *me*. 'Tis, *to me*, just as plain that these Words are *not* to be understood *literally*, as it is that Christ's Crucifixon is not to be understood *figuratively*. Yet, is not this very Proposition, in *some respect*, *ambiguous*? i. e. Is it *plain* and *certain* what another Man means by it? Do all mean the same Thing by the *Sacrament of the Lord's Supper*? If I ask a *Papist*, or a *Roman-Catholick*, the Doctrine is *Transubstantiation*, and a *real Sacrifice*: If a *Lutheran*, *Consubstantiation*, or *Impanation*. If another, *Real Presence*: A Fourth tells me of an *unbloody Sacrifice*; a Fifth, of *Spiritual Privileges* annexed to the receiving the Elements of Bread and Wine. The next gives me what he calls a "Plain Account of the Lord's "Supper," which, indeed understood, as I would willingly understand his Meaning, is not, perhaps, justly exceptionable: Another frankly declares, with all Plainness of Speech and Simplicity, that he really means nothing more by the *Communion of the Body, and Blood of Christ*, than the *true Spiritual Communion* of Christians, in mutual Love and Charity. Now, Sir, say, I beseech you, How can I possibly discover the Meaning of *any One* of these Persons, merely from his telling

ling me, that he believes the Truth of our Lord's Word's when he says, *This is my Body?* Or, is it not *ambiguous*, what he *means* by those Scripture-Words?

Once more----*Christ came into the World to save Sinners.* He saves Sinners, says the *Papist*, or the *Roman Catholick*, not only by his Doctrine and Example, and the Merit of his Sufferings; but by purchasing, by his own Blood, an *Infallible Church*; by joining with, or being added to which, Men are saved.----- Christ saves Sinners, says the *Supralapsarian*, by making the indispensible, necessary, infinite Satisfaction to infinite Justice.---He saves Sinners by making full Satisfaction to the Divine Justice, so that nothing remains on our Part, but *true justifying Faith*, which is *of Course attended* with, or is *productive* of Obedience. So says the *Antinomian*, or *Solifidian*. Another says (and says rightly) That Christ saves Sinners by the Morality of his Gospel, Repentance, Obedience, and Perfection; by leaving Men a complete Example of all Virtue and Holiness in his own spotless Life; by enforcing the Practice of his Laws by the Sanctions of eternal Rewards and Punishments; and by enabling all those who are *willing to do his Will*, with the Grace and Assistance of his Holy Spirit; but, *principally* by suffering upon the Cross a *proper vicarious Punishment*, and being an *expiatory Sacrifice* for the Sins of the whole World; the great Method of Reconciliation between God and Man, *freely appointed* by the *original essential Goodness* of the *Father*.---But if you inquire of a *Christian-Deist* (one who will readily subscribe to a *Scripture-Creed*,) whether, or not, he believes, that Christ came into the World to save Sinners, he will reply, undoubtedly he did; and for that End, he preached very excellent *Morality*, and withal gave an Instance

Instance of the Practicableness of it in his own Life, beyond any *other Moralist*, or Prophet; and that he died in *Confirmation* of the Truth of it. As for any *proper Sacrifice* in the *Death of Christ*, that Notion, it seems, took its Rise from some Passages in Scripture, where the Apostles, (St. *PAUL* in particular, whose manner it was to *become all Things to all Men*) are speaking in Accommodation to the gross Notions and Prejudices of the *unmetaphysical Jew*; but *we*, who understand the *Nature and Reason of Things*, have not so learned the Apostles: Thus the *Socinian*.---Now is it not *ambiguous*, what any Person *means* by these Scripture-Words, *Christ came into the World to save Sinners?* Are they not understood in several *different* Senses? And is there not therefore a Necessity for *Explanation?*

The Conclusion is, that it being thus *ambiguous* and *indeterminate*, *what Sense* any Person affixes to the *Words of Scripture*, amidst the several *different* Senses and Interpretations; therefore some *Explanation* is *necessary* to be assented to, or subscribed by those who are Candidates for the Christian Ministry, as a *Test* of their *Qualification* for the Office of the Ministry; which Qualification is their holding the *Faith* of the Gospel.

If Mr. *Chandler* now ask that Question of Questions, *Who shall judge?* who shall judge and determine *what* is the *Faith* of the Gospel? *Which* it is, of the various, and perhaps contradictory Senses and Interpretations that Men have put upon the *Words* of Scripture, that *is the True Sense?* I answer, that, in the present Case, where the believing the Doctrines, or holding the Faith of the Gospel, is *a Qualification* for the Office of the Ministry; *undoubtedly*, those Persons whose Right it is, or who are delegated, or appointed by others,

others, to examine and determine concerning the *Qualification* of Candidates for the Ministry, who are qualified, and who not; THEY must judge *what is that Qualification*, which is the *Rule* by which these judgments are to be directed. But that Qualification, as before observed, is the Believing the *Principles of the Doctrine of Christ*, the *Faith* of the Gospel. Who then, in the Name of Common Sense, must judge what *are* the Principles of the Doctrine of Christ? or, *what is* the *Faith* of the Gospel, but *They* who are to judge of the Qualification of others for the Ministry? Nothing is more evident. If I am to judge of *your* Qualification for the Ministry; if such Qualification be your Belief of the Truths of the Gospel; and, if it be *ambiguous*, *what are* the Truths of the Gospel; what is the *true Sense* of Scripture Texts relating to any Doctrine; *who*, I pray, is to determine, in this Case, what *is* the Doctrine of Scripture, *You*, or *I*? If *You* are, 'tis a flat Contradiction to the Supposition that *I* am to judge. Certainly, if *I* am to judge, whether *you* are qualified for the Ministry, or not; *I* must be determined, not by *your* Opinion, but by *my own*. The Right of *private Judgment* stands just where it did, and is not in the least affected by these Considerations. Private Judgment is *supposed* on all Sides. The Candidate has judged for himself, what is the true Sense of Scripture; and the Examiner is to judge for himself, whether the Candidate be *qualified* or not. Every Man's Judgment must be, *to him*, *the True Judgment*, the *Truth of the Case*; nor can it be otherwise without a Contradiction; For, if you think your Own Judgment, or Opinion, *not to* be *true* or *right*; 'tis plainly, *not your* Judgment, or Opinion, but what you perceive to be *Error*. Whatever a Man judges to be the *true Sense*

and

and Meaning of Scripture, *that is*, and must be, *to him*, *the Doctrine* of Scripture, the *Faith of the Gospel*; and consequently, whosoever holds or maintains *another sense*, cannot but appear *to him*, *not to hold the Faith of the* Gospel. Indeed, not being *infallible*, he cannot *absolutely affirm*, as a certain Truth, that whosoever so differs from him, does *not* hold the Christian Faith; but yet he cannot but *think*, and *judge*, and be *of Opinion*, that he does not; and therefore, if a Candidate for the Ministry give an Explication of the Words of Scripture, an Account of the Truths of the Gospel, as his Faith, which the Person who is Judge of his Qualification for the Ministry, thinks to be erroneous; he cannot consistently admit him, *as qualified*, to the Office of the Ministry. Therefore, *whatever Sense of Scripture* appears, to those who are to judge of the Qualification of Candidates for the Ministry, to be the *true Sense* of Scripture; *That* must be *Their Rule* in judging of such *Qualification*.

I have purposely omitted to take notice of that wild Scheme of Subscription, *viz. Subscription to the Scripture, as the Word of God*; the beloved Project of the Friends of an *unlimited Comprehension*. Because, 'tis indeed the same Thing in Effect and Consequence, with the Subscription to a *Scriptural-Creed*. In shewing, therefore, the Vanity of one Scheme, I expose both. 'Tis evident, that all who will subscribe to the *Scripture-Creed*, will subscribe as readily to Scripture *as the Word of God*; and, equally, that all who will subscribe to Scripture as the Word of God, will subscribe to the *Scripture-Creed*; supposing always that they mean *the same Thing* by *Scripture*, and hold the *same* Writings to be *authentic*; and that the only Difference between these two Sorts of Subscribers, is, that

[Archives copy is incomplete.]

One

WESTERN VIEW OF "POQUETANNOCK," PRESTON.
The church, built soon after 1734, is seen at the extreme right of the picture.

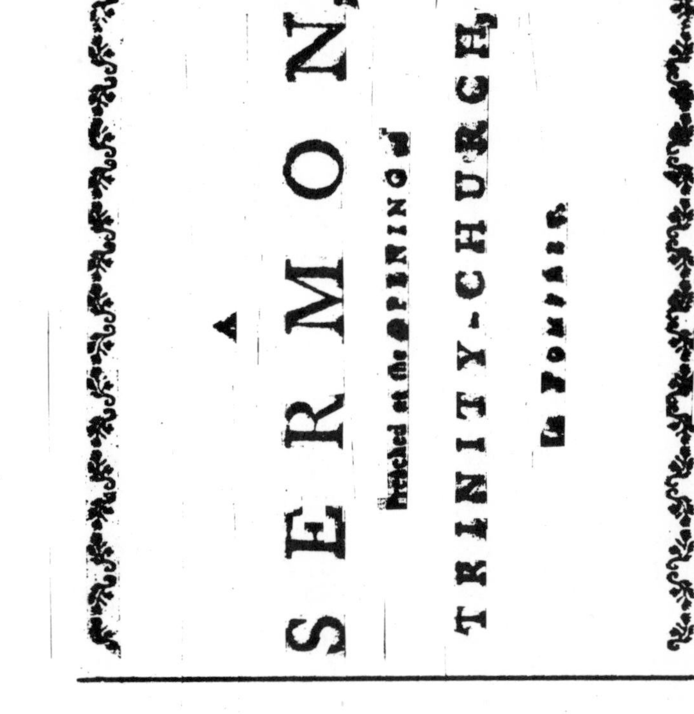

A
SERMON,
Preached at the OPENING of
TRINITY-CHURCH,
in Pomfret.

CHRIST CHURCH, STRATFORD.
Second Building, 1744.

TRINITY CHURCH, NEW HAVEN.
First Building, 1752.

THE

SANCTITY

OF A

CHRISTIAN TEMPLE;

Illuſtrated in a

SERMON,

At the OPENING of

TRINITY-CHURCH, in *Pomfret*,

On *Friday*, *April* 12, 1771.

By *JOHN TYLER*, A.M.
MISSIONARY from the venerable *Society for the Propagation of the Goſpel*, at NORWICH, in CONNECTICUT.

Reverence my Sanctuary: I am the Lord. JEHOVAH.
O come, let us worſhip, and bow down; let us kneel before the Lord, our Maker. K. DAVID.
With one Mind, and one Mouth, glorify God.
Glorify God in your Body, and in your Spirit, which are God's.
St. PAUL.

PROVIDENCE: Printed by JOHN CARTER, at *Shakeſpear's Head.* M,DCC,LXI.

TO

Simon Peaſe, Eſq;

OF NEWPORT, RHODE-ISLAND.

SIR,

THE laudable and pious activity you have ſhown, among the many and very worthy benefactors at Newport, by whoſe generous aſſiſtance the Church at Pomfret was principally erected, has induced me to offer this diſcourſe to your acceptance, in compliance with the deſires of the members of it, as a monument of their ſincere thanks to you and them, and an acknowledgment of their gratitude for that noble piety and zeal for goodneſs, which, from your firſt appearance among men, have ever been viſibly predominant in you, and eminently conſpicuous in promoting the building of their edifice, to the honour of God, and their very great comfort and relief.

They

DEDICATION.

They alſo acknowledge their obligations for the few helps they have received elſewhere; and promiſe that nothing, on their parts, ſhall be wanting to afford the moſt convincing proofs, by their earneſt and devout attachments to religion, that their pious contributions have not been ill-placed.

I now beg of Almighty GOD, that he may be pleaſed to make this Church effectual to his own honour and ſervice; and to bleſs you, and all its other promoters, in the practice and continuance of all virtuous excellencies in this world, until ye may all finally receive your never-ending reward in that which is to come.

I have the honour to be, with very great eſteem and reſpect,

Sir, your moſt obedient,

And very humble Servant,

JOHN TYLER.

Norwich, Dec. 1771.

THE

SANCTITY of a *Chriſtian Temple.*

2d CHRONICLES vi. 40, 41.

Now, my God, let, I beſeech thee, thine Eyes be open, and let thine Ears be attent unto the Prayer that is made in this Place.

Now therefore ariſe, O Lord God, into thy reſting Place, thou, and the Ark of thy Strength: Let thy Prieſts, O Lord God, be cloathed with Salvation, and let thy Saints rejoice in Goodneſs.

THIS houſe being built to the honour of God's holy name, with much unanimity and diſpatch, through the favour of divine providence; and it being, from this time forward, to be devoted, ſet apart and dedicated, to the more ſolemn, public and immediate worſhip and ſervice of the one ſupreme Lord of the univerſe, was the reaſon of my chooſing theſe words of the wiſe King Solomon (uttered on a like occaſion) for your conſideration at this time.—My text is a part of that ſolemn and excellent prayer, which the wiſe man offered up to his maker, when he conſecrated to his ſacred ſervice an elegant and beautiful edifice, even that rich and magnificent Temple, which he had erected to that noble purpoſe. And although the workmanſhip and ornamental glory of the houſe, in which we are now aſſembled, are incomparably beneath thoſe of Solomon's Temple; yet the words under conſideration, may be as properly uſed at the dedication

tion of this Houſe, as they were at the conſecration of that Temple. For the preſence of God is as neceſſary in this Sanctuary, as in that of Solomon: You as really need God's favourable attention to your prayers offered in this Church, as the Iſraelites did in their Temple. And if you *worſhip in ſpirit and in truth*, with ſincere devotion and hearty affection; the God of heaven will as mercifully hear, and anſwer with as bountiful a bleſſing, thoſe prayers you offer in this Church; and as readily afford you his gracious preſence and acceptance in this Houſe, as he did the Iſraelites in that ſplendid Temple, which was adorned with all the wealth and art of a potent empire. For, under the Chriſtian œconomy, *Wherever two or three are gathered together in* Chriſt's *name, there will* he *be in the midſt of them*. And notwithſtanding *heaven, and the heaven of heavens, cannot contain* God; yet he will afford his preſence to the faithful, in thoſe Houſes which are built for his honour, and devoted to his ſacred worſhip and ſervice. For, *thus ſaith the high and lofty one that inhabiteth eternity, whoſe name is holy; I dwell in the high and holy place, with him alſo that is of a contrite and humble ſpirit, to revive the ſpirit of the humble, and to revive the heart of the contrite ones. Thy way, O God, is in the ſanctuary*, ſaith the royal Pſalmiſt. So that, although the magnificence of this Houſe will not compare with that of Solomon's Temple; yet if you are properly qualified for the divine favour, and in theſe courts offer up unfeigned, pure and holy worſhip, God will in a peculiar and glorious manner be preſent with a bleſſing. And ſince the occaſion of our being now aſſembled together, is ſimilar to that upon which the words of my text were firſt uſed; let us conſider them, and attend to the peculiar inſtruction which they are proper to afford.

Solomon entreateth the Lord God, that in caſe his people, for their ſins, ſhould be diſtreſſed by their *enemies*—by *drought*—by *dearth*—*peſtilence*—*blaſting*—*mildew*—*locuſts*—*caterpillars*—or any kind of ſickneſs, and ſhould repent and pray to God, in or toward that houſe, he would hear and except their prayer, forgive their ſin, and deliver them out of their calamity. And then, the wiſe King, drawing towards a concluſion, deſires that God would be ready to hear, and graciouſly anſwer, all the faithful prayers, which ſhould be offered up in that Houſe upon any occaſion whatſoever: *Now, my God, let, I beſeech thee, thine eyes be open, and let thine ears be attent unto the prayer that is made in this place.* And then he requeſts of God to accept of that Houſe for his Sanctuary; his reſting place, where he might at all times be graciouſly preſent: That he would direct and bleſs the endeavours of the prieſthood for the good of the people; and grant his faithful worſhippers great occaſion to rejoice in his mercy, favour and protection: *Now therefore ariſe, O Lord God, into thy reſting place; thou, and the ark of thy ſtrength: Let thy prieſts, O Lord God, be cloathed with ſalvation, and let thy ſaints rejoice in goodneſs.*

This text is one remarkable inſtance of the religious cuſtom among God's people, in former ages, of ſetting apart, and dedicating Houſes to the ſolemn worſhip of their maker. This cuſtom, among the Jews, was under the direction and approbation of God: And performed by Solomon, with the immediate aſſiſtance of the divine ſpirit. And this has been almoſt the univerſal cuſtom of Chriſtians, ever ſince

since they have been suffered to erect decent houses of worship. Hence we may infer from the text,

I. That God affords his more peculiar presence in those Houses which are devoted to his sacred worship; and hath a greater regard for them than for other places.

II. That God is treated with greater respect, honour and reverence, by the public worship of his people; and will more graciously hear and answer their grateful praises, and sincere prayers, when offered up in *his* Sanctuary, than elsewhere. And,

III. The respect which is due from you to this House, considered as the Temple of God; and how you ought always to behave when you tread the courts of the Lord's House.

First, then, we learn that God affords his more peculiar presence in those Houses which are devoted to his sacred worship; and hath a greater regard for them than for other places. *Arise, O Lord God, into thy resting place, thou, and the ark of thy strength.*

That allwise providence of the supreme Lord of nature, which surveys, and constantly presides over the whole universe, doth nevertheless fix its peculiar attention upon some particular places*. *God hath loved the gates of Sion, more than all the dwellings of Jacob*; saith the Psalmist. Again, *the Lord hath chosen Zion; he hath desired it for his habitation. This is my rest for ever: Here will I dwell; for I have desired it.* And accordingly, in the first ages of the Church, to have places set apart for religious worship, was the care of divine providence. The Patriarch Jacob was admonished from heaven to build an altar to the Lord, in that place where he had before appeared to him in a dream, where the Patriarch had set

* *Vide* South *in eundem.*

set up a stone for a pillar, and *vowed*, that *if God would be with him,—that stone should be God's house:—This*, said he, *is the gate of heaven.*—How particular were the directions which God gave to Moses concerning the Tabernacle! And how exact was he about the Temple! Though David was a *man after God's own heart*, and had made a prodigious preparation of materials, yet, because he had shed blood, though it was the blood of the open enemies of the true God, he was not suffered so much as to lay the foundation of that sacred building: But the whole glory of the work devolved upon Solomon; whose heavenly wisdom, shining forth in a blessed time of uninterrupted peace and plenty, rendered him a more pleasing and unexceptionable instrument for so noble a purpose.

Again, when the Temple, for the sins of the people, was levelled with the ground, by an Assyrian army, yet, after the chastisement of a long captivity had fitted the Jews for the precious enjoyment of God's peculiar presence among them again, how wonderfully did God influence the heart of Cyrus, though a heathen Prince, to set forward the building of another Temple! And was not that shining miraculous cloud, which was often seen in and over the Tabernacle and Temple, called, by the Jews, *Shekina*, or majestic divine presence?—Was not this, I say, a most sensible and wonderful token of God's peculiar regard for, and special presence in that House, which was devoted wholly to his solemn worship?

Neither the horrible schism and rebellion of Corah, and his company, nor the sudden and awful vengeance of heaven upon them, could desecrate or unhallow their censers, because they had been devoted to the service of God. Said the Lord to Moses, *the censers*

censers of these sinners against their own souls, let them make broad plates for a covering of the altar; for they offered them before the Lord, therefore they are hallowed. And the case is just the same with respect to places which are consecrated to the worship of God.

Again, that God is peculiarly present in, and hath a greater regard for Houses and other things which are devoted to his service, than for those which are not, appears by the exemplary vengeance of God, executed upon the profaners and impious violators of them.

Sacrilegious depredations have ever been attended by the secret curse of God, and the invisible vengeance of heaven *. This kind of wickedness hath consumed the families of Princes, demolished thrones, and laid whole kingdoms waste. When the Philistines routed the armies of Israel, and took from them the ark of God, what a dreadful curse was it to them, like a devouring plague in their very bowels!—The vengeance of heaven struck Uzzah dead in a moment, for touching the ark; because, though he was zealous for its preservation, yet he had no right to meddle with it. When God delivered the law to Moses at Sinai, any beast that touched the mountain, was to be struck through with a dart; and to fall a sacrifice for a crime, which it was utterly unconscious of. We read that in the reign of Rehoboam, King of Judah, Shishak, King of Egypt, came up to Jerusalem, and took away the treasures of Solomon's Temple, even those utensils which had been devoted to sacred use: And we are told by Josephus what happened to *him*, after this sacrilegious robbery.—When he returned to Egypt, great mischiefs befel his family; he burnt to death two of his chil-

* *Vide* South *in eundem.*

children; his brother conspired against him; and his son, who next possessed the throne, was struck blind. Afterwards the great Nebuchadnezzar robbed God's Temple: And we also read what judgments followed his sacrilege.—For being puffed up with his own greatness, and what he had done, we are told that his kingdom was taken from him; and he himself, by a judgment before unheard of, driven from human society, and made to feed on grass with the beasts of the field; his impiety rendering him more proper to associate with brutes, than with those who were capable of religion.—And when his son Belshazzar became King, at an impious feast, he sent for the sacred vessels, which had been taken from God's Temple in Jerusalem, and made use of them to drink out of, in derision of their being devoted to the religious service of the God of Israel: And while he was profaning and polluting them with his sensuality, he saw part of an hand upon the wall of his apartment in the palace, and the fingers writing his doom there in legible characters, *viz. God hath numbered thy kingdom, and finished it.—Thou art weighed in the balances, and art found wanting.—Thy kingdom is divided, and given to the Medes and Persians.* And the prophet Daniel, immediately before he interpreted the sentence, told him what this judgment was for: He declared to him, that though he knew the impiety of his father, yet he had *not humbled his heart; but* thou *hast lifted up thyself,* said the prophet, *against the Lord of heaven, and they have brought the vessels of his House before thee, and thou and thy Lords, thy wives and thy concubines, have drunk wine in them.*— And we are informed that the sentence was speedily executed upon him; for that very night, Cyrus with his army broke into the city of Babylon, and took from

from Belshazzar both his kingdom and his life. And many other remarkable instances of the execution of divine vengeance, upon the profaners, and sacrilegious violators of those things which were sacred to God, under the Jewish œconomy, might be produced.

Under the Christian dispensation also, history abounds with accounts of the same thing. "There "is nothing (says an ingenious * author) that the "united voice of all history proclaims so loud, as "the certain unfailing curse, that hath pursued and "overtook sacrilege." All this shows that God hath a peculiar regard for Houses, and other things, that are religiously devoted to his worship and service.

I will now just mention some of the reasons why God affords his more peculiar presence in those Houses which are devoted to his sacred worship, and hath a greater regard for them, than for other places.

One reason is, ‡ that God esteems himself peculiarly honoured by his people, when they pay him that respectful reverence, which the meeting together of considerable numbers in one place, and uniting in religious homage, doth express. And therefore he is pleased to be more peculiarly present among them at such times.

Another reason is, that in Houses wholly devoted to the worship of God, the minds of men, being in some measure separated from all worldly objects, and removed from their temporal concerns, are less subject to be diverted from devotion.

Another reason is, that Houses devoted to God, and used only in his service, do naturally inspire the minds of men with reverence for God and religion; which

* Dr. South.

‡ *Vide* Johnson *in eundem.*

which tends to fit them for the divine presence and blessing.

Another reason why God so peculiarly regards his House, as commonly to punish the profaners and violators of it with exemplary vengeance, is because that such proceedings tend to the disrepute of religion, and are a daring insult upon the majesty of the invisible God: For assaulting a man's house, is insulting his person.

The last reason I shall mention (and that not the least of them) why God manifests a * particular regard for Houses and other things which are devoted to his service, is because they are peculiarly his property. There is no holiness in these things, considered in themselves, that occasions his regard for them; not even the most holy place in Solomon's Temple had inherently any more sanctity than any other place; but it was relatively holy, being in a peculiar manner God's property. Not but that God is the absolute proprietor of all things; yet nevertheless those things, which men have no right to use, except in his immediate service, may be peculiarly called *his* property; while he hath granted to them the free use of all other things which come in their way, for their temporal comfort and support.

These things are peculiarly the property of God, which he hath chosen, and set apart for his own use and service. *Of every tree of the garden thou mayest freely eat,* said God to Adam; *but of the tree of the knowledge of good and evil thou shalt not eat.*—Thus also God chose the *gates of Sion, and the tribe of Levi.*

That is likewise the peculiar property of God, which men set apart and devote to his immediate ser-

* *Vide* South.

ſervice. In this caſe, men give, or more properly return, as an offering to God, that which he hath firſt given to them. They relinquiſh, quit and deliver up to God, all their right or liberty to uſe thoſe things as their own property, as for any worldly purpoſe, which God hath freely granted to them, for their own ſecular uſe. Upon which donation or dedication, the property of the things given, and the uſe of them, are alienated and abſolutely changed: So that men have no manner of right to the uſe of them, except in that immediate ſervice of God, to which they were appropriated. And God will endure no rival or competitor in them: But the man who profanes, invades or violates them, is guilty of a ſacrilegious uſurpation; for which the vengeance of heaven is armed againſt him, and the curſe of God will conſume him. Man's giving up, and devoting to the immediate ſervice of God, Houſes, or other things, is now, under the Chriſtian œconomy, the foundation of his peculiar property in them.

That man who takes upon him the office of a prieſt in Chriſt's Church, doth ſo give himſelf up to God and to his ſervice, that he hath no more right to diſpoſe of himſelf to any other employment, than he hath to command the ſervice of one who is ſuperior to, and abſolutely independent of him. And Houſes given up to God, and devoted to his immediate ſervice, are peculiarly his property. And men have no more right to appropriate them to any other uſe, than they have to diſpoſe of other mens eſtates: Nay, the crime is, almoſt beyond compariſon, greater and more aggravated, becauſe it is ſacrilege—an hoſtile robbery, perpetrated againſt the ſupreme ruler of the univerſe, who is an infinite benefactor, in

in open contempt of his authority, and the inſtituted means of his grace.

And conſidering with what bold and undaunted confidence men are ſometimes apt to invade the property of an inviſible, though almighty avenger, a religious and public dedication of Houſes to the ſacred worſhip and ſervice of God, as it doth impreſs a more ſenſible reſpect and reverence, a deeper awe and veneration upon the minds of the people, is certainly a matter of no ſmall importance.

And for dedicating Houſes to the public worſhip of God, and imploring his preſence and favourable acceptance of the prayers and praiſes offered up in them, we have the expreſs warrant of ſcripture; particularly in the account of Solomon's dedicating the Temple: For *when Solomon had made an end of praying* (as a teſtimony of divine approbation) *the fire came down from heaven, and conſumed the burnt-offering and the ſacrifices; and the glory of the* Lord *filled the Houſe.*

Now, ſome of the reaſons (beſides thoſe already mentioned) why God hath required, and is more eſpecially pleaſed with public worſhip, are theſe; * that as we are made ſocial beings, and are ſenſibly affected by each other, ſo we are commonly more zealouſly affected with what we tranſact in ſociety and fellowſhip one with another.—Again, as we all enjoy the ſame common bleſſings, both temporal and ſpiritual; ſo theſe enjoyments do moſt certainly demand a common and ſocial return of praiſe. And as we all, in general, have the ſame neceſſities; ſo for the attainment of what we all equally need, it is, in all reaſon, moſt fitting we ſhould make our joint addreſſes and ſupplications to God. And as public wor-

* *Vide* Johnſon *in eundem.*

worſhip is our moſt reaſonable ſervice, and is expreſſive of peculiar reſpect and veneration; ſo nothing on earth is more beautiful and amiable, than an aſſembly of rational creatures, joining together with one heart, and one voice, in offering up their grateful homage to their ſupreme Lord and benefactor; as St. John, in the Revelations, repreſents the worſhip of heaven, performed in the moſt perfect manner, before the throne of God.—Such ſocial and public worſhip tends to knit our hearts together in Chriſtian love and unity.

On ſuch accounts as theſe, God doth require, and is, in an eſpecial manner, pleaſed with the public and united worſhip of his creatures: And this is what occaſioned holy David to ſay, that *one day ſpent in the Houſe of God, was better than a thouſand elſewhere.*—Indeed that our Maker is to be worſhipped publicly, —that the more ſolemn, general and unanimous, our adorations and acknowledgments of him are, the more are they for his honour, and the more becoming our duty; is not only the voice of revelation, but even of nature and reaſon: Which appears by the univerſal conſent of mankind, in every age and nation; ſo that there never have been any communities of men, who did not cultivate ſome kind of public religious worſhip. And from the earlieſt ages of Chriſtianity, it hath ever been the practice of its profeſſors (as appears from their conſtantly meeting on the firſt day of the week, to break bread) unanimouſly to join, in devoting themſelves to God, in his ſolemn worſhip and ſervice. Accordingly St. Paul exhorts Chriſtians, *not to forſake the aſſembling of themſelves together.*—And we read that the Apoſtles *lifted up their voice to God with one accord*; and our Church is ſo happy as to follow their excellent example. St. Paul

Paul exhorts us, *with one mind, and one mouth,* to *glorify God.*

But then public worſhip requires ſome particular place for the performance of it. Private devotions may be performed in any place; though ſome are more convenient than others. We read that God is *about our path, and about our bed:* And the more ſolitary the place, the better we may perform ſuch addreſſes. But public worſhip demands a decent Houſe, a convenient reception for numbers to reſort to, at ſtated times; a building ſet apart and diſtinguiſhed from common uſe, to which we may retreat from the world and its cares. And ſuch Houſes being given up by us, as an offering to God, and devoted to his immediate ſervice, ought to be as commodious, elegant, and magnificent, as our abilities will admit of.

But if any are inclined to blame the cuſtom of the profeſſors of the Church of England, for expenſively adorning their Houſes of public worſhip, where they are able, I would aſk them, whether being ſparing in our offerings to God, doth not manifeſt, in *us*, as ungrateful, ſordid narrowneſs of ſoul, and as great diſreſpect to our Maker, as was ſhown by thoſe *Jews* of old, who *offered* up *for ſacrifice the blind and the lame*, whoſe offerings God abhorred? And is not a liberal offering to God, an indication of reſpect to him, and regard for the honour of religion? Did God, who changeth not, ever diſapprove of the prodigious magnificence, and coſtly ornaments of Solomon's Temple? And did he not, by the mouth of his prophet Haggai, ſeverely reprove his people for their ſparing contributions to the ſecond Temple? *Is it time* (ſaid he) *for you, O ye, to dwell in your ceiled houſes, and this Houſe lie waſte? Build the Houſe, and* I will

I will take pleasure in it, and I will be glorified, saith the Lord.

That the Houſe of God ſhould be at leaſt commodious, decent, clean, and comely, is what we might reaſonably expect every one would approve of, who pretends to any reverence for God or religion. Saith the pious and worthy Dean Stanhope, " Far " from us be all ornaments, miſbecoming the worſhip " of a ſpirit, or the gravity of a Church. But " ſure it hath a very ill aſpect, for men to be content" edly and ſordidly frugal, and to think *that* well " enough in God's Houſe, which they would not en" dure, even in the meaneſt apartments of their own. " Religion ſhould not be dreſſed in the habit of a " wanton; but do not deny her that of a matron.— " Let her be modeſt in her garb; but withal comely " and clean; and allow her enough, not only to pro" tect her from ſhame and contempt, but to draw " ſome reſpect too. If ſome have injured her by a " falſe and too artificial beauty, this is no reaſon why " we ſhould think it a virtue, to turn pious clowns " and ſlovens, by running into the contrary extreme, " and," inſtead of *worſhipping the Lord in the beauty of holineſs*, addreſs him " in the dirt and deformity" of ſlovenlineſs. If we are contented with meanneſs and uglineſs in the Houſe of God, and being able, are however penuriouſly unwilling to provide what is honourable for his worſhip, though it be under pretence of regarding only *ſpiritual worſhip, heart worſhip*, and the like; yet do we not tempt, nay, even provoke mankind to diſtruſt and ridicule our profeſſions of piety, and to deſpiſe the ſervice of God? And do we not alſo incur the peculiar indignation of heaven? *If ye offer the blind for ſacrifice, is it not evil? And if ye offer the lame and ſick, is it not evil? Offer it now to thy Governor, will he be pleaſed with thee, or accept thy perſon? ſaith the Lord of hoſts.* If we are willing to enjoy the beſt of every thing ourſelves, and think any thing good enough for God's ſervice, we may call him *Father*, *Lord*, or *Maſter*, or what we pleaſe; yet theſe ſentiments and proceedings are plain indications, that he is not the ſupreme object of our love and reverence.

In the next place, as no reaſon can be given, why God ſhould not be as graciouſly preſent in each Houſe, that we now dedicate to his worſhip, as he was in the one Jewiſh Temple; ſo theſe words of the Lord, uttered by the Prophet Iſaiah (among many other teſtimonies of ſcripture) ſeem fully to evince it: *My Houſe ſhall be called the Houſe of prayer for ALL people.* By which the introduction of the Gentiles into the Church of God, is plainly foretold; and that whatſoever Houſe they ſhould devote to his ſervice, and aſſemble in for worſhip, ſhould be called God's Houſe of prayer, as the Jewiſh Temple was. And agreeable to this, St. Paul wrote to Timothy, who was then at Epheſus, *hoping*, ſaid he, *to come unto thee ſhortly; but if I tarry long, that thou mayeſt know how thou oughteſt to behave thyſelf in the Houſe of God, which is the Church of the living God.* Theſe words of the Apoſtle are a ſufficient explanation of thoſe recorded by the Prophet Iſaiah, which were juſt now mentioned.

Accordingly it is the cuſtom of the Church of England, when Houſes are built and reſigned up to God for the purpoſes of his worſhip, to aſſemble in them, and to join, with one accord, in public prayers and praiſes; to have ſermons preached ſuitable to thoſe occaſions, in which public declarations are made, that thoſe Houſes are devoted to God,—de-

dedicated to his religious worſhip and ſervice, and from that time forward are to be eſteemed ſacred to God and religion. The peculiar preſence of God is invoked, and his favourable attention to, and eſpecial bleſſing upon thoſe perſons, who ſhall faithfully ſeek him in thoſe places. This tends to make ſuch places venerable in the eyes of men, and to draw down a divine bleſſing on worſhipping aſſemblies.

If any ſhould be inclined to cavil, and ſay, notwithſtanding what hath been offered, that ſuch formal dedications are either needleſs or ſuperſtitious; I would recommend to their conſideration, the grand ſolemnity of dedicating Solomon's Temple, and the miraculous teſtimony of divine approbation, conſequent thereupon. And why are ſuch dedications leſs proper now? * Euſebius (the firſt Chriſtian hiſtorian, after the Apoſtles) mentions the dedication of Churches, as generally practiſed by the primitive Chriſtians. He tells us the particular manner in which this ceremony was performed, and ſtiles it a cuſtom of the Church becoming God. In a word, all nations who have retained any venerable ſentiments of God and religion (whether Chriſtians, Jews, or even heathens) have ever practiſed ſolemn, formal dedications, when they ſet apart Houſes for religious worſhip and ſervice.

But though, after our Churches are dedicated, we attribute no inherent holineſs to them, but only relative, as being ſet apart from worldly uſes, and devoted wholly to religious purpoſes, yet ſome are apt to accuſe us of having a ſuperſtitious regard for the Houſes themſelves. Are they not wood and ſtone, ſay they, as well as other buildings? I anſwer; this cavil is the language of that recent kind of refined

* *Vide* South *in eundem.*

and ſpiritualized piety, to which Jeſus Chriſt and his Apoſtles were utter ſtrangers. Our Lord had ſuch zeal for the honour of God's Houſe, that he himſelf drove out of it the buyers, ſellers, and other invaders of it. And St. Paul reproved the Corinthians, for profanely eating or feaſting in their Churches. *Have ye not houſes to eat and drink in? Or deſpiſe ye the Church of God?* ſaid he.—I have now done with the firſt general head of diſcourſe, and proceed to ſhow,

II. That God is treated with greater reſpect, honour and reverence, by the public worſhip of his people; and will more graciouſly hear and anſwer their grateful praiſes and ſincere prayers, when offered up in *his* Sanctuary, than elſewhere. *Now, my God, let, I beſeech thee, thine eyes be open, and let thine ears be attent unto the prayer that is made in this place*, ſaid Solomon, when he dedicated the Temple. And ſoon after God anſwered him, ſaying, *now mine eyes ſhall be open, and mine ears attent unto the prayer that is made in this place*. And no reaſon can be given, why God ſhould not be as well pleaſed *now*, with public worſhip in his own Houſe, as he was under the Jewiſh œconomy; for numbers publicly to aſſemble, in order to worſhip God, is evidently a token of reſpect and reverence for him: But it is ſtill more ſo, when they wait on him for that purpoſe, at his own Houſe. And conſequently God will more graciouſly hear and anſwer prayers and praiſes, when offered up in his Sanctuary, than elſewhere. Public worſhip, for ſeveral reaſons, is extremely neceſſary and becoming, (as I have ſhown under the preceding head of this diſcourſe) and ſo is peculiarly entitled to the divine attention and bleſſing.

I have

I have already proved that God is peculiarly preſent in Houſes which are devoted to his worſhip: But what other valuable purpoſe can his peculiar preſence there anſwer, or what elſe can be meant by it, but his being peculiarly ready to hear, anſwer, and bleſs thoſe who worſhip him, as they ought to do, in his own Houſe? What elſe can the ſpecial preſence of God ſignify? The author and governor of all worlds is not a corporeal being: He cannot be confined within any place, or contained within any particular limits; *for heaven, and the heaven of heavens, cannot contain him:* But univerſal extent is filled with the immenſity of his preſence and exiſtence. The ſpecial preſence of God, in any particular place, muſt therefore ſignify, that he is, in that place, peculiarly gracious and merciful. Hence David prayed that God would *ſend help from the Sanctuary*—and declared that *his way is in the Sanctuary*—that *from Mount Zion, the Lord commanded his bleſſing, even life for evermore.*—And Chriſt hath told us, that *where two or three are gathered together in his name* (for public worſhip, in acknowledgment of him) *there he is in the midſt of them.*—From theſe obſervations it plainly appears, that God is treated with greater reſpect, honour, and reverence, by the public worſhip of his people; and will more graciouſly hear and anſwer their prayers and praiſes, when offered up in his Sanctuary, than elſewhere. But I proceed to ſhow, in the

III. And laſt place, the reſpect which is due from you to this Houſe, conſidered as the Temple of God; and how you ought always to behave when you tread the Courts of the Lord's Houſe.

There is ſomething ſo great and affecting, ſo beautiful and ſolemn, in the appearance of a congregation, when united in religious worſhip, each one join-

joining both with heart and voice, in paying homage to the Almighty King of glory in his own Sanctuary; that nothing on earth beſides can ſo nearly reſemble the tranſcendently glorious exerciſes of heaven. For the bleſſed angels are repreſented as jointly paying, with united voices, their grateful, ſolemn, and joyous addreſſes, to the ſupreme governor of the univerſe, in ſuch a language as this, *holy, holy, holy* LORD GOD *of hoſts, which was, and is, and is to come; heaven and earth are full of thy glory: Great and marvellous are thy works,* O LORD GOD *Almighty; juſt and true are thy ways, thou King of ſaints.—Bleſſing, and honour, and glory, and power, be unto him that ſitteth upon the throne, and to the Lamb for ever and ever.*—What can be more delightful at preſent, than to imitate the worſhipping choirs of heaven, and to make that our pleaſing employment now, which hereafter is to be our buſineſs and delight for ever? If we hope to enjoy the company of pure and holy ſpirits above, is it not extremely proper and neceſſary for us to learn their bleſſed practice while here on earth, by habituating ourſelves to thoſe religious exerciſes, in which the happineſs of heaven conſiſts, and by which we ſhall become more and more fit *to be partakers of the inheritance of the ſaints in light,* until we are ready to join our kindred ſpirits above?

And as this Houſe is built for the honour of the Deity, and given up to theſe religious exerciſes, ſo let it be devoted entirely to this uſe. And as it is now ſet apart for the convenience of public worſhip and religious ſervice, ſo take notice and remember, that it is dedicated to this holy purpoſe, and reſigned up to the ſupreme Majeſty of heaven. Let it therefore be, from this time forward, ſacred to ALMIGHTY GOD, by the name of TRINITY-CHURCH.

D Now

Now then let us all heartily and devoutly address the throne of grace, as Solomon did on a like occasion.——*Arise, O Lord God, into thy resting place; Let thy priests, O Lord God, be cloathed with salvation, and let thy saints rejoice in goodness. Let, we beseech thee, thine eyes be open, and let thine ears be attent unto* all *the prayers that are made in this place.* May the holy spirit of God attend the exercises of this House, and the means of grace be ever successful here. May the reading of the word of God, and the preaching of the gospel in this House, through the rich blessing of God, produce the heavenly fruit of holiness, and lead many souls to eternal life. May all those, that shall here be taken into the covenant of grace, by baptism, be sanctified and constantly led by the blessed influences of the divine spirit: May they stedfastly adhere to their sacred engagements; "ever remain in the number of thy faithful and elect "children; and be everlastingly rewarded by thee," O heavenly Father. And may all those who shall here devote themselves to God, in the participation of the Lord's supper, in commemoration of the death of their dear Redeemer, receive plentiful communications of the divine spirit; never disgrace their holy profession, but faithfully perform their sacred obligations, and *grow up in holiness and comfort through faith, unto eternal salvation.*

And grant, O heavenly Father, that thy people who shall wait upon thee, and devoutly offer up pure and holy worship, in this *House of prayer*, may enjoy all the privileges, and blessings of the covenant of grace, *which is in all things well ordered and sure.*—And *when thy judgments are abroad in the earth*, to punish the wickedness of men, and thy people in this place shall be distressed with mortal sickness, or any other

other sore calamity, if they shall repent and turn to thee, *then, whatsoever prayer or supplication shall be made by any man, or by all thy people*, in this place, *when* any, or *every one shall know his own sore and his own grief, and shall spread forth his hands in this House: Hear thou from heaven, thy dwelling place, and forgive*; deliver them out of their calamity, send forth thy blessing upon them, grant thy mercy and favour unto all those who implore it, through the atonement of thy Son; and cause *the hearts of the disobedient to turn unto the wisdom of the just; that thy people* in this place *may fear thee, and walk in thy ways.* And being *planted in the House of the* Lord, *may* they *flourish in the courts of* thy *House*, O God, bring forth *the fruit of thy spirit*, even *goodness, and righteousness, and truth*; and enjoy both the blessings of thy House here, and life for evermore!

Grant that this people may speedily be supplied with an able, spiritual guide, who shall profitably explain to them *the word of truth*; be an ornament to his profession, a worthy Ambassador of God, and Messenger of Christ, a bright shining light in this Sanctuary: And give thy people in this place occasion to cry out, *how beautiful are the feet of them that preach the gospel of peace, and bring glad tidings of good things!* Grant this, O Lord God, for Jesus Christ's sake, our only Mediator and Redeemer. Amen.

And now, my brethren, you are to consider this House, as it truly is, the Temple of the living God: And to behave in it, at all times, "as under God's "more immediate presence and observation." *How dreadful is this place! surely this is none other than the House of God; this is the gate of heaven*, said the astonished Patriarch Jacob, when he arose from his dream or

or vision, in which the divine presence appeared in a glorious view. What can be expressed with a more majestic solemnity than this sentence which he uttered? *How dreadful!* as much as to say, though this is a desert which is wild and solitary, destitute of cultivation and the conveniences of life, where I have reclined my head on a pillow of stones; yet how awfully venerable is it, since the immortal God hath consecrated it with his holy presence! *Surely the* LORD *is in this place,* said he, *and I knew it not.*

When God appeared in visions formerly, and wheresoever he was publicly worshipped, his people had a powerful sense of his presence, and, when in such places, always expressed the most awful veneration. So, my brethren, ought you to behave, when you are in this House. And to wait upon God here, ought to be your peculiar delight. LORD, *I have loved the habitation of thy House, and the place where thine honour dwelleth,* said holy David. And he knew no happiness on earth, equal to that of resorting to the Sanctuary of God: For when he was under the greatest personal distresses; when his own children rebelled against him, and sought his life, when his friends deserted him, and his enemies triumphantly reviled him; no trouble seemed to be so deeply fixed in his heart, as his banishment from the House of the Lord. *My soul longeth,* said he, *yea even fainteth for the courts of the Lord: My heart and my flesh cry out for the living God.—O send out thy light and thy truth, let them lead me, let them guide me unto thy holy hill, and to thy Tabernacle! Then will I go unto the altar of God; unto God, my exceeding joy: Yea upon the harp will I praise thee, O God! my God!* How earnestly did the Prophet Daniel entreat his Maker that the Temple might be rebuilt? *Cause thy face to shine upon thy Sanctuary, that is desolate. Thy servants take pleasure in her stones,* said he, *and favour the dust thereof.* They had a veneration for the very ruins of the House of God; and loved the meer dust and rubbish of Sion, more than all the sumptuous palaces of Babylon. So ought you to regard and reverence this House, this Temple of the living God.

Now the very notion of reverential respect, properly includes two things: * An inward esteem of what we regard or reverence, and the expression of that esteem by suitable external actions. No one can properly be said to reverence any thing, unless from his heart he bears a regard to it. Without this, all outward show is but meer hypocrisy. And the esteem ought always to be in proportion to the worthiness of the object. There is a degree of reverence due to God, which can be due to none *but God:* He justly claims our supreme veneration. But then his House, and every thing besides, that relates immediately to divine worship, claim a lower degree of our reverence and respect.

In the present case, the reverence which we owe to this House of God, doth not arise from the meer building itself; but from its being a place solemnly dedicated to religious worship; where we, as being his children, are to receive the blessings of the Father of spirits: And where, as being the work of his hands, we are to *worship, fall down, and kneel before the Lord our Maker.* The inward esteem and reverence which is due to the House of God, is in scripture expressed in the most affectionate language:—*How amiable are thy Tabernacles, O Lord of hosts!* said David. How hearty was the respect which our Sa-

* *Vide* Warren *in eundem.*

Saviour paid to the Temple, when, with a pious indignation, *he cast out them that sold and bought therein?* And while we remember the pious regard and zeal of our blessed Lord, for *his Father's House of prayer*, and reverence this House only on God's account; we need not be afraid of carrying our veneration for it too high. The danger, my brethren, is that you will not retain in your minds such a powerful sense of the holiness of this House, and of the special presence of God in it, as becomes you. You are always to remember that the lofty Majesty of heaven is peculiarly present here; and that it is your duty to approach him with respectful awe; with godly fear and reverence, with an holy dread, and most profound submission.

But this brings me to speak of the other part of that reverence, which is due to the sacred Majesty of the invisible God, and to this edifice, wherein he is peculiarly present. This consists in such actions or outward behaviour, as are most expressive of your inward respect, and venerable regard for them. And I entreat you all to consider, that whosoever bears a sincere regard to any thing, will not fail, on proper occasions, to express it, by his outward carriage and demeanour. When we see a man treat another with rudeness or indifference; we do not fail to conclude that he wants a real respect for him. And so, when you see a man behave in God's House of prayer with an air of vanity and irreverence, you may also reasonably conclude, that he regards neither the House he is in, nor the presence and authority of that being, who hath commanded him to *keep his Sabbaths, and reverence his Sactuary.*

But, for creatures so weak and degenerate, so mean and sinful as we are, the most submissive postures

tures that we are capable of, are hardly low and humble enough, when we approach the supreme Majesty of heaven and earth, in his own House; a God of infinite holiness, in whose presence the very angels, though a more noble order of beings than we are, and free from all guilt; yet are said to *veil their faces*, to express their solemn respect and reverence; and to *bow down* before him, in token of awful submission.

Therefore, whensoever you assemble in this House for worship, as a public acknowledgment of the most high God, by no means allow yourselves in any idle, inattentive, irreverend gestures, lest, under the hypocritical pretence of giving God your *hearts*, you afford him not even so much as the service of your *bodies*. And I entreat all those, who are fearful of showing the supreme God of heaven too much outward reverence and respect, to remember that *he* is the creator of their bodies as well as their souls: That *he* preserves and supports them both; and that *he* requires, and hath an equal right to the worship and service of both. *Glorify God in your body*, saith St. Paul, *and in your spirit, which are God's.* And again saith he, *I beseech you therefore, brethren, by the mercies of God, that ye present your bodies a living sacrifice, holy and acceptable unto God, which is your reasonable service.* Such a service is very agreeable to reason, which teaches us, that he who made the body, hath a right to the worship and service of it.

One would think experience alone sufficient to prove to a Christian, the efficacy of a serious, humble, outward deportment of the body, in order to excite and cherish in the soul a sincere and lively devotion. Christ, our blessed Redeemer, who did not come into the world to encourage superstition; yet, when he earnestly prayed, just before his crucifixion, that *if it*

it were possible, that cup might pass from him, did not refuse the most humble posture; but *kneeled down upon the ground.* And can any who pretend to *name the name of Christ,* refuse to follow his example? Will they presume to address God with less deference than his own Son our Lord and Master did! Will they dare to be so rude and indecent, so bold and unbecoming, when they are in the special presence of the sacred Majesty of heaven, as to compose themselves into a sleepy posture, or behave themselves as carelesly as though they were in their own houses; without appearing to have the least veneration for God's Sanctuary, and the worship of their Maker, who can destroy them in a moment, with the breath of his mouth! Is it not, my brethren, prodigious strange, that men, while they pretend to honour God, should affront him to his face! But it is still more wonderful, if possible, that any of the professors of Christianity should be deluded with such false notions of reverence, as to imagine that their outward behaviour, such as *kneeling at prayers, bowing at the name of Jesus,* in the rehearsal of what they believe, *standing up* when the Psalms are read or sung, and the like, is so far from being any part of religious reverence, or divine worship, as justly to deserve the name of superstition! Not considering that the worship of the body, is as really our duty as that of the soul: And that it is absolutely impossible for our souls to be well affected and piously devout, while we do *wilfully* or *scornfully* refuse to honour and reverence God with our bodies, in the manner that St. Paul exhorts us to do.

Therefore, my brethren, I do entreat you, by no means to neglect bodily worship, which is your indispensable duty, and very useful to recall your wan-

wandering thoughts, to the exercises of inward devotion, and to increase and keep up your religious zeal and piety. Be very careful to avoid all indecent, careless, indifferent, lolling, slovenly gestures, in the public worship of Almighty God. Do not stand up when you are commanded to kneel, nor sit down when the rules of the common prayer require you to stand; but know assuredly, that all inclination to oppose these rules and orders is irregular, and proceeds either from inattention, laziness, indifference, a disputatious temper of mind, or from that perverse pride and obstinacy, which are owing to the vile suggestions of the great enemy of mankind.

A mind truly pious and devout, will unavoidably show its sincerity, by an humble, religious, and reverential deportment of body in the House of God. And I think it must be morally impossible, for men, who have a sincere regard for religion, to come to Church, without discovering, while in the peculiar presence of their Maker, some tokens of religious reverence, in their bodily behaviour. A sincerely good man is sensible of the great duty and advantage of waiting upon God in his House: He so well considers his own infirmities, and hath so solemn a veneration for the divine presence, that, while he is in the exercise of devotion, and all the time that he remains in the House of God, he imagines no care nor circumspection too great, for the suitable conduct both of body and soul. Whereas many people attend public worship in God's Sanctuary, with such a careless indifference, as amounts to a strong indication of a wicked and perverse, of an obstinate and profane temper of mind: So that we have just reason to suspect, and fear, that the inward disposition of

their souls is of the very same cast with the haughty negligence, and lazy indecency, of their bodily deportment.

But, "in order to your duly reverencing this Sanc-"tuary" of the most high God, you must behave in it "with that inward piety, and that outward hu-"mility, which so august a presence, and so mo-"mentous a concern, require of you." And that ye may do these things the better, you ought to prepare yourselves well beforehand: Which is peculiarly proper for *us* of the Church of England, since we may know, before we begin, exactly what we have to do: And have therefore a great advantage in preparing for the due performance of it.

When you offer up your public addresses to God in this House, though the words are ready prepared for you to utter, yet you have enough to employ you, in presenting them to the throne of grace, with zealous attention and undisturbed devotion. They only, who heartily and affectionately offer up to God the words which they use (whether by the assistance of a book, or without) can be truly said to pray as they ought. But since we are weak and imperfect creatures, unable to transact many things at one and the same time, it is evidently most proper for us, when we publicly worship God in his own House, to have nothing else to do, for the exercise of the soul, but to employ it in offering up, with fervent devotion, what we have very often considered, and do well understand: That we may not spend our time in studying how to tickle each other's ears, and rack our heads with invention, while our hearts ought to glow with the most solemn devotion: And that we may not be employed in considering the new petitions which we hear, and whether they are fit for us

us to join in, while we ought to do homage to God with our voices, and to reverence him with the warm affections of our hearts. He that useth our liturgy in public worship, with that holy devotion of soul which he ought, "can never complain that forms of "prayer stint the spirit, or make men lazy and "idle."

To make you sincerely good and pious, whether you will or no, is not in the power of the Church of England. All our Church can do, is to assist you, in the best manner, concerning your devotions, and to lead you in the surest and most direct course to heaven. And this she hath done with peculiar wisdom and piety. And if you comply with her directions, you will reap the blessed benefit, and rejoice in so great a privilege. But if you will not observe the rules prescribed, and accordingly should not receive any manner of *good* to your souls; yet that will not be the fault of the Church, but entirely your own.— Therefore I exhort and intreat you all, for the honour of Christianity, for the glory of God, and for the benefit of your own immortal souls, to make a right use of our public liturgy. In order to which, you must often peruse it; take care to understand it; and prepare yourselves for the due performance of *your part* in it. And to assist you, I will now, in a few words, explain to you the right use of our morning and evening service.

Our public devotions begin with two or three short sentences of scripture, expressive of our wickedness, and of the mercy of God: After which is pronounced by the minister, "a serious exhortation to repentance; that the minds of the people may be impressed with a humble sense of their sins, that they may recollect their many iniquities, and that they

E 2 may

may be properly difpofed to enter upon the great duty of repentance: Accordingly, then followeth a general confeffion of fins, imploring forgivenefs; to be faid by the whole congregation, by minifter and people alternately, with a folemn voice, *all kneeling*, and with a truly humble and penitent heart. After which, the prieft alone uttereth the abfolution; which is a declaration that God will be merciful to all true penitents. And when this is performed, the remembrance of God's mercy will tend to make us fubmiffive, dutiful, and thankful. Then we may, with comfortable affurance, call God our Father, in that form which Chrift hath taught us. Accordingly the minifter and people, all as one, repeat the Lord's prayer. Thus the honeft Churchman, the pious Chriftian, receives divine comfort in the Houfe of God. For though he frequently offendeth through the infirmity of his nature; yet he doth as often repent, and always, when he is in the Sanctuary, implore pardon. And fo, by conftantly mortifying and bewailing his fins, he obtains an habitual averfion to them: And from the fincerity of his repentance, derives a joyful hope of pardon, and of the favour of his Maker, through the gracious mediation of his kind Redeemer.

The Pfalms, which confift chiefly in praifes, come next in our liturgy: And in order to the due performance of this part of our worfhip, we muft frequently and attentively confider the Majefty and goodnefs of God. And our minds, being properly affected therewith, will be prepared to hear, with dutiful attention, the portions of fcripture read by the minifter: And we fhall be difpofed to receive them as fpoken to ourfelves; fince *all fcripture is given by infpiration of God; and is profitable for doctrine, for reproof,*

reproof, for correction, and inftruction in righteoufnefs. —And if we are thankful to God, as we ought to be, for the light of revelation, we fhall be difpofed to utter, with a heavenly tranfport of joy and devotion, among others, that moft divine anthem, "we "praife thee, O God, we acknowledge thee to be "the Lord." Thus we fhall *ferve the Lord with gladnefs*, praife him publicly with chearfulnefs, and take peculiar delight in the courts of the Houfe of our God.

The remaining part, both of our morning and evening fervice, doth moft intimately concern our temporal and eternal intereft: And confifts in a number of petitions, for all thofe good things which we need, relating both to *this* life, and to *that* which is to come. And that we may perform this part of our public fervice to God's acceptance, and by his bleffing obtain what we afk for, it is abfolutely neceffary that we pray with faith and humility: And be alfo well perfuaded, that we afk for nothing but what is both lawful and expedient. And in order to this, we muft frequently and ferioufly confider what it is we pray for. Therefore it is very neceffary for you to read and examine, with diligent attention, the common prayers, and the feveral directions contained in the rubricks. And I affure you, that the liturgy of the Church of England is the beft collection, both of prayers, and rules for public worfhip, that can be found among all human compofitions. And as you have the beft affiftance for publicly worfhipping the fupreme Lord of the univerfe, that human wifdom hath ever yet contrived; fo it will greatly increafe your condemnation, if you neglect to make a good ufe of it.

I fhall

I ſhall not, at this time, undertake to conſider, in any particular manner, the caſe of thoſe who diſſent from our ſolemn and divine method of worſhip, for the ſake of extemporary prayers, and undigeſted effuſions. Let me only obſerve, that thoſe who complain, that they cannot be religiouſly devout in our form of worſhip, will hardly be ſincerely ſo in their own.

He that intimately knows the ſecrets of all hearts, ought not to be addreſſed with raſhneſs and inconſideration: Nor to be treated with idleneſs or wantonneſs. But we muſt pray with faith and zealous attention, with humble reverence and ſincere devotion, in order to meet with divine acceptance. And he that is not affected with the humility, ſolemnity and piety of the public prayers of the Church of England, muſt, I am ſure, be either ſtupidly inattentive, or perverſely ſtubborn, or perhaps otherwiſe extremely vicious in his diſpoſition and behaviour.

And as to bodily worſhip, it muſt be very improper to leave every one to follow all the whims that can be ſtarted by his own private fancy, either to ſit, ſtand, or kneel, juſt as he pleaſes. Therefore, like a wiſe and good mother, tenderly concerned for the true intereſt of her ſpiritual children, our Church hath directed and commanded us, to behave in each part of our public worſhip, as ſhe judged to be moſt becoming. When we earneſtly implore the greateſt of mercies, ſuch as the forgiveneſs of our ſins, the influences of the divine ſpirit, deliverance from all calamities, the continual preſervation of our ſouls, of our bodies and eſtates, and the mercy and favour of God towards others, we are required to kneel. While the word of God is read or preached to us, we are allowed to ſit down, provided we are ſerious and attentive,

attentive, and behave with proper decency. And when we are rehearſing the creeds, which contain the ſubſtance of our Chriſtian belief, or while ſome part of the goſpel, particularly adapted to the ſeaſon, is read to us, we are commanded to ſtand up, in token of reſpectful reverence. And, at all times, when we either read or ſing the praiſes of God, as they are contained in the Pſalms, or thoſe Hymns which we uſe, let us by no means refuſe to ſtand up, which is the moſt becoming poſture for thanſgiving and praiſe. David exhorts to *praiſe the Lord*—STANDING *in the Lord's Houſe.* And we read, concerning the worſhip at the dedication of Solomon's Temple, that when *the Prieſts and Levites praiſed the Lord—all Iſrael* STOOD. Therefore, my brethren, you ought ſtrictly to conform to all the rules and directions of the Church of England, reſpecting public worſhip, ſince they are agreeable to the higheſt reaſon, plainly warranted by ſacred ſcripture, and the moſt of them no leſs than divine commands.—I need not explain to you any more of the particulars of our worſhip: They are all to be found diſtinctly ſet down in the Common Prayer-Book; to that I refer you.

After what hath been ſaid, is it not ſurpriſing, that any ſhould be ſo ſtubborn and diſobedient, as to diſſent from the directions of our liturgy, which are ſo wiſe and rational; or from our method of worſhip, which is ſo eaſy and becoming, ſo pious and humble, ſo plain, beautiful and ſolemn? Since the worſhip of the Church of England doth agree ſo exactly with reaſon, with the commands, exhortations, and pious examples which are recorded in holy ſcripture; let it be ſuitably impreſſed on your minds, that if you wilfully refuſe to comply with it, you will moſt certainly incur the vengeance of heaven, for diſobedience to your

your proper governors, both in Church and State; Because your compliance with the liturgy, is required and commanded by the authority of both; whom you are bound to obey in every thing that they enjoin, which is not forbidden by the laws of God, But though I accuse people of irreverence, for not standing when public praises or thanksgivings are offered up, or for not kneeling in the time of solemn public prayer; yet I know very well, that many will speak of these attitudes as matters of indifference, notwithstanding they are both absolutely commanded in holy writ, and are also agreeable to the constant example of all the scripture worthies. But suppose they were indifferent, one might reasonably imagine, that no wise or good man would run the risque of drawing upon himself the displeasure of heaven, for not complying with the commands of lawful authority, in what is so easy to be performed, and in what he confesseth to be indifferent, and so not sinful. *Submit yourselves*, saith St. Peter, *to every ordinance of man, for the Lord's sake.*—And to the same effect are the following words of St. Paul, *let every soul be subject unto the higher power; for there is no power but of God: The powers that be are ordained of God. Whosoever therefore resisteth the power, resisteth the ordinance of God: And they that resist shall receive to themselves damnation.*

You may, with very little trouble, stand and kneel in public worship, as you are commanded: But the evils which you incur by refusing so to do, are great. A small portion of knowledge, with an honest, humble, and obedient heart, renders us capable of the spiritual graces of the Holy Ghost. But when we wilfully and stubbornly refuse to comply with the ordinances both of God and men; and *hew out* for ourselves *broken cisterns*, by our own invention; it

it must be just and right for God to resign us up to hardness of heart. For it is altogether just, that he, who will not be happy, in the method which Christ hath provided, should be left to be miserable in his own way. Let this consideration be a motive with you, always to behave in this House of God, as he hath commanded you, in these words, namely, *reverence my Sanctuary*; and in subordination to him, comply with all the directions of your lawful superiors. And I intreat you to suffer no evasions or excuses to deter you from it. Do not consider it as a small, indifferent matter: For be assured, you will find it far otherwise in the end.

But to conclude, I intreat of you all, seriously to consider what you have now heard: And I earnestly wish it may have its due effect upon you. —You have heard that God is peculiarly present in, and hath a great regard for, his House.— This should fix in your minds a respectful reverence for this House, which hath now been, in a solemn manner, dedicated to the most high God. You are to consider it as his peculiar property; so that you have no right to use it, except in his immediate service. And you ought to be awfully afraid of profaning it; since God is jealous for his honour, and for *the place where his honour dwelleth*: Remember therefore, and never forget, that this is the Temple of God.

Again, you have heard that public worship, performed in the House of God, is peculiarly expressive of reverence for him, and very acceptable to him. This ought to make you zealous and constant in attending public worship in this House: Since you have more reason to expect a blessing here, than elsewhere.

F And

SEAL OF THE SOCIETY FOR THE PROPAGATION OF THE GOSPEL.

REV. SAMUEL JOHNSON, D.D.
Ordained 1722.

36 A DEDICATION SERMON.

And in the last place, you have heard very particularly, what respect you owe to this House; and how you ought to behave in it. I beseech you therefore, to let these instructions sink deep into your hearts. Whensoever you come here, remember that you are in the immediate presence of him, who made and supporteth all worlds; who knows your most secret thoughts, and will hereafter reward or punish every one of you *according to the deeds done in the body*. Remember that the inhabitants of heaven are represented to us as worshipping God jointly and in unity: Not by one, representing the remainder; but each acting for himself, in uniformity *with* the rest. Therefore accustom yourselves *now* to worship God jointly and uniformly in public, and to carry on an open and apparent part of divine service in God's Sanctuary on earth, that it may be natural and easy for you hereafter to join the Church triumphant, in alternate and uniform, in public and united worship, at the throne of divine Majesty in heaven. And that this may be the delightful employment of us all, for ever and ever, God of his infinite mercy grant, through Jesus Christ our Lord.

Now therefore to the one, infinitely wise, good, and eternal God, in three persons, be rendered all honour and glory, thanksgiving and praise, might, majesty and dominion, world without end. Amen.

F I N I S.

THE

COMMUNION-OFFICE

FOR THE USE OF THE

CHURCH

OF

SCOTLAND,

AS FAR AS CONCERNETH THE

MINISTRATION

OF THAT

HOLY SACRAMENT,

WITH

PRIVATE DEVOTIONS.

EDINBURGH:
M.DCC.LXXXI.

THE

COMMUNION-OFFICE

FOR THE USE OF THE

CHURCH OF SCOTLAND,

As far as concerneth the Miniſtration of that HOLY SACRAMENT.

¶ *The Exhortation.*

DEARLY beloved in the Lord, ye that mind to come to the holy Communion of the body and blood of our Saviour Chriſt, muſt conſider what St Paul writeth to the Corinthians; how he exhorteth all perſons diligently to try and examine themſelves, before they preſume to eat of that bread, and drink of that cup. For as the benefit is great, if with a true penitent heart and lively faith we receive that holy ſacrament, (for then we ſpiritually eat the fleſh of Chriſt, and drink his blood; then we dwell in Chriſt, and Chriſt in us; we are one with Chriſt, and Chriſt with us;) ſo is the danger great, if we receive the ſame unworthily; for then we are guilty of the body and blood of Chriſt our Saviour; we eat and drink our own damnation, not conſidering the Lord's body; we kindle God's wrath againſt us; we provoke him to plague us with divers diſeaſes, and ſundry kinds of

 death.

death. Judge therefore yourſelves, brethren, that ye be not judged of the Lord; repent you truly for your ſins paſt; have a lively and ſtedfaſt faith in Chriſt our Saviour; amend your lives, and be in perfect charity with all men: ſo ſhall ye be meet partakers of theſe holy myſteries. And, above all things, ye muſt give humble and hearty thanks to God the Father, the Son, and the Holy Ghoſt, for the redemption of the world, by the death and paſſion of our Saviour Chriſt, both God and man, who did humble himſelf even to the death upon the croſs for us miſerable ſinners, who lay in darkneſs and the ſhadow of death, that he might make us the children of God, and exalt us to everlaſting life. And to the end that we ſhould always remember the exceeding great love of our Maſter and only Saviour Jeſus Chriſt thus dying for us, and the innumerable benefits which by his precious blood-ſhedding he hath obtained to us, he hath inſtituted and ordained holy myſteries, as pledges of his love, and for a continual remembrance of his death, to our great and endleſs comfort. To him, therefore, with the Father, and the Holy Ghoſt let us give (as we are moſt bounden) continual thanks, ſubmitting ourſelves wholly to his holy will and pleaſure, and ſtudying to ſerve him in true holineſs and righteouſneſs all the days of our life. *Amen.*

¶ *Then*

¶ *Then the Presbyter, or Deacon, ſhall ſay,*

Let us preſent our offerings to the Lord with reverence and godly fear.

¶ *Then the Presbyter ſhall begin the offertory, ſaying one or more of theſe ſentences following, as he thinketh moſt convenient by his diſcretion, according to the length or ſhortneſs of the time that the people are offering.*

IN proceſs of time it came to paſs, that Cain brought of the fruit of the ground an offering unto the Lord. And Abel, he alſo brought of the firſtlings of his flock, and of the fat thereof. And the Lord had reſpect unto Abel, and to his offering: but unto Cain and to his offering he had not reſpect. *Gen.* iv. 3, 4.

Speak unto the children of Iſrael, that they bring me an offering: of every man that giveth it willingly with his heart, ye ſhall take my offering. *Exod.* xxv. 2.

Ye ſhall not appear before the Lord empty. Every man ſhall give as he is able, according to the bleſſing of the Lord your God which he hath given you. *Deut.* xvi. 16, 17.

Give unto the Lord the glory due unto his name: bring an offering, and come into his courts. *Pſal.* xcvi. 8.

Lay not up for yourſelves treaſures upon earth, where moth and ruſt doth corrupt, and where thieves break through and ſteal: but

A 3 lay

lay up for yourfelves treafures in heaven, where neither moth nor ruft doth corrupt, and where thieves do not break through nor fteal. *Matth.* vi. 19, 20.

Not every one that faith unto me, Lord, Lord, fhall enter into the kingdom of heaven: but he that doth the will of my Father which is in heaven. *Matth.* vii. 21.

Jefus fat over-againft the treafury, and beheld how the people caft money into it: and many that were rich caft in much. And there came a certain poor widow, and fhe threw in two mites, which make a farthing. And he called unto him his difciples, and faith unto them, Verily I fay unto you, that this poor widow hath caft more in, than all they which have caft into the treafury. For all they did caft in of their abundance: but fhe of her want did caft in all that fhe had, even all her living. *Mark* xii. 41, 42, 43, 44.

Who goeth a warfare any time at his own charges? who planteth a vineyard, and eateth not of the fruit thereof? or who feedeth a flock, and eateth not of the milk of the flock? 1 *Cor.* ix. 7.

If we have fown unto you fpiritual things, is it a great thing if we fhall reap your carnal things? 1 *Cor.* ix. 11.

Do ye not know, that they which minifter about holy things, live of the things of the temple? and they which wait at the altar, are partakers with the altar? Even fo hath the

the Lord ordained, that they who preach the gofpel, fhould live of the gofpel. 1 *Cor.* ix. 13, 14.

He who foweth fparingly, fhall reap alfo fparingly: and he who foweth bountifully, fhall reap alfo bountifully. Every man according as he purpofeth in his heart, fo let him give; not grudgingly, or of neceffity: for God loveth a chearful giver. 2 *Cor.* ix. 6, 7.

Let him that is taught in the word, communicate unto him that teacheth, in all good things. Be not deceived; God is not mocked: for whatfoever a man foweth, that fhall he alfo reap. *Gal.* vi. 6, 7.

Charge them that are rich in this world, that they be not high-minded, nor truft in uncertain riches, but in the living God, who giveth us richly all things to enjoy: That they do good, that they be rich in good works, ready to diftribute, willing to communicate; laying up in ftore for themfelves a good foundation againft the time to come, that they may lay hold on eternal life. 1 *Tim.* vi. 17, 18, 19.

God is not unrighteous, to forget your work and labour of love, which ye have fhewed toward his name, in that ye have miniftered to the faints, and do minifter. *Heb.* vi. 10.

To do good, and to communicate, forget not; for with fuch facrifices God is well pleafed. *Heb.* xiii. 16.

¶ *While the Presbyter distinctly pronounceth some or all of these sentences for the offertory, the Deacon, or (if no such be present) some other fit person, shall receive the devotions of the people there present, in a bason provided for that purpose. And when all have offered, he shall reverently bring the said bason, with the oblations therein, and deliver it to the Presbyter; who shall humbly present it before the Lord, and set it upon the holy table, saying,*

BLESSED be thou, O Lord God, for ever and ever. Thine, O Lord, is the greatness, and the glory, and the victory, and the majesty: for all that is in the heaven and in the earth is thine: thine is the kingdom, O Lord, and thou art exalted as head above all: both riches and honour come of thee, and of thine own do we give unto thee. *Amen.*

¶ *And the Presbyter shall then offer up, and place the bread and wine prepared for the sacrament upon the Lord's table: and shall say,*

The Lord be with you.
Answer. And with thy spirit.
Presbyter. Lift up your hearts.
Answer. We lift them up unto the Lord.
Presbyter. Let us give thanks unto our Lord God.
Answer. It is meet and right so to do.
Presbyter. It is very meet, right, and our bounden

bounden duty, that we should at all times, and in all places, give thanks unto thee, O Lord, * [holy Father,] Almighty, everlasting God.

* *These words* (holy Father) *must be omitted on Trinity-Sunday.*

¶ *Here shall follow the proper preface, according to the time, if there be any especially appointed; or else immediately shall follow,*

Therefore with angels and archangels, *&c.*

¶ *Proper Prefaces.*

¶ *Upon Christmas-day, and seven days after.*

BECAUSE thou didst give Jesus Christ thine only Son, to be born * [as on this day] for us, who, by the operation of the Holy Ghost, was made very man, of the substance of the blessed Virgin Mary his mother, and that without spot of sin, to make us clean from all sin. Therefore with angels, *&c.*

* *During the seven days after Christmas, say,* as at this time.

¶ *Upon Easter-day, and seven days after.*

BUT chiefly are we bound to praise thee, for the glorious resurrection of thy Son Jesus Christ our Lord: For he is the very Paschal Lamb which was offered for us, and hath taken away the sin of the world; who by his death hath destroyed death, and by his rising to life again, hath restored to us everlasting life. Therefore with angels, *&c.*

¶ *Upon Ascension-day, and seven days after.*

THROUGH thy most dearly beloved Son, Jesus Christ our Lord; who, after his most glorious resurrection, manifestly appeared to all his apostles, and in their sight ascended up into heaven, to prepare a place for us; that where he is, thither might we also ascend, and reign with him in glory. Therefore with angels and archangels, *&c.*

¶ *Upon Whitsunday, and six days after.*

THROUGH Jesus Christ our Lord; according to whose most true promise the Holy Ghost came down* [as on this day] from heaven, with a sudden great sound, as it had been a mighty wind, in the likeness of fiery tongues, lighting upon the apostles, to teach them, and to lead them to all truth, giving them both the gift of divers languages, and also boldness with fervent zeal constantly to preach the gospel unto all nations, whereby we are brought out of darkness and error into the clear light and true knowledge of thee, and of thy Son Jesus Christ. Therefore with angels, *&c.*

* *During the six days after Whitsunday, say,* as at this time.

¶ *Upon the feast of Trinity only.*

WHO art one God, one Lord; not one only person, but three persons in one substance. For that which we believe of the glory of the Father, the same we believe of the Son, and of the Holy Ghost, without any difference or inequality. Therefore with angels, *&c.*

¶ *After which prefaces shall follow immediately this doxology.*

THEREFORE with angels and archangels, and with all the company of heaven, we laud and magnify thy glorious name, evermore praising thee, and saying, Holy, holy, holy Lord God of hosts, heaven and earth are full of thy glory. Glory be to thee, O Lord most high. *Amen.*

¶ *Then the Presbyter standing at such a part of the holy table as he may with the most ease and decency use both his hands, shall say the prayer of consecration, as followeth.*

ALL glory be to thee, Almighty God, our heavenly Father, for that thou of thy tender mercy didst give thy only Son Jesus Christ to suffer death upon the cross for our redemption; who (by his own oblation of himself once offered) made a full, perfect, and sufficient sacrifice, oblation, and satisfaction, for the sins of the whole world; and did institute, and in his holy gospel command us to continue a perpetual memorial of that his precious death and sacrifice until his coming again. For, in the night that he was betrayed, (a) he took bread; and when he had given thanks,

(a) *Here the Presbyter is to take the paten in his hands:*

(b) And here to break the bread:

(c) And here to lay his hands upon all the bread.

(d) Here he is to take the cup into his hand:

(e) And here to lay his hand upon every veſſel (be it chalice or flagon) in which there is any wine to be conſecrated.

thanks, (*b*) he brake it, and gave it to his diſciples, ſaying, Take, eat, (*c*) THIS IS MY BODY, which is given for you: DO this in remembrance of me. Likewiſe after ſupper (*d*) he took the cup; and when he had given thanks, he gave it to them, ſaying, Drink ye all of this, for (*e*) THIS IS MY BLOOD, of the new teſtament, which is ſhed for you, and for many, for the remiſſion of ſins: DO this as oft as ye ſhall drink it in remembrance of me.

The Oblation.

WHEREFORE, O Lord, and heavenly Father, according to the inſtitution of thy dearly beloved Son our Saviour Jeſus Chriſt, we thy humble ſervants do celebrate and make here before thy divine majeſty, with theſe thy holy gifts, WHICH WE NOW OFFER UNTO THEE, the memorial thy Son hath commanded us to make; having in remembrance his bleſſed paſſion, and precious death, his mighty reſurrection, and glorious aſcenſion; rendering unto thee moſt hearty thanks for the innumerable benefits procured unto us by the ſame.

The Invocation.

And we moſt humbly beſeech thee, O merciful Father, to hear us, and of thy almighty goodneſs

neſs vouchſafe to bleſs and ſanctify, with thy word and Holy Spirit, theſe thy gifts and creatures of bread and wine, that they may become the body and blood of thy moſt dearly beloved Son. And we earneſtly deſire thy fatherly goodneſs, mercifully to accept this our ſacrifice of praiſe and thankſgiving, moſt humbly beſeeching thee to grant, that by the merits and death of thy Son Jeſus Chriſt, and through faith in his blood, we (and all thy whole church) may obtain remiſſion of our ſins, and all other benefits of his paſſion. And here we humbly offer and preſent unto thee, O Lord, ourſelves, our ſouls and bodies, to be a reaſonable, holy and lively ſacrifice unto thee, beſeeching thee, that whoſoever ſhall be partakers of this holy Communion, may worthily receive the moſt precious body and blood of thy Son Jeſus Chriſt, and be filled with thy grace and heavenly benediction, and made one body with him, that he may dwell in them, and they in him. And although we are unworthy, through our manifold ſins, to offer unto thee any ſacrifice; yet we beſeech thee to accept this our bounden duty and ſervice, not weighing our merits, but pardoning our offences, through Jeſus Chriſt our Lord: by whom, and with whom, in the unity of the Holy Ghoſt, all honour and glory be unto thee, O Father Almighty, world without end. *Amen.*

¶ *Let*

¶ *Let us pray for the whole ſtate of Chriſt's Church.*

ALMIGHTY and everliving God, who by thy holy Apoſtle haſt taught us to make prayers and ſupplications, and to give thanks for all men; We humbly beſeech thee moſt mercifully to accept our alms and oblations, and to receive theſe our prayers, which we offer unto thy divine majeſty; beſeeching thee to inſpire continually the univerſal church with the ſpirit of truth, unity, and concord: and grant that all they that do confeſs thy holy name, may agree in the truth of thy holy word, and live in unity and godly love. We beſeech thee alſo to ſave and defend all Chriſtian Kings, Princes, and Governors, and eſpecially thy ſervant our King, that under him we may be godly and quietly governed: and grant unto his whole council, and to all who are put in authority under him, that they may truly and indifferently miniſter juſtice, to the puniſhment of wickedneſs and vice, and to the maintenance of thy true religion and virtue. Give grace, O heavenly Father, to all Biſhops, Prieſts, and Deacons, that they may both by their life and doctrine ſet forth thy true and lively word, and rightly and duly adminiſter thy holy ſacraments: and to all thy people give thy heavenly grace, that with meek heart, and due reverence, they may hear and receive thy

thy holy word, truly ſerving thee in holineſs and righteouſneſs all the days of their life. And we commend eſpecially to thy merciful goodneſs the congregation which is here aſſembled in thy name, to celebrate the commemoration of the moſt precious death and ſacrifice of thy Son and our Saviour Jeſus Chriſt. And we moſt humbly beſeech thee of thy goodneſs, O Lord, to comfort and ſuccour all thoſe who in this tranſitory life are in trouble, ſorrow, need, ſickneſs, or any other adverſity. And we alſo bleſs thy holy name for all thy ſervants, who, having finiſhed their courſe in faith, do now reſt from their labours. And we yield unto thee moſt high praiſe and hearty thanks, for the wonderful grace and virtue declared in all thy ſaints, who have been the choice veſſels of thy grace, and the lights of the world in their ſeveral generations: moſt humbly beſeeching thee to give us grace to follow the example of their ſtedfaſtneſs in thy faith, and obedience to thy holy commandments, that at the day of the general reſurrection, we, and all they who are of the myſtical body of thy Son, may be ſet on his right hand, and hear that his moſt joyful voice, Come, ye bleſſed of my Father, inherit the kingdom prepared for you from the foundation of the world. Grant this, O Father, for Jeſus Chriſt's ſake, our only Mediator and Advocate. *Amen.*

¶ *Then*

¶ *Then ſhall the Presbyter ſay,*

As our Saviour Chriſt hath commanded and taught us, we are bold to ſay,

OUR Father who art in heaven, Hallowed be thy name. Thy kingdom come. Thy will be done on earth as it is in heaven. Give us this day our daily bread. And forgive us our treſpaſſes, as we forgive them that treſpaſs againſt us. And lead us not into temptation; but deliver us from evil. For thine is the kingdom, the power, and the glory, for ever and ever. *Amen.*

¶ *Then the Presbyter ſhall ſay to them that come to receive the holy communion, this invitation.*

YE that do truly and earneſtly repent you of your ſins, and are in love and charity with your neighbours, and intend to lead a new life, following the commandments of God, and walking from henceforth in his holy ways; Draw near, and take this holy ſacrament to your comfort; and make your humble confeſſion to Almighty God.

¶ *Then ſhall this general confeſſion be made, by the people, along with the Presbyter; he firſt kneeling down.*

ALMIGHTY God, Father of our Lord Jeſus Chriſt, maker of all things, judge of all men; We acknowledge and bewail our manifold

ſins and wickedneſs, which we from time to time moſt grievouſly have committed, by thought, word, and deed, againſt thy divine Majeſty; provoking moſt juſtly thy wrath and indignation againſt us. We do earneſtly repent, and are heartily ſorry for theſe our miſdoings; the remembrance of them is grievous unto us; the burden of them is intolerable. Have mercy upon us, have mercy upon us, moſt merciful Father; for thy Son our Lord Jeſus Chriſt's ſake, forgive us all that is paſt; and grant, that we may ever hereafter ſerve and pleaſe thee, in newneſs of life, to the honour and glory of thy name, through Jeſus Chriſt our Lord. *Amen.*

¶ *Then ſhall the Presbyter, or the Biſhop, (being preſent,) ſtand up, and, turning himſelf to the people, pronounce the abſolution, as followeth.*

ALMIGHTY God, our heavenly Father, who, of his great mercy, hath promiſed forgiveneſs of ſins to all them who with hearty repentance and true faith turn unto him; Have mercy upon you; pardon and deliver you from all your ſins; confirm and ſtrengthen you in all goodneſs; and bring you to everlaſting life, through Jeſus Chriſt our Lord. *Amen.*

¶ Then

¶ *Then ſhall the Presbyter alſo ſay,*

Hear what comfortable words our Saviour Chriſt ſaith unto all that truly turn to him:

COME unto me, all ye that labour, and are heavy laden, and I will give you reſt. *Matth.* xi. 28.

Refreſh, O Lord, thy ſervant, wearied with the burden of ſin.

God ſo loved the world, that he gave his only begotten Son, that whoſoever believeth in him, ſhould not periſh, but have everlaſting life. *John* iii. 16.

Lord, I believe in thy Son Jeſus Chriſt, and let this faith purify me from all iniquity.

Hear alſo what St Paul ſaith.

This is a faithful ſaying, and worthy of all acceptation, that Chriſt Jeſus came into the world to ſave ſinners. 1 *Tim.* i. 15.

I embrace with all thankfulneſs that ſalvation that Jeſus has brought into the world.

Hear alſo what St John ſaith.

If any man ſin, we have an advocate with the Father, Jeſus Chriſt the righteous: and he is the propitiation for our ſins. 1 *John* ii. 1, 2.

Interceed for me, O bleſſed Jeſu! that my ſins may be pardoned, through the merits of thy death.

¶ *Then ſhall the Presbyter, turning him to the altar, kneel down, and ſay, in the name of all them that ſhall communicate, this collect of humble acceſs to the holy communion, as followeth.*

WE do not preſume to come to this thy holy table, O merciful Lord, truſting in our own righteouſneſs, but in thy manifold and great mercies. We are not worthy ſo much as to gather up the crumbs under thy table: But thou art the ſame Lord, whoſe property is always to have mercy. Grant us therefore, gracious Lord, ſo to eat the fleſh of thy dear Son Jeſus Chriſt, and to drink his blood, that our ſinful bodies may be made clean by his moſt ſacred body, and our ſouls waſhed through his moſt precious blood, and that we may evermore dwell in him, and he in us. *Amen.*

¶ *Then ſhall the Biſhop, if he be preſent, or elſe the Presbyter that celebrateth, firſt receive the communion in both kinds himſelf, and next deliver it to other Biſhops, Presbyters, and Deacons, (if there be any preſent,) and after to the people, in due order, all humbly kneeling. And when he receiveth himſelf, or delivereth the ſacrament of the body of Chriſt to others, he ſhall ſay,*

THE body of our Lord Jeſus Chriſt, which was given for thee, preſerve thy ſoul and body unto everlaſting life.

¶ *Here the perſon receiving ſhall ſay,* Amen.

¶ *And*

¶ *And the Presbyter or Minister that receiveth the cup himself, or delivereth it to others, shall say this benediction.*

THE blood of our Lord Jesus Christ, which was shed for thee, preserve thy soul and body unto everlasting life.

¶ *Here the person receiving shall say,* Amen.

¶ *If the consecrated bread or wine be all spent before all have communicated, the Presbyter is*

is to consecrate more, according to the form before prescribed, beginning at the words, All glory be to thee, *&c. and ending with the words,* that they may become the body and blood of thy most dearly beloved Son.

¶ *When all have communicated, he that celebrates shall go to the Lord's table, and cover with a fair linen cloth that which remaineth of the consecrated elements, and then say,*

Having

Private Devotions for the Altar.

BLESSED Jesus! Saviour of the world! who hast called me to the participation of these thy holy mysteries, accept my humble approach to thy sacred table; increase my faith, settle my devotion, fix my contemplation on thy powerful mercy; and while with my mouth I receive the sacred symbols of thy body and blood, may they be the means of heavenly nourishment to prepare my body and soul for that everlasting life which thou hast purchased by thy merits, and promised to bestow on all who believe in and depend on thee. *Amen.*

Prayer to God.

O Gracious and merciful God, Thou supreme Being, Father, Word, and Holy Ghost, look down from heaven, the throne of thy essential glory, upon me thy unworthy creature, with the eyes of thy covenanted mercy and compassion: O Lord my God, I disclaim all merit, I renounce all righteousness of my own, either inherent in my nature, or acquired by my own industry: And I fly for refuge, for pardon and sanctification, to the righteousness of thy Christ: For His sake, for the sake of the blessed Jesus, the Son of thy covenanted love, whom Thou hast set forth to be a propitiation for fallen man, and in whom alone Thou art well pleased, for His sake, have mercy upon me, receive my prayers, pardon my infirmities, strengthen my weak resolutions, guide my steps to thy holy altar, and there feed me with the meat which perisheth not, but endureth to everlasting life. *Amen.*

After Receiving.

BLESSED Jesus! Thou hast now blest me with the food of thy own merciful institution, and, in humble faith of thy gracious promise, I have bowed myself at thy table, to receive the precious pledges of thy dying love, O may thy presence retire with me from this happy participation of thy goodness, that when I return to the necessary labours and employments of this miserable world, I may be supported by thy grace to obey thy commandments, and conducted by thy watchful care thro' all trials, till, according to thy divine wisdom, I have finished my Christian course here with joy, that so I may depart out of this world in peace, and in a stedfast dependence on thy merits, O blessed Jesus, in whose prevailing words I shut up all my imperfect wishes, saying,

Our Father, &c. Amen.

Having now received the precious body and blood of Chriſt, let us give thanks to our Lord God, who hath graciouſly vouchſafed to admit us to the participation of his holy myſteries; and let us beg of him grace to perform our vows, and to perſevere in our good reſolutions; and that being made holy, we may obtain everlaſting life, thro' the merits of the all-ſufficient ſacrifice of our Lord and Saviour Jeſus Chriſt.

¶ *Then the Presbyter ſhall ſay this collect of thankſgiving, as followeth.*

ALMIGHTY and everliving God, we moſt heartily thank thee, for that thou doſt vouchſafe to feed us, who have duly received theſe holy myſteries, with the ſpiritual food of the moſt precious body and blood of thy Son our Saviour Jeſus Chriſt; and doſt aſſure us thereby of thy favour and goodneſs towards us, and that we are very members incorporate in the myſtical body of thy Son, which is the bleſſed company of all faithful people, and are alſo heirs thro' hope of thy everlaſting kingdom, by the merits of his moſt precious death and paſſion. We now moſt humbly beſeech thee, O heavenly Father, ſo to aſſiſt us with thy grace and Holy Spirit, that we may continue in that holy communion and fellowſhip, and do all ſuch good

works

works as thou haſt commanded us to walk in, thro' Jeſus Chriſt our Lord; to whom, with the Father, and the Holy Ghoſt, be all honour and glory, world without end. *Amen.*

¶ *Then ſhall be ſaid or ſung,* Gloria in excelſis, *as followeth.*

GLORY be to God in the higheſt, and in earth peace, good will towards men. We praiſe thee, we bleſs thee, we worſhip thee, we glorify thee, we give thanks to thee, for thy great glory, O Lord God, heavenly King, God the Father Almighty; and to thee, O God, the only begotten Son Jeſu Chriſt; and to thee, O God, the Holy Ghoſt.

O Lord, the only begotten Son Jeſu Chriſt; O Lord God, Lamb of God, Son of the Father, who takeſt away the ſins of the world, have mercy upon us. Thou that takeſt away the ſins of the world, receive our prayer. Thou that ſitteſt at the right hand of God the Father, have mercy upon us.

For thou only art holy, thou only art the Lord, thou only, O Chriſt, with the Holy Ghoſt, art moſt high in the glory of God the Father. *Amen.*

¶ *Then the Presbyter, or Biſhop, if he be preſent, ſhall let them depart, with this bleſſing.*

THE peace of God, which paſſeth all underſtanding, keep your hearts and minds

in

in the knowledge and love of God, and of his Son Jesus Christ our Lord: and the blessing of God Almighty, the Father, the Son, and the Holy Ghost, be amongst you, and remain with you always. *Amen.*

THE END.

THE

ADDRESS

OF THE

Episcopal CLERGY of CONNECTICUT,

TO THE RIGHT REVEREND

BISHOP SEABURY,

WITH THE

BISHOP's ANSWER.

AND, A

SERMON,

Before the CONVENTION at MIDDLETOWN,

AUGUST 3d, 1785.

By the Reverend JEREMIAH LEAMING, *A.M.*

Rector of CHRIST's CHURCH, Stratford.

ALSO,

Bishop SEABURY's first CHARGE, to the CLERGY of his DIOCESS,

Delivered at MIDDLETOWN, August 4th, 1785.

With a LIST of the Succession of SCOT's BISHOPS, from the Revolution in 1688, to the present Time.

NEW-HAVEN:

Printed by THOMAS and SAMUEL GREEN.

To the Right Reverend Father in GOD, SAMUEL, by divine Providence, BISHOP of the Episcopal CHURCH in CONNECTICUT.

The ADDRESS *of sundry of the Episcopal Clergy in the State of Connecticut.*

REVEREND FATHER,

WE, who have hereunto subscribed our names, in behalf of ourselves, and other presbyters of the Episcopal Church, embrace with pleasure this early opportunity of congratulating you on your safe return to your native country; and on the accomplishment of that arduous enterprise in which, at our desire, you engaged. Devoutly do we adore and reverently thank the Great Head of the church, that he has been pleased to preserve you thro' a long and dangerous voyage; that he has crowned your endeavours with success, and now at last permits us to enjoy under you, the long and ardently desired blessing of a pure, valid, and free episcopacy— A blessing which we receive as the precious gift of GOD himself; and humbly hope that, the work he has so auspiciously begun, he will confirm and prosper, and make it a real benefit to our church, not only in this state, but in the American states in general, by uniting them in doctrine, discipline and worship; by supporting the cause of Christianity against all its opposers: and by promoting piety,

peace, concord and mutual affection, among all denominations of Christians.

Whatever can be done by us, for the advancement of so good a work, shall be done with united attention, and the exertion of our best abilities. And as you are now, by our voluntary and united suffrages (signified to you, first at New-York, in April, 1783, by the Rev. Mr. JARVIS, and now ratified and confirmed in this present convention) elected Bishop of that branch of the catholic and apostolic church to which we belong, We, in the presence of Almighty GOD, declare to the world, that we do unanimously and voluntarily accept, receive, and recognise you to be OUR BISHOP, supreme in the government of the church, and in the administration of all ecclesiastical offices. And we do solemnly engage to render you all that respect, duty and submission, which we believe do belong, and are due to your high office, and which, we understand, were given by the presbyters to their bishop in the primitive church, while, in her native purity, she was unconnected with, and uncontrouled by, any secular power.

The experience of many years had long ago convinced the whole body of the clergy, and many of the lay-members of our communion, of the necessity there was of having resident bishops among us. Fully and publicly was our cause pleaded, and supported by such arguments as must have carried conviction to the minds of all candid and liberal men. They were, however, for reasons which we are unable to assign, neglected by our superiors in England. Some of those arguments were drawn from our being members of the national church, and

and subjects of the British government. These lost their force, upon the separation of this country from Great-Britain, by the late peace. Our case became thereby more desperate, and our spiritual necessities were much increased. Filial affection still induced us to place confidence in our parent church and country, whose liberality and benevolence we had long experienced, and do most gratefully acknowledge. To this church was our immediate application directed, earnestly requesting a bishop to collect, govern, and continue, our scattered, wandering, and sinking church: and great was, and still continues to be our surprise, that a request so reasonable in itself, so congruous to the nature and government of that church, and begging for an officer so absolutely necessary in the church of CHRIST, as they and we believe a bishop to be, should be refused. We hope that the successors of the apostles in the church of England have sufficient reasons to justify themselves to the world and to GOD. We, however, know of none such, nor can our imagination frame any.

But blessed be GOD! another door was opened for you. In the mysterious œconomy of his providence he had preserved the remains of the old episcopal church of Scotland, under all the malice and persecutions of its enemies. In the school of adversity, its pious and venerable bishops had learned to renounce the pomps and grandeur of the world; and were ready to do the work of their heavenly Father. As out-casts, they pitied us; as faithful holders of the apostolical commission, what they had *freely received* they *freely gave*. From them we have received a free, valid, and purely ecclesiastical

clesiastical episcopacy, are thereby made complete in all our parts, and have a right to be considered as a living, and, we hope through GOD's grace shall be, a vigorous branch of the catholic church.

To these venerable fathers our sincerest thanks are due, and they have them most fervidly—May the Almighty be their rewarder, regard them in mercy, support them under the persecutions of their enemies, and turn the hearts of their persecutors; and make their simplicity and godly sincerity known unto all men! And wherever the American episcopal church shall be mentioned in the world, may this good deed which they have done for us, be spoken of for a memorial of them!

JEREMIAH LEAMING,
RICHARD MANSFIELD,
ABRAHAM JARVIS,
BELA HUBBARD,
JOHN R. MARSHALL,
and OTHERS.

Middletown,
August 3d, 1785.

BISHOP SEABURY's ANSWER.

Reverend Brethren, beloved in our Lord, Jesus Christ,

I HEARTILY thank you for your kind congratulations on my safe return to my native country; and cordially join with you in your joy, and thanks to Almighty GOD, for the success of that important business, which your application excited me to undertake—May GOD enable us all to do every thing with a view to his glory, and the good of his church!

Accept

Accept of my acknowledgments for the assurances you give me of exerting your best abilities, to promote the welfare, not only of our own church, but, of common Christianity, and the peace and mutual affection of all denominations of Christians. In so good a work, I trust, you will never find me either backward or negligent.

I should, most certainly, be very apprehensive of sinking under the weight of that high office to which I have been, under God's providence, raised by your voluntary and free election, did I not assure myself of you ready advice and assistance in the discharge of its important duties—grateful, therefore, to me, must be the assurances you give, of supporting the authority of your bishop upon the true principles of the primitive church, before it was controuled and corrupted by secular connexions and worldly policy. Let me entreat your prayers to our supreme Head, for the continual presence of his Holy Spirit, that I may in all things do his blessed will.

The surprise you express at the rejection of your application in England is natural. But where the ecclesiastical and civil constitutions are so closely woven together as they are in that country, the first characters in the church for station and merit, may find their good dispositions rendered ineffectual, by the intervention of the civil authority: and whether it is better to submit quietly to this state of things in England, or to risk that confusion which would probably ensue, should an amendment be attempted, demands serious consideration.

The sentiments you entertain of the venerable bishops in Scotland are highly pleasing to me. Their

Their conduct through the whole business was candid, friendly, and christian; appearing to me to arise from a just sense of duty, and to be founder in, and conducted by, the true principles of the primitive, apostolical church. And I hope you will join with me in manifestations of gratitude to them, by always keeping up the most intimate communion with them and their suffering church.

SAMUEL, Bp. Ep[l] Ch. Connect.

Middletown, August 3d, 1785.

A

SERMON,

Preached before the

Convention of the CLERGY,

OF THE

Episcopal CHURCH in Connecticut,

AT MIDDLETOWN, AUGUST 3d, 1785;

The Day on which they recognised Bishop SEABURY.

BY THE REVEREND

JEREMIAH LEAMING, A.M.

Rector of Christ's Church, in Stratford.

NEW-HAVEN:

Printed by THOMAS and SAMUEL GREEN.

To the Right Reverend Father in GOD,

SAMUEL,

BY DIVINE PROVIDENCE,

Bishop of the Episcopal Church in Connecticut,

And to the Reverend,

The CLERGY of the same State;

THIS DISCOURSE,

PUBLISHED at their REQUEST, is,

With all Humility, DEDICATED.

2 TIMOTHY, III. 16, 17.

"All ſcripture is given by inſpiration of
"God, and is profitable for doctrine,
"for reproof, for correction, for in-
"ſtruction in righteouſneſs:
"That the man of God may be perfect,
"throughly furniſhed unto all good
"works."

SAINT Paul in his epiſtles to Timothy has pointed out the true characters of thoſe that are to adminiſter in the ſacred offices of the Chriſtian church. And he has alſo given the rule, by which, they are to conduct themſelves, both as to the *doctrine*, *diſcipline*, and *inſtruction of the church*.

The ſame method that was proper for planting the Chriſtian church, in the firſt ages of it; muſt, with great prudence, be made uſe of, for perpetuating the ſame church, in this new world, under a new form of civil government.

The ſtrange things that have paſſed under our view for ſeveral years paſt, muſt naturally lead us to recollect, in what manner God conducted the affairs of the great empires of the world, before, and at our Saviour's appearing.

In this view of the ſubject, we ſhall ſee ſome ſtriking evidence that God's providence was employed

ployed in an uncommon manner, to make it appear to the ſons of men, that the Deſire of all nations, was about to make His appearance in the world; and give a religion, by which, they might be happy.

To favour this great event, and render the firſt appearance of our holy religion more *auguſt*—and more *ſecure*, the ſtruggle for empire—the long conteſt for dominion, which had been in the world, *all* ſubſided at once.

That ſtormy ocean which had been, for ages, in continual agitation, now all of a ſudden, ſunk into a ſurprizing calm; and the earth was inſtantly overſpread with tranquillity, to receive the Prince of Peace, and his holy Religion.

The introduction of Chriſtianity was preceded likewiſe by remarkable degrees of knowledge; and the illumination of ſcience, ran before the light of the Goſpel. Egypt—Perſia—Greece, and Rome, thoſe ſeats of learning, formed the Roman empire.

Thus the Chriſtian Religion was able to give the moſt illuſtrious proof, that it really came from Heaven; by its diffuſing all over the world, at once, a light ſuperior to all human wiſdom collected, in its brighteſt ray of glory.

At the very ſame period of time, in which the Chriſtian Religion was publiſhed to the world, the largeſt empire that ever exiſted, was in its greateſt glory.

The hand of Providence is manifeſt beyond a doubt, to place evidence in ſuch a light, as to prove, that the *wiſdom of religion*, is ſuperior both to *earthly power*, and *human learning*. Empire which ſprang up amidſt the ſeven hills of Rome,

—*Science*

—*Science* nurst amidst the academic groves—and *Religion* from the obscure vales of Judea, all met, at this grand crisis, when Christianity first appeared.

The *power* of *Rome*—the *wisdom* of the *sage*—and the *Religion of Jesus*, were *unknown* to each other. They must have been conducted by the hand of Providence, or they never could have come together. They met. Power could find no fault with Religion, for it was friendly to government: Wisdom could not confute it, for Religion was supported by the most clear evidence: And the consequence was, that *Religion* very soon triumphed over both *power* and *wisdom*; the whole empire, and all the sages in it, became Christian. Thus you see, how GOD's providence has been concerned all along in support of true Religion.

And that we may comply with GOD's all-wise, disposing providence, in the present state of Christianity in this land; let the greatest care be observed, in admitting persons into Holy Orders; that they be such, as will be true Shepherds, and faithful Pastors in the Church of Christ.

Those bid fairest for the faithful discharge of their office, who are endowed with a competent share of *Divine Knowledge*—*with Holiness of Life*—*with Zeal for* GOD's *Honor in the Salvation of Souls*, and with a *Christian Sincerity*.

A man endowed with these qualities will seldom fail of being an eminent instrument, under GOD, in promoting the true interest of the Church of Christ.

As to *Divine Knowledge*, this certainly leads to the advancement of true Religion: Skill in any art or science will create respect for the man; much more.

more, proficiency in *Divine Knowledge*: So that with the greatest propriety it deserves the name of *Wisdom*: as proposing to itself the noblest end, our ETERNAL SALVATION—and the surest methods to attain it—and to teach others how they may arrive at it.

If ever *Learning* and *Divine Knowledge* were requisite to preserve the Clergy in *due esteem*, and true religion in *countenance*, they will be found absolutely necessary at this day.

The very business of teaching supposes, that the man is not only designated to that office, but well furnished with all useful knowledge. Ministers are to be living oracles of GOD, to whom any member of the Church may resort for advice, when ever they need it. They should be such, as are of ability to apply the general rules of *reason* and *scripture*, to the particular cases, in which, every doubting conscience, desires to be informed.

It is true, the first preachers of Christianity were *endowed with power from on high*, or *immediate inspiration*; but when the evidence for Christianity was compleated by miracles, *then*, as the manna ceased when the children of Israel came to the Holy Land; so inspiration ceased in the Church, when the canon of scripture was compleat. Since that time, the ministers of the Gospel, are to acquire their knowledge by labour and industry; yet by the blessing of the same GOD, who gave the inspiration.

Let us therefore consider the great importance of understanding what true Religion is, and the way to obtain the benefits of it. Too many mistake even in the terms.

Redemption

Redemption is *one thing*, and *Salvation* is *another*; yet they have been very often taken for the same: *Redemption* is what Christ has done; *he trode the wine-press alone; and of the people there were none with him*: *Salvation* is the consequence of Redemption; the benefit man receives from being redeemed. Man is not commanded to work out his *redemption*: *this is done by Christ*. But man is exhorted to work out his own *Salvation*: Since Christ has redeemed him, man is to fit himself, by obedience to the laws of Christ, with the assistance of the Divine Spirit, to be able to receive the benefits of redemption. These things must be distinctly understood by the *preacher*; otherwise he will never be able to make them plain to the *bearer*.

A second qualification of a Clergyman is, *Holiness* or in other words, *The life of* GOD *in the soul of man*. Indeed a religious life, is the only way to attain, the heavenly knowledge, I mentioned under the former head. *The secret of the Lord, is only with them that fear him*. This divine wisdom, delights to dwell no where, but in the *upright* and *pure heart*.

If therefore we would follow the advice of the apostle, *Let no man despise us*, we must be very careful to live a holy life, which certainly deserves the *greatest esteem*; and will be the best means, to prepare the way for our instructions to be properly attended to.

A minister whose character is amiable will find, that people will give attention to what he says. Bad as the world is, yet they do pay reverence to conspicuous virtue. Nothing is so beautiful as virtue, adorned with prudence.

Some

Some profane persons have pretended indeed to make holiness of life their *scorn* and *derision*; yet true piety carries such an awe with it, that even the wicked will revere it: honoring that virtue in their *hearts*, which they neglect in their conduct: Whose laws they must approve, tho' their beloved pleasures forbid to obey them. Thus you see how amiable virtue is, in the opinion of the profane: otherwise there never would be any hypocrites.

Certainly, all truly pious men, will most industriously endeavour, to perform all those duties which are incumbent upon all Christians; they will always strive to be *good*—*devout*—*just*—*bountiful*—and *merciful* Christians. But they will never suppose it a part of Religion, to rush into the office of a minister of Christ, till they are set apart to that office, according to Christ's appointment. The

Third Qualification to fit a man for a minister in the Church of Christ, is a *true, Christian zeal*.

I have mentioned knowledge as a requisite to the ministerial office: and here observe, that *Christian zeal*, must be governed by *Gospel knowledge*: Not only according to its *truths*, but its *precepts*: not only according to its *free grace*, but its *necessary duties*: not only according to its *mysteries*, but *the end for which those mysteries are to be believed*. It should be according to the original design—the fundamental principles, and eternal end of the Gospel; not so, as to exalt, or set any one doctrine at variance with another; which are all consistent with each other.

True zeal neither is, nor ought to be a solitary, or

or melancholy grace. It ought to have many other endowments of nature, joined with it: such as a *discreet judgment*—a *clear understanding*—a *well ordered devotion*—an *exemplary charity*; this will give the brightest lustre to true religion.

Zeal ought to be composed of the highest degrees of all pious affections. That zeal which has the greatest mixture of the *gentle*—the *benign*—and *charitable affections*, is the most likely to be the *best*. That wherein the contrary passions prevail, is in most danger of being *immoderate*.

This shews which is most agreeable to the *great, primitive purpose* of Christianity: that in the love of God, and desire to please him, man can never be *too affectionate*.

It is also true, tho' at first sight it may seem a paradox, that in the hatred of sin, men are some times too passionate; the more we love God, and those that bear his image, the better: but that which goes under the name of hatred of sin, insensibly carries men farther than against the sin, which we should hate altogether; it too often involves the person; which we should not hate at all: for all hatred to a person, is directly contrary to the spirit of the Gospel.

It is proper to observe this, because it is very evident, and a deplorable thing it is, that Religion, which was intended to reconcile mankind to Almighty God, whom we have infinitely offended, should not universally have the *same*, or *like effect*, in reconciling mankind among themselves.

It is too often the case, that men in religious matters, prefer *anger* and *censure*, before *brotherly love*, and *good will*. Too many there are, who

believe *no religion* to *be true*, but what is *intemperately rigid*; no *zeal* to be *spiritual*, but what is *censorious*, or *vindictive*; whereas *no religion is true*, that is not *peaceable*, as well as *pure*; no *zeal* is *spiritual*, that is not *charitable*.

True zeal in *religion*, should be what true courage is in human nature; none but minds truly pious are capable of the *one*; none but minds that are truly *great*, are capable of the *other*: and they both alike dispose and qualify the hearts, which they possess. That is the truest courage, which is not *only firm*—*brave*—and *undaunted*;—but also *calm*—*inoffensive*—*slow to anger*—*hard to be provoked*—and soon *reconciled*.

So should true zeal be; not only *constant*—*daring*—*fearless*;—but *meek*—*compassionate*—*long-suffering*—*easy* to be *entreated*. All other courage, besides that, is not *true valour*, but *rashness*. All other zeal besides this, is not a *Christian grace*, but *religious madness*.

Is there not some other qualification for a Christian preacher? Let us recollect——Yes, there is; and such an one, as is of no small consequence, which is Christian sincerity.

As it is the chief part of the minister's office, both by *arguments*, *examples*, and *discourses*, to persuade men to embrace the offer of mercy; so nothing is more conducive to this end, than for mankind to have a full assurance of our *faithfulness* and *sincerity*. We ought to imitate our heavenly Father, as far as possible, in the perfections of *divine wisdom*, and *unbiassed sincerity*. This will be the best way, to persuade our *hearers*, to *believe the truth we assert*, and *to follow the advice we give*.

On the contrary, the least suspicion of *duplicity* and *insincerity*, will defeat all our designs of doing good in the world.

This virtue of *sincerity* is so necessary in a Christian preacher, that there can be no need of enlarging on the subject.

To close the whole, Let all candidates for holy orders, acquaint themselves thoroughly with the service of our Church ; for it is the best school to teach *pure, genuine Christianity* that can possibly be formed. For the scriptures appointed to be read, from *Christmas* to *Trinity Sunday*, lay before us, the various steps, and the whole history of what Christ has done to redeem fallen man : and from *Trinity Sunday* to *Advent*, the Church hath wisely pointed out those scriptures to be read, which acquaint fallen man, what he, by the assistance of the Divine Spirit, must do, in order to obtain the benefits of that redemption. And as at the close of this mortal scene, we must all appear at the bar of Christ's judgment seat, to receive a sentence according to our conduct ; so the Church has provided, that in the close of the year, in the four Sundays in Advent, we are taught in the genuine language of Heaven, That we must all be judged by that very law, which Christ himself hath given to the Church.

So that in the compass of the year, we are taught, from pure scripture, this short, but comprehensive lesson, that the whole of our Religion, *Is to believe what Christ has told us, and to do what he bids us.*

Thus, my Reverend Brethren, I have laid before you, some of those qualifications, which in my opinion, appear requisite for those we are to recommend to the Bishop, for Ordination. We must not

not recommend any out of *favour*, or *affection* ; they must be only such, as will, in our best opinion, be able to build up the *Church—edify the saints —convert sinners*—and *enlarge the Redeemer's Kingdom*. Nothing will be more fatal to the Church, than to bring improper persons into the ministry. And much, very much depends upon our being faithful in this affair.

A very great and weighty charge has devolved upon us ; and may God's grace, be extended to us, in proportion to the importance of the subjects we shall deliberate upon.

It is our indispensible duty, in our undertaking to perpetuate the *primitive episcopal Church*, in these new States, to take the utmost care, that we do not move one step, by which any injury may accrue to the Church. In this view of the subject, we are bound to act, with the *coolest deliberation*, and the *most firm resolution*. If any mistakes are committed, we must bear the blame forever. Therefore let all unite as one man in carrying on the arduous work of building up the Church, in this land. *Proper* and *prudent measures* must be taken, to prevent our crumbling into parties.

To preserve us from these fatal mistakes, we ought to imitate as near as we can, some eminent characters : If a number of the Clergy in each State were endowed with the *prudence*, the *address*, and *eloquence* of a *Hering* ; the *humility, meekness*, and *piety* of a *Secker* : and the *good sense, learning*, and *fortitude* of a *Markham* : how powerfully, might such men, under God, preserve peace and unity among us ? Especially, if they imbibe the spirit of that prayer, for the Unity of the Church, which

which Christ addressed to GOD in these words, *Holy Father, keep, thro' thine own name, those whom thou hast given me, that they may be one, as we are.*' In this prayer, the Unity of the God-head, is proposed as a pattern for the Unity of the Church. Let us therefore, by the exercise of a *fervent, extensive,* and *exalted charity,* perform our parts towards uniting the divided body of Christians; and healing the unhappy wounds the Church has received; *that we may become one fold, under one shepherd.* Were this done, our Religion would appear in its native form; and look with that lovely and inviting aspect, that would win over its *enemies*, as well as make its *votaries* happy.

The providence of GOD was not more conspicuous, in preparing the world for the reception of the Gospel at the first, than it has been in bringing about a method for perpetuating the Church in this State. This might be painted in the most lively colours, and in the most striking manner; but some certain circumstances attending it, requires a more delicate hand than mine, to touch it. Therefore, I shall leave every one to enjoy their own sentiments about it.

And shall pass on to observe, that our Church is now compleatly organized with all its proper officers to continue her existence, upon a constitution, which we believe to be primitive; as it is unconnected with any civil establishment; it will appear to be truly the work of GOD, not of man.

I have the pleasure to see the day when there is a Bishop here, to act as a true Father towards his Clergy, supporting *their dignity*, as well as his *own*; to govern them with *impartiality*, as well as *lenity*; and

and to admit none to the altar, by ordination, but the *worthy*: to *uphold* a Church beaten with storms on every side; to *support* a Church that has been a bulwark against infidelity on the one hand, and Romish superstition on the other: But by the Divine Providence it has continued to this day. And upon this auspicious day, I cannot forbear to mention (and I do it with pleasure) the conduct of the Civil Rulers of this State, respecting our Church: they have not only manifested a spirit of *benevolence*, but an exalted *Christian charity*; for which, our gratitude is due, and shall be paid, in obeying all their just commands.

As the same disposition appears in the Ministers of our neighbouring Churches, to live in Christian harmony with us; we are all ready to meet them upon the same ground, with a *sincerity like their own.*

And the consequence of this will be, to lead our Bishop to seek the peace and welfare of all Christian Churches. To do all this, requires such uncommon talents, and such liberal supplies from Heaven, that it may be justly said, *Who is sufficient for these things?* Without the Divine assistance, none. But we are to believe, when GOD's providence advances any man to a public station, he gives the Divine Spirit to him, as he did to Saul, when he was *turned into another man, and God gave him another heart.*

A Bishop who puts his trust in GOD, may have the *spirit of wisdom*, (to manage happily the public affairs of the Church) the *spirit of understanding*, (to penetrate into all matters that require his inspection) the *spirit of counsel*, (to direct what is best

best to be done, in all intricate emergences) the *spirit of might*, (to resist and conquer all opposition) the *spirit of knowledge*, (to unfold the mysteries of faith) the *spirit of the fear of the Lord*, (to rule with an awful sense of being accountable to God) a *spirit of piety*, (to maintain a constant communion with God.)—A man endowed with all these gifts, may go forward in his work with *chearfulness* and *success*.

I shall, my dear fellow-labourers in the Gospel, in the next place, put you in mind of some few things, that may be worth your attention at this time.

As the Constitution of the Church in this State, will be formed upon the model of the primitive Church, antecedent to the time, in which, the Civil Powers undertook to patronize it; so your Bishop, will always consult his Clergy, as the primitive Bishops did, in all matters of importance. And you must be prepared to give the best advice, in all such cases: And constantly, for the time to come, preserve that same unanimity and harmony, for which you have been so justly famed.

Let us behave with the *dignity*, and *condescension*, that belongs to the office we bear; for honor and respect is due to the *Calling*, abstracted from the *Man*. This we may say without being suspected of *preaching up ourselves*: for our blessed Saviour hath given an eternal honor to the Priesthood, by being partaker of it himself.

A true Pastor of the Church of Christ, is required to take the greatest care, to watch over the flock committed to his charge; and should he meet with any opposition, he ought to resolve the more firmly

ly

ly, to perform every part of his duty; which will not only be most pleasing to God, but will secure our Holy Office in due esteem *among men*.—Indeed, *learning*, *wisdom*, and *sincerity*, *holiness*, *obedience to our civil rulers*, and an *unwearied zeal for the salvation of souls*, with *undaunted courage* in *defence of what* God *hath revealed*, are such ornaments, as the enemies of our holy Religion may be *displeased* at, but, for which, they can never *despise* us.

Having placed several things before you, that in a more particular manner concern the Clergy:

I shall close with an Application to the Laity; by putting them in mind how much they ought to exert themselves to support true Religion: and to do *this*, they are required to pay the Ministers of Christ that respect which is due to their sacred office.

Upon the first tho't, it can scarce be imagined, that an order of men instituted by Christ himself, to promote the eternal welfare of souls, should meet with any ill treatment: That they who bring glad tidings of reconciliation, between God and man; who, publish freedom to the captive—happiness to the miserable—and pardon to the greatest offenders; one would think, *such men*, might reasonably hope, to be received with *respect*, as well as *joy*.

But sad experience shows, *that there are men*, who because they *slight the offers of grace*, wish to render those that publish them, *despicable*. This must be very pleasing to the devil, for he knows how much the *discredit* of the Clergy, tends to the *destruction of souls*; and how little, the generality of men will regard the *doctrine* when they either

contemn,

contemn, or *despise* the *Preacher*. St. Paul himself could not escape the censure of such men, who, though they acknowledged his letters to be *weighty* and *powerful*, yet, they found fault with his *bodily presence*, as *weak*—and *his speech*, as *contemptible*.

Thus men who hate pure Religion, will wound it, by exposing the Ministers of it to scorn. To excuse their *own vices*, they will lay some of them upon the Clergy.

The principal part of the Religion we teach, is *Love*. For the soul which animates all societies, *civil* or *sacred*, is the *great* and *generous spirit* of *Charity*; that violates no *compacts*—that raises no *commotions*—that interrupts no good man's *peace*—that assaults no innocent man's *person*—that invades no man's *property*—that grinds no poor man's *face*—that *envies* no *man*—that *supplants* no *man*—that submits *private convenience* to *public utility*:—And recommends those duties to your *practice*, that will receive an infinite reward; and you may see, from the few following instances, what will be the rewards of the whole.

If we deal out our bread to the *hungry*, God will give us the *bread that came down from Heaven*: If we give *drink* to the *thirsty*, God will give us, *that living water, which will not suffer us to thirst again*: If we *clothe* the *naked*, God *will clothe us with Christ's righteousness, and immortal glory*: If we take in the *stranger*, we shall, after our pilgrimage is over, be *received into Christ's own family, with saints and angels*: If we *visit the sick*, we *shall be freed from all infirmities, and enjoy an eternal state of health*: If we *relieve* the *prisoner*, we shall be *released from eternal chains* and *darkness*: If we *plead* the cause of the *widow* and *fatherless*,

therless, *Christ will plead our cause*: If we *love our enemies*. *Christ will love us*.

To close the whole. Let both the Clergy and Laity consider, that our Religion requires us to act with a Christian fortitude *whenever trials attend us*. When storms arise—when dangers threaten—when inward or outward enemies attack our peace—when we cannot maintain our integrity without the sacrifice of some darling passion, of almost irresistible power—when we can walk no longer in the paths of truth, without the loss of some considerable temporal advantages—when we are summoned by our blessed Master, to fly from the soft allurements of pleasure, to burst the bonds of *avarice* or *ambition*—to disclaim all dependence upon the *world*, *ourselves* or any *created being*: In a word, *to forsake all, take up our cross and follow Christ*. Then, indeed is our hour of trial; then the sincerity of our attachment to Christ will be made manifest to ourselves, and to the world; our conduct will determine to whom we most assuredly belong; when thou canst abide with Christ in the *darkness of the vale*, as well as in the *splendors of the mount*; when you can follow Christ without the loaves and fishes, as well as when they were multiplied under his creating hand; then you have reason to think your faith is such, that your blessed Saviour will own you as true disciples in the last great day; and that you will be justified by his merits. Let us remember so much of what has been said, as may influence our lives, and direct us to the attainment of that reward, which God has promised, thro' the intercession of Christ, to all that *love*, *fear* and *obey* him.

BISHOP

BISHOP SEABURY's FIRST CHARGE TO THE CLERGY OF HIS DIOCESS,

Delivered at MIDDLETOWN,

AUGUST 4th, 1785.

Bishop SEABURY's first CHARGE, &c.

REVEREND BRETHREN,
Beloved in our LORD JESUS CHRIST.

IT is with very great and sincere pleasure, that I meet you here at this time, and on this occasion; and I heartily thank GOD, our heavenly Father, for the joyful and happy opportunity with which his good providence has favoured us; and do beseech him to direct and prosper all our consultations and endeavours, to his glory and the benefit of his Church.

At your desire, and by your appointment, I consented to undertake a voyage to England, to endeavour to obtain those Episcopal powers, whose want has ever been severely felt and deeply lamented, by the thinking part of our communion. The voyage has been long and tedious, and the difficulties that arose, perplexing, and not easily surmountable. Yet, by the favour of GOD, the important business has been happily accomplished; and the blessing of a free, valid and purely ecclesiastical Episcopacy procured to our infant Church; which is now compleatly organized in all its parts, and being nourished by sincerity and truth, will, we trust, under the guidance of the Holy Ghost, *grow up in him in all things, which is the head, even Christ: From whom the whole body fitly joined together, and compacted by that which every joint supplieth, according to the effectual working in the measure*

measure of every part, will *make increase of the body, unto the edifying of itself in love.* *

As under GOD, the Bishops of the remainder of the old episcopal Church of Scotland, which, at the revolution, fell a sacrifice to the jealous apprehensions of William the third, were the sole instruments of accomplishing this happy work: to them our utmost gratitude is due; and I hope the sense of the benefit we have, through their hands, received, will ever remain fresh in the minds of all the members of our communion, to the latest posterity.

Under the greatest persecutions, GOD has preserved them to this day, and I trust will preserve them; that there may yet be some, to whom destitute Churches may apply in their spiritual wants —some faithful shepherds of Christ's flock, who are willing to give *freely*, what they have *freely* received from their Lord and Master.

With us then, my venerable brethren, it remains, to make this precious gift which we have received, conducive to the glory of GOD, and the good of his Church. Long have we earnestly desired to enjoy the full advantage of our religious constitution; let us then carefully improve it, to all those holy purposes for which it was originally designed by our divine Head, the august Redeemer of sinful men.

Sensible as I am of my own deficiencies, and of the infirmities of human nature, I shall, by GOD's grace, be always ready to do my duty, according to my best ability and discretion; and, I trust, I shall, by him, be enabled to avoid every thing that may bring a reproach on our holy Religion, or be a

* Eph. iv. 15, 16.

a hindrance to the increase and prosperity of that Church, over which, I am, by GOD's providence, called to preside. On your advice and assistance, reverend brethren, next to GOD's grace, I must rely for support in the great work that is before me, and to which I can, with truth, say, I have devoted myself without reserve. Your support, I know, I shall have; and I hope for the support of all good men. Let us then trust that GOD will prosper our honest endeavours to serve the interests of his Church, and to make his Gospel effectual to the conversion of sinners to him, that their souls may be saved by the redemption and mediation of his Son. Worldly views can here have no influence, either on *you* or *me*. Loss, and not gain, may, and probably will be, the consequence of the step we have taken, to procure for our Church the blessing we now enjoy. But however our worldly patrons may be disposed towards us, our heavenly Father knoweth whereof we are made, and of what things we have need: And HE is able to *open his hand, and fill all things living with plenteousness.* * Let us then *seek first his kingdom and the righteousness thereof*,† and depend upon the gracious promise of our Redeemer, that all things necessary to our bodily sustenance shall, in the course of his providence, be given unto us.

In our endeavours to promote the interests of Christ's Church in this world, much, I know, will depend upon me: Much also, my beloved in Christ, will depend on you. Permit me then, in this my first charge, to mention two or three things of great importance in themselves, and which require your immediate attention.

The

* Psalm cxlv. 16. † Mat. vi. 33.

The first is, the obligations you are all under to be very careful of the doctrines which you preach from the pulpit, or inculcate in conversation.— You will not suppose that I am finding fault, or that I have reason so to do. General cautions of this kind must make part of almost all the charges from a Bishop to his Clergy. Should any Clergyman be censurable in this respect, it would be ungenerous to attack him in this public way, and unfair to correct him by wounding the body of his brethren. Should such a case ever happen, which I pray God never may, there are other modes of proceedings more likely to be effectual, and which therefore ought to be adopted. But when you consider, as I doubt not you do often and seriously, that many of the people under your care have little or no other instruction in religion but what they get from you—that the care of their souls is by Christ and his Church committed to you—and that you must give an awful account of them in the day of judgment, you cannot think such cautions as I just now interposed, can at this, or at any other time, be either impertinent or unnecessary. You are, and it is expected of the people that they account you as *ministers of Christ, and stewards of the mysteries of* God; * let us all then remember that *it is required of stewards that a man be found faithful*: And our own hearts will inform us, that the first instance of fidelity is, that the pure doctrines of the Gospel be fairly, and earnestly, and affectionately proposed, explained, and inculcated; and that we suffer nothing else to usurp their place, and become the subject of our preaching.

Another matter which my duty requires me to mention,

* 1 Cor. iv. 1. 2.

mention, relates to a business in which you will probably be soon called upon to act—I mean the very important one of giving recommendations to candidates for Holy Orders. It is impossible that the Bishop should be personally acquainted with every one, who may present himself for Ordination. He must, therefore, depend on the recommendation of his Clergy, and other people of reputation, for the character and qualifications of those who shall be presented to him. By qualifications, I mean not so much literary accomplishments, though these are not to be neglected, as aptitude for the work of the ministry. You must be sensible that a man may have, and deservedly have, an irreproachable moral character, and be endued with pious and devout affections, and a competent share of human learning, and yet, from want of prudence, or from deficiency in temper, or some singularity in disposition, may not be calculated to make a *good* Clergyman; for to be a *good* Clergyman implies, among other things, that a man be a *useful* one. A Clergyman who does no *good*, always does *hurt*: There is no medium. Not only the moral character, and learning, and abilities of candidates are to be exactly inquired into, but also their good temper, prudence, diligence, and every thing by which their usefulness in the ministry may be affected. Nor should their personal appearance, voice, manner, clearness of expression, and facility of communicating their sentiments, be altogether overlooked. These, which may by some be thought to be only secondary qualifications, and therefore of no great importance, are however those that will require your more particular

E

ticular attention, and call for all your prudence. They, who shall apply for recommendations, will generally be such as have passed through a course of academical studies, and must be competently qualified in a literary view. Examination, however, will ascertain the matter with sufficient certainty. And it is improbable that the openly vicious, or even they whose characters will not bear to be scrutinized, will ever apply for your testimonials: But should they be so hardy, the matter will soon be decided. You cannot recommend them, and there is an end of it. But the other qualifications I mentioned—good temper, prudence, diligence, capacity and aptitude to teach, and all those requisites necessary to make a worthy, useful Clergyman, may probably be sometimes doubted. And then a question arises, whether such a person ought to be recommended? The general consideration that a Clergyman should be useful to others, and should not merely consult his own emolument, but the benefit of Christ's Church principally, ought, in my opinion, to determine this point; and if there be real ground to suspect that a person will not make a useful Clergyman, whatever his moral character and literary attainments may be, he ought not to be recommended. He may serve GOD usefully and acceptably in some other station: and he cannot justly esteem it an injury that he was not admitted to a station in Christ's Church, where the probable chance was, that he would do more *harm* than *good*. It is always easier to keep such persons out of the ministry, than to get rid of them when once admitted. Open immorality exposes a man to the public censure

sure of his superiors, and he may, by due authority, be deposed, and dismissed from the ministry. But a Clergyman's conduct may be so guarded, as to be always within such a line as shall skreen him from public censure, and yet be such, as does manifest disservice to religion; and brings reproach on the order to which he belongs: And however uneasy you may be with having him in your number, no fair occasion to get rid of him may ever present itself.—*Lay hands suddenly on no man*, * was one of the things St. Paul gave in charge to Timothy, whom he had appointed Bishop of Ephesus: And if not *suddenly*, without *sufficient* deliberation and trial, certainly not in *doubtful* cases, especially where the probability is against the man, with respect to his usefulness as a minister. And all the reasons why the Bishop should *lay hands suddenly on no man*, are so many strong arguments against recommending any man *suddenly*, or in *doubtful* cases, to the Bishop for ordination.

The third thing which my duty calls upon me to mention to you at this time, because it requires your immediate attention, is that old and sacred rite, handed down to us from the apostolic age, by the primitive Church—*the laying on of hands* upon those who have been baptised, and, by proper authority, admitted into the Christian Church; and which is now commonly called *Confirmation*. Though, in truth, there seems to me to be more in the rite than a bare confirmation of the baptismal vow; and that it implies, and was originally understood to imply, the actual communication of the Holy Spirit to those who worthily received it.

It has not hitherto been in the power of the members

* 1 Tim. v. 22.

members of our Church to comply with this rite, for want of the proper officer to administer it. And we trust that the mercy of God, will pardon those omissions of duty, in his faithful servants, which arose merely from the necessity of their situation. But the case is now altered, and, through his gracious providence, that, and every other rite and ordinance which he has instituted for the government and edification of his Church, may be obtained and enjoyed. It becomes therefore our duty to attend to this matter; and as it is unreasonable to expect that people should comply with a rite before they are convinced of their obligation to do so, it lies upon us to explain to them its nature and meaning, the foundation on which it stands, the obligations they are under to comply with it, and the benefits they will receive from the institution, if they come worthily to it; and then, it is to be hoped, there will be no backwardness in the members of our Church to submit to it.

It is, I am sensible, unnecessary to point out to you, the several arguments and reasons by which your instructions in this point may be supported. You have undoubtedly often and seriously reflected on them. But as your duty, in that respect, is now to be more particularly regarded, and very soon carried into execution, permit me, by way of remembrance, to make a few general observations on the authority, nature and benefits of the institution.

We suppose, and I think justly, that the rite is founded on apostolical practice. In Heb. vi. 2, St. Paul enumerates the fundamental principles of the Christian Religion, such as were necessary for all

all Christians—viz. *Repentance from dead works—faith in* God—*the doctrine of baptisms—and of laying on of hands—and of the resurrection of the dead, and of eternal life.* No commentator or expositor of the holy Scriptures, ever understood this text of any other *laying on of hands*, but that in Confirmation, till since the reformation; and the celebrated Calvin himself, gives it as his opinion, *that this one text shews evidently, that Confirmation was instituted by the Apostles.* *

In the 8th Chapter of the Acts it is recorded, that when many of the Samaritans had been converted and baptized by St. Philip the deacon, the College of Apostles at Jerusalem sent two of their own number, Peter and John, who, when they had prayed for them, that they might receive the Holy Ghost, *laid their hands on them, and they received the* Holy Ghost.

In the 19th Chapter St. Paul finding some disciples at Ephesus who had been baptized only with the baptism of John, had them baptized in the name of the Lord Jesus, and when *he had laid his hands upon them, the Holy Ghost came on them; and they spake with tongues and prophesied.*

I know that the usual way of evading the force of these two last authorities is, by saying that this imposition of hands was for the sole purpose of conferring the miraculous gifts of the Holy Spirit: But this will not reach the first case, where St. Paul mentions *the laying on of hands* among the rudiments of the doctrines of the Gospel. In the infancy of Christianity *extraordinary, or miraculous gifts* were necessary for its establishment and propagation in the world. But have we reason sufficient

* Vid. Calvin, in loc.

cient to justify the opinion, that all upon whom the Apostles laid their hands received these miraculous powers? Is it not surprising that twelve men at Ephesus who had not even heard that there was any Holy Ghost till St. Paul's visit, should be pitched upon by him for receiving these extraordinary gifts? The miraculous powers of the Holy Spirit are communicated when, and where, and how, it pleases Infinite Wisdom: And very probably St. Paul was surprised at this extraordinary display of the power of the Holy Spirit upon the twelve men at Ephesus, as well as St. Peter had been, when the Holy Ghost fell upon the whole company of Cornelius to whom he was preaching, even before they had been baptized.* Because God sometimes departs from the ordinary institutions in his Church, are we to suppose that there is no virtue in those ordinary institutions, except when God shall please to accompany them with miraculous powers? The Holy Spirit is given for the sanctification of the heart, and to lead all those who will be governed by him, from one degree of holiness to another, till they shall become fit inhabitants of the kingdom of Heaven. And in truth there is as great a miracle in the conversion of a sinner from the error of his ways, as in speaking with tongues and prophesying. Both are beyond the power of nature, and both require Almighty Interposition.

In Confirmation, by the imposition of the hands of the Bishop and prayer, we believe the Holy Spirit to be given for sanctification, i. e. for carrying into effect that regeneration which is confered in Baptism. By Baptism we are taken out of our natural

* Acts x. 44, &c.

tural state of sin and death, into which we are born by our natural birth, and are translated, transplanted, or born again into the Church of Christ, a state of grace, and endless life; and by Confirmation, or the imposition of the hands of the Bishop, when we personally ratify our baptismal vow and covenant, we are endued with the Holy Spirit, to enable us to overcome sin, and to perfect holiness in the fear of God. If it can be proved that the Holy Spirit is not necessary for these purposes, but that his influence is only necessary when miraculous powers are to be confered, I will confess that Confirmation is unnecessary at this time, for it is not pretended that the miraculous powers of the Holy Spirit are now confered by *the laying on of hands.*

You must have observed that though the Samaritans were converted and baptized by St. Philip the deacon, yet the Apostles sent two of their own order to *lay hands* on them. And St. Paul, when the twelve disciples at Ephesus had been baptized in the name of the Lord Jesus, *laid* HIS *hands* on them. For these reasons, the Christian Church has always appropriated this rite to the successors of the Apostles, the supreme order of the Christian priesthood.

The time when Confirmation is to be used is not restricted to any particular age. When the person is of competent reason and understanding to comprehend the nature of the baptismal covenant, and is duly instructed in it, and sensible of his duty to fulfil it, and disposed to ratify and confirm it before God and his Church, with full purpose of continuing God's faithful servant to his life's end, he is properly qualified for the rite. And of these qualifications

lifications his minister is to be the judge, and is to certify the Bishop thereof.—A God-father or God-mother are to attend with them, to witness their Confirmation, and to *put them in mind*, if they perceive them to be afterward negligent of their duty, or departing from the solemn vows and promises they then made.

The benefits resulting from this institution have in some measure been anticipated; permit me however just to enumerate them. It enters us into a new engagement to be the Lord's, and to lead a Holy and Christian life; it is a lasting admonition not to dishonor or desert our profession: it preserves the unity of the Church, by making men sensible of their obligations to maintain communion with those ecclesiastical superiors who are the successors of the holy Apostles; and it is a testimony of GOD's mercy and favour to them, if they receive it worthily; because his minister declares authoritatively that GOD accepts their proficiency, and advancing them to the higher rank of the faithful, gives them a right to approach his Table and feast with their brethren on the sacrifice of the Holy Eucharist, the memorials of Christ's death; and by it also GOD condescends to communicate supernatural strength, even the gift of his blessed Spirit, to enable them to encounter and vanquish their spiritual enemies, and fulfil the terms of the Gospel.

These things, Reverend Brethren, you will explain and inculcate in your several congregations, that all may be informed of the nature of their duty, excited, on proper motives, to comply with it, and instructed how to come worthily to this holy rite,

rite, that they may receive the full benefit of it, and the Church be edified with sound and living members.

You will also put God-fathers and God-mothers, as well as the natural Parents, in mind, to see that the children they have answered for at the Font, be properly instructed, and in due time brought to the Bishop to be confirmed by him, that they may discharge themselves of the obligation which their Christian charity excited them to undertake.

And the GOD *of all grace, who hath called us unto his eternal glory by Jesus Christ—make you perfect, stablish, strengthen, settle you**—bless and prosper your ministry in his Church, and reward your faithful labours with the blessings of his own heavenly kingdom. *To him*, the holy triune GOD, be *glory* and dominion for ever and ever. Amen.

* 1 Pet. v. 10. 11.

A LIST of the Conſecration and Succeſſion of SCOT's BISHOPS, ſince the Revolution 1688, under William the third, as far as the Conſecration of Biſhop Seabury is concerned.

1693. *Feb.* 23. DR. GEORGE HICKES, was conſecrated Suffragan of Thetford, in the Biſhop of Peterborough's Chapel, in the Pariſh of Enfield, by Dr. William Loyd, Biſhop of Norwich, Dr. Francis Turner, Biſhop of Ely, and Dr. Thomas White, Biſhop of Peterborough. *N. B.* Dr. Loyd, Dr. Turner, and Dr. White, were three of the Engliſh Biſhops who were deprived at the Revolution, by the civil power, for not ſwearing allegiance to William the third. They were alſo three of the ſeven Biſhops who had been ſent to the Tower, by James the ſecond, for refuſing to order an illegal Proclamation to be read in their Dioceſſes.

1705. *Jan.* 25. Mr. John Sage, formerly one of the Miniſters of Glaſgow, and Mr. John Fullarton, formerly Miniſter of Paiſley, were conſecrated at Edinburgh, by John Paterſon, Archbiſhop of Glaſgow, Alexander Roſe, Biſhop of Edinburgh, and Robert Douglas, Biſhop of Dunblane. *N. B.* Archbiſhop Paterſon, Biſhop Roſe, and Biſhop Douglas, were deprived at the Revolution, by the civil power, becauſe they refuſed to ſwear allegiance to William the third.

1709. *April* 28. Mr. John Falconar, Miniſter at Cairnbee, and Mr. Henry Chryſtie, Miniſter at Kinroſs, were conſecrated at Dundee, by Biſhop Roſe of Edinburgh, Biſhop Douglas of Dunblane, and Biſhop Sage.

1711. *Aug.* 25. The Honorable Archibald Campbel, was conſecrated at Dundee, by Biſhop Roſe of Edinburgh. Biſhop Douglas of Dunblane, and Biſhop Falconar.

1712. *Feb.* 24. Mr. James Gadderar, formerly Miniſter at Kilmaurs, was conſecrated at London, by Biſhop Hickes. Biſhop Falconar, and Biſhop Campbel.

1718. *Oct.* 22. Mr. Arthur Millar, formerly Miniſter at Innereſk, and Mr. William Irvine, formerly Miniſter at Kirkmichael in Carrict. were conſecrated at Edinburgh, by Biſhop Roſe of Edinburgh, Biſhop Fullarton, and Biſhop Falconar,

After the Biſhop of Edinburgh's death.

1722. *Oct.* 7. Mr. Andrew Cant, formerly one of the Miniſters of Edinburgh, and Mr. David Freebairn, formerly Miniſter of Dunning, were conſecrated at Edinburgh, by Biſhop Fullarton, Biſhop Millar, and Biſhop Irvine.

1727. *June* 4. Dr. Thomas Rattray of Craighall, was conſecrated at Edinburgh, by Biſhop Gadderar, Biſhop Millar, and Biſhop Cant.

1727. *June* 18. Mr. William Dunbar, Miniſter at Cruden, and Mr. Robert Keith, Preſbyter in Edinburgh, were conſecrated at Edinburgh, by Biſhop Gadderar, Biſhop Millar, and Biſhop Rattray. *N. B.* They who were deprived of their pariſhes at the

Revolution.

Revolution, are in this list called, Ministers; but they who had not been parish-ministers under the civil establishment, are called Presbyters.

1735. *June* 24. Mr. Robert White, Presbyter at Cupar, was consecrated at Carsebank, near Forfar, by Bishop Rattray, Bishop Dunbar, and Bishop Keith.

1741. *Sept.* 10. Mr. William Falconar, Presbyter at Forress, was consecrated at Alloa, in Clacmannanshire, by Bishop Rattray, Bishop Keith, and Bishop White.

1742. *Oct.* 4. Mr. James Rait, Presbyter at Dundee, was consecrated at Edinburgh, by Bishop Rattray, Bishop Keith, and Bishop White.

1743. *Aug.* 19. Mr. John Alexander, Presbyter at Alloa, in Clacmannanshire, was consecrated at Edinburgh, by Bishop Keith, Bishop White, Bishop Falconar, and Bishop Rait.

1747. *July* 17. Mr. Andrew Gerard, Presbyter in Aberdeen, was consecrated at Cupar, in Fife, by Bishop White, Bishop Falconar, Bishop Rait, and Bishop Alexander.

1759. *Nov.* 1. Mr. Henry Edgar, was consecrated at Cupar, in Fife, by Bishop White, Bishop Falconar, Bishop Rait, and Bishop Alexander, as Co-adjutor to Bishop White, then *Primus.*
N. B. Anciently no Bishop in Scotland had the stile of Archbishop, but one of them had a precedency, under the title of, *Primus Scotiæ Episcopus:* And after the Revolution they returned to their old stile, which they still retain; one of them being entitled *Primus*, to whom precedency is allowed, and deference paid in the Synod of Bishops.

1762.

1762. *June* 24. Mr. Robert Forbes, was consecrated at Forfar, by Bishop Falconar, *Primus*, Bishop Alexander, and Bishop Gerard.

1768. *Sept.* 21. Mr. Robert Kilgour, Presbyter at Peterhead, was consecrated Bishop of Aberdeen, at Cupar, in Fife, by Bishop Falconar, *Primus*, Bishop Rait, and Bishop Alexander.

1774. *Aug.* 24. Mr. Charles Rose, Presbyter at Down, was consecrated Bishop of Dunblane, at Forfar, by Bishop Falconar, *Primus*, Bishop Rait, and Bishop Forbes.

1776. *June* 27. Mr. Arthur Petrie, Presbyter at Meiklefolla, was consecrated Bishop Co-adjutor, at Dundee, by Bishop Falconar, *Primus*, Bishop Rait, Bishop Kilgour, and Bishop Rose: And appointed Bishop of Ross and Caithness, July 8th, 1777.
N. B. After the Revolution, the Bishops in Scotland had no particular Diocess, but managed their ecclesiastical affairs in one body, as a college: But, finding inconveniencies in this mode, they took particular Diocesses, which, though not exactly according to the limits of the Diocesses under the former legal establishment, still retain their old names.

1778. *Aug.* 13. Mr. George Innes, Presbyter in Aberdeen, was consecrated Bishop of Brechen, at Alloa, by Bishop Falconar, *Primus*, Bishop Rose, and Bishop Petrie.

1782. *Sept.* 25. Mr. John Skinner, Presbyter in Aberdeen, was consecrated Bishop Co-adjutor, at Luthermuir, in the Diocess of Brechen, by Bishop Kilgour, *Primus*, Bishop Rose, and Bishop Petrie.

N. B. The foregoing list is taken from an attested copy, in the possession of Bishop Seabury.

1784.

1784. *Nov.* 14. Dr. Samuel Seabury, Presbyter, from the State of Connecticut, in America, was consecrated Bishop, at Aberdeen, by Bishop Kilgoure *Primus*, Bishop Petrie, and Bishop Skinner,—as, by the deed of consecration, now in his possession, does fully appear.

SAMUEL, Bp. Epl. Ch. Connect.

New-London, }
August 26, 1785. }

BISHOP SEABURYS

SECOND CHARGE,

TO THE

CLERGY

OF HIS

DIOCESS,

DELIVERED AT DERBY,

IN THE

STATE OF CONNECTICUT,

On the 22d of September, 1786.

Published at the earnest desire of the CONVOCATION.

NEW-HAVEN;

PRINTED BY THOMAS AND SAMUEL GREEN.

A CHARGE, &c.

Reverend Brethren,

IT having pleaſed Almighty God, our heavenly Father, that we ſhould again come together, to compare the progreſs each of us has made in the great work committed to his charge—the preaching the Goſpel of Chriſt, and reclaiming ſinners from the errors of their ways ;—to deliberate on the moſt prudent and effectual means of building up the Church, and enlarging the kingdom of our Redeemer ; and to encourage each other to proceed with ſteadineſs and zeal in the arduous undertaking—moſt ſincerely do I bleſs God for the happy meeting, earneſtly beſeeching him to enable us by his grace, to proſecute our buſineſs with prudence, and meekneſs, and a ſincere love for the ſouls of them that are under our care ; and that he would bleſs and proſper our endeavours, and render them effectual to the purpoſe for which they are intended.

In the Charge delivered the laſt year at Middletown, particular mention was made of the neceſſity of Confirmation, and of the propriety of your explaining to your people the nature of the holy Rite, and the authority on which it ſtands, that ſo they might come to it with due preparation, and a mind convinced of its reaſonableneſs and uſefulneſs. I have every reaſon to ſuppoſe that this has been done with the greateſt care and fidelity. The numbers of ſerious

and

and well-informed perſons who have preſented themſelves for Confirmation in the various Churches where it has been miniſtred, are a ſufficient and pleaſing proof that the ſubject has not been neglected. This is a matter of ſincere joy to me ; and muſt be ſo to you, and to all good men ; and opens a fair proſpect of my finding all thoſe Congregations ready for the Holy Solemnity, which I ſhall at this time be able to viſit.

The general ſtate of the Church, however, is ſuch as muſt fill every ſerious mind with anxious concern for its proſperity. Its old patrons, who, under God, were its great ſupport, have withdrawn their countenance, and left it to ſtand by its own ſtrength. The time, and ſudden manner of doing this, are attended with ſuch circumſtances as really double the inconveniences. The members of the Church had in no degree recovered from the loſs and damage ſuſtained in the late commotions. Nor had time enough elapſed, to give them an opportunity of arranging any matters, or eſtabliſhing any funds, for the ſupplying of that deficiency, which the withdrawing of the ſalaries from England would neceſſarily make in the ſupport of their miniſters. One years notification previous to the withdrawing of the ſalaries, would in a great meaſure have prevented the inconveniences which we now feel : And it is hard to conceive that this would materially have injured the Societys funds, or have diſobliged thoſe benevolent perſons who ſo generouſly contribute to that excellent inſtitution.

But duty requires that every thing relating to that venerable body, in whoſe ſervice many of us were lately employed, ſhould be conſidered in the moſt favorable light. And, in juſtice to them, it ought to be noted, That their Charter enables them to ſend Miſſionaries only into the Britiſh Colonies, Plantations, and Factories, beyond ſea. When therefore the American

rican

rican States ceased to belong to the British empire, they ceased, in a legal sense, to be the objects of their Charter. Thus candor obliges us to think and say. But gratitude has further obligations on us. We ought to bless God for his mercy in raising up that Society for our assistance. We have been benefited by it: And we ought to be grateful to him, and to those worthy characters who composed and supported it. The memory of those that are dead, ought to be revered by us: Nor should the present apparent unkindness obliterate the sense of the former benefits we have received from the present members. May God reward them! And as they are now exerting their benevolence in other countries—may HE bless and prosper their endeavours to establish true religion, piety, and virtue in them.

On our part, this, as well as every other misfortune, is to be received as the dispensation of God—as the chastisement of our heavenly Father: Whether intended to correct something amiss in us and the congregations to which we minister; or to exercise and prove our faith and patience, must be left to every persons judgment and conscience to determine for himself. Probably something of both may be in the case. Our duty therefore requires, that we call ourselves to account, and see wherein we have offended; that we humble ourselves before God for our negligences and omissions—for our want of diligence and zeal in our Masters service; that we beg of him his merciful forgiveness of all that is past, and the grace of his Holy Spirit, to amend our lives, and make us more careful and exact in our duty for the time to come. And let us inculcate the same sentiments and conduct on the people of our several cures.

Let this dispensation also teach us patience, and humility, and resignation, and faith; and excite us to obtain that poverty of spirit to which the heavenly

kingdom

kingdom is promised. We shall thereby resemble him the more, who humbled himself, that he might exalt us; who became poor, that he might make us rich; who patiently resigned himself to the will of his Father, that he might pay the ransom of our souls, and redeem us from destruction: Setting us an example that we might follow his steps.

Our dependence must now be on our own efforts, the benevolence of our Congregations, and the merciful providence of him who "openeth his hand and filleth all things living with plenteousness." He has cut off one resource, and he can open others: And he will open others, should he see it best for us. To him let us commit ourselves and our Church, in humble confidence, that he who feeds the ravens, who clothes the grass, who protects the sparrow, who numbers the hairs of our heads, who knoweth whereof we have need, who hath promised all necessary things to them who seek his kingdom and the righteousness thereof, will extend his providential care to us also. And while we thus put our trust in God, let us not be negligent in using an honest and decent means for our own support, that shall be in our power. Little indeed can a Clergyman do, out of the line of his profession, to increase his income; and out of the line of his profession, it is not always right and proper that he should step. His principal efforts then must be in the way of economy and frugality: By moderation in his enjoyments and expences, to make his income go as far as possible in the support of himself and family, and so that something also may be left to answer the necessary demands of benevolence and charity. If these efforts fail us, and our present income be really too little to support us as becomes the Ministers of God, we must, with all meekness and patience, explain our circumstances and situations to the Congregations where we officiate; and endeavour to convince them of their duty to exert their abilities in making some

further

further provision for our support; that so we may attend on our duty without anxious solicitude for the comforts of life, and they may enjoy the public worship of God, and the sacred offices and ordinances of Religion, which he has appointed in his Church, for their growth in grace and christian knowledge. It is to be hoped and presumed, that these representations will have their influence. Should they not, I know of no human remedy, but a removal to some place where there is a chance of doing better. But be the issue whatever it may, let us remember that it is the dispensation of our heavenly Father, who knows, and who will do, what is best for us. And,

That we may with the more confidence look to him for his gracious protection, we must take especial care faithfully to do our duty to him, as good stewards of those heavenly mysteries with which he has entrusted us. Now,

One great instance of fidelity in our duty, and which we have all solemnly engaged at our ordinations, attentively to regard, is to drive away all erroneous and strange doctrines, by which the truth of the Gospel may be obscured, or corrupted, and the salvation of the people endangered. And certainly there never was greater need of the discharge of this duty, or of contending earnestly for the faith, as it was once delivered to the saints, than at this time.

Deism, with its necessary consequence—no religion at all, or rather adverseness to all religion, if I am rightly informed, has within a few years, made great advances in the United States. Other causes may have concurred; but I cannot help thinking, that the wild, ill-founded and inconsistent schemes of religion, and systems of divinity, which have obtained in the world—I fear I may say, particularly in this country—have opened the way for the progress of infidelity. People of sober reason and common sense may hence be

be tempted to think, that Reason and Religion can never be reconciled. They too who have been beguiled into a belief of such ill-founded systems, or enthusiastic opinions, finding that they cannot be supported, when properly attacked, may be led to suppose that all religious principles are equally unfounded with their own. The next step is to become proselites to the opinion that all religions are equal, and no religion as good as any.

Our only weapons, are sober reason and fair argument—drawn from the nature of God and of man—from the relation we stand in to God—from our real state and condition in this world—and from that immortal state which awaits us in the next. That our reasons and arguments may have effect, they should be proposed with perspicuity, and urged with meekness and good temper. All ostentation, and vanity, and every appearance of superiority, should be carefully avoided. We must therefore understand our religion, and be able to give a good account of it, or we shall not be able to defend it, or to convince gainsayers. And we must understand ourselves too—be acquainted with our own tempers, and able to command our passions, or we shall probably be foiled, through want of knowledge, or through the impetuosity of passion. Religious disputes, no doubt, ought commonly to be avoided: But sometimes duty requires us to enter into them: And that we may do so with advantage, we ought to be acquainted with the principles and doctrines of our religion, the ground on which they stand, and the topics from which reasons and arguments may be drawn, to illustrate and defend them.

Duty obliges me to take notice of another circumstance that will call for our attention.—The prevalence of Arianism and Socinianism. The former of these heresies early infested the Church, and nearly destroyed

ftroyed the true faith. The latter fprung from the former, and is the produce of more modern times: And their advocates feem now to be incorporating their fyftems, and joining their efforts, to difcard the divinity of Chrift from the Chriftian fyftem.

It is fomething extraordinary, that men who profefs to believe the Holy Scriptures, fhould difcard a doctrine fo plainly and ftrongly afferted in them, and on which the whole ftructure of our religion is apparently built. To get rid of the pofitive declarations of Holy Scripture in favour of Chrifts divinity, the patrons of thefe herefies are obliged to recur to forced and unnatural conftructions of particular paffages, and to affix new meanings to words and phrafes, of which the early Chriftians had no knowledge. Attachment to philofophical fyftems, firft adopted, and then made the ftandard of truth, feems to be the fource of thefe, as it is of many other evils to Chriftianity. Objections have been made to the Mofaic account of the creation, becaufe it was thought not to comport perfectly with the fyftem of Copernicus. And, if I rightly remember, Dr. Prieftly in his letters to the Archdeacon of St. Albans, attempts to overthrow the doctrine of the Trinity of Perfons in the Godhead, becaufe he fuppofes it inconfiftent with mathematical principles—1+1+1=3— therefore there cannot be THREE perfons, and ONE GOD.

It would be well if men would referve pofitive affertions, and dogmatical pofitions, for thofe fubjects they do underftand; and would learn to fpeak with more modefty and diffidence of matters which it is impoffible they fhould fully comprehend. We know nothing of GOD but what he has been pleafed to reveal to us. And though there muft of neceffity be many things myfterious in his nature, and works, and revelations, when contemplated by fuch limited underftandings as we poffefs; yet as his revelations

are intended for our information; we muft fuppofe the terms in which they are conveyed are, as much as poffible accommodated to our capacities, and to be underftood according to the analogy they have to our own mode of expreffion, and not in a fenfe totally different from, and utterly incongruous with that in which we are accuftomed to ufe them. When Chrift fays, "I and my Father are one"—are we to fuppofe that he intended to convey an idea that He and his Father were as abfolutely diftinct in effence as are two mathematical unites? When St. John fays, "There are three that bear record in heaven, the "Father, the Word, and the Holy Ghoft: And thefe three are one"——EN EISI——one thing—one fubftance—one effence—are we to fuppofe them to be totally diftinct, fo that if the Father be God, and the Word be God, and the Holy Ghoft be God, there fhall be three Gods? Three diftinct witneffes they are, and therefore they muft be three diftinct perfonalities: But they are one effence, and therefore one GOD.* We cannot comprehend this myftery—muft we then refufe to believe it? Let us alfo refufe to believe our eyes, for we can as little comprehend how they perceive objects at ten or twenty miles diftance.

When Dr. Prieftly can by fearching find out GOD; when he can comprehend the Almighty to perfection, —then let him pronounce pofitively on the nature of GOD, and adjuft it as fchool-boys adjuft their fums in addition. He may then too be qualified to correct the errors of expreffion in divine revelation, and teach the Almighty to exprefs himfelf better. But let us bow in humble reverence before the majefty of hea-

* I am not ignorant that the authenticity of 1 John 5. 7, is difputed: Nor am I ignorant that it has been inconteftibly eftablifhed by the Rev. Mr. Travis, in his letters to Mr. Gibbon.

ven and earth: And as we know nothing of his nature, or of his will, but by revelation, let us attend to that—be content to ſubmit our ignorance to his knowledge, and to think of him, and believe in him, as he has repreſented himſelf to us.

It is always a diſagreeable taſk to be obliged to mention any matter with cenſure, or even diſapprobation; and I am very happy that the meaſure of which I am now to take notice, can call for animadverſion, only by way of caution. A number of the Clergy and Laity in the ſouthern States, have undertaken to reviſe and alter the Liturgy, and Offices, and Government of the Church; and have exhibited a Prayer-book to the public. The time will not permit me to ſay any thing of the merit of the alterations in the Liturgy: But, I am perſuaded, by an unprejudiced mind, ſome of them will be thought for the worſe, moſt of them not for the better. But the authority on which they have acted, is unknown in the Epiſcopal Church. The government of the Church by Biſhops, we hold to have been eſtabliſhed by the Apoſtles, acting under the commiſſion of Chriſt, and the direction of the Holy Ghoſt; and therefore is not to be altered by any power on earth, nor indeed by an angel from heaven. This government they have degraded, by lodging the chief authority in a Convention of clerical and lay Delegates—making their Church Epiſcopal in its orders, but Preſbyterian in its government.

Liturgies are left more to the prudence and judgment of the governors of the Church: And the primitive practice ſeems to have been, that the Biſhop did, with the advice, no doubt of his Preſbyters, provide a Liturgy for the uſe of his dioceſs. This ought to have been the caſe here. Biſhops ſhould firſt have been obtained to preſide over thoſe Churches. And to thoſe Biſhops with the Proctors of the Clergy, ſhould

ſhould have been committed the buſineſs of compiling a Liturgy for the uſe of the Church, through the States. This would have enſured unity in doctrine, worſhip and diſcipline through the whole, which upon the preſent plan will either not be obtained, or, if obtained, will not be durable.

And ſhould we ever be ſo happy, through the merciful providence of God, as to obtain ſuch a meeting, great regard ought to be had to the primitive Liturgies and Forms, in compiling a book of Common-Prayer. The Chriſtians who lived in the next age after the apoſtles, muſt have converſed with apoſtolic men, i. e. with thoſe who had converſed with the Apoſtles, and were acquainted with their opinions and practice, in the conduct of the public worſhip, and adminiſtration of the ſacraments, and diſcipline of the Church. Nor is it likely they would eaſily, or quickly depart from that mode which they knew had been approved by them; eſpecially at a time, when perpetual perſecution and diſtreſs kept men cloſe to God and their duty: And the world and its concerns could have but little power over thoſe, who daily expected to yield up that life in martyrdom, which they paſſed in continual devotion to God, and in the ſervice and edification of his Church. It would therefore be a good rule, in altering any thing in our ſtated Liturgy that might be thought to need it, to go back to early Chriſtianity, before it was corrupted by Popery, and ſee what was then the practice of the Church—what its rites and ceremonies—and to conform our own as nearly to it as the ſtate of the Church will permit; always remembering that the government, and doctrines, and ſacraments of the Church, are ſettled by divine authority, and are not ſubjected to our amendment, or alteration.

And the beſt way to aſcertain the Government, doctrines, Liturgies or forms of public ſervice of the primitive

primitive Church, is to conſult and attend to the early chriſtian writers. They were the beſt judges of apoſtolic practice, becauſe they lived neareſt to the apoſtolic times; at leaſt, they could not be miſtaken with regard to the practice of their own times and churches. And whenever we find by theſe writers, that the Churches of Aſia, Africa, and Europe agreed in any particular relating to government, doctrine, diſcipline, or public worſhip, we may conclude it to have been according to apoſtolic uſage and judgment. For theſe Churches were ſettled by different Apoſtles and Evangeliſts; and conſequently, what they did, and held, and taught, in common with each other, muſt have been from the general doctrine, practice, judgment, and authority of the Apoſtles. We ought therefore to be very careful not to weaken that government, or warp thoſe doctrines, or contravene the principles of the public liturgies of the early period of the Chriſtian Church: For the probable chance is, if we do, we ſhall run counter to apoſtolic doctrine and practice.

You ſee, that it is not my aim to ſet up the judgment or opinions of particular men—of Origin, Chryſoſtom, or Jerom, for inſtance—as the foundation of our religious principles, but the general judgment and practice of the primitive Church, as the beſt ſtandard of apoſtolical practice.

It is upon the authority and teſtimony of the primitive Church that we ſettle the canon of the new-teſtament. Give up this authority and teſtimony, and there will be no good proof left, that the ſeveral books of the new-teſtament were written by the perſons whoſe names they bear. But when it is known from the primitive writers, that theſe books were univerſally received by, and redde in, all the Churches, as the writings of thoſe perſons to whom they are aſcribed,

cribed, their authenticity, and divine authority will be eſtabliſhed beyond all reaſonable diſpute.

The ſame mode of reaſoning will apply to the interpretation of ſcripture. The preſent, ſeems to be the age of refinement, and of what is called reformation, but which does not always prove to be for the better. Every thing human and divine ſeems to be in the way of being new modelled. Religion in particular, is turned, and twiſted, into a variety of appearances; ſome of them aukward enough; and ſome tending to very miſchievous conſequences—the deſtruction of true religion and virtue, by confounding truth with error, right with wrong, good with evil. Yet all appeal to the Bible, and from it pretend to derive proof to their ſyſtem. None that I know of, have profeſſedly ſet about making a new Bible, i. e. writing a new book, with that title: But if they alter the old one, in its ſenſe and meaning, they, in truth, make a new one. And what better do they do, who put new and ſtrange meanings on old words and phraſes—who alter the tranſlation, or force the ſenſe, till it bows and bends into a compliance with a favourite ſyſtem; and where this fails, boldly charge the original with error and interpolation. The ſureſt way to guard againſt this miſchief, is to attend to the interpretations of the oldeſt Chriſtians, and of the univerſal Church. Having converſed with the Apoſtles, or with apoſtolic men, they were beſt acquainted with the mind and intention of the writers. They knew the force, and idiom of the language in which thoſe books were written. The manners and cuſtoms to which many paſſages allude, were familiar to them: For they were the language, and manners, and cuſtoms of their own country, and nearly of their own age. A prudential regard to our own characters, juſtice to the ſacred books, and to the people of our charge, will therefore require, that we pay a due regard to the more early interpretations

interpretations of the Holy Scriptures in the primitive Church: For we may rest assured, that those doctrines, and that interpretation of scripture, which was common to all Churches in their early period, was from the Apostles, and therefore may be depended on by us. By this conduct we shall secure ourselves against new-fangled notions in religion; against its corruption, by vain philosophy, metaphysical reasonings, and the perplexities of school divinity, which have, one or other of them, been the perpetual corrupters of the true religion: And let us remember, that in religion novelty and truth can scarcely come together: For nothing in religion is now true, that was not true seventeen hundred years ago. Philosophy may shift its fashion, metaphysics may be in or out of vogue, or may change its principles, or its appearance, school divinity may be nice in its definitions, exact in its methods, and positive in its decisions, but none of them alter the nature of the Christian Religion; that remains the same, and its true principles, doctrines, and practice continue the same now that they were in its early period. It teaches the means of reconciliation with God, through Christ: And it teaches the same things now which it ever did, and none other. It is therefore our business to hold the same faith, teach the same doctrines, inculcate the same principles, submit to the same government, recommend the same practice, enforce the same obedience, holiness, and purity, and to administer the same sacraments, that the Apostles, and primitive Christians did. And we ought to do all this, plainly and fully, leaving ourselves, our own interests, and honor, and aggrandisement, out of the case. If men will receive our testimony, we must bless God, and be encouraged in our duty: If they reject it, we must pray more earnestly to God for them. But let us never think of accommodating our systems, or our sermons to popular humor or fancy; nor

nor to the flattering of the pride and vanity of the human heart; nor to the bolstering of men up, in an opinion of their own worthiness, ability or sufficiency; nor to the lessening of the obligation of holiness and purity; nor to the weakening of the influence of the government and discipline of the Church, or of the necessity and efficacy of the holy sacraments. If we do, we shall be false to God and our Saviour, to the people under our care, and to our own most solemn vows and promises; and we must expect to receive the recompence of traitors—the condemnation of unfaithful stewards.

Having mentioned the sacraments of our holy religion, forgive me, if I trespass a few minutes longer on your patience, in speaking more particularly on that subject. The inattention of many to these holy institutions, must be a matter of grief to all good Clergymen.

I hope that the members of our own Church are not generally reprehensible with regard to the presenting of their Children to holy Baptism. But the instances of adult Baptisms that do occur, shew that there is somewhere a blameable remissness. If children are suffered to grow up to maturity without being initiated into the christian Church, the want of due consideration, too often keeps them away from the solemn Rite, or bashfulness induces them to insist on its private administration. And should they while unbaptised, become masters or mistresses of families, their children will probably grow up in the same unregenerate state. We ought therefore to be constant, and earnest, in explaining the nature of Baptism to our people; pointing out its benefits, and, in all meekness and love, urging them to a conscientious compliance with their duty: That being regenerate, and made members of Christ's mystical body, by baptism, they may be sealed with the seal of the Holy Spirit, in Confirmation, advanced to the rank of adult Christians,

ans, and entitled to the privilege of celebrating the Holy Eucharist with their brethren,—commemorating the death and sacrifice of their dear Redeemer, and participating in all the blessings of his atonement. And,

Was the nature of this last mentioned institution better understood, I must suppose people would more generally comply with it. In some congregations the number of Communicants is indeed respectable; in others but small.* Be it our care then, to set this matter in its true light, by explaining the nature and design of the Holy Communion to our several Congregations, making them sensible of the inestimable blessings to be thereby obtained.

Some writers on this subject, under the idea of making it plain to ordinary capacities, have, I fear, banished all spiritural meaning, by discarding all mystery, from it—making it a mere empty remembrance of Christs death. Others have considered it as an arbitrary command, and an instance of Gods sovereignty over us—requiring our obedience for wraths sake. Others represent it simply as the renewal of our Christian Covenant, and expecting no particular benefits

from

* It must be acknowledged in honor to the female sex, that they are much more numerous in their attendance at the holy Communion, than the men. It may be said, that the softness and tenderness of heart which they possess, the nature of their education, and their mode of life, render them more susceptible of religious impressions, and dispose them better to the exercise of gratitude and devotion. Should it be so, the fact remains the same. They were the first believers, witnesses, and preachers, of our Saviours resurrection, and seem always to have been the chosen instruments of God, to keep up a sense of religion, piety, and devotion in the world. May God bless and reward them, and grant that their example may have a proper influence on the other sex! It is certain the same truths do not make the same impression on them. And yet they have the same need of redemption and salvation—The same sinful nature, from which to be delivered—Are under the same curse and condemnation for sin,—and must be saved by the same means, and the same Saviour.

from it. The primitive Christians had very different sentiments from these, concerning the Holy Communion, and so I suppose our Church has also. They considered it not as the renewal of the Christian Covenant, but a privilege to which the Christian Covenant, into which we had been admitted by Baptism, and which had been ratified in Confirmation, entitled us. Nor as an arbitrary command of God, to shew his sovereign authority over us. Nor as a bare remembrance of Christs death. But as the appointed means of keeping up that spiritual life which we received in our New-birth; and of continuing that interest in the benefits and blessings of Christs passion and death, which was made over to us, when we became members of his mystical body. They called and esteemed it to be the Christian Sacrifice, commemorative of the great sacrifice of atonement which Christ had made for the sins of the whole world; wherein, under the symbols of bread and the cup, the body and blood of Christ which he offered up, and which were broken and shed upon the cross, are figured forth; and being presented to God our heavenly Father, by his Priest here on earth, the merits of Christ for the remission of sins, are pleaded by him, and we trust, by our great High Priest himself in heaven: And being sanctified by prayer, thanksgiving, the words of institution, and the invocation of the Holy Spirit, are divided among the Communicants as a Feast upon the Sacrifice. And they did believe, that all who worthily partook of the consecrated Elements, did really and truly, though mystically and spiritually, partake of the Body and Blood of Christ. Our Church evidently teaches the same thing in her Catechism, defining "the inward part, or thing signified," by the bread and wine in the Holy Communion, to be "the body and blood of Christ, which are verily and indeed, taken and received by the faithful in the Lords-supper."

This

This doctrine ſeems to be founded on what our Saviour ſaid in the ſixth chapter of St. Johns Goſpel, concerning eating his fleſh and drinking his blood, which when compared with the inſtitution of the bleſſed Euchariſt, as recorded by the Evangeliſts, will ſufficiently juſtify the Church in her opinion and judgment. We have therefore a right to believe and ſay, That in the Holy Communion, the faithful receiver does, in a myſtical and ſpiritual manner, eat and drink the Body and Blood of Chriſt repreſented by the conſecrated bread and wine; and does thereby partake in the atonement made by the paſſion and death of Chriſt, having remiſſion through him, of all paſt ſins, and eternal life aſſured to him.

And now, Reverend Brethren, that you may ſee how neceſſary it is for you to exert yourſelves in ſupport of the Holy Catholic Faith, let me requeſt you to direct your attention particularly to this country; and when you obſerve how low ſome have ſet the doctrines and principles of religion—How others are depreſſing the Offices, corrupting the Government, and degrading the Prieſthood of Chriſts Church—on the one ſide,—his divinity denied on the other,—Two of the old Creeds, the guards of the true faith againſt Arianiſm and Socinianiſm, thrown out—The deſcent of Chriſt into Hell, the inviſible place of departed ſouls, by which his perfect humanity, and our perfect redemption, of ſoul, as well as of body, are aſcertained, rejected from the Apoſtles Creed—Baptiſm reduced to a mere ceremony, by excluding from it the idea of regeneration—And you will own with me, that the ſtrongeſt obligations lie upon us, to hold faſt, and contend earneſtly for, the faith as it was once delivered to the Saints—To abide by the government, ſupport the doctrines, retain the principles, explain the true nature and meaning of the ſacraments and offices of the Church, and endeavour to reſtore them to that ſtation

ſtation and eſtimation, in which the primitive Chriſtians placed and held them. Error often becomes popular and contagious, and then no one can tell how far it will ſpread, nor where end. We muſt in ſuch caſes, recur to firſt principles, and there take our ſtand. The Bible muſt be the ground of our faith. And the doctrines, practices and old Liturgies of the primitive Church will be of great uſe to lead us to the true meaning of the Holy Books. Judgment and prudence, muſt no doubt be exerciſed: But truth muſt not be ſacrificed to prudence, nor muſt judgment be warped by attachment to ſyſtem, or compliance with popular error and prejudice.

THE END.

Mr. *ANDREWS*'s

Farewell DISCOURSE.

A

DISCOURSE

ON

St. MARK, XVI. 15, 16.

" AND HE SAID UNTO THEM, GO YE," &c.

BY

Samuel Andrews, A. M.

Late Missionary at Wallingford, from the venerable Society for the Propagation of the Gospel in foreign Parts: And now Missionary at St. Andrews, (New-Brunswick.)

NEW-HAVEN: Printed by DANIEL BOWEN, in *Chapel-street*, near the COLLEGE. (M.DCC.LXXXVII.)

To the CONGREGATIONS of *Wallingford, Cheshire*, and *North-Haven*, lately under my Care.

GENTLEMEN,

THE following Discourse was intended to have been delivered on my taking leave of you; but, my present infirm state of health rendering that impracticable: I take the liberty of presenting it to you in this manner, and beg you will receive it as a testimony of my regard for you, and of my solicitude for Your spiritual interest.

The AUTHOR.

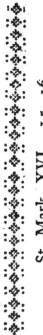

St. Mark, XVI. 15, 16.

AND HE SAID UNTO THEM, GO YE INTO ALL THE WORLD; AND PREACH THE GOSPEL TO EVERY CREATURE: HE THAT BELIEVETH AND IS BAPTIZED, SHALL BE SAVED; BUT HE THAT BELIEVETH NOT, SHALL BE DAMNED.

THIS is the important commission given by the blessed Head of the Church to the apostles, the first ministers in his kingdom; and in them to all who should be in future authorized to publish the glad tidings of his salvation, in all succeeding generations to the end of the world. In these words, the extent of our mission is mentioned—the nature of our errand unfolded,—and the conditions of salvation, we are to publish in the name of our blessed master, are expresly declared. To this divine rule you are then to look, would you know whether we deviate from our commission or not.

This Discourse is not designed to prove the truth of the christian religion: It is addressed to those only who declare themselves christians, and profess to believe that the gospel is the only charter of hope to men: It therefore proceeds upon christian principles, takes for granted that the bible is true, and undertakes to shew by scripture what the gospel promiseth to do for men, and upon what terms we may hope for the rewards of it.

The gospel scheme is built upon a sufficient atonement,

atonement, which is already made to divine justice for sin. The bible informs, that originally *God made man upright*, put him under a certain law, and declared death to be the award of disobedience to it—that man however transgressed, and stood exposed to the penalty—but that Jesus Christ, the second person in the sacred trinity, undertook his restoration, and accomplished it by his own sufferings and death in the place of the offender.

The generally received doctrine of the christian church is, and has been, that Jesus Christ, having ransomed human nature by paying the price of our redemption, steps forth in his own right, as our Proprietor, King and Judge; enacts laws for us to observe; and offers all the rewards of his purchase upon such terms as to his infinite wisdom seem proper. In a word, that the terms proposed are repentance of sin, and faith in the Redeemer.

In conformity to this faith of the Church of God, judging it to be fully and clearly supported in divine revelation: I have constantly maintained, that there is no other name under heaven, than that of Jesus Christ, by which men can be saved—that HE hath redeemed mankind—paid the price of our ransom; and is become our law-giver and judge—that in consequence of his dominion over us, he has treated us as agents; enacted laws to bind us; and condescended to make a gracious

covenant

covenant with us in the gospel, in which covenant he promises to give us his salvation, upon condition that we believe in him, submit to his laws, and repent of our sins—but has threatened to exclude us from the benefits of his purchase, if we continue in impenitence and unbelief—and that we must therefore comply with these conditions, or submit to a miserable eternity.

Many of you are my witnesses, that *this* has uniformly been the great burden of my instructions from my youth to the present day. The doctrine has also been universally believed in this society, where, for a course of many years, unless I am mistaken, there has been as perfect an uniformity of religious sentiment, as ever was in any congregation.

Happy, I sincerely believe, it had been for the town at large, and for this society in particular, had the doctrine never been opposed: Of late, however, there are those who deny the human race to be agents—that the gospel is a covenant between God and men—or that it has any conditions of life in it—and who assert, that Jesus Christ having paid the whole debt to divine justice, which every human creature had contracted by sin, that a second payment cannot be justly required; and therefore, however men may live here, the whole human nature must and will be finally happy. This doctrine is in direct opposition to what

you

you have early and ever been taught. It appears to clash with the words of our text; and it opposeth the whole system of the faith, I have ever believed and taught. Can I do less than to examine it candidly by the word of God?

I am now to take my final leave of my country, and of this my charge; upon both which I earnestly wish and implore every divine blessing, which may conduce to their comfort here, and their happiness forever. But how can I expect the accomplishment of this wish, unless I leave them established in the truth?—rooted and grounded in the faith and order of the gospel? Should the doctrine I oppose be found true, I should think it an honor to retract my present mistake; and this disposition I hope to find in others. However, should the doctrine you all have till of late received, be found supported by God's word, it must be my duty to call upon you, to *hold fast the beginning of Your confidence and hope.* My obligation to you as a spiritual instructor, and my higher obligation to the great Head of the Church as his embassadour, conspire to demand this of me.

" Men, Brethren and Fathers, hear ye therefore my defence, which I now make unto you". The words of the text prove, that all men shall not be saved by gospel, unless all men shall believe it.—They are the very words

of

of the great Redeemer himself, who has ransomed us from death; and they contain the terms upon which only HE has ordered the gospel to be published.

The words are addressed to the apostles; and these first christian ministers are directed to *go into all the world, and preach the gospel to every creature*; then follow the very words of the gospel they were to publish. *He that believeth and is baptized, shall be saved; but he that believeth not, shall be damned.* When we know the true import of these words, we shall also know what the conditions of salvation are, which Christ has fixed.

To believe and be baptized must signify, not only to believe that Jesus is the Christ; but to repent of our sins, and submit to his government; for so much Christ hath elsewhere expressly required. So, to be *saved*, ' as this is Christ's gift,' must intend the enjoyment of *his* salvation.

And on the other hand, not to *believe*, must signify, not only to deny Christ before men, but to reject his government: And to be *damned* must be, to be rejected from the above salvation.

Let the meaning of the word *damned* be *condemned*, or *judged*, or however you interpret it, it stands in direct opposition to the word *saved*. And if the unbeliever is not rejected from the salvation to which the believer is admitted, the

B passage

paſſage is left without meaning, nor can it be reconciled with common ſenſe. In the paſſage above, Chriſt admits the believer to his ſalvation; but he condemns, or judgeth the unbeliever to be unworthy of his ſalvation; and this is to reject him from it. Neither does this interpretation reſt upon my authority; but upon the authority of the Redeemer himſelf, for thus he hath explained it. **He that believeth on the Son, hath everlaſting life; and he that believeth not on the Son, ſhall not ſee life; but the wrath of God abideth on him.* Chriſt here declares, the unbeliever ſhall not ſee the life, which is given to the believer. Chriſt's ſalvation is the life he has given to the believer, therefore he has rejected the unbeliever from his ſalvation. He has declared he ſhall not even ſee it. Can we have higher evidence that all men ſhall not be ſaved by goſpel, unleſs all men ſhall finally believe it, that is, fulfil the conditions of it, than this explicit declaration of our bleſſed Redeemer and final Judge? But why do I mention conditions, when it is denyed, that there are conditions in the goſpel? or indeed, that men are agents? or the goſpel a covenant between God and men? We will examine theſe particulars, before we proceed to the principal enquiry; which is, whether all men ſhall finally believe the goſpel?

The firſt inquiry is, whether men are *agents*?

What

* John 3d, 36th.

What we underſtand by an agent is, a being capable of inſtruction, or able to underſtand, and to be governed by laws, or to be influenced by the ſanctions of law. The laws and civil conſtitutions of every country prove, it is, and has been, the common conſent of mankind, that *we* are ſuch beings; that is, beings capable to learn the meaning of law, and to be governed by the precepts of it; otherwiſe why were civil conſtitutions ever framed? To give men laws, is to treat them as agents: that is, as beings capable of government by law, and to acknowledge it proper to enact laws to bind us, is to grant we are agents, or proper ſubjects of law: but God has given laws to bind us: he therefore has treated us as agents.

Should it be ſaid, though we can obey the laws of *men*, we cannot obey the laws of *God*; therefore, though we are agents under human laws, we are not agents, or proper ſubjects of divine laws. This objection muſt ſuppoſe, either that God *has* given us no laws: or that he he has not treated us properly according to our condition. We grant (as indeed we ought to do) that in our own ſtrength we are unable to keep even thoſe divine laws on which our ſalvation is ſuſpended: But Chriſt in the goſpel has declared, that the aids of his ſpirit ſhall be of equal extent with his laws—that we ſhall not be tempted above our ability—that his ſtrength ſhall be perfected in our weakneſs—

and

and that it ſhall be ſufficient for us. However impotent we are in ourſelves, we want no other ſtrength than that which is *ſufficient* for us—and as the goſpel promiſes to give us *ſufficient* ſtrength, though it did not find us agents, it has raiſed us to that capacity. All who believe God has given a revelation to teach men their duty, muſt believe them able to learn it: and they who grant that God has given laws to regulate our lives, ought to grant that we are agents, and able to be governed by law.

Will any men then, who acknowledge the authority of revelation, deny that God has given laws to mankind? Who can deny that God gave a law to the firſt two in innocency, and declared death to be the penalty of diſobedience to it? Who can deny the Decalogue, and the whole law of Moſes, to be divine laws given to regulate the manners of men? Who will deny that God by Moſes ſet life and death before the Jewiſh nation, and referred it to them which they would chuſe, as though they really had the power of choice. Finally, who can deny that faith and repentance are laws of the goſpel, deſigned to bind men, when Chriſt commands men to repent and believe the goſpel, declares they ſhall be ſaved, if they do, but affirms they ſhall not ſee life, if they do not? The truth is, from the day God made man to the preſent time, he has uniformly given laws to govern us: he has treated us as

beings

beings capable of government by law, or as creatures able to chooſe and refuſe. And this is to treat us as agents. Clearly nothing more can be neceſſary to make man an agent, than to be able to be governed by laws, inforced by rewards and puniſhments. God has always given ſuch laws to men. However long we contend therefore, it will follow, either that we are agents, or that God has treated us improperly. Which ſide of the alternative ſhall we take?—we ought not, and we dare not ſay, God has treated us improperly: We therefore muſt believe we are agents, ſince God has treated us as ſuch.

But the next point is, whether there are *conditions* of life in the goſpel? A condition, is any thing upon which the enjoyment of a favour is ſuſpended. When we do the thing required, we receive the benefit: When we do it not, we are rejected from the favour. The thing thus required is a condition of enjoyment; becauſe the enjoyment is not to take effect without a compliance with the condition. Let us examine whether ſuch conditions of life are not to be found in the goſpel.

Our bleſſed Lord came to ſave men by the remiſſion of their ſins. When he entered upon his public miniſtry, he declared the approach of his kingdom, and commanded men to repent and believe his goſpel. That he requires faith and repentance is clearly legible to every

one

one who looks into his bible: He hath made faith and repentance the terms of his pardon and salvation, and requires them, as the conditions of life which himself has fixed. Luke 24, 47. *He has commanded repentance and remission of sins to be preached in his name*,—not remission of sins without repentance, but repentance first, as a condition without which there should be no remission. As *repentance* is one condition of life in the gospel; so *faith* is another: Our blessed Redeemer saith, St. John, 3, 16, and 36. *God so loved the world, that he gave his only begotten son, that whosoever believeth in him should not perish, but have everlasting life. He that believeth on the son, hath everlasting Life; and he that believeth not the son, shall not see Life.* Christ, the purchaser and giver of life, has promised it to the believer; but declared the unbeliever shall not see life, but shall remain under the wrath of God. Is not faith then a condition of life? Without faith, life is not promised in the gospel;—with faith, it is promissed. Faith is then a condition upon which the enjoyment of life is suspended by the gospel. If we expect salvation by Christ, we must look for it in the way in which he has promised it. Christ has not said, we shall be saved without faith: Who dare say we shall? Christ has declared the believer shall receive his salvation; but that the unbeliever shall not receive it: Who dare say he shall re-

ceive

ceive it? To close the argument:—If the believer shall enjoy life, and the unbeliever shall not enjoy it, then faith is a condition of life. Jesus Christ has expressly declared this to be the case: therefore Jesus Christ has made faith a condition of life.

Having proved that there are conditions of life in the gospel, it will soon appear that the gospel is a *covenant* between God and men. A covenant is an agreement between two or more parties. In this case God is one party, and men are the other. On his part, God promises life to men, upon the conditions of faith and repentance: On men's part, when they take the christian profession upon them, they promise to comply with the above conditions, as the way to enjoy the good things promised. They who take this profession upon them, are said to enter into covenant,—nay, and baptism, the rite by which we compleat this agreement, is called the *seal* of the covenant. A covenant then there must be, or there could be no *seal* to it. But who are the parties in the covenant? Unquestionably God and men are the parties: For they are the two parties which agree. Indeed, it is impossible the covenant should be betwixt God and Christ. Tho' there might originally have been a covenant between the Father and the Son; yet this of which we now speak, is not: For we are told, that Christ is the *mediator* of this covenant. A mediator

diator

diator is a middle perſon, and an interceſſor: But Chriſt cannot intercede betwixt God and himſelf,—nor can he ſtand in the middle between God and himſelf: But he muſt mediate between God and his people, the two parties who have entered into the agreement. In conformity to this idea, the apoſtle obſerves, that Chriſt is a mediator; but ſaith, that **a mediator is not a mediator of* ONE; *but God is one*,—therefore he tells us, both that ‖*he is the mediator betwixt God and men*, and ‡*the mediator of the new covenant*. I ſee not then why it does not follow, with a force of evidence equally convincing with a mathematical demonſtration, that ſince Chriſt is the mediator of the new covenant—ſince he cannot be a mediator of one, nor mediator betwixt God and himſelf,—but is the mediator between God and men, that the new covenant of which he is mediator, muſt be a covenant between God and men.

The above obſervations ſhew, that men are agents, becauſe God treats them as ſuch—that the goſpel is a covenant between God and men, that it contains conditions of life—and that faith and repentance are the conditions of this covenant. It will from hence follow, that we muſt fulfil the conditions of the covenant, or not expect the rewards of it. As we are agents, we are accountable to God for the improvement of

* Galatians 3d, 20th. ‖ 1ſt Timothy, 2d, 5th. ‡ Heb. 12, 24th.

of the powers he has given us. As goſpel promiſes are conditional, we muſt comply with the conditions, or not inherit the promiſes. Jeſus Chriſt has paid the price of our ranſom: We are his in right of purchaſe: and he has an undoubted authority to diſpoſe of us as he ſhall judge proper.

Chriſt has promiſed his ſalvation to the believer: he has rejected the unbeliever from it. In the text he declares, he that believeth ſhall be *ſaved*; and he who believeth not, ſhall be *damned*. If we diſagree in the meaning of this laſt word, our Lord has declared it ſignifies, not to ſee or enjoy the life he has given to the believer. Theſe are his words: *He that believeth on the ſon, hath everlaſting Life; he that believeth not the ſon, ſhall not ſee Life.* Theſe are the words of our final judge, and they abſolutely exclude the unbeliever from the life which is given to the believer; they declare he *ſhall not ſee* or enjoy it. The life here promiſed to the believer is Chriſt's ſalvation. Chriſt's ſalvation is eternal life: For ſpeaking of his ſheep, he ſaith **I give unto them eternal Life.* The ſalvation then, which is given to the believer, is eternal life; the unbeliever is rejected from the ſalvation given to the believer; he therefore is rejected from eternal life; and this too by the declaration of the judge himſelf.

It follows, either that we muſt acknowledge

* St. John 10th, 28th.

ledge the final unbeliever is rejected from eternal life, or deny the positive, clear and express declaration of our Redeemer and Judge.

Moreover, this sentence of the judge will be executed upon the final unbeliever in the great day of retribution. For judgment is then to proceed according to the gospel: And the business of that important day is only to execute the promises and threatnings of the gospel. As the unbeliever is totally excluded from eternal life, it will follow, either that all men will not be finally happy; or that all men will finally believe; Since without faith no one can be happy, no one can please God, or enjoy him.

We therefore enquire whether all men shall finally believe, or fulfil the conditions of the gospel? That all men do not fulfil these conditions in the present life, may be thus argued. St. John observes, that *without* (or out of the kingdom of Heaven) ‡" are sorcerers, whoremongers, murderers, and idolaters." Had these men obeyed the gospel in this life, they had not been excluded from Heaven: but would have taken part of the inheritance given to *him who overcometh*.

The same thing may be argued from the case of Dives and Lazarus. Lazarus died, and was carried by Angels into Abraham's bosom—a place of joy and comfort. The other died, and lift up his eyes in torment. Why is this difference

‡ Revelations 22d, 15th

difference made betwixt the two? The only reason which can be given is, the one had fulfiled the conditions of life, and the other had not. The one had faith, the other had it not. Had Dives in this life fulfiled the conditions to which Christ had promised his salvation, we now should not find him in torment, and hear him beg in vain for releif; but we should find him with Lazarus in a place of comfort. These instances are a demonstration, that all men do not fulfil the conditions of the gospel in this life, because we find some men excluded from the rewards of it at death.

As all men do not fulfil gospel conditions in this life, it remains to be done after death, if it is ever done. But surely it cannot be done between death and the resurrection. For our blessed Lord tells us, death is a §*night in which no man can work*. And the apostle, that we are to be judged for *the things only* which are *done in the body*. Soul and body are separated at death, and will remain in a separate state till the judgment shall commence:—then they will be re-united—not for a second probation however; but to receive the just award of the deeds done in the body before its separation from the soul. Hence the apostle, ‖*we must all appear before the judgment seat of Christ, that every one may receive the things done in his body, according to that he hath done, whether it be good or bad* So in the description

§ St. John 9th, 4th. ‖ 2a. Corin. 5th, 10th.

defcription of the final judgment recorded by St. Matthew, our bleffed Redeemer awards thofe on his right hand to happinefs, becaufe they had fed the hungry, &c. Things which could be done no where but here in the body: and he alfo fentences thofe on the left to mifery, for no other reafon than becaufe they had neglected to do fuch good deeds upon earth.

I know it has been faid, that *devils* only are on the left hand, and all mankind, bad and good, on the right: But this interpretation deftroys the great defign, both of this paffage, and of the gofpel at large. For doubtlefs the defign of both is, to encourage virtue, and difcourage vice, by the different awards they fhould receive at this grand period: But place all men, good and bad, on the right hand, and adjudge them indifcriminately to happinefs, and this great defign is totally loft. It contains no motive to virtue, or difcouragement to vice; nor can you reconcile it with the wifdom of God, or the reafon of men. Befides, the crime for which thofe on the left hand are punifhed, does not agree with devils, but with men. Men are expected to feed the hungry; I never knew that devils were: Nor is this the crime for which they are to fuffer. The apoftle tells us, that "God fpared not the angels which finned, but caft them down to hell." They finned before they were caft down; and they are referved in chains to the judgment of the great day, becaufe

caufe they rebelled againft God in Heaven;—not becaufe they did not vifit the fick upon earth.†

From the above obfervations it clearly follows, that the judgment of the great day is the award of the things done in the body, and only of the things fo done. This award is made according to the terms of the gofpel.—For the apoftle teftifies, **that God fhall judge the fecrets of men by Jefus Chrift, according to the gofpel.* It appears further, that all men do not fulfil the terms of the gofpel in this life—that between death and judgment they cannot fulfil them, becaufe in this period nothing can be done for which we are to be judged: And it muft follow, that as fome men are not within the conditions of life at the time of judgment, they muft then be rejected from falvation.

The conclufion is unavoidable. The word of God is exprefs, that the fentence of the laft judgment is given according to the gofpel, for thofe things only which are done in the body. The gofpel has in plain words rejected the unbeliever from falvation. Some men die unbelievers. At this period they therefore muft be rejected

† In the paffage of fcripture referred to above, it is faid that *all nations* fhall be gathered before the Judge. The objector faith, the devils are comprehended in the words *all nations*.——Mat. 28th, 19th, the apoftles are commanded to go and teach *all nations*, and baptize them. If impure fpirits are comprehended in the above expreffions; *all nations* they are within the commiffion given to the apoftles, and fhould have been inftructed and baptized by them; did they mifunderftand their commiffion? or did they perverfely neglect to execute one grand part of it; or finally did they underftand it better than the objector?

* *Rom.* 2d. 16.

rejected by the judge; becauſe the goſpel has already rejected them, and judgment is only the execution of the goſpel ſentence.

We have now arrived at the period of the general judgment. We have found that ſome men at this period have not fulfiled the conditions of life—that in conſequence they are, and muſt be, rejected from Chriſt's ſalvation by this judgment. It alſo appears that Chriſt's ſalvation is *eternal*; that they therefore are rejected from eternal ſalvation by the laſt ſentence of the judge; becauſe they have not fulfiled the conditions of life. Theſe conditions then remain to be fulfiled after the general judgment, when the ſentence of rejection from eternal life is paſſed, or they never can be fulfiled. But after the general judgment there will be no goſpel conditions; therefore there can be none to fulfil. Judgment is the laſt act of goſpel. It is to fix the condition of thoſe who have been tryed by the goſpel—to reward its friends and puniſh its enemies. It is to put all things in ſubjection to Chriſt. And when this is done, goſpel has accompliſhed its whole deſign, and muſt ceaſe.

As judgment is the execution of goſpel promiſes and threatnings, it cannot take place till the end of the diſpenſation. It is not time to reward or puniſh men by goſpel, till they have been firſt proved by it. Therefore the judgment of the laſt day cannot commence, till

all

all thoſe have ſtood their trial by goſpel, whom the wiſom of God hath decreed to try by it. firſt to inflict goſpel puniſhments upon men, and after this to put them under tryal by the goſpel, would be like puniſhing a man for a breach of law which was never given him; and after this putting him under the law, to try if his future diſobedience would not merit the unjuſt ſentence already executed upon him.

In the nature of the thing, we muſt begin with probation, and end with judgment, and thus God has repreſented the judgment of the great day. *So ſhall it be in the *end of the world*, ſaith Chriſt; *the Angels ſhall come forth, and ſever the wicked from among the juſt.* In the parable of the tares of the field, our bleſſed Lord being the interpreter, the harveſt, or judgment, is the *end of the world:* And the repreſentation is, that as the reapers do not begin harveſt till the corn is fully ripe; ſo judgment ſhall not commence till all the ſubjects of it have finiſhed their probation; and are ripe for the award. Hence judgment is alſo repreſented as a work of the *laſt day.* ||*He that rejecteth me, and receiveth not my words, hath one that judgeth him: The word that I have ſpoken, the ſame ſhall judge him* IN THE LAST DAY. The ſentence Chriſt has pronounced againſt the unbeliever ſhall condemn him in the general judgment, the *laſt day*, the winding up and

conclusion

* Matt. 13th, 49th. || St. John 12th, 48th.

conclusion of the gospel dispensation. "The last enemy to be destroyed is death:" And this enemy is destroyed by the resurrection: Judgment follows, and puts all enemies under Christ's feet. Devils and wicked men receive their final doom. And then the apostle saith, the end cometh: then Christ will deliver up his kingdom, as mediator, into the hands of the father. The *second death* is not the last enemy here intended. The second death must be destroyed before the final judgment, or never— It must be destroyed by the effect the gospel has upon our lives. If we believe, it has no power over us. If we believe not, we shall be hurt of the second death. For thus saith God, * *He that overcometh shall inherit all things, and I will be his God, and he shall be my son: But the fearful and unbelieving, and the abominable murderers, &c. shall have their part in the Lake which burneth with fire and brimstone, which is the second death.*

Reason and revelation unitedly declare, that judgment is the last act of gospel, the concluding scene of the dispensation. When the gospel ceases, the conditions of it must cease. Judgment shuts up the gospel: It therefore must shut up the conditions of the gospel. Faith is a condition or law of the gospel. Judgment closes the gospel. After judgment therefore, faith is not rewardable by the gospel, because it is not required by it.

* Rev. 21, 7, 8.

The sum of all is, that there can be no probation under the gospel after the general judgment, because gospel itself is then at an end, and ceases to command. Between death and judgment nothing can be done to alter our state. Nothing can be done for which we are to be judged; for judgment only takes cognisance of the things done in the body. It follows, that if we ever fulfil the conditions of the gospel, it must be in this life, while we are in the body. We have adduced several instances, which prove incontestably that some men do not fulfil these conditions in this life, and as they cannot be fulfiled after death or judgment, it must follow, that some men, at the final judgment, must have the sentence of rejection executed upon them; and that they being filthy must remain filthy, and the wrath of God abide upon them. Where then is *universal salvation*? It is not found in the gospel, the last act of which excludes some men forever from a possibility of it.

We will answer a few *objections*, and close the subject.

The first objection is, that Jesus Christ has paid the *whole debt* which we had contracted by sin; and that justice cannot demand a second payment.

Christ has indeed ransomed us from the penalty of the law of innocence. He has paid the whole debt to this law, and redeemed us

D from

from the curſe of it. If we are condemned therefore, it will be by another law. Chriſt has redeemed us from the *Law*; but has he redeemed us from the *Goſpel* too? If we are under no obligation to the law, who dare ſay we are under none to the goſpel? The goſpel was given to us: But why was this done, if we are under no obligation to obey it? Tho' the law has been fulfiled, Chriſt who did fulfil it, has placed us under the goſpel which is not fulfiled, and has threatened to exclude us from his ſalvation, if we do not comply with the conditions of it. If we are finally condemned then, it will be by the goſpel, from the laws of which Jeſus Chriſt has never excuſed us. Our Lord could neither believe nor repent. Innocency foreclofed him from repentance; and infinite knowledge from faith:—Theſe two are the leading terms of the goſpel,—Terms adapted only to ſinners, and beings of limited knowledge—which can be fulfiled only by ſuch beings;—and as they are required of us, will remain a debt upon us till we comply with them; and if we do not comply, we may be condemned by the goſpel, without the charge of a ſecond payment.

The next objection is, that puniſhment is a *medicine*, deſigned by God for the cure of offence; and that it will have its effect either in this, or in ſome future trial. We grant, the puniſhments of this life are deſigned to purge

purge from offence; but that this is the caſe with the puniſhments of the future ſtate, is not a doctrine of the goſpel. In the book of God, the puniſhments of the future judgment are uniformly repreſented, not as the *cure*, but the *award*—the proper wages and deſert of ſin, as a judicial recompence which the juſtice of God is concerned to execute upon the offender. Thus the apoſtle *"The *wages* of ſin is death." And in the laſt day Chriſt is to appear ||*in flaming fire, taking vengeance on them that know not God, and that obey not the goſpel of our Lord Jeſus Chriſt: who ſhall be puniſhed with everlaſting deſtruction from the preſence of the Lord, and from the glory of his power.*

Should it be ſaid, God is not a Being of *paſſion*: The reply is, he is a Being of *juſtice* however; and has told us, if his mercy does not reclaim us, his vengeance or his juſtice ſhall purſue us; that there ſhall be no remedy or eſcaping.

As the poſition, that future puniſhment is purgative, is unſcriptural: ſo the hope of a *ſecond trial* under goſpel is merely viſſionary and ideal. For it has been proved, that after judgment there can be no trial, becauſe goſpel is then cloſed. Indeed, that after the ſeparation of ſoul and body there can be none—for judgment takes cogniſance only of the things done in the body. It therefore follows, that this life is the only time of probation under the goſpel, and

* Rom. 6, 23d. || 2d Theſſ. 1, 8, 9.

and that NOW only *is the accepted time and day of ſalvation*, agreeably to the expreſs words of ſcripture.

Laſtly, it is objected, that we are *finite* beings; our crimes therefore muſt be finite; but the puniſhment of them is repreſented to be *infinite*, and muſt exceed the weight of the offence. No being knows the weight of offence ſo perfectly, as *he* who has adjuſted the puniſhment to it: This being hath declared that **that ſervant which knew his Lord's will, and prepared not himſelf, neither did according to his will, ſhall be beaten with many ſtripes—but he that knew not, and did commit things worthy of ſtripes, ſhall be beaten with few ſtripes, for unto whomſoever much is given, of him ſhall be much required.—‡Take therefore the talent from him, and give it unto him which hath ten talents, For unto every one that hath ſhall be given, and he ſhall have abundance; but from him that hath not ſhall be taken away, even that which he hath. And caſt ye the unprofitable ſervant into outer darkneſs: there ſhall be weeping and gnaſhing of teeth.* If the offender remains an offender forever, it is as juſt to continue his puniſhment, as it was at firſt to inflict it, Whether any ſhall continue offenders forever is then the queſtion.—Were men machines, the puniſhment God inflicts in this life, would infallibly reclaim the vicious. But as we are agents, the concluſion will not follow. The puniſhments inflicted upon Pharaoh were by infinite wiſdom adapted

* Luke 12, 47, 48th. ‡ Matt. 25, 28, 29, 30th.

to the cure of his proud and ſtubborn heart; they did however prove ineffectual. Experience teaches, and the word of God declares, that the longer habits of vice are continued, the more inflexible they grow. The truth is, all men are not reclaimed in this world, either by human or divine puniſhments. Every man muſt be reclaimed in the time of his trial, or never. It has been proved, that this life is the only time of trial: for judgment takes cogniſance of the things only which are done in this life: and after judgment there can be no time of trial under goſpel: for the goſpel itſelf is then cloſed. It follows then, that ſome men are not reclaimed by goſpel in the only time of trial under it, and therefore muſt forever remain offenders againſt it. And ſurely it is as juſt to *continue* as to *begin* to puniſh an offender. It has been proved that judgment is the laſt act of goſpel. As men muſt be firſt tried, before they can be judged by goſpel, they who plead for a time of probation after judgment, plead for a thing clearly impoſſible under the goſpel: becauſe at this period, there will be no goſpel to prove us.

If theſe future trials are ſuppoſed to be under ſome future diſpenſation of grace, the goſpel knows nothing of them: nor will I concern myſelf further with the hypotheſis than to obſerve, that though it may be ingenious, it hath nothing but conjecture to ſupport it. To ſuppoſe goſpel has told us of ſuch future

trials,

trials, is to ſuppoſe it militates againſt itſelf, and has rendered its own motives feeble. They therefore who build their hopes of happineſs upon ſuch conjectures, are *removed from the hope of the goſpel*, and place their expectations only in *cunningly deviſed fables*, built upon mere dream and enthuſiaſm.

It has been proved, that we are probationers, that faith and repentance are conditions of the goſpel—that our redeemer and judge has excluded us from his ſalvation, if we refuſe to comply with them—that judgment muſt proceed according to the conditions of the goſpel, that all men do not, in this life fulfil theſe conditions—that after death they cannot be fulfiled, till goſpel is finally cloſed—and it therefore follows, that all men ſhall not be finally ſaved by goſpel,

After the moſt critical examination, in the fear of God, I ſincerely believe theſe concluſions are fairly drawn from undoubted principles, if the cleareſt and moſt poſitive declarations of God's word are granted to be undoubted principles. And indeed the capital arguments are founded upon the expreſs declarations of our bleſſed Redeemer and judge. Can it be denied, that our Redeemer has rejected the unbeliever from his ſalvation? as judgment takes cogniſance only of the things done in the body. Can it be denied that judgment muſt execute the above ſentence of the Redeemer

Redeemer upon all who die in unbelief? Can it be denied that we are bound to obey the conditions of the goſpel, though Chriſt has anſwered the demands of the law of innocence? Can it be denied that judgment is the laſt act of goſpel, as it is deſigned only to reward or puniſh thoſe who have had their trial under it? Can it then be denied that after judgment all probation under goſpel muſt be at an end? Can it be denied that judgment takes cogniſance of the things only which are done in the body, and executes ſentence according to the conditions of the goſpel? And can it be denied that Dives and others have died deſtitute of the conditions of life? But if there is one perſon rejected from ſalvation by the goſpel, there may be more, and muſt be as many as die in impenitence and unbelief. *One inſtance at leaſt has been adduced. *Univerſal Salvation* muſt therefore be rejected.

From the above reaſons it appears, that the ancient doctrine of the Church of God is the true doctrine—that the doctrine we have oppoſed is deſtitute of goſpel ſupport—and that faith and repentance are conditions of the goſpel

* Perhaps it may be objected, that the inſtance of Dives is a parable, and therefore improperly adduced.—But the circumſtance of its being a parable adds weight to the argument: for though Dives and Lazarus are mentioned as particular perſons, they are deſigned to repreſent different characters; and it is clear from the context that Lazarus repreſents all who obey the goſpel, and Dives all who diſobey it.—therefore the declaration is, that all they who obey the goſpel, do find themſelves at death in a place of joy and comfort; and all who diſobey it, feel themſelves in a place of miſery and diſtreſs, nor will it do to ſay there will be no ſuch different characters at this period, for this would be to deny there was a foundation for the parable itſelf.

goſpel which we muſt fulfil, or be rejected from the hope of the goſpel.

As the doctrine I have here attempted to maintain, is (at leaſt in my own judgment) founded in truth, and ſupported by the word of truth; but has lately, however, been warmly oppoſed by ſome, I ſhall publiſh the arguments adduced in ſupport of the ancient doctrines of the Church, and leave the world to judge of the validity of them. I do this the rather, in teſtimony of affection to my country; and particularly to the reſpected people of my charge, to whom I ſhall leave this Diſcourſe as a legacy. Let me entreat them all, let me entreat you in particular before whom I have walked from childhood to this day, to conſider ſeriouſly, and examine impartially the arguments here advanced. I claim this as due for long and unremitted friendſhip. I claim it as your inſtructor for many years, and one who has never failed to attend you, and take a part with you in every diſtreſs; and I claim it as a meſſenger from God, an ambaſſador of the bleſſed Jeſus. I believe the doctrine oppoſed in this Diſcourſe to be contrary to God's holy and eternal truth, and ſubverſive of the great deſign of the goſpel of Chriſt; and how can I bid you a final adieu, while I fear any of you, by imbibing this doctrine, may be *removed from the hope of the goſpel*. I am clear in it, that faith and repentence are neceſſary to

goſpel

[Archives copy is incomplete.]

AN

EARNEST PERSUASIVE

TO

FREQUENT COMMUNION;

Addreſſed to thoſe Profeſſors of the

Church of England,

IN

CONNECTICUT,

Who neglect that HOLY ORDINANCE,

By the Right Reverend Father in GOD, SAMUEL, their Dioceſan Biſhop.

NEW-HAVEN:

PRINTED BY THOMAS AND SAMUEL GREEN.

M,DCC,LXXXIX.

✣✣✣✣✣✣✣✣✣✣✣✣✣✣✣✣✣✣✣✣✣✣✣✣✣✣✣✣✣

An Earnest Persuasive, &c.

Brethren, beloved in Christ,

THE title has informed you, that my design is to address you on the subject of frequent Communion in the Holy Eucharist, or Sacrament of the body and blood of Christ, commonly called, The Lords-Supper. The subject is an important one, and claims your serious attention: And the great neglect of the duty requires plainness of speech, and freedom of admonition on my part. I have, therefore, to request, that you will carefully read and consider what is here addressed to you: and bear patiently that plain dealing which proceeds only from a desire to stir you up to the practice of a duty which I suppose an indispensable one, and in the neglect of which you live in a constant state of sin against your God.

"Sin" said the apostle, "is the transgression of the law." ‖ The will of God, when made known to us, is his law to us, and binds us in all cases whatsoever. Nothing is sinful any further than it is contrary to Gods will; and every thing is sinful in the same degree that it is contrary to his will: For to contradict the will of God constitutes the nature and essence of sin.

The will of God is made known to us by Revelation, and is declared in the Holy Bible, which is intended by God to be the standard of our faith and practice, that we may know at all times what he requires us to believe and do.

Some of Gods commands are prohibitory, i. e. they forbid us to do certain things because they are contrary to his will: And they are contrary to his will, because, as far as we can judge, they are destructive of

our

‖ 1 John 3. 4.

our own happiness, and of the happiness of others. Other commands are positive, requiring us to do certain things in obedience to God. In many instances we can perceive that what God commands is conducive to our welfare, and to the welfare of others, and reason will teach us to believe, all Gods commands proceed from the same benevolent principle,—a desire of doing us good—though our blindness may not perceive it.

However, The essence of all sin consisting in acting contrary to the will of God, there must be the same sin and danger in neglecting to do what God commands, as in doing what he forbids. In either case we transgress the will or law of God, and commit sin: And, whether it be by wilfully doing what God has forbidden, or wilfully omitting what he has commanded, we equally transgress his law, and are equally guilty in his sight.

That Christ declared the will of God, and that whatever he commanded is the command or law of God, must be owned by all who acknowledge his Divinity —indeed by all who acknowledge He acted by divine authority. Now, He gave no command more positive than the one relating to the Holy Ordinance of which I am treating. The institution is as solemn as it possibly can be, and was made at the commencement of the most solemn period of his ministry on earth. The injunction on his Apostles to do as he had done, and thereby keep up the memorial he appointed, is as absolute as any command that ever was given.*

From the account the Holy Evangelists, have left us, the universal and perpetual obligation of this command, is very apparent. It is true, it does not appear there were any persons present at the institution, besides the Apostles, but this will furnish no argument against the universal obligation all Christians are under to comply with it. They are all as much interested

in

* S. Matt. 26. 26. S. Mark 14. 22. S. Luke 22, 19.

in it as the Apoſtles were. Chriſt died equally for us, and for all Chriſtians, as he did for the Apoſtles. We, therefore, and all Chriſtians are as much obliged to regard the inſtitution as the Apoſtles were. Nothing in the inſtitution peculiarly related to them, except the power of adminiſtration. By the command, "Do this in remembrance of me;" they were impowered and obliged to adminiſter the Holy Ordinance: And conſequently Chriſtians were obliged to receive it; for unleſs they did receive it, the Apoſtles could not adminiſter it.

That the Apoſtles were, by our Saviours command, obliged to this adminiſtration, appears from the inſtitution compared with the command. For the command, "This do in remembrance of me," relates not barely to eating bread & drinking wine in remembrance of Chriſt, as the Socinians teach, and ſome ill-informed Chriſtians ſuppoſe, but to the whole tranſaction. By it the Apoſtles were enjoined, when they adminiſtred the Holy communion, to do as Chriſt then did—take bread and break it, and offer it up to God, by thankſgiving and prayer, conſecrating it to be His myſtical body—the memorial or repreſentative of that body which Chriſt in the inſtitution willingly offered up and devoted to God, a ſacrifice and propitiation for the ſin of the world; and which, in conſequence of his offering, was ſoon after ſlain upon the croſs for our redemption—the body of Chriſt in virtue and efficacy. They were then to deſtribute it to the Chriſtians who attended the Holy ſolemnity, as Chriſt diſtributed it to them. Likewiſe they were to take the cup, and offer it up to God, by prayer, thankſgiving, and bleſſing, conſecrating it to be the ſacramental blood of Chriſt—the repreſentative, or memorial of His blood which Chriſt devoted to God to be ſhed for ſin—the blood of Chriſt in virtue and efficacy to all worthy receivers. They were then to give it to all the Chriſtians preſent to drink of it in remembrance,

brance, or for a memorial of Chriſt. So that all they who received the ſacramental body and blood—i. e, the bread and wine thus bleſſed and conſecrated by Chriſts authorized miniſter—with true penitence and faith, might, at the ſame time, receive, in a ſpiritual and miſterious manner, the life-giving body and blood of Chriſt, i. e. all the benefits of his paſſion, death, and reſurrection.

This memorial, I ſay, the Apoſtles were obliged to make in obedience to their Lords command. And the Chriſtians of their time were of courſe obliged to communicate with them. or their Lords command could not be fulfilled.

As it appears that the very inſtitution of the Holy Euchariſt laid an obligation upon the Apoſtles to adminiſter, and upon all Chriſtians of their time to communicate with them in the celebration of it; ſo a little reflection will convince us, that the ſame obligation lay upon their ſucceſſors, the Biſhops of the Chriſtian Church, and upon all duly authorized by them, and upon all Chriſtians of every period, from their days to ours, to make the ſame holy memorial of his bleſſed body and blood which Chriſt commanded. The command of Chriſt, "This do in remembrance of me," has no limit of time annexed to it. It muſt therefore continue in force till he who gave ſhall repeal it. We are as much intereſted in the ſacrifice of Chriſts death, and therefore as much obliged to commemorate it as the firſt Chriſtians were. We need the benefits of his redemption as much as they did. It muſt, therefore, be as much our duty to commemorate his ſacrifice for ſin, in the way he appointed, as it was theirs—that receiving his bleſſed body and blood in the Holy Communion, we may be made partakers of all the benefits of his death. Was there any doubt of this matter the authority of St. Paul would fully remove it.—"As oft "as ye eat this bread and drink this cup, ye do ſhew "the

"the Lords death till he come."*—Ye do represent, set forth, exhibit the Lords death till he come at the end of the world to judge the quick and the dead—according to his most true promise to his Apostles—"If "I go and prepare a place for you, I will come again "and receive you to myself."§

In this sense the early Christians understood their Lords command. And so strong a sense had they of their duty to commemorate their Redeemers love in dying for them, that they never assembled for divine worship but the Holy Eucharist made a principal part of the solemnity: Nor was it till the love of Christians abated, and their faith declined, that the memorial of Christs death came to be celebrated only on particular occasions.

Consider these things, and let your own consciences determine, whether your neglect of the Holy Communion can be justified on any principles of Christianity or reason? Whenever you compare your conduct with Christs command, sure I am, your own hearts must condemn you: Remember then, "God is great-"er than your heart, and knoweth all things."‖ It is not so much with me, as with your God, you have this matter to settle; and did you attend to it, you would make no more excuses, but immediately prepare yourselves to become worthy guests at Gods table.

It is to be feared there are some who never think enough of the subject to make excuses about it. To these I have nothing to say at present. Till they come to

* Or, *Shew ye* the Lords death till he come.—Probably there is here an allusion to the Shew-bread—the bread of the presence, or bread of representation, under the Œconomy of the Law—That as *that* pointed to the true (not figurative) bread—the bread of God which should come down from heaven to be given for the life of the world—even Christ Jesus: so the Shew-bread under the Gospel—the Eucharistic Bread and Wine—points to the same Lord Jesus Christ already come.

§ St. John 14. 3. ‖ 1 St. John, 3. 20.

a better mind, they will give no attention, and till they do, no reason or persuasion can take any hold of them. I flatter myself there are few, I hope none, among you in so hopeless a condition. Most people intend to consider the subject of religion some time or other, and to make up for all deficiences by their after diligence. The misfortune is, this *some time or other* is long in coming; and there is danger lest it never come at all. Negligence, and indisposition to reflection, and attachment to the world, and the lust of sensual pleasure, by continuance, grow stronger, and death closes the scene, before any resolutions of the future amendment are carried into effect.

The great excuse for not coming to the Communion, and to which all others, where there is any hope of doing good, may be referred, is that of *unworthiness*. And it is probable, a sense of their deficiences, and a strong apprehension of the sin of unworthy receiving, keep more well disposed people from the Communion than any other reason. Let such well disposed people consider the danger of disobeying God, as well as the danger of unworthy receiving. By refusing to communicate, they sin against Gods positive law; but by communicating, it is not certain they would incur the guilt of unworthy receiving—for with some tender consciences, there is more of apprehension than reality in the case. And why should any one keep himself in such a state as that he must sin against God, either by disobeying his positive law, or by unworthy attendance upon his ordinance? Why does he not rather repent of his unworthiness, and amend his life? God is ready to bless his efforts if they be sincere, and to accept his penitence.

It is to be regretted that the word *damnation* is used by our Translators in rendering a passage of St. Paul to the Corinthians†—for that seems to be the occasion of

† 1 Cor. 11. 20.

of the great terror of unworthy receiving. The literal meaning of the word is *judgment*, and it is ſo rendered in the margin of our Bible; and had it been in the text—"He that eateth and drinketh unworthily, eat-"eth and drinketh judgment to himſelf," it would have prevented much uneaſineſs to many pious people. That St. Paul uſed the word here to expreſs temporal judgments and not eternal damnation appears from the next verſe—"For this cauſe"—on account of this unworthy receiving—"many are weak and ſickly among you, and many ſleep"—are dead. He then obſerves, that the way to avoid theſe judgments was, to judge ourſelves and amend our lives, and then "we ſhould not be judged"—the judgments of God, ſickneſs and premature death, would not be inflicted on us. But he ſays not a word of giving up the thoughts of receiving the Communion, leſt by their unworthineſs they ſhould bring Gods judgments on them. The obligation to communicate he ſuppoſed ſtill remained, and exhorts them to repentance and amendment, that they might communicate worthily. He makes another obſervation, viz. That thoſe judgments were the chaſtiſements of the Lord, ſent to reclaim them, and bring them to repentance and a better mind, that they might "not be condemned with the world."

It is, however, certain, there was ſome great unworthineſs among the Corinthians which St. Paul condemned, and on account of which Gods judgments were inflicted on them: And he ſeems to have pretty clearly pointed it out.

The firſt converts to Chriſtianity being Jews, and having a ſtrong attachment to their own religious cuſtoms, they carried ſome of them into the Chriſtian Church. On many occaſions it was their cuſtom, and their law required it, to have a feaſt upon the ſacrifice, and all who eat of it were ſuppoſed to have an

interest

intereſt in its efficacy. Their annual Paſſover particularly was a feaſt of this kind—And as our Saviour had inſtituted the Holy Communion at the concluſion of this feaſt, conſecrating the paſchal bread and the cup of bleſſing as it was called, to be the memorials of his body and blood, the Apoſtles and firſt Chriſtians carried the cuſtom into the Chriſtian Church of accompanying the Chriſtian ſacrifice of bread and wine with a feaſt. This feaſt was called, The Feaſt of Love: To it the rich and the poor brought their proviſions, and ate them together at a common table, in token of their mutual good will and affection, of their fellowſhip, and unity in Chriſts religion, and of their belief that the benefits of Chriſts death were not reſtrained by any conſideration of bond or free, high or low, rich or poor.*

However well calculated theſe love-feaſts which accompanied the Lords-ſupper were, to promote and ſecure Chriſtian charity and unity, at Corinth they were perverted. The rich deſpiſed the poor—the powerful thoſe beneath them. They waited not till the brethren were come together, but they who came firſt ate their own ſupper by themſelves. The rich, who could provide plenty of delicate food, ate and drank to exceſs; while the poor, who could bring little or nothing, not being permitted to partake with the rich, went away hungry from a feaſt of charity.—At ſuch diſorderly feaſts the Holy Supper was celebrated among them.

This is the conduct which St. Paul ſo frequently cen-

* Where the Chriſtians had all things in common, as at Jeruſalem, it is probable the love-feaſts were provided out of the common ſtock. And in other places they may have been furniſhed from what was given at the Offertory; which Offerings, in thoſe early ages, were called the *Devotions* of the faithful, from the Latin word *devoveo*—to *conſecrate* or *devote*—becauſe thoſe offerings were conſecrated or devoted to God. It is true ſince the duty of communicating at the Holy Table has become leſs the practice, *prayer* has peculiarly obtained the name of *devotion*, though it is ſo only in a ſecondary ſenſe.

cenſures, as any one may ſatisfy himſelf by reading carefully his diſcourſe upon the ſubject.* He affirms, that ſuch diſorderly celebration of the Communion was not to eat the Lord's ſupper but to prophane it; and directs them who were hungry to eat at home, and not make the Church a ſcene of diſorder and riot by their exceſs, nor their love-feaſts an occaſion of pride and inſolence, by deſpiſing and putting to ſhame the poor, unprovided members of the congregation, whoſe hunger ought, at leaſt at their love-feaſts, to be relieved by the rich. To convince them of the impropriety of their conduct, and reclaim them to a decent and worthy behaviour, he then ſets before them the ſolemn inſtitution of the Holy Ordinance, as he had received it by revelation, from Chriſt himſelf. And the force of the Apoſtles argument ſeems to be—that Chriſt diſtributed the ſacramental elements equally to all the Apoſtles, in token that he devoted himſelf to death equally for them all, and directed them to eat of it at one table in remembrance of, and as a memorial before God, of his love to them all, and in token of their mutual love and union. For the Corinthians, therefore, to exclude the poor for whom Chriſt equally died, to whom the ſacred ſymbols of his body and blood were equally diſtributed, from a due ſhare in their feaſt of love, without ſupplying their hunger with neceſſary bread—was ſo far from worthily eating the Lords ſupper, that it was not even to diſcern the Lords body, i. e. It put no difference, made no diſtinction, between the Lords-ſupper, & a common meal--at leaſt did not ſanctiſy the Lords body--treat it as a holy, but common thing.‖—This was the unworthineſs which the Apoſtle cenſured in the Corinthians, and this, the not diſcerning the Lords body, which, he ſays cauſed the judgments of God, ſickneſs, and death, to come upon them.

I have

* 1 Cor. 11. 17. &c. to the end.
‖ See Hammond, Whitby, Lock upon the place.

I have been the more particular in this matter to convince you, that in the Church to which we belong, all opportunity of incurring that unworthineſs which the Apoſtle cenſured in the Corinthians is precluded.*

It may, I know, be ſaid, and ſaid juſtly, that tho' all opportunity of incurring that unworthineſs which St. Paul condemned in the Corinthians be cut off, by the abolition of the love-feaſts, yet there may be people in ſuch a ſtate as makes them really unworthy to partake in the Holy Communion. I readily own too, that a perſon who approaches the Holy table without due reverence and devotion, without conſidering the dignity of the Holy myſtery, and the difference between receiving the body and blood of the Lord, and eating and drinking common bread and wine, does not receive the Lords body, is guilty of the body and blood of Chriſt, and is in danger of bringing Gods judgments upon him by his unworthy receiving. But I repeat it; there is no reaſon why he ſhould continue in this evil ſtate but what comes from himſelf. Let him judge himſelf by the rule of Gods commandments, and ſee wherein he has done amiſs. Let him compare his ſentiments of the Holy communion with our Saviours inſtitution, and with the doctrines of the Catholic Church, and correct his unworthy notions. Let him be inſtant in prayer to God for the gift of his grace and Holy Spirit. Let him deny his evil propenſities, and mortify his vicious appetites; and in this way prepare himſelf to do honor to God by obeying his command.

But to treat of this ſubject of general unworthineſs a little more particularly. The qualifications requiſite to make a worthy Communicant, and to make an adult a worthy ſubject of Baptiſm, as far as I can ſee are the ſame,

* The diſorders attending the love-feaſts at Corinth and in other places became too great to be reſtrained; they were therefore aboliſhed by the Church. Though poſſibly they continued longer in ſome places than others.

ſame. They who have kept their Baptiſm undefiled are undoubtedly always fit to approach the Chriſtian altar —More knowledge may be requiſite to the Communion than to Baptiſm ; In other reſpects, the qualifications are the ſame.

That habits, and groſs acts of ſin, render a perſon unworthy to communicate, there can be no doubt. There is, as little doubt, that the ſame ſtate renders him unfit to pray, or do any act of religion, acceptably to God. I will go further, and ſay, that it would be a profanation of the Holy Communion for him, while in this ſtate, to come to it.—And it would be ſo far from doing him good, that it would do him hurt, by hardening the heart in impenitency. And is not this as true of prayer as of the Holy Communion ? Is it not a profanation of Gods name to pray to him, while we wilfully live in the habits, or practice of known ſin, without any deſign or deſire of becoming better ? In this ſtate every prayer is an act of hypocriſy, and hardens the heart againſt the impreſſions of Gods. Spirit. Therefore it is, that "the ſacrifice of the wicked," and the "prayer" of him "that turneth away his ear from hearing the law"—that refuſeth to obey the commandments of God—"are an abomination to the Lord." *

But ſhould ſuch a perſon have any deſire to become better—any wiſh to get rid of the ſlavery and guilt of ſin ;—as ſuch a deſire and wiſh muſt come from God, ſo the only effectual means of bringing them to good effect is, conſtant and earneſt prayer to God for the ſupport of his Holy Spirit, carefully to do his duty according to his beſt knowledge and ability, and ſteadily to avoid all occaſions of ſin. In this way his good deſires would be encouraged, his reſolutions of amendment ſtrengthened, his love of God increaſed, habits of virtue and holineſs formed and confirmed—while thoſe

* Prov. 15. 8. and 28. 9.

thoſe of ſin and vice would decline and die away, His prayers would no longer be an abomination, but highly acceptable to God. And he would then too become a worthy gueſt at the Lords Table, where receiving the outward elements with true penitence and faith, he would alſo receive the precious body and blood of Chriſt, "to his great and endleſs comfort." For the Holy Communion is, at leaſt, as great an inſtrument of holy living as prayer, and the efficacy of both, on our part, reſts on the ſame circumſtances—penitence and faith : The former denoting our converſion or departure from ſin, the latter our reliance upon God, and truſt in his mercy and goodneſs. Should I go further, and ſay that prayers offered up at the altar have more efficacy with God than other prayers have, it would be ſaying no more than the Catholic Church has always ſaid and taught.

But though ſinful habits, and ſingle acts of groſs ſin, render us unworthy to approach God's table, till repentance reconcile us to him, yet ſins, as they are called, of infirmity, ignorance, ſurpriſe, are not attended with that malignity. Our preſent ſtate ſubjects us to them. They proceed from that luſt of the fleſh, or original corruption of nature, which, according to the 9th article of our Church, remains even in the regenerate. And though they have in them the nature of ſin, being contrary to the holineſs and purity of God, yet by the merciful terms of the Chriſtian covenant, they ſhall not finally condemn us, provided we do not willingly live in them, but watch and ſtrive againſt them, humble ourſelves before God under the ſenſe of them, pray earneſtly to him to be delivered from their power by the might of his Spirit, and truſt to his mercy through the Redeemer that he will not impute them to us.

To people who have a lively ſenſe of their imperfections and failings of this kind—who conſcientiouſly refrain

refrain from the Holy Communion, becauſe they fear they are not good enough to come to it, and who do not make the excuſe merely for excuſe ſake, without any intention of ever complying with their duty of frequenting the Holy Table, I would propoſe the following conſiderations.

1. That if they ſtay till they are worthy, in the ſenſe in which they ſeem to underſtand it, before they will venture to partake of the Sacrament of Chriſts body and blood, they will never partake of it at all, but will live all their life, and die at laſt in the neglect of Chriſts command. For however they may wiſh it, they never will be free from the unworthineſs of coming ſhort of their duty, from mere weakneſs of nature. Every created being muſt be imperfect in this ſenſe. And did thoſe lapſes which proceed from infirmity and imperfection render us unworthy to partake in the Chriſtian ſacrifice, no mortal could approach the altar without ſin. Upon this ſuppoſition, Apoſtles and Martyrs, and the beſt Chriſtians that ever lived, have offended in commemorating their Saviour, and have ſinned even by obeying him. They were all men of like paſſions with us, and felt the weakneſſes of nature as we feel them.—Conſcious of their extreme inability to do any good thing without ſome degree of alloy or mixture of ſin, they moſt humbly acknowledged their unworthineſs to perform any of thoſe ſervices which God required of them; but their ſenſe of duty, and fear of diſobeying God, made them cheerfully do whatever his law required of them, knowing that God accepteth of what a man hath, and requireth not that which he is unable to give.—The Angels themſelves, high and holy as they are in their nature, ſeem to have ſome deficiences of this kind, for God, ſaith Job, charged even them with folly.*

2. That the Holy Communion is not only a commemoration

* Job 4. 18.

memoration of Chriſts death, but a memorial or repreſentation of his ſufferings and death made before the Almighty Father, to put him in mind of the meritorious ſacrifice of his bleſſed Son on our behalf.

Chriſts offering himſelf up to death, and yielding his life for us upon the croſs is certainly the moſt aſtoniſhing event that ever happened. And when we conſider the benefits thereby procured for us—the pardon of paſt ſin upon our repentance—the gift of the Holy Spirit—and the aſſurance of a heavenly inheritance to all who believe in and obey him—we muſt feel that his ſacrifice deſerves our grateful remembrance above all other events. But to ſuppoſe that the whole duty and benefit of the Holy Euchariſt reſts here is a miſtake. As we are to commemorate and confeſs Chriſt before men, and gratefully to acknowledge the wonderful works of love and mercy he has done for us; ſo we are to make a commemoration or memorial of his precious death and ſacrifice before the Almighty Father, and plead before *him* the merits of his dearly beloved Son dying for the ſin of the world: Not that God will forget, unleſs we refreſh his memory; but becauſe, in ſo doing, we uſe the means that Chriſt has appointed to convey to us the benefits of that ſacrifice which he offered for ſin. To refuſe, or neglect the Holy Ordinance of the Euchariſt looks as though we had no grateful ſenſe of Chriſts love in dying for us; or that we did not fully truſt to his merits for pardon of our ſins, the gift of the Holy Spirit, and eternal life in the kingdom of God.

3. That the Holy Euchariſt is a covenanting rite, and by it we keep up communion with God.

By Baptiſm we enter into covenant with God: Being born of Water and the Spirit we are born into Chriſts Church, and become members of his body.* By the Holy Euchariſt the new life begun in baptiſm is

* St. John 3. 5. 1 Cor. 6. 15.

is nouriſhed, and fed, and ſtrengthened. This undoubtedly is the caſe with thoſe happy perſons who keep their baptiſm undefiled. But a broken covenant is of no force : And when it is our unhappineſs to break our baptiſmal covenant, and forfeit our right to Gods promiſes, by our ſins and miſdoings—how gracious is God, to permit us, upon our repentance, again to renew it at his Holy table ! again to repeat our vows of obedience, and regain our title to his heavenly promiſes !

It has ever been the doctrine of the Catholic Church, that as when we worthily receive baptiſm, we obtain through Chriſt remiſſion of all paſt ſins, * ſo when we worthily communicate at Gods altar we obtain remiſſion of all the ſins committed ſince baptiſm. And that it is ſo, fully appears from the Holy Euchariſts being an act of communion with God. For when Gods Prieſt offers up the elements of bread and wine upon the Holy altar, they are thereby made Gods property ; and being bleſſed and ſanctified by prayer and thankſgiving, they become, through the operation of the Holy Ghoſt, the body and blood of Chriſt in power and effect. ‖ They are then returned by the hand of Gods miniſter, and diſtributed among the Communicants as a feaſt upon the ſacrifice : And all who partake of them with true faith and repentance are fed with Gods food, and eat at Gods table ; and are thereby aſſured of his favour and goodneſs towards them : and conſequently muſt obtain remiſſion of all paſt ſin, otherwiſe they could not be in favour with God. Accordingly,

C

* Acts 2. 28. and 22. 16.

‖ This is not to be underſtood as though the elements became upon Conſecration, the natural Body and Blood of Chriſt, as the Church of Rome affirms.—The natural Body and Blood of Chriſt are in heaven, and not here on earth.—But they become his repreſentative or ſacramental Body and Blood ; of which, whoſoever partaketh with due repentance and faith, and in the unity of his Church, receives ſpiritually all the benefits of his death and mediation.

cordingly, when our Saviour gave the firſt intimation of this Holy inſtitution, he expreſſed himſelf in terms that imply not only remiſſion of ſins, but all other benefits of his paſſion, " Whoſo eateth my fleſh, and drinketh my blood, hath eternal life, and I will raiſe him up at the laſt day." * Behold the Chriſtians privilege ! and conſider what injury ye do to God, what injuſtice to yourſelves, by your wilful neglect of the heavenly feaſt.

4. That the Holy Euchariſt is one of the inſtituted means of grace and holy living—the appointed inſtrument of conveying the Holy Spirit to us. That this is the doctrine of the Church appears from her Catechiſm and Office of Communion. In anſwer to the queſtion, " What are the benefits whereof we are partakers thereby"—by receiving the body and blood of Chriſt in the Euchariſt—ſhe anſwers, " The ſtrengthening and refreſhing of our ſouls by the body and blood of Chriſt, as our bodies are by the bread and wine." And in one of the exhortations to the Communion ſhe ſpeaks of Chriſts being given, " not only to die for us, but alſo to be our ſpiritual food and ſuſtenance in that Holy ſacrament."

If then you ſeriouſly wiſh to become better Chriſtians and more worthy to communicate with God at his Holy altar, the moſt effectual method is, to prepare yourſelves for the ſolemn office by careful examination of your paſt lives—by ſettled reſolutions to forſake your ſins and live better for the time to come—by mortifying your unruly appetites and paſſions by faſting and ſelf-denial—by earneſt prayer to God that he would give you true repentance, and his Holy Spirit, to enable you to bring your good reſolutions to a happy iſſue—and then to go to the Holy altar—humbly and firmly truſting that God will accept you and bleſs you, and ſeal to you the remiſſion of your

ſins—

* St. John 6. 54. See the whole chap. particularly ver. 48 to 58.

ſins—that he will impart to you the ineſtimable bleſſing of his Holy Spirit, and make you partakers of all the benefits of Chriſts redemption.

To me it is, and to all good Chriſtians it muſt be, an afflicting circumſtance, in congregations who ſeem to have a ſerious ſenſe of religion, and of their duty to frequent the worſhip of God, and who apparently join with devotion in the common ſervice of the Church, to ſee ſo few who act as though they really believed the religion they profeſs. For when people turn from the higheſt act of Chriſtian worſhip, and refuſe to commemorate the love of their Saviour in dying for them by communicating at the Holy table in the unity of his Church, How is it to be known that they are Chriſtians, beyond the mere profeſſion?

Moſt of you, I truſt, would undergo great uneaſineſs ſhould your children, through your fault, die without baptiſm. But to receive baptiſm is not a more expreſs command of Chriſt than to receive the Holy communion; and why there ſhould be more ſolicitude about the one than the other, I cannot conceive.—It is juſt as neceſſary that the new life we receive in baptiſm ſhould be continued, as that it ſhould be begun. Now all life muſt be continued by the uſe of ſuch food as is proper to it—the natural life by natural food—the ſpiritual life by that which is ſpiritual. God has provided and ordained the food of this world for the ſupport of our natural life; and he has provided and ordained food in his Church for the ſupport of our ſpiritual life. If we refuſe this food held out to us in the Holy communion, we deprive ourſelves of our ſpiritual ſuſtenance, and leave the ſoul to famiſh, juſt as the body would famiſh without the nouriſhment of bodily food. To complain, therefore, of your weakneſs and unworthineſs, while you neglect the means God has appointed to increaſe your ſpiritual ſtrength, and all holy and chriſtian tempers and graces, is as unfair

unfair and uncandid, as for a man to complain of a weak and ſickly habit of body, while he wilfully refuſes the food that is neceſſary to his bodily health.

And,

What account can you give to God for the abuſe or neglect of the means of grace and holy living which he has appointed and required you to uſe? You muſt not plead weakneſs, for you refuſe to be ſtrengthened—nor unworthineſs, for you reject the moſt powerful means of becoming better. In any thing but religion, the abſurdity of ſuch a conduct would not eſcape your cenſure. And why it ſhould not be condemned in religious matters as much as in any other, I ſee not. Religion is of more importance to you than any worldly buſineſs can be, and ought more ſenſibly to affect you.

The ſick man, who complains of his achs and pains, and who laments his misfortune in being obliged to bear ſuch a load of miſery and diſeaſe as muſt ſhortly put a period to his life, and yet obſtinately refuſes all the remedies which can alleviate his diſtreſs and reſtore him to health, becauſe they are bitter, or not exactly ſuited to his taſte, becomes the object of our compaſſion—we pity his unreaſonable and fooliſh conduct. Is then his conduct more reaſonable, who complains of his ſpiritual maladies, confeſſes "there is no health in him," laments his unworthineſs and weakneſs, and bemoans his deficiencies in chriſtian virtue, and yet refuſes the means God has directed to cure the diſeaſes of the ſoul, to ſtrengthen the weakneſs of nature, and make him partaker of the worthineſs of his own beloved Son, becauſe the proceſs is diſagreeable to his ſenſual nature?

Could you flatter yourſelves with the opinion that you are as good as you need be—as good, and pious, and holy as God requires you to be—it would be unreaſonable in me to wiſh any alteration in your conduct.

duct. But when I compare your behaviour in respect to the Holy communion with Christs positive command, "This do in remembrance of me," and see you live in the open violation of it, I cannot but be anxious for you—and anxious for myself too, lest my remissness should encourage you in a conduct so irreconcilable with the word of God, and the directions of his Church. And as nothing but a regard to my duty, and an earnest desire to do you good in your most essential interest, could have drawn these free expostulations from me; so I beg you will receive this address as the effort of a heart disposed to do you every service—that wishes to lead you to the embraces of the God of love, to the arms of the blessed Redeemer, and to the consolations of the Holy Spirit of peace.

If what I have said be agreeable to the truth and nature of our Holy religion, your own good sense will enable you to see how indispensibly necessary your attendance at the Holy altar is, to keep up your union with Christ, and through him with the Father. For how can you be living members of Christs body, without partaking of that nourishment by which the whole body is fed and kept alive? And you will at the same time see the necessity of your communicating frequently—even as frequently as God shall bless you with the opportunity. The cravings of natural hunger make you impatient till it is appeased with food; and the health of the body requires that this food be supplied several times in a day. Faith is the hunger—the earnest desire of the soul. They who are blessed with it will hunger and thirst after righteousness, i. e. obedience to God. They need no exhortation: For they will bless God for, and gladly embrace, every opportunity of testifying their ready obedience to a command from which they receive such large supplies of grace and consolation.

The Church of England repuires that all her members

bers "shall communicate at the least three times in the year, of which Easter to be one." * This regulation evidently proceeded from necessity, and was occasioned by the backwardness of the people to communicate frequently. For in Cathedral and Collegiate Churches all the Clergy are directed to communicate every Sunday at the least, except they have a reasonable cause to the contrary. * And in the Communion-office she directs the proper prefaces to be used for several days together—upon Christmas-day, and seven days after—upon Easter-day, and seven days after—upon Ascension-day, and seven days after—and upon Whitsunday, and six days after. It is evident it was her intention that the Communion should be administred on all these days, and I believe it is done in all the Cathedral and Collegiate Churches.

The general practice in this country is to have monthly Communions, and I bless God the Holy ordinance is so often administred. Yet when I consider its importance, both on account of the positive command of Christ, and of the many and great benefits we receive from it, I cannot but regret that it does not make a part of every Sundays solemnity. That it was the principal part of the daily worship of the primitive Christians, all the early accounts inform us. And it seems probable from the Acts of the Apostles, that the Christians came together in their religious meetings chiefly for its celebration. § And the antient writers generally interpret the petition in our Lords prayer, "Give us this day," or day by day, "our daily bread," of the spiritual food in the Holy Eucharist. Why daily nourishment should not be as necessary to our souls as to our bodies, no good reason can be given.

If the Holy Communion was steadily administered whenever there is an Epistle and Gospel appointed, which

* The Rubrics after the Communion-office.

§ Acts 2. 42, 46, 20. 7.

which ſeems to have been the original intention—or was it on every Sunday—I cannot help thinking that it would revive the eſteem and reverence Chriſtians once had for it, and would ſhew its good effects in their lives and converſations. I hope the time will come when this pious and chriſtian practice may be renewed. And whenever it ſhall pleaſe God to inſpire the hearts of the Communicants of any congregation with a wiſh to have it renewed, I flatter myſelf, they will find a ready diſpoſition in their miniſter to forward their pious deſire.

In the mean time, let me beſeech you to make good uſe of the opportunities you have; and let nothing but real neceſſity keep you from the heavenly banquet when you have it in your power to partake of it.

May the conſideration of this ſubject have its proper effect upon every one of you! And the God of peace be with you—"make you perfect in every good work to do his will"*—keep you in the unity of his Church, and in the bond of peace, and in all righteouſneſs of life---guide you by his Spirit through this world, and receive you to glory, through Jeſus Chriſt our Lord. Amen.

All glory to God.

* Heb. 13. 21.

The duty of conſidering our ways.

A

SERMON

PREACHED

BY

ST. JAMES' CHURCH,

NEW-LONDON,

ON ASHWEDNESDAY, 1789.

By the Right Reverend Father in GOD,

SAMUEL, Biſhop of Connecticut

NEW-HAVEN.

PRINTED BY T. AND S. GREEN.

The duty of confidering our ways.

HAGGAI I. 7.

Thus faith the Lord of Hofts, Confider your ways.

BY the prefervation of Gods good providence, we are again come to that holy feafon, in which the Church calls all her members to ferious reflection on their paft lives; that, comparing themfelves with the rule of Gods commandments, they may fee wherein they have departed from their duty; and, confidering the awful threatnings of his word againft fin, may be brought to repentance and amendment.

Juftice to ourfelves requires that this examination be frequent. The pious Chriftian will

will not clofe his eyes in fleep, till he has reflected how he has paffed the day, and has begged Gods forgivenefs for the errors and fins he has committed: And the prudent Chriftian will end the week in the fame way—that humbling himfelf before God, for his failings, he may obtain the comfort of his forgivenefs, and his grace to enable him to live more carefully for the time to come: Thereby too he will be better prepared to attend upon God in his houfe, and offer him an acceptable fervice, at the return of the folemn feafon of public worfhip.

The neceffity of this method, in the management of worldly bufinefs, is apparent. The merchant is obliged frequently to examine into the ftate of his affairs, that he may keep his accounts free from perplexity, know what he gains and what he lofes, correct paft miftakes, avoid future errors, and purfue advantages that are before him with greater profpect of fuccefs. Now they do it to obtain the riches and enjoyments of this world; And fhall not Chriftians take equal pains to obtain the riches of eternity? the good things that God has prepared for them that love him?

It is not that this duty is to be performed once only in a year, that the Church annually

ly calls on us at this ſeaſon, to enter ſeriouſly into it; but becauſe our thoughtleſſneſs may put it off from week to week, and month to month, and year to year, and it never be done at all.

If you have attended to the ſolemn ſervice that has been before you, with that ſeriouſneſs which its importance demands, you muſt perceive that your beſt obedience comes far ſhort of the holineſs of Gods laws; and muſt on that account feel your hearts impreſſed with an awful ſenſe of his divine majeſty. If you fear him as you ought, you will tremble at his juſtice: If you love him as you ſhould, you will loath and deteſt thoſe ſins by which you have offended your beſt friend; and you will need no exhortation to humble yourſelves before him, for your vile ingratitude in ſinning againſt him—Confeſſion and lamentation will flow ſpontaneouſly from the contrite heart. Let me hope this of you all—that you do feel that "godly ſorrow" for your ſins, which "worketh repentance to ſalvation, not to be repented of:"* And that its worthy fruits will appear in your "carefulneſs" and diligence, to repair what is amiſs, and do better for the time to come——in holy "fear," leſt you ſhould again forfeit Gods favour by new offences—in "indignation"

* 2 Cor. 7, 10, 11.

on" againſt your luſts and paſſions, which have been the occaſion of your ſins—and in "revenge" againſt yourſelves, that you have ſo fooliſhly offended your heavenly Father.

That the Church requires theſe ſentiments, and this conduct from you, is evident from the manner in which ſhe has directed the ſeaſon of Lent to be employed, viz. in faſting and abſtinence; not only as a chaſtiſement for our ſins, and a teſtimony of our deteſtation of them, but alſo, that the appetites and paſſions being reſtrained from their uſual indulgence, and mortified by that reſtraint, may be "ſubdued to the ſpirit," ſo that "we may obey all godly motions in righteouſneſs and true holineſs, to the honour and glory" of Chriſt our redeemer.*

That I might promote the pious intention of the Church, to bring her members to ſuch reflection as may end in repentance, and ſhew itſelf in all proper expreſſions of it, I have choſe to addreſs you, at this time, from the ſhort, but ſolemn exhortation of the prophet Haggai to Gods old people, the Jews—"Thus ſaith the Lord of Hoſts, Conſider your ways."

This is not barely a meſſage delivered in the name

* C lect for the firſt Sunday in Lent.

name of the Lord: It is God ſpeaking by the mouth of his prophet.—"Thus ſaith the Lord of Hoſts"—the almighty Lord—he that rules, not only in the armies of men, giving the victory to whom he pleaſes, but in the armies of heaven alſo—To whom angels, and powers, and principalities, and thrones, and dominions, and cherubim, and ſeraphim, are ſubject—whoſe word created, and whoſe will governs them—who employs them as meſſengers to carry his commands, and as mighty ſpirits to execute his decrees. When the majeſty of this God ſpeaks to "vile earth and miſerable ſinners," it muſt be our duty to attend—when He commands, inſtantly to obey. "Conſider your ways" ſaith this God.

Our ways are all before his ſearching eye: For "he is about our path, and about our bed, and ſpieth out all our ways." There is not a ſtep of our foot, nor a word of our lips, nor a thought of our heart, but he knoweth it altogether.* Careleſs and thoughtleſs, we may "ſtray like loſt ſheep from his ways," nor heed the dangers into which we run: But he ſees the tendency of every motion. The fatal precipice to which our erring ſteps lead, and the gulph of perdition which opens to ſwallow up the impenitent, are in his view—and in mer-

cy

* Pſalm 139.

cy he calls—"Conſider your ways" ye children of men—reflect on the tendency of your lives—ſee whither ye are going—open your eyes to the dangers before you.

In a ſimilar ſtrain of mercy and love did he call by his holy prophet Ezekiel—"Turn ye, turn ye from your evil ways; for why will ye die, O houſe of Iſrael!"*—May we regard this admonition of our God! For if the wicked "will not turn, he will whet his ſword: He hath bent his bow, and made it ready: He hath prepared for him the inſtruments of death." † Judgments follow unregarded admonitions, and they who will not hear reproof, muſt feel the rod of correction. They are both the efforts of mercy and love to reclaim us, that our ſin may not be our ruin. When admonition produces repentance, the bent bow in Gods hand is unſtrung, and the rod of correction is laid aſide. The Ninevites repented at the admonition of Jonah, and the threatened vengeance was withheld. The Jews repented not at the admonition of the old prophets, and their city and nation were given up to the king of Babylon. Again, they repented not at the admonition of Chriſt, and God delivered them into the hand of the Romans.

God,

* Ezek. 33. 11. † Pſalm 7, 13, 14.

God, who ſees not as man ſees, and whoſe diſpenſations are always directed by mercy as well as juſtice, ſometimes ſends chaſtiſement before admonition, that feeling his hand, we may regard his words. This may have been the caſe with the Jews when Haggai ſpake Gods words to them. Returning from Babylon, they leſs regarded the laws, and ordinances, and worſhip of God, who had brought them back from the bondage of ſeventy years captivity, than the ſettling themſelves in eaſe and plenty on their lands. From their hiſtory we learn, that they diſregarded the laws of God concerning marriage and affinity with people of idolatrous and ſtrange religions, they oppreſſed the poor by uſury and extortion, they defrauded the labourer of his hire, they deprived the widow and fatherleſs of their right, they withheld the tythes or ſtated allowance of Gods prieſts, they ſupplied not his altar with ſacrifices, or offered to him the lame and the blind—the refuſe of their flocks and herds—they polluted his ſabbaths with worldly buſineſs, and though they builded elegant houſes for themſelves to dwell in, they ſuffered Gods houſe to lie waſte.†—That is, they regarded the riches and enjoyments of the world, more than the law and ſervice of God.

To

† See the books of Ezra, Nehemiah, Haggai, Zacheriah and Malachi.

To correct their evil practices, and bring them to a ſenſe of their duty, God viſited them with drought, and unfruitful ſeaſons, and devouring inſects, and famine.—Under theſe circumſtances he ſpeaks to them—"Conſider your ways"—Compare your conduct with my law, and judge whether it be right to regard only your own eaſe and profit, and neglect juſtice, and mercy, and religion? By Malachi, God challenged them to try him—To do juſtice, relieve the oppreſſed, defend the fatherleſs and the widow, bring honeſtly into his houſe what was due to him, both in tythes and offerings, and then ſee, whether he would not open to them the windows of heaven, bleſs their flocks and their tillage, and make them rich with his favour.¶

The ſpirit of prophecy God has reſtrained; and having completed the revelation of his will, hath left us to the direction of that revelation, for the rule of our conduct, and to its admonitions, for reproof and correction. For this purpoſe was the holy "ſcripture given, by inſpiration of God, and is profitable for doctrine, for reproof, for correction, for inſtruction in righteouſneſs."† In his word, God has declared that war, and peſtilence, and famine, and drought, and ravenous beaſts. and devouring

inſects,

¶ Malachi 3. 10, 11. † 2 Tim. 3. 16.

infects, are his judgments, to correct the fins of men, or fcourge them for their impenitency. When any of them, therefore, come on us, they are Gods vifitation—his hand is on us—and his voice is calling to us—"Confider your ways"—"Turn ye, turn ye from your evil ways; for why will ye die?" May his voice reach our hearts! He is now calling to us by his judgments—May he not call in vain!

Several years are now paft, fince an infect before unknown to us, began, in a neighbouring State, to prey upon the labour of the hufbandman, and deftroy his hopes. Its ravages were, at firft, confined to a fmall tract, and were little regarded, from an opinion, that its appearance was cafual, and that its depredations would be foon at an end. But, on the contrary, it has continued to fpread gradually over the country every way, annually widening its circle, fo that it has reached to the diftance of an hundred and fifty miles from the place where it firft appeared. All kinds of grain are in fome degree injured by it; but its principal deftruction is of the wheat, the nobleft produce of our fields, and the grand material of our bread. No means have yet been difcovered to prevent its fatal effects, or to ftop its progrefs: And how long its depredations will continue, or how far extend, is impoffible for us to know.

In a country fo wide extended, and fo fruitful in various kinds of grain, as the territory of the United States of America is, the failure of one kind, and in a fmall tract, cannot materially effect the whole. But fhould this deftroyer pervade the whole, or a large part of the States, the confequence will be very alarming. At prefent, in the parts infefted by it, one principal refource of the hufbandman is cut off, and it has become more difficult for him to fupport his family, to defray the neceffary expence of his bufinefs, or to difcharge thofe dues to government, which its unavoidable exigencies require.

I truft in God, that in the midft of judgment he will remember his mercy, and will "rebuke the devourer, that he may not deftroy the fruit of our grounds."§ To implore his mercy, the devout prayers of all our congregations in the State, have this day afcended to heaven, and I truft have been prefented to the Father almighty, by Him who "ever liveth to make interceffion for" us.† But let us remember, that repentance on our part muft qualify us for Gods mercy, being the condition on which his mercy is promifed. This fhould excite us to attend to the duty enjoined in the text—to confider our ways, and fee in what we have offended:

§ Malach 3. 11. † Heb. 7. 25.

fended: And this examination of ourſelves, when the chaſtiſement of God is on us, ſhould be more particularly directed to thoſe crimes which, when they become general, bring down the vengeance of God in national judgments. The crimes charged with this particular malignity, are idolatry, profaneneſs, contempt of religion and diſregard of its inſtitutions, violence, oppreſſion of the poor and friendleſs, by with-holding their due, by uſury or exceſſive intereſt, by unjuſt and vexatious law-ſuits.

How far any perſon lives in theſe crimes muſt be left to his own conſcience to determine; but whenever they become general, the curſe of God will follow them, and will ſhew itſelf in ſome way out of the common methods of his providence. Nothing is ſo inſignificant in itſelf, but he can make it the inſtrument of his chaſtiſement. The duſt of the earth became a ſore plague to Pharaoh and his people, when God commanded it to be ſo: And it is worthy of remark, that ſeveral of the judgments, by which the inſolence of that unhappy prince and people was chaſtiſed, were effected by thoſe we think the weakeſt and moſt contemptible of Gods creatures. Nothing appears weaker, or leſs able to help itſelf, than the inſect by which we ſuffer: Yet it endures heat, and drought, and rain, and froſt, and tranſports itſelf

ſelf a good many miles in the courſe of a ſummer: And wherever it goes, the richeſt harveſts fall immature before it.

That it is the viſitation of God, no Chriſtian can doubt, who reads that chapter of the prophet Joel, † from which the ſcripture appointed for the Epiſtle on this day, is taken. There the "locuſt, and canker-worm, and caterpillar, and palmer-worm," are ſtiled Gods "great army:" And, in the beginning of the chapter, are deſcribed in all the horrible majeſty of a diſciplined and well appointed hoſt, ſetting out to ſpread deſolation through an enemies country. The voice of God which accompanied that viſitation of his old people was —"Turn ye even to me with all your heart, "and with faſting, and with weeping, and "with mourning. And rent your heart, and "not your garments, and turn unto the Lord "your God: For he is gracious and merciful, "ſlow to anger, and of great kindneſs, and re"penteth him of the evil"—"Then will the "Lord be jealous for his land, and pity his "people. Yea the Lord will anſwer and ſay "unto his people, Behold I will ſend you corn, "and wine, and oil, and ye ſhall be ſatisfied "therewith"—And, "I will remove far off "from you the northern army"—and "I will "reſtore

† Joel 2.

" restore to you the years that the locust hath
" eaten, the canker-worm, and the caterpillar,
" and the palmer-worm, my great army which
" I sent among you. And ye shall eat in plenty,
" and be satisfied, and praise the name of the
" Lord your God."

This is the voice of God to us now: And if we regard it as we ought—consider our ways, and turn to him with penitence of heart and amendment of life—cleave to him with all our soul—regard his worship, and honour his ordinances—deal justly with our neighbour, and mercifully with the poor and helpless—God will turn from his anger, remove the devourer from our country, and bless our tillage with abundant increase.

I have hitherto considered you as members of civil society, and parts of that whole which makes the national body: But we should all remember, that as we are accountable to God in our national capacity, and stand exposed to those judgments, which by our sins we may have contributed to bring on: So we are accountable to him in our single capacity—as his servants. Nations can be punished only in this world, for here only they subsist. But individuals may be punished in this world, or in the next, as God shall see best. That God does

does punish the sins of nations, is a sure indication that he will punish the sins of individuals: Because national judgments make not an exact distribution of justice—the less and the more guilty generally suffering alike. That he does not always punish the sins of individuals in this life, is a certain argument that he will punish them in the next. His justice requires that every man should be dealt with, according as his life has been: And his character of moral governor of the world, requires, that the penalty of transgressing his laws should be inflicted, or an atonement made for the offender. That God has accepted an atonement for the sins of the whole world, even the blood of his own Son, his revelation gives the amplest testimony. The same revelation informs us of the circumstances under which the benefits of this atonement will be extended to us—repentance and faith. "Consider," therefore, "your ways"—Examine yourselves, and see whether you do "repent truly for your sins past, and have a lively and steadfast faith in Christ our Saviour?"

Lest your carelessness should omit ever to do, what ought often to be done, the Church calls you at this season, to the solemn exercise of both—that with firm faith in the atoneing blood of Christ, you rend your hearts rather than your garments, and turn to the Lord your God

God, with weeping and fasting and mourning. Then, "though your sins be as scarlet, they "shall be as white as snow; though they be "red like crimson, they shall be like wool"§ from the fullers hand—For the merits sake of the Redeemer, and through the intercession he now makes for us in heaven, God will forgive and pass them over, and they shall never come into judgment against us. But he has declared, if we live and die impenitent, our sin shall remain unatoned by that blood of the covenant which we have accounted an unholy thing; and instead of placing our faith and confidence in it, have, by our sin and impenitency, trodden it under foot.† On such God hath declared he will "render indignation and wrath; "tribulation and anguish upon every soul of "man that doeth evil"—"in the day when" he "shall judge the secrets of men by Jesus "Christ."*

"Repent ye therefore and be converted, that your sins may be blotted out, and that times of refreshment may come from the presence of the Lord; and that he may send Jesus Christ who before was preached unto you"—to bring you this refreshing, or consolation, by giving you a final acquittal or absolution from all your sins in the great day of account—even him, "whom

§ Isaiah 1. 18. † Heb. 10. 29. * Rom. 2. 6, 8, 16.

"whom the heavens must receive, until the time of the full completion of all things, which God hath spoken by the mouth of his holy prophets since the world began."†

† See Dr. Whitby on Acts 3. 19, &c.

AN ADDRESS

TO THE MINISTERS and CONGREGATIONS

OF THE

PRESBYTERIAN and INDEPENDENT

PERSUASIONS

IN THE

UNITED STATES of AMERICA.

By a MEMBER of the EPISCOPAL CHURCH.

[Attributed to Bp. Seabury.]

We took sweet Counsel together, and walked unto the House of God in Company. DAVID.

Now I beseech you, Brethren, by the Name of our Lord Jesus Christ, that ye all speak the same Thing, and that there be no Divisions among you; but that ye be perfectly joined together in the same Mind, and in the same Judgment. St. PAUL.

PRINTED IN THE YEAR M,DCC,XC.

An ADDRESS, *&c.*

GENTLEMEN,

IT is neither from a whimſical nor pragmatical diſpoſition that I addreſs you at this time, and in this manner; but, if I know my own heart, ſolely from a wiſh to do good to the general intereſt of chriſtianity, and to the ſtate of religion in this country, by uniting the great body of Preſbyterians and Independents with the Epiſcopal Church. The Epiſcopal Church, you well know, is deſcended from the Church of England, from which the Preſbyterians and Independents withdrew themſelves in the ſixteenth century. My encouragement to this undertaking ariſes from obſerving, that candour and liberality of ſentiment are increaſing in the country, and that moſt of thoſe objections againſt the Church of England which cauſed a ſeparation from it, have in a great meaſure ceaſed to operate in the United States of America.—People of your perſuaſion can now look upon a gown or ſurplice without horror; and ſome of your own clergy make a reſpectable and dignified appearance when clothed in the former of thoſe garments, or, at leaſt, one very like it. They can be preſent at divine ſervice in our churches, and uſe the Common-Prayer-Book with every appearance of ſincere devotion. They can pay attention to Chriſtmas and Good-Friday, and ſeem to be ſenſible of the propriety of obſerving *thoſe* days, at leaſt, for the commemoration of the nativity and death of the bleſſed Redeemer: and your clergy, particularly in the eaſtern ſtates, have generally adopted, and ſeem to be well pleaſed with, the ſtile and title of Biſhop.

From theſe circumſtances, I cannot but hope that the great difficulties in the way of an union between you and the Epiſcopal Church are at an end, and that all leſſer matters may be obviated or removed by mutual explanations and conceſſions.

Another reaſon that has induced me to make this attempt is, the great importance of unity in Chriſt's Church.

Chriſt has but one church, and I know of no medium between being in this church and out of it. It muſt appear, at firſt view, that different modes of church government, and of public worſhip in the ſame country, muſt have unfavourable effects on chriſtian unity. And as Chriſt's Church is and can be only one, why ſhould not its government and worſhip be the ſame in the ſame country? The peace of the church and of civil ſociety would be better ſecured, and the edification of chriſtian people better promoted under the ſame mode of church government, than where the modes are various and diſcordant. And their aſſembling, though in different congregations, to worſhip God by the ſame form, and to profeſs their faith in the ſame words, would prevent many of thoſe diſputes and jealouſies that now too frequently happen, and which, under ſuch circumſtances, muſt for ever happen. It muſt therefore be the wiſh of every man who deſires the proſperity of his country, and to ſee the kingdom of the Redeemer flouriſh in peace and unity, that all the different parties of chriſtians were cemented together by the ſame faith, and doctrines, and diſcipline, and government, and form of worſhip—making one great body—living together, and ſerving God in unity of ſpirit, in the bond of peace, and in righteouſneſs of life.

That I am a member of the Epiſcopal Church I have no deſire to conceal. It is from a full perſuaſion of the excellency of that church in its doctrines, government, and mode of worſhip, that I wiſh all others to be of the ſame profeſſion with myſelf. I can eaſily believe that others may have as ſtrong an attachment to their religious profeſſion as I have to mine, and may be as fully perſuaded of its ſuperior excellency. But then, I imagine this attachment and perſuaſion ariſes from education, habit, and ſometimes from prejudice, and from an undue regard to the opinion and judgment of others. I perſuade myſelf, that on a fair examination, matters would appear otherwiſe to them than they do at preſent. It is to this fair examination that I now invite them. Candid inquiry can hurt nobody—it is a friend to truth, and therefore to human happineſs.

I am very ſenſible, that great addreſs and good temper are neceſſary in conducting ſuch an inquiry with any proſpect

prospect of doing good, and I am not sure that I possess those qualities in a sufficient degree to promise much success: nor, though I am conscious that I have, through my whole life (and I am not a young man) endeavoured to keep myself free from prejudice and narrow principles, am I certain that I have entirely succeeded. I am sure, however, that I have a love for all men, and wish to do them good; and this, I hope, will be thought to be a sufficient apology for my present undertaking.

If I can induce you, gentlemen, to review the principles of your present religious system, which I think erroneous, and productive of much evil to yourselves, to civil society, and to the church of Christ—if I can help, in any degree, to dissipate that mist of prejudice which, I apprehend, prevents your seeing the truth, or lessen the force of that bias which turns you away from it; it will both increase my happiness and promote yours.

That some things are right, in most denominations of christians, I see with pleasure; and in every thing that is so, I can heartily bid them *God speed*. But it can be no part of christian charity to say they are *right*, and bid them God speed, when I think they are *wrong*. I can, however, judge of their errors with candour, knowing, that I also am subject to the same infirmities, and need the candour of others. Gracious is God—and happy for us it is, that he will look with pity on human frailty, and make every allowance for involuntary error. But whether he will overlook voluntary errors, is another consideration.

That religion is of importance, all allow. The Deist, the Infidel, the Atheist (if such a one there can be), must confess that religion, by curbing the passions, and checking the malevolent tempers of men, contributes to the happiness of civil society. But the christian looks further, and believes that his religion will secure to him eternal felicity, through the Redeemer. If so, its importance is increased, and it becomes an object of great consequence to ascertain in what it consists—or what he ought to believe and do, in order to obtain the full benefit of it.

The Deist supposes religion to consist entirely in moral virtue, and that man is capable, by the strength of his

A 3 own

own reason, to discover and practise that virtue. He therefore rejects revelation and all supernatural assistance, as superfluous and unnecessary. Was he right, every religion which teaches a pure morality, would be a good and true religion; and that would be the best religion, which teaches and enforces the best morality.

I mean not to disparage moral virtue. I feel its obligation, and readily acknowledge that no religion can be good which disregards it. But did religion consist of morality alone, I see not how it could extend its influence beyond this world, or do us service in the life to come: because our morality is imperfect, in many things we have all offended against its laws, and stand exposed to the justice of God, the moral governor of the world. I must therefore give up the idea of being accountable for my actions, or I must abide the rigour of divine justice. To the mercy of God I can have no title: mercy and justice can never be at variance in him, whose being is perfection infinite, *" and with whom there is no variableness, nor shadow of turning."* If then man be not merely a creature of this world, but must live in eternity; without a mediator, who, by making atonement for sin, can reconcile justice and mercy together, he is lost and undone, notwithstanding the exactest morality he can perform.

Some christians have run into the contrary extreme, and seem to suppose that all religion consists in doctrine, and that if they have a right faith, all is well, and they are perfectly safe. I will not say these christians despise morality and good works, because I hope better things of them. I am ready to own with them, that morality and good works can give us no title to salvation. But then, it ought to be remembered, that faith, properly speaking, can do no more for us than works. On the foot of merit, our faith, and our works, are equally insignificant—neither of them make any atonement for sin. If, then, the man who has this true and right faith, commit sin, he stands exposed to the justice of God, equally with him who trusts to his imperfect morality.*

Was

* It seems to be the opinion of many Calvinists, that God sees no sin in his elect—that Christ, having made atonement for their sins, God will impute no sin to them; but, on the contrary, all their sins

Was I to define christian religion, I would say, It is the method appointed by God to reconcile sinful man to himself, so as to make him capable of happiness with him. In this view it consists not merely of morality, nor merely of faith; but of every thing which God has commanded. The word of God must be the standard of this religion. Whatever He commands, must be done—whatever He forbids, must be avoided:—True faith will therefore consist in believing whatever God has revealed; and true morality, in doing whatever he has enjoined. The word of God, by which our religion is to be regulated, we all acknowledge to be the Bible, or that revelation from God which is contained in the books of canonical scripture, as they were received, and have been handed down to us, by the primitive church.

In the Bible we are informed, that God sent his Son into the world to be its redeemer, and to rescue man from that state of sin and misery into which he had fallen by the instigation of the devil—and, that through the Son, as mediator, a new covenant is made with man, or new conditions of life are held out to him. As God was the party offended, and man the offender—*He* infinite in power, knowledge, and goodness; *man* weak, and frail, and ignorant—it belonged to God to appoint the method or terms of reconciliation, and it was the duty

of

are not only now forgiven, but were so from eternity; or, at least, that they are forgiven as fast as they are committed; and that Christ having fulfilled the law in their nature, his holiness is imputed to them. This seems to have been the opinion of the celebrated Bishop Beveridge: and from what I hear (for I have not the honour of his acquaintance) this seems to be the opinion of Mr. Murray; only Mr. M. has generously extended that benefit of salvation through Christ, to the whole human race, which the Calvinists confine to here and there one, whom the arbitrary decree of God has picked out, leaving the rest to their merciless fate. When all are wrong, to say who is most so, is sometimes a difficult point. The notion that God sees no sin in his elect, I cannot reconcile with his being of *purer eyes than to behold iniquity*. If sin be forgiven as fast as it is committed, it amounts to a direct licence to sin. To say that sin is forgiven from eternity, or from any time before its commission, is absurd. Sin is the transgression of the law. Until the law be transgressed, sin is not in being, and therefore cannot be forgiven. Permit me to recommend to the candid reader, a tract of Dr. Whitby on the imputation of Christ's righteousness, inserted at the end of his Commentary on the first Epistle to the Corinthians.

of man humbly to receive, and gratefully to acquiefce in them.

Hence appears the abfurdity of an attempt in a man, or any number of men, to frame their own religion; for be its morality ever fo exact and pure, and its doctrines ever fo agreeable to the judgment of their own minds, unlefs they be alfo agreeable to the will and inftitution of God, there can be, ftrictly fpeaking, no religion in them. It all comes under the true notion of felf-righteoufnefs, and can have no warranted claim upon the acceptance of God.

From hence alfo it is evident, that the common opinion, that every man has a right to choofe his own religion, is an error: for God having inftituted and appointed the true religion, it becomes every man's duty to embrace *that*, and be of it, and of no other—His own contrivances are out of the queftion. In the prefent unhappy divifion of chriftians into fects and parties, every man has not only a right, but is bound in duty to exercife his own reafon and judgment, in order to diftinguifh which the true religion is. But this gives him no right to choofe wrong. If he do, he does it at his peril; for God requires that he choofe right, and has given him reafon, confcience, and revelation to enable him to do fo. For though it be admitted, that prejudice of education, deference to the opinion of others, weaknefs of underftanding, or want of better information, may excufe errors in this matter, they never can be pleaded in juftification of a wrong choice in religion which has arifen from views of intereft, ambition, or party. This is a confideration worthy of the attention of all thofe who have chofen their religion from fuch bad motives, or who, from the fame motives, continue in a wrong religion in which they have been educated, after they have had opportunity of fuch information as ought in reafon to correct their judgment.

What has been faid may, in a good degree, be applied to the private right of interpreting holy fcripture. The Bible, we are agreed, is the ftandard of our religion: but who is to interpret the Bible for us? I am fenfible, it will be an unpopular ftep to controvert the right of private judgment. Where it is prudently exercifed, I

fee no great inconveniency in it. It is not the right, therefore, but the abufe of it, that is to be cenfured. Under its patronage, men fometimes *bend* and *twift* the fcripture to make it comport with fome pre-conceived, favourite opinion. If fcripture and their opinion differ, their opinion is not to be given up. It is the child of their own begetting, and they have a fondnefs for it; or, it is faft rooted in education and habit, and they know not how to part from it; or, it opens the door to popular applaufe, and fmooths the path to honour and preferment, and they muft hold it faft. What is to be done? A religious opinion for which no fcripture can be adduced, looks oddly among chriftians. The remedy is to hunt out fome interpretation of fcripture which nobody ever thought of, but yet, fuch a one as comports with their opinion; and then all is right. But this is not to try opinions by fcripture, but fcripture by opinions.

And from this fource we may, in a great meafure, deduce all the religious fects which divide chriftendom. Afk any other denomination, Why fuch a fect errs fo much from the truth? the anfwer is, They mifunderftand the fcripture. This made a gentleman of wit fay, that, among religious difputants, holy fcripture fared like an open town in time of war—each party ufed it to ferve its own purpofe.*

Something of this fpirit feems to pervade almoft all religious partizans. They will worm about moft miferably,

* A gentleman of good character, but rather of an enthufiaftic turn, and confequently of weak judgment, having embraced the plan of univerfal falvation according to the fcheme of Mr. Murray, which denies all future punifhment, being hardly preffed with a paffage in St. Matt. ch. xii. v. 32. "Whofoever fpeaketh againft the Holy Ghoft, "it fhall not be forgiven him, neither in this world, neither in the "*world* to come;" denied that the paffage was fairly cited. A Bible was produced, and the paffage read. He then denied it to be a true tranflation. A Greek Teftament was brought, and the tranflation juftified. Thus entangled, he faid the text muft have been corrupted, and could not have originally been written in that manner. Being called upon for authority to fupport his affertion, he had none to produce: And no wonder—the diligence of Mills not having noted a various reading, or even a different punctuation in the text. It may be expected that the gentleman was convinced, and converted from his error: no fuch thing; he was right—St. Matthew's Gofpel had in that text been corrupted, and was of no force.

ably, and put the fcripture to the rack, and ftretch it beyond all bearing, till they think they have made it comport with their fyftem, and then their fyftem is truly fcriptural: they can quote fcripture for it—no matter how much fcripture is diftorted or mangled in the application.

I know of but one remedy adequate to this difeafe, and that I fear will fare as many good remedies have done—be rejected as foon as propofed—becaufe its complexion or confiftence does not pleafe the eye, or its tafte the palate. A good phyfician will, however, direct his remedy, and leave it to the patient to determine whether he will avail himfelf of its virtues, or linger under his difeafe. The remedy is, to abate our own pride and felf-importance, and pay a due regard to the doctrines and practice of the primitive church; and where the fenfe of fcripture, with regard to any doctrine or practice, appears to be doubtful, to enquire how the firft chriftians underftood it, and acted upon it.

From the Bible we learn, that when the Son of God came into the world to redeem it, he made atonement for the fins of it by his own death; and that to make men partakers of that falvation which he purchafed, he formed and inftituted a fociety called his church, which is to fubfift to the end of the world, and to confift of all thofe who, in every age, believe in him; that is, of thofe who, receiving and regarding him as their mediator, renounce their apoftacy from God, believe his word, obey his precepts, and rely on him for remiffion of fins and eternal life. In this church he appointed facraments, to be outward figns and feals of inward and fpiritual grace. Over it he conftituted governors, and directed them, as well by his inftructions as by the Holy Spirit whom he fent on them, how to build up his church, and eftablifh it in the world, according to his will. To this church all his promifes of fupernatural grace, of forgivenefs of fins, and of eternal life, are made.

No one fuppofes the Apoftles acted unfaithfully in the difcharge of the commiffion they received to teach and govern the church of Chrift. We muft therefore conclude, that the chriftians who lived in the next age after the apoftles, efpecially thofe to whom they committed the

the government of the church, underſtood their doctrine and practice. They had their information from the apoſtles themſelves; and this information, together with the apoſtolical writings, they communicated to the ſucceeding generation. In a great part of the world, Greek, the language in which the apoſtles wrote, was the common tongue, and well underſtood. The manners and cuſtoms of the age and countries, to which the apoſtles allude, and from which they draw many of their expreſſions, were familiar to them. On theſe accounts (and more might be mentioned) they muſt have been better judges of the writings of the New Teſtament eſpecially, than we poſſibly can be. To ſuppoſe that thoſe chriſtians did not underſtand their religion, or did not practiſe agreeably to it, when too, the ſupernatural proofs of its divine original were ſo recent, and they, in conſequence of their profeſſion, were obliged to relinquiſh all wordly hopes and views, is an abſurdity too great for common ſenſe to admit.

In aſcertaining the meaning of old laws, we recur to the opinions and practice of the judges and lawyers who lived at, or near the time of their promulgation; and ſuppoſe that to be their true meaning which their deciſions have warranted and handed down to us. If this be reaſonable, why ſhould it not alſo be reaſonable to recur to the firſt ages of chriſtianity, to aſcertain the laws and doctrines of the goſpel, ſhould any doubt ariſe concerning them?

Tradition, is, at preſent, an ill-ſounding word, and the ill uſe which the church of Rome has made of it, juſtifies the proteſtant chriſtian in liſtening to it with a cautious ear. Yet that there were traditions, and oral traditions too, delivered by St. Paul to the churches which he planted, appears from his charge to the Theſſalonians, (2 Theſſ. ii. 15.) "Therefore brethren, ſtand "faſt, and hold the *traditions* which ye have been "taught, whether by *word* or our epiſtle." Again, Ch. iii. 6. "Withdraw yourſelves from every brother "that walketh diſorderly, and not after the *tradition* he "received from us"; and that it might make the greater impreſſion, this injunction is laid, "in the name of our Lord Jeſus Chriſt". He uſes the ſame expreſſion in

in 1 Cor. ii. 2. Our tranſlators have indeed rendered the Greek word παραδόσεις by the Engliſh word *ordinances*, and have put *traditions* in the margin as equivalent. Why this was done it is impoſſible to tell. The Greek word here is the ſame that is uſed in the two places cited from the epiſtle to the Theſſalonians, which they have there rendered according to its literal meaning, viz. *Traditions*, or things to be delivered from one to another.

The regarding of traditions, and the prefering of them to the commandments of God, is, it is true, in ſeveral inſtances, condemned by our Saviour and his apoſtles; but the context informs us, that they were unwarranted Jewiſh traditions which they condemned, and not thoſe delivered by apoſtolical authority to the chriſtian church.

In ſome inſtances the generality of chriſtians pay a due regard to the traditions of the church. By tradition they aſcertain and receive the canon of holy ſcripture, infant baptiſm, the obſervation of the Lord's day, the celebration of the holy communion in the morning, and not in the evening, the adminiſtration of it to women as well as men: Why then ſhould it not be equally regarded in other inſtances, if it be of equal clearneſs and authority.

It may be thought a matter of difficulty to aſcertain, when a tradition is of ſuch clear and full authority, as to give it a title to a ready reception. The old rule is certainly the beſt—*That which was held by all conſiderable churches, in all places, and at all times, muſt be by apoſtolical authority.* By this rule, we pin our faith on no particular church, writer, nor body of men, but depend on the teſtimony of the church catholic, or univerſal.

The apoſtles ſeparated, and diſperſed themſelves through the world, to preach the goſpel, as they had been commanded—and they founded churches in all countries, as God gave them ſucceſs. If we find the ſome inſtitutions, doctrines, and practices in different churches, founded by different apoſtles, we may fairly conclude they owed their origin to apoſtolical authority---nothing elſe can account for the fact. The apoſtles all taught the ſame doctrines, adminiſtered the ſame ſacraments,

ments, inſtituted the ſame government, directed the ſame mode of worſhip, enjoined the ſame rules---for they were all inſpired by the ſame bleſſed ſpirit. The churches therefore founded by them would be alike;—and however we may ſuppoſe error, in a greater or leſs degree, to have crept into ſome or all of them afterwards, making diſtinctions among them; yet thoſe things in which they all agreed muſt have been from ſome common ſource, and that could be no other than apoſtolical inſtitution; eſpecially if they are ſo ancient, that their beginning cannot be fixed to a later period, than the apoſtolic age.

It has been obſerved that Chriſt inſtituted a ſociety in the world which we call his church*—that he appointed governors over it, and inſtructed them how to build up and eſtabliſh it according to his will. It has been alſo obſerved, that the apoſtles, whom he appointed governors of his church, cannot be ſuppoſed to have acted unfaithfully in their commiſſion; becauſe they abandoned all worldly hopes, when they ſet out upon the diſcharge of it, and could have no temptation to prevaricate in it; becauſe they expected, and endured the perſecutions of the world, and, one only excepted,† all died the death of violence, in atteſtation of the truth of their miſſion, and of their own fidelity in the execution of it; and becauſe they had the conſtant preſence of the Holy Ghoſt with them, to guide them in the truth, and ſecure them againſt error. We may therefore ſafely rely upon what they taught and practiſed, whether it come to our knowledge by their writings, or by the teſtimony of the univerſal church.

B I mean

* The Greek word for Church is Εκκλησία, from ἐκκαλεω, to *call out of*, or *from among*; and means thoſe who are *called out of*, or *from the world*, to be the ſubjects of Chriſt's kingdom, which is not of this world.

† Eccleſiaſtical hiſtory informs us, that St. John the beloved apoſtle, and who ſurvived all the reſt, died a natural death at Epheſus. Yet the church always gave him the honour of a martyr; becauſe, by the command of Nero, he had been thrown into a veſſel of boiling oil; from which however, by the miraculous interpoſition of Almighty God, he came out alive and well. He was then baniſhed into the iſle of Patmos, where he continued during the life of that Emperor, and where he received and wrote his revelation.

I mean not to set the authority of tradition upon an equality with that of holy scripture. I know there is an evident distinction between them; and am sensible, that if they come in competition, the tradition of the church must be given up, and the scripture regarded as the standard of faith and practice. But where the testimony of the church does not disagree, but rather coincides with the scripture, I can see no good reason why it may not be safely admitted. To make myself understood, I will give an example or two of what I mean.

The Anabaptists reject infant-baptism, and, some of them the observation of the Lord's day. To dispute with them from scripture is fruitless. They will impose their own interpretation, and abide by it. They moreover demand positive texts, and direct commands for these observances; and we have none to give them. Must we, then, abandon these institutions, because there are no texts which say, *Ye shall baptise infants—Ye shall observe the first day of the week for the christian sabbath?* By no means: We have, I take it, as good authority to retain and observe them, as though they had been positively enjoined in scripture. For we have the consentient testimony of the universal church in favour of them both—that they were practised in all churches, and at all times, so that no body can tell when the observance of them first began. They must, therefore, have been from the beginning of the christian church, and consequently, from apostolical practice. We are of course not only justified in retaining them, but it is our duty to do so; especially as there is nothing in scripture against them, but several passages and expressions which are evidently in favour of them, and which seem incapable of being applied to any thing else. Did scripture contradict them, the matter would be soon ended—the testimony of scripture must be regarded, and the tradition of the church abandoned.

The same mode of reasoning, and that only, would establish the canon of scripture, was there any dispute among protestant christians about it. The present books were ever received and read in the church as canonical scripture; that is, not only as being written by the authors whose names they bear, but as being written by divine

divine inspiration. On this ground we part from the church of Rome respecting the books called Apocryphal. —We have not the same united testimony of the church, that they were written by the authors whose names they bear; and if they were, we are not sure of their divine inspiration. The church therefore reads them in her public assemblies, not as canonical scripture, but on account of the excellent instruction contained in them.

Permit me, without offence, to apply this mode of reasoning to two other instances, that we may see whether its conclusions, with respect to them, be not as strong, as they are for infant-baptism and the Lord's day.

One instance is the government of the church by bishops, as successors to the holy apostles, and as an order superior to presbyters. I mean not that the present bishops of the christian church are successors to the apostles in their extraordinary capacity, as they were the inspired penmen of holy scripture, workers of miracles, and witnesses of the resurrection of Christ; but as they were the stated rulers and governors of his church. The commission Christ gave them points to these ordinary powers, "As my father hath sent me, even so send I you"—— "Receive ye the Holy Ghost. Whose soever sins ye "remit, they are remitted unto them; and whose soever "sins ye retain, they are retained," John xx. 21, 22, 23.

Every word implies commission and authority. He sent them to send others, for so the Father had sent him. He gave them power to admit men into his church, and to exclude them from it, as circumstances should require, and thereby committed the government of his church to them. He promised to be with them, by his power and spirit, even to the end of the world; to the end of the world therefore, their office was to continue. Now we have the concurrent testimony of the church, that it was always governed by bishops who had under them presbyters and deacons: And so universally did this prevail, that no time nor country can be found in which it did not obtain. The opposers of episcopal government have in vain attempted to find some time or place where presbyterian government had been established; and too many of them have shewn great dexterity in torturing words, and darkening plain expressions; but they are yet at fault,

fault, and are likely so to continue. It remains, therefore, for us to conclude, that the government of the church by bishops, as superior to presbyters, was, and is of apostolical authority; nothing else can account for its universality in all times and places, till the reformation.

This conclusion will be much strengthened by recurring to holy scripture. There we find that several persons were admitted to the apostolic office, in the early period of the ministry of the eleven.---St. Matthias, St. Paul, St. Barnabas. These are expresly called apostles in our bible (Acts i. 26.—xiv. 14.) The apostolic power, therefore, was not confined to the eleven original apostles: But besides these, there are others who, though called *apostles* in the Greek testament, are in our bible stiled *messengers*—as Epaphroditus, Titus and others, (Philip ii. 25. 2 Cor. viii. 23). Andronicus and Junia are also by fair implication stiled *apostles* in Rom. xvi. 7. Why our translators rendered the Greek word, Αποςολος, sometimes apostle, and sometimes messenger, when no evident reason required it, is hard to say. The verb αποςελλω, from which the word *apostle* is derived, signifies indeed to *send*; and the apostles were so named from Christ's sending them, as his messengers to the world. From this manner of rendering the Greek word sometimes by *apostle*, and sometimes by *messenger*, an obscurity is thrown on our translation, from which the Greek testament is intirely free; and the English reader is led to understand the matter in a sense different from what I apprehend the Greek testament will justify. For instance, Philip ii. 23.—"Epaphroditus, my brother—but your *messenger*." The idea that will probably strike the English reader is, that Epaphroditus was a messenger whom the Philippians had sent to St. Paul, on some business. But the Greek ὑμων δε αποςολον, means an apostle, or messenger of Christ, who had been set over them as the governor of their church. In Rom. xi. 13. St. Paul stiles himself, *the apostle of the Gentiles*; in the Greek, εθνων αποςολος. Was St. Paul a messenger whom the Gentiles had sent to do their business? or was he the apostle, or messenger of God to them, set over them in the Lord, to preach the gospel to them, and direct and govern them in the christian faith, according to Christ's command? These

These instances afford undeniable proof that it was not the opinion of the apostles that their office was to cease with their lives. On that supposition, why should others be admitted into it? Do they not prove more? Do they not prove that the apostolic office is transmitted down to us in the present Episcopacy of the christian church? If not, where is their office to be found? If it be not to be found, what becomes of the promise of Christ—"Lo, I am with you always even unto the end of the world"? The promise of Christ is certain. The apostolic office, therefore, still subsists some where. We claim it for the present bishops of the christian church—I mean bishops as superior to presbyters, to whom the government of the church is committed, who have the power of ordination, and to whom the presbyters are subject. They who deny these bishops to be the successors of the apostles, ought, in all reason, to inform us where the successors of the apostles are to be found, and not leave those who confide in them under the temptation of thinking, that Christ's promise to be with his apostles to the end of the world, has failed.

That there has been a change of names by which the governors of the church were distinguished, is readily granted. When this change happened we know not. It therefore happened early—probably soon after the death of the original apostles; for in the next age, the chief governors of the church are mentioned under the stile of the Bishops, and not of apostles, unless rarely. The opinion of those seems best founded, who suppose that on the death of the first apostles, the christians applied the name of apostles to *them* by way of eminency, and distinguished their successors by the stile of Bishops, one of the names by which the second order of the christian priesthood had been distinguished. Be this as it may: It is certain that by the middle of the second century, the title of Bishop became the common term, by which the chief governors of the church were distinguished.

That there was a subordination of power and order among the governors of the church, even in the time of the apostles, is evident from St. Paul's epistles to Timothy and Titus. I mean not a subordination to the original apostles only, but to those whom they had admitted

mitted into their own order. Timothy and Titus appear to me to have been of this number. They had powers superior to the other church-officers or bishops at Ephesus and Crete. They ordained, directed, and governed the other overseers of the church—called them to account, and censured them when it was necessary; at least, they had power to do so: and no authority is mentioned as superior or equal to theirs, in those places.

To say that they were extraordinary officers in those churches is begging the question. Let it be proved that that they were so, and all dispute with regard to them will be ended. Timothy, it is true, was an evangelist, or rather had been so: But a *preaching* apostle or bishop could be no such extraordinary thing as to give him, on that account merely, a pre-eminency over the other overseers of the church at Ephesus.

I will not pursue this argument here, but shall now only observe, that the testimony of the church universal, in favour of episcopal government, taken in conjuction with allusions, expressions and events, which we find in the apostolical writings, afford as strong an argument of its being of apostolical institution, as can well be conceived: Full as strong as the argument for infant-baptism, or the observation of the Lord's day; or for the divine authority of the books of the New Testament.

The other instance to which this mode of reasoning may with propriety be applied, respects the mode of celebrating public worship in christian congregations.

There is ample testimony that public worship among the primitive christians was conducted by a prescript form, or liturgy. Those ascribed to St. James of Jerusalem, St. Mark of Alexandria, St. Clement of Rome, &c. &c. are still extant—And though some may doubt their being the liturgies of those eminent men whose names they bear; and though all should acknowledge that errors have got into them, which favour of the corruptions of the Greek and Roman churches; yet they incontestibly prove the great antiquity of public liturgies for public worship. Their antiquity is so great that it cannot be ascertained. Whereas extempore prayers in public worship are of modern date—we know when they began; for till the reformation the churches of God had no such custom. The

The public worship of the Jewish church was conducted by set forms; and as the first converts to christianity were from among the Jews, it is probable they carried the custom into the Christian Church. This is the more probable, as our Saviour not only said nothing which can be construed into a censure of forms of prayer; but, on the contrary, at their own request, gave his disciples a form, apparently to be added to, or used with, their other devotions. Nor is there a syllable in the writings of the apostles which can, by any tolerable construction, be made to militate against forms of prayer.

That the apostles, when they presided in public worship, always used forms, I do not presume to say. They were persons divinely inspired; sometimes, at least, prayed and preached, as the Holy Ghost gave them utterance. There is no absurdity in supposing that at other times they joined in the ordinary liturgy of the church where they were; and, most probably, their inspired prayers were only in addition to the common offices of their public devotions, according to the good pleasure of the Holy Ghost.

Be this as it may—their extempore praying; I mean as a part of public worship—cannot be adduced as an example for our imitation, unless we have the inspiration of the spirit, as they had. Some of the first dissenters from the Church of England set up the claim of praying by the inspiration of the Spirit, and it served as an engine to draw away weak and enthusiastic minds from the offices and communion of the church; because, as it was said, prescribed forms stinted the Spirit. The world, I trust, is grown too wise to suppose, that a man who prays extempore in the congregation, must of course pray by the dictates of the Holy Ghost. And to do justice to the successors of the first dissenters, they seem sensible of the arrogancy of such a pretence, and are content with the modest expedient of composing their prayers and getting them by heart, before they venture on a public exhibition. Was I to be a constant attendant on their ministrations, I should feel myself much obliged by this prudent management. Much of the extravagance which marked the original extemporizers in prayer would be avoided by a prudent minister; and if he had a tolerable

a tolerable turn for devotional compoſition, or judgment enough to avail himſelf of many good forms that are in print, he could not fail of making his prayers more acceptable to God, more advantageous to the people, and more honourable to himſelf; as he could moſt certainly acquire the reputation of a *gifted man in prayer*.

I preſume it will appear from the view we have taken, that forms of prayer may be lawfully uſed in the public worſhip of the church:—They are not forbidden in holy ſcripture:—They are countenanced by our Saviour and his apoſtles: He gave a form to his diſciples—and he and they attended the public worſhip in the temple, which was conducted by forms—they are recommended by the practice of the primitive church in its pureſt ages; and, moſt probably, they were in uſe in the chriſtian church from the beginning. The queſtion then will be concerning their expediency, whether they are more proper, and better calculated to anſwer the purpoſe of public, ſocial worſhip, than extempore prayers. As I do not wiſh to lengthen this addreſs beyond what is neceſſary, I ſhall not indulge myſelf in writing a panegyric on forms of prayer, but ſhall content myſelf with mentioning ſome diſadvantages which I think inſeparable from extempore prayer in public worſhip, againſt which a good form would be an effectual guard. But before I proceed, I beg leave to make two or three ſhort obſervations.

1. That whatever may be the diſadvantages of extempore prayers—and however I may prefer a good, that is, a ſound form before them, I preſume not to cenſure them as ſinful in themſelves. Pious people may, for any thing that I know, conduct their public worſhip by them with a ſafe conſcience; and, in the unity of Chriſt's church, I ſhould not heſitate to hold communion with ſuch a congregation. But I muſt not conceal my ſentiments, that if the fondneſs for extempore prayers lead people off from the unity of the church into ſchiſms and diviſions, they become highly criminal, and cannot, under thoſe circumſtances, be attended on without ſin. Should this be cenſured as a narrow principle, I apprehend it to be no narrower than the truth—not a whit more ſo than the way that leadeth unto life.

2. By

2. By extempore prayers, I mean not only thoſe that are uttered *ex improviſo*, juſt as the mind conceives them on the emergency; but thoſe alſo which, according to the preſent general practice, have been ſtudied and committed to memory.

3. That extempore prayer, under either of the above deſcriptions muſt, of neceſſity, be as much a form to the congregation, as though it was read out of a book. They muſt pray in the words of their miniſter, whether he conceive the words on the inſtant, or has ſtudied them, and treaſured them up in his memory. So that all the great advantages which the warm partizans for extempore prayer have aſcribed to it, come juſt to—nothing: And a monſtrous clamour has been raiſed againſt forms of prayer, without which, when matters are fairly ſtated and conſidered, no ſocial worſhip at all can be carried on. For whether the congregation who are to worſhip together, conſiſt of three or a thouſand, he who utters the prayer is the mouth of the whole, and his prayer their form: They can neither add to it, nor diminiſh from it, nor vary its expreſſion, but are as ſtraitly confined by it, as any Epiſcopalian can be by his liturgy.

The only point then to be ſettled is, Whether a form of prayer, compoſed on the inſtant for the congregation, (for a form they muſt have, and cannot pray together without one) or previouſly digeſted and committed to memory; or whether a form deliberately compoſed by a number of men, of character for piety and learning, printed, and put into the hands of the congregation, be the more eligible mode of conducting the public worſhip of chriſtian aſſemblies?

Againſt the former method, there are ſome objections which to me appear conſiderable: They may be trite ones; but as I aim at truth and not at novelty, their being old can be no diſadvantage to them, unleſs it ſhall appear that they have at any time been fairly and ſolidly anſwered.

1. My firſt objection to extempore prayer is, that the particular opinions of the miniſter will be apt to intrude themſelves into his prayer, and tincture it with his peculiar ſentiments.

The

The congregation muſt put up ſuch petitions to Almighty God as their miniſter ſhall dictate. Should any of thoſe petitions not be perfectly agreeable to the goſpel, there is no remedy; they muſt pray them, or not pray at all. For ſhould any one attempt to winnow the prayer, that he may get rid of the chaff, and preſent only the pure wheat to God—while he is doing ſo, the miniſter goes on, and he muſt make long ſtrides indeed to overtake him. Should the miniſter have imbibed the *extravagances* of Calviniſm, or Arminianiſm, or Arianiſm, or Socinianiſm, or any other hereſy, his principles will give a colour to his prayer; and ſuch as his prayer is, ſuch muſt be the principles of the people for that turn, or they worſhip not God together.

Such is the ſituation of ſome congregations, that changes of miniſters, from the intercourſe of ſtrangers, or otherwiſe, are frequent in them. It appears not impoſſible to me, that a congregation may, at one time, worſhip on the rigid principles of Calvin; the next ſunday, perhaps, Arminius may dictate their prayers: Arius and Socinus may alſo have their turn; and how many more I ſhall not pretend to ſay. Nor is this all—Should the miniſter's principles be corrupt, he has the greater chance of corrupting thoſe of his people, and of drawing them away from the pure doctrine of the goſpel. I believe it will be found true, on obſervation, that the principles of the people depend more on the prayers they hear, than on the ſermons. And though ſermons may be made the inſtrument of ſpreading corrupt principles—yet, where the miniſter makes his own prayers as well as ſermons, he has the greater opportunity of doing miſchief, becauſe he can work with two engines, inſtead of one. Beſides—there is a great difference between preaching erroneous principles (bad as that may be) and making the people obtrude thoſe principles on Almighty God, in a ſolemn prayer.

Now, though it may not be practicable to prevent every miniſter from diſſeminating errors in his ſermons and converſation, yet a good liturgy will effectually prevent the ſacred duty of public prayer from being proſtituted to that purpoſe: Nor is that all—a good liturgy would become a kind of ſtandard to the people, and

would

would enable them to judge with more precision concerning the doctrines delivered in sermons. Art and sophistry may pervert expressions of holy scripture and apply them to purposes foreign from the truth. Its language is, in many respects, hard to be understood, even by those who have learning enough to enter into a critical study of it. That this observation is true, will appear from the great number of sects and parties into which the christian world, to its great shame and reproach, is so miserably divided—all pleading the authority of scripture, yet all disputing about its genuine interpretation. But a good liturgy, drawn up on true christian principles, and expressed in plain language, is not so easily perverted. People become habituated to it, and enter into its spirit, and comprehend its meaning, so that they will readily perceive any deviation the minister may make in his sermon from the principles and doctrines on which it is founded.

And here, though some may think it foreign to my subject, I take the liberty to say a few words on the use of Creeds, or short summaries of christian faith, to be repeated by the congregation every time they assemble for public worship. By means of these, the people are much better guarded against errors in doctrine, than they could be without them. The grand points of christian faith being expressed in few and plain words, the memory can easily retain them, and the mind readily advert to them. Let me also just observe, that the design of creeds is not to establish doctrines, but to represent them, or declare what they are. The doctrines are to be drawn from holy scripture, and to be established by it.—The creed is designed to bring those doctrines together, which the holy scripture teacheth; at least the fundamental ones—that they may be seen at one view. They also serve as a bond of faith and uniformity of doctrine among the clergy, and between the different congregations and members of the same church; and also between the different branches of the church universal.

Against the insinuations of error it is difficult, I know, to place an effectual guard. The crafty hypocrite, the interested partizan, and the zealous enthusiast, will find opportunity to do mischief by spreading false principles, and

and debauching the weak and unsteady from the pure simplicity of the gospel. The question then is not, whether the creeds of the church and a good liturgy will absolutely secure her members from all error, but, whether they do not afford greater security than can be found where they are wanting. If they do, it is one good reason why they should be adopted in all christian assemblies.

2. Another objection which I have to extempore prayer in public worship, is, that not only the principles, but the temper also of the minister may give a tincture to his prayers. Should he be proud, or passionate, or morose, or whimsical, or melancholic; or whatever may be his prevailing disposition, it is a great chance, that it will, at some times, form the complexion of his prayer. If his temper be good, well—if not, the congregation are in danger of having their devotions coloured by his irregular disposition of heart, and may be obliged to offer up petitions to God, which savour more of revenge than of christian charity. There have been instances where a clergyman, upon some misunderstanding with a parishioner, has so far departed from his character, as to point him out in his sermons. Suppose such a man to have the forming of his prayers, would there be no danger of his particularizing such a person in his prayer, as well as sermon, and literally *pray against him*, as well as *preach at him*.

Or suppose the minister to be of a melancholic cast, and to be occasionally troubled with fits of despondency—a malady to which gentlemen of a studious turn and sedentary life are particularly liable. Has he any security that the gloom of his disease shall not attend him to the house of worship? and when there, that it shall not tincture his prayers, and give them a hue of darkness inapplicable to the circumstances of the generality of his congregation?

One supposition more—should the minister be of that class usually distinguished by the name of *preachers of terror*—Is there no danger lest his terrific temper should affect his prayer, and excite him to direct the Almighty how to aim his judgments and level the darts of his displeasure? It is not the setting before sinners the indignation

nation of God, and persuading them to repentance from the certainty and weight of the judgments of his justice, to which I object; but to a minister's usurping the prerogative of God, and either discharging the bolts of divine vengeance himself, in his sermons; or, in his prayers, directing the Almighty how to employ them to the best advantage.

All these inconveniencies, and more which I could mention, did I not apprehend it to be needless, would be prevented by a good liturgy. In its use, the worst that could happen, and that is bad enough, is, that the congregation may not have their devotion heightened by the mode of the minister's reading it.

He may be careless and unaffected by the solemn service in which he is engaged;—he may hurry, or he may drawl; but he can introduce no improper petitions. The people have their proper prayers before them, and are acquainted with them; and it is their own fault, if they do not keep their hearts right towards God, though their minister should be deficient in his devotion.

3. Another objection I have against extempore prayers in public worship, is, that they are generally too particular. Confessions, prayers, thanksgivings, praises are often so exact and precise, that many in the congregation are excluded from some part or other of them.

Public worship being of a social nature ought to be so conducted as to be common to the whole congregation. If it be so particular that the whole cannot join in it, it ceases to be social worship, and becomes partial. To say that some parts of the prayers may suit one man's condition, and other parts the condition of another, and that in this way they may all be suited, is not sufficient to take off the force of the objection. This would make the different parts of the prayer the distinct worship of individuals, not the joint worship of the whole. If confessions of sin, petitions, thanksgivings to God, be not so general that the whole congregation can join in them, as a congregation they cannot worship by them. To this inconvenience extempore prayer in public worship must for ever be liable. The minister will pray his own sentiments and sensations, and he cannot help it. His own situation of mind and state of heart must, therefore,

fore, in a great degree, become the ſtandard of worſhip to the whole congregation.

This inconveniency can be prevented only by a good form of prayer, in which the common ſtate of chriſtians is duly regarded; and the prayers and praiſes, confeſſions and thankſgivings ſo expreſſed, as to have a direct tendency to make the whole congregation feel themſelves intereſted, and be thereby excited to join in them with a ready heart and will.

4. Another objection againſt extempore prayer in public worſhip, is, that it is not calculated to excite and enliven, but tends to repreſs and deaden, devotion. This effect ariſes from two cauſes, both inherent in the very idea of extempore prayers, as they are conducted in the congregations of the Preſbyterians and Independents, and, I ſuppoſe, of the Anabaptiſts alſo. 1. From the length of the prayers, and ſameneſs of the geſture and tone of voice. 2. From the congregation's being excluded from bearing any vocal part in the public worſhip.

It has been remarked of the writings of ſome of the beſt Engliſh poets, particularly of Mr. Pope, that notwithſtanding the ſmoothneſs and harmony of his lines, the beauty of the imagery, and the good ſenſe which adorn them, the pleaſure which a reader of taſte firſt perceives, ſoon abates; languor ſucceeds, and the attention cannot be commanded, but the mind calls for the relaxation of variety. I have obſerved ſomething of this effect in reading ſome of the more highly-poliſhed proſe-writers; eſpecially in the ſermon way—what at firſt was delightful, became at length cold, lifeleſs, and inſipid. The inference I would make from this obſervation is, that the human mind cannot be long employed on one ſubject, without fatigue, unleſs variety be called in to relieve, and give new vigour to the palled attention. What, then, muſt be the ſituation of a congregation at a long extempore prayer where the ſame tone of voice, the ſame attitude, the ſame expreſſion of countenance, are exhibited before them, for, poſſibly, near an hour? where petitions, praiſes, invocations, narrations, confeſſions, thankſgivings, are all jumbled together—a little of one and a little of another, *ſtratum ſuper ſtratum?* Granting that there is devotion in this, which I apprehend may reaſonably be doubted, can it be kept up? can the attention be commanded? impoſſible—

In conjunction with this, the ſecond cauſe of want of devotion in extempore prayers, is to be taken into account, viz. That the congregation are excluded from bearing any vocal part in the public worſhip—they have nothing to do; and, in truth, do nothing—not even ſay, *Amen*, at the concluſion of the prayer. Can it now be a wonder, that there ſhould be all that appearance of languor, inattention, and fatigue, which I have ever remarked in thoſe meetings which I have attended—ſtanding up, ſometimes with the face, ſometimes with the back to the miniſter, and ſometimes ſide-ways—lolling over the pews, or ſitting down a while, and then up again—every poſture indicating uneaſineſs, and a wiſh that the prayer was done?—But enough—probably ſome may think too much has been already ſaid on this ſubject. I cannot however cloſe it, without propoſing two or three queries, which they who are intereſted may conſider at their leiſure.

1. Whether in meetings where extempore prayer is uſed, the geſture and behaviour of the congregation, during the prayers, be different from that during the ſermon?

2. Whether, to judge from appearance, for God only can judge the heart, they do not meet together as literally to *hear* the *prayer*, as to hear the *ſermon.*

3. Whether, if hearing a prayer be praying, hearing a ſermon be not preaching?

4. Whether a congregation who keep their lips cloſe ſhut during the whole ſolemnity, can, with any propriety of ſpeech be ſaid to worſhip God, except it be in dumb ſhow?

5. Whether it be not a monſtrous perverſion of public, ſocial worſhip, for one man to monopolize it all to himſelf, and not ſuffer his congregation to offer up one petition, or utter one reſponſe of adoration and praiſe to the God of their ſalvation?

Let it not be irkſome, if I again call the attention of the candid reader to the benefit of a good form of prayer for public worſhip. By it all the above diſagreeable appearances might be remedied, as far as human frailty will permit.

In it the different parts of divine worſhip may be ſo intermixed, that it could not be tedious to any perſon who had goodneſs enough to conſider what he was doing. Short energetic prayers, the interpoſition of pſalms and devout hymns, the reading of leſſons, the reſponſes which would be frequently expected from the congregation, would keep attention alive, and carry devotion to its higheſt pitch. No one but he who has tried it can be ſenſible, how much the worſhipping and praiſing of God, by way of reſponſe, enlivens the devotion of both miniſter and people. There is alſo great advantage in ſhort prayers or collects, where every part tends to one point, eſpecially where the people have the prayers before them, and are at no loſs what ſentence is to follow the preceding one. As the prayer is, ſo is their devotion, *concentered*; and its energy may be kept up without flagging, till its concluſion be ſealed with a hearty, *Amen*. It is ſuppoſed that every perſon in the congregation is furniſhed with a book, and that he will attend to it, and conduct himſelf by the directions there laid before him. The bodily geſtures will, therefore, be uniform, and ſuch as encourage and expreſs humility, reverence, and adoration, as the different parts of the ſervice require. This is doing the moſt that can be done to enſure a proper behaviour, and an acceptable ſervice; and if it fail, it is not the fault of the church, which has, by providing a good liturgy, endeavoured to enliven devotion and guard againſt impropriety of behaviour.

Should it be replied, that there is as much devotion among thoſe who worſhip in the way of extempore prayer, as among thoſe who uſe a liturgy—I beg to be underſtood as ſpeaking of *appearance* only. Of the devotion of the heart I cannot judge. But I do flatter myſelf that, upon obſervation, there will be found greater indications of devotion in the congregations of Church-people, than in thoſe of the Preſbyterians. Should this point be determined againſt me, I take the liberty to remark, that it may be accounted for, by the contagious nature of evil example. The irreverence which extempore prayers have introduced into chriſtian aſſemblies may have corrupted the church people, and tainted

tainted them with the idea of going to church literally to *bear* prayers; and to this the too little attention of some of them to the service of the church may be owing. If they behave at church, as they see people behave where extempore prayer is used, they may think themselves irreproachable. To this we may impute the inconsiderate gazing of some, instead of attending to the service; the sitting posture of others, while prayer and supplication are made to God, instead of devoutly kneeling; or instead of standing up when his praises are recited. What makes me insist the more on this point is, the remark I have several times heard made by people who did not belong to the church—that they go sometimes to church, and would go oftener, but they did not like the frequent sitting down and rising up, now kneeling, and then standing. Such remarks often repeated may have an effect on weak minds, and lead them away from that pure devotion with which the service of the church is calculated to inspire them.

5. Another objection to extempore prayer is, that it operates to the exclusion of reading the holy scriptures in the congregations. Whether this defect be the fault of the ministers or people, or of both, I know not—whether the minister is so fond of shewing his gift in prayer, that he cannot spare the time to read lessons; or whether he thinks that reading lessons would degrade his dignity, and put him on a level with a school-boy; or whether the people think they can read the Bible at home, as well as their minister can at meeting, they must answer who can: But, it always appeared odd to me, that people who affected so great a veneration for the Bible, should have so little to do with it in their public assemblies. When I was young, I was a frequent, though only an occasional attendant of their meetings; and I do declare, I never heard more of the Bible in them, than the preacher's text, and passages occasionally introduced in the prayer and sermon. Another circumstance that appeared odd to me, was to hear Presbyterians, who read no part of the Bible in public, find fault with the church of England for not reading the whole Bible through in course, from the first of Genesis, to the last of Revelation. The beam in their

own

own eye surely could trouble them but little, when they had eye-sight enough left to see so small a mote in the eye of another.

I am ready to acknowledge, that, upon inquiry, I have been informed that some of their ministers and congregations are so sensible of the impropriety of so palpable a deficiency, that they have endeavoured to remedy it: And, that in some of the congregations a chapter is read forenoon and afternoon; and that there is a prospect that the practice will gradually prevail and become general. I bless God for it; and hope that the selecting of chapters will not be left to the minister, but that proper lessons will be appointed, and he obliged to attend to them.

6. There is only one objection more to extempore prayer in public worship, which I shall, at this time, mention, and that is, that it symbolizes too much with the Papists, and that in a very faulty particular.

It has always been made on objection to the church of Rome that her public service and offices are in latin—a language which the people do not understand; and I do not see how she can get over the objection, since it seems necessary, if the congregation are to offer up to God a reasonable service, they should by all means understand the language in which it is performed. I suppose that the objection does not lie against *latin* considered merely as a language, but as a language not generally understood; and, that if the congregation did understand latin, there would be no impropriety in having public prayers in that language.

It hurts me to make remarks which may appear invidious. But I will submit it to any competent judge (not excepting a Presbyterian of candour) who has attended on any considerable variety of ministers, who use the extempore mode of public prayer, Whether they do not frequently introduce sentences, and phrases in their prayers, which there is the highest probability a great part of the congregation do not understand, and which they cannot understand without explanation, or reflection? And while one of these unintelligible phrases employs their power of investigation, the minister is gone on, God only knows how far; and so, a large part of

the

the prayer, because they could not attend to two things at once, becomes as unintelligible, as the hard words he had uttered some time before. Now this is downright *latin*, as much so as if it had been picked from the Mass-Book.

It is so far from being improbable that this should ever happen, that in a country where there are a considerable number of ministers who use the extempore method, it would be very strange indeed if it never did happen. Only figure to yourself a young man, just set loose from college, smitten with the vanity of praying well, and thinking to recommend himself by florid expressions, quaint phrases, scholastic distinctions, and grammatical precision—exhibiting his utmost efforts before a country congregation—I will not except even a city one—and if he does not more or less pray in *latin*—as unintelligible as a popish *Ave*—I am no judge of young extempore prayer-makers.

It cannot seem foreign to my subject, if I here mention another source of obscurity in extempore prayers; and that is the absurd custom some of your ministers have fallen into, of addressing declamatory speeches, rhetorical flourishes, and historical narrations to Almighty God, instead of pouring out the devout supplications of penitent hearts before him.

I do not mention these as the faults of every minister among you, nor of every young minister, but as matters that sometimes do happen, and which therefore call for redress; and which nothing but a good form of prayer can effectually remedy.

It may be observed in reply, that all I have said about the obscurity of extempore prayers, depends on circumstances which may, or may not happen; and I confess it: yet they are circumstances which it is next to impossible should not happen, and therefore it is necessary to guard against them.

But the difficulty of understanding extempore prayers does not arise merely from the imprudence of the minister; their very nature renders them less intelligible than forms. The congregation must watch for the words, for they know not what is to come. They must then attend to their coherence, ascertain their meaning, and

and determine on their propriety, before they can, as reasonable, devout christian worshippers, offer them up to Almighty God. If any thing drop from the minister which a person does not approve, it makes a gap in the prayer; if any thing which he does not understand, it is to him an unknown language. This I suppose to be the reason why there is no *Amen* said at the conclusion of the prayer—some things are disapproved, some are not understood; and it is thought best to let the prayer go, and shift for itself—it has their minister's sanction, and they hope that will do.

Now all this is remedied by a good form. The people can examine it at their leisure, and make themselves acquainted with its matter and spirit; so that when they come to church to pay their joint homage and adoration to their Almighty Creator—the God of their salvation—Father, Son, and Holy Ghost—with humble, contrite hearts, to confess their sins, and implore his mercy; to celebrate his divine majesty, and make their supplications before him; they have nothing to do but to attend to the matter and spirit of their prayers, and to keep the heart engaged in the solemn and sublime service in which their body is employed. Neither the imprudence of a young man, nor the bad principles of one that is involved in error, nor the infirmities of the aged or diseased, can corrupt the purity of their prayers, or sully the sacred offices of their religion.

And should any difficulty arise with the weak and more illiterate, they can always avail themselves of the advice and assistance of their minister, or of their more understanding brethren; and, by their help, obtain a competent knowledge of the whole system of the public liturgy, and of the intention of its component parts, and of the expressions by which its meaning is conveyed.

In this way christian congregations may be enabled to worship God, in their joint or social capacity, with understanding and devotion—in body and in spirit, in unity of heart and of mind, and in uniformity of external gesture and behaviour; and how it can otherwise be done to the same advantage, I see not.

Thus I have delivered my sentiments on two of the principal points of distinction between the Episcopal church

church on the one side, and the Presbyterians and Independents on the other, viz. The government of the Christian Church, and its mode of worship. On both subjects I have spoken with freedom; on the latter, perhaps, with more freedom than will be agreeable to gentlemen who are attached to the extempore mode of public worship. My apology is, that it is now a long time since the clamour against forms of prayer was set a-going; that it has, with only occasional intermissions, been continued ever since; that the whole force of sophistry, as well as all the artillery of reviling language, has been diligently employed against the church which enjoined them: That, on the other side, the highest eulogiums on extempore prayers in public worship, which their admirers could invent, have been published and re-published, echoed and re-echoed, vended, repeated, and retailed, till the subject seems pretty well worn down. In defence of forms of prayer, though many excellent treatises and tracts have been published, abounding with solid sense, strong arguments, and christian piety; yet the minds of the beguiled people for whose information they were written, were so fettered with prejudice, poisoned with misrepresentation, and hood-winked by the undue influence and overbearing authority of their ministers, every one of whom had the power of a little Pope in his parish, that they either would not read, or would not consider—Fed with Calvinism and extempore prayers till they were gorged, they could not hunger or thirst for any thing better.

It is a happiness that prejudice, in being handed down from generation to generation, will at last be dissipated by the gradual influence of the rays of truth, which, little by little, will find their way into the mind. It is also a happiness that the undue stretch of power, and over-exertion of influence, commonly work their own destruction. Human nature, though it bear much, will eventually feel and assert its own right to freedom, both of mind and body.

That, at the present period, the prejudices of the Presbyterians and Independents in America against the government and liturgy of the Episcopal Church are much abated; and the despotic authority, and reputation

tion of infallibility, in which their ministers have long triumphed, are a good deal declined, must be evident to every careful observer. We hope the time is come when free enquiry in religion, as well as in politics, shall have its *free* course. To this free enquiry into the government of the Christian Church, and the best mode of conducting its public worship, it is the design of this address (as has been already announced) to invite, more particularly, the ministers and congregations of the Presbyterian and Independent persuasions in this country. The author does not mean this invitation as a challenge to a public dispute. Had *that* been his intention, he would not have with-held his name. But he does earnestly desire that the gentlemen to whom this address is made, would seriously and candidly review the grounds of the difference between them and the Episcopal Church: And he persuades himself, if they do, they will find abundant reason to correct that judgment on the subject, which, he apprehends, education and partial examination have induced them to make; and will then be ready, on liberal and catholic principles, to form a coalition with the Episcopal Church—an event devoutly to be wished by all good men.

He, therefore, thought it right to express himself without reserve, when treating on the government of the Church, and the mode of divine service, or public worship in it: Not with a design to irritate, but to convince those gentlemen, that the church has, at least the appearance of, strong arguments for her mode of government; and that her mode of worship, by a form of common-prayer, is not that mean, low, driveling contrivance which they have been too apt to consider it: But that it is founded, most probably, on apostolical authority—most certainly in true and accurate knowledge of human nature. And also, that their own plan of church government is essentially deficient in the origin of its authority, and consequently in all spiritual powers. —That their scheme of conducting public worship, by extempore prayers, not only does not deserve the high encomiums that have been lavished on it, but is actually absurd in itself, betrays great ignorance of human nature,

ture, and is, on all fides, open to the impreffions of fair argument, and to the keen fhafts of ridicule and fatire.

There are feveral reafons which ought to induce confiderate people of all denominations to attempt the accomplifhing of an uniformity of religion, throughout the United States of America, both as good citizens and as good chriftians. The greater the unity of the Americans in religion, the greater, probably, will be their unity in political fentiments and conduct. However detrimental parties in the ftate may be in themfelves, they are always moft fo, when inflamed by religious animofity; and while oppofite, or difcordant fchemes of religion prevail in a country, however friendly their general intercourfe may be, there is always fome danger of religious diffenfions breaking out, on particular occafions. At beft, religious diftinctions will make fome difference of interefts, and prevent the people from cementing fo cordially as they otherwife would do. If unity in religion fhould not intirely prevent all parties in the ftate, yet it would probably be fome reftraint upon their violence: At leaft it would prevent religious animofity from adding fuel to the flame. I know it is the opinion of fome people, that differences in religion are a fecurity to public and political liberty; becaufe the different denominations will watch each other, and counteract the encroachments that any particular denomination may be difpofed to make.

There are fome reafons that appear to militate againft this theory. It feems to make the fecurity of political freedom depend on the difunion of the people in religion, and reprefents it not as any thing real, and good in itfelf, but as merely depending on the ftruggles for power, and fo only good *per accidens*, as it prevents any one party of a divided people from encroaching on the reft. But it is forgotten that if the people were not divided, there would be no difcordant interefts, and confequently no temptations to encroachments.

That different religious denominations watch each other with a jealous eye, is allowed; and while they have feparate interefts, it is owned this is a fecurity to political liberty. But take away the diftinction, and though their jarring interefts and jealoufies would hap-

pily,

pily ceafe, political liberty would remain the fame. Befides, there is great danger left the public good fhould fuffer from this jealous oppofition of different religious denominations. A meafure calculated to do fervice to the public may be defeated, becaufe it is patronifed by a particular denomination; or, becaufe their opponents think it may eventually be of benefit to them. In the violence of party, public good is oftener the cry, than the object. A good citizen would wifh to get rid of all party in the ftate, that the public good might folely be regarded; and will, therefore, join his influence to promote uniformity in religion, that at leaft one fource of party may be cut off.

That it is the duty of chriftians to promote unity and uniformity among the profeffors of their holy religion, will appear from even a curfory reading of the New Teftament. It is not my defign to enter on a long difquifition of this fubject, nor fhall I produce many authorities to prove a point, the truth of which, I fuppofe, no well informed chriftian will controvert. I fhall, however, call the candid reader's attention to the divine prayer our bleffed Saviour made for his difciples, and for all thofe who fhould believe on him through their word—*That they all may be one, as thou Father, art in me, and I in thee; that they alfo may be one in us* (John xvii. 20, 21.) And I would afk, Whether this prayer of Chrift be fulfilled in modern chriftians? Whether, in particular, the differences which fubfift between the Church-people and the Prefbyterians be confiftent with fuch a union? Whether it ought not to be the wifh and endeavour of every good man to promote and accomplifh it? And whether it can be done without fome fuch coalition as is now propofed—fome nearer approach to each other—fome greater uniformity in their church government and mode of worfhip, than at prefent fubfifts? The holy apoftle St. Paul, alfo, writing to the Corinthians (1 Cor. i. 10.) ufeth thefe ftrong and perfuafive words, *Now I befeech you, brethren, by* (or in) *the name of our Lord Jefus Chrift, that ye all fpeak the fame thing, and that there be no divifions among you; but that ye be perfectly joined in the fame mind, and in the fame judgment.* I afk again, Is this exhortation, and earneft intreaty of

that

that bleffed apoftle regarded by modern chriftians? Has it any more influence on their conduct than if it was written only in an old almanack? Do the different parties and denominations of chriftians *all fpeak the fame thing?* Are there *no divifions among them?* Are, for inftance, the Church-people and Prefbyterians *perfectly joined in the fame mind, and in the fame judgment?* Every tongue muft anfwer, *no*. There is, therefore, a great fault fome where, and why fhould it not be corrected? Every one muft fay it ought to be done. Why then will not every one contribute his aid to accomplifh it?

It appears from thefe authorities, that different denominations of chriftians, living together in peace, and what is called charity, are not perfectly blamelefs; for, though this be beyond all comparifon better than worrying and perfecuting each other; yet, it does not come up to that union and uniformity among chriftians, which our Saviour and his holy apoftles have pointed out to us. It is undoubtedly much eafier to lament, than to remedy thofe divifions which prevail among chriftians. It is, however, a fhame to them all, that there is fo little of that charity, of which they all boaft; that they all appear to think more of ftrengthening their own party, than of ftrengthening the church of Chrift, by promoting unity—*famenefs of mind and of judgment* among the difcordant parties, who all profefs to worfhip the fame God, through the merit and interceffion of the fame Mediator.

The author does not pretend to more charity than his neighbours, but he apprehends that his notion of that divine grace may be fomewhat different from that which is commonly entertained of it. He, for inftance, does not fuppofe that there is any charity in the opinion that all religions are equal, and one juft as fure a road to heaven as another, provided a man be fincere in his profeffion. He prefumes he has as great efteem for fincerity in religion as any man; but he cannot fee how fincerity can make that which is wrong, to be right, or what is falfe, to be true. Charity will incline us to impute the errors of chriftian profeffors to want of judgment, or of information—to any thing rather than to perverfenefs of heart: But charity can never make us

D think,

think, and ought never to tempt us to say, *that* is *right*, which, on deliberate judgment, we are convinced is *wrong*, whatever our opinion of sincerity may be. This would confound truth and falshood, and take away that distinction which God has placed betweem them. The proper business of charity here, is to point out, not to approve, their errors: to endeavour to remove their prejudices, inform their understandings, and thereby enable their sincerity to make a better judgment. They who are continually repeating that we ought to have charity for those who differ from us, that sincerity is all in all, that Church-people, Presbyterians, Independents, &c. &c. are all in the good road to heaven, provided they be sincere and honest, are ignorant people, and understand not what they say, nor whereof they affirm—They gabble by rote, and repeat what they think to be pretty sentences, because they have heard them, and thought they sounded well. St. Paul has given many characteristic marks of charity, but he does not say it is *blind*, and cannot see truth from error; nor that it is so very good natured and complaisant, as to confound them together, to please the squeamish affectation of tenderness and humility.

Leaving these people to the enjoyment, if they choose it, of their own crude notions of christian charity, I shall take the liberty to go on in my own way; only beseeching them to take heed how they make the next step, which is to think that no religion is as good as any. For having confounded right and wrong, error and falshood, what privilege have they to exclude from their charity the unhappy man who professes no religion. He too may be sincere, and live as uprightly as they who pride themselves in this figment of unbounded charity: he too may be as charitable as they are, and it is pity any love should be lost between them.

Understanding christian charity to mean the heavenly disposition of doing *good* to all men, at all times, and on all occasions, according to our best ability—I suppose I have acted a real charitable part towards these very charitable people, in pointing out their misconceptions of that divine virtue: And I shall now, under the influence of the same benevolent principle, go on to finish this

this address to our fellow-professors of Christ's religion, the Presbyterians and Independents of the states of America—hoping that their candour and liberality will dispose them to take in good part what has been already said, as well as what is yet to come; and that their sincerity will incline them as strongly to abandon errors, now they are pointed out to them, as it has hitherto done to retain them.

In this coalition which I have proposed, it may be a matter of delicate hesitation, who shall make the first advance. Every man has a right to give his opinion in this matter, and consequently that right, in common with others, belongs to me also. Now there are some reasons which induce me to propose that the first overtures be made by the Presbyterians and Independents; and I hope, on mature deliberation, they will be thought to be just and strong ones.

1. They are the more numerous.

Now if there be any humiliation in taking the first step, which I do not conceive there is, it will be the less felt where there are many to bear it. There will also be the more merit in it; because it is the more extraordinary, and therefore meritorious, for a large body to concur in doing what they think is making a concession, than for a less number to do the same. But where is the humiliation of doing what is right? If a man be in an error, to continue in it is more dishonourable, and ought to be more humiliating to him, than breaking loose from it, and returning to a better mind. But I conceive the matter may, with tolerable prudence, be so managed, as to prevent all appearance of abasement. There are now three Bishops in the states. It is not improbable, that some of your clergy may have an acquaintance with one or other of them. There can be no impropriety in bringing a subject of such consequence into conversation. It would require no great penetration to form an estimate of his opinion and temper. If it did not succeed with one, I would try another, and the third; and if it did not produce happy consequences, my good opinion of those gentlemen would be greatly lessened. The same conduct might be tried with some of the more elderly and respected Episcopal clergy.

That

That the issue would be favourable I can have no doubt. And indeed I would press it strongly on *them* to make the first advance, did I think they have the same chance of succeeding with you, that you have with them. Though I am not authorised to give an opinion for them, I am confident they would receive the proposal with joy, and do every thing in their power to ensure its success.

But why do I talk of first advances? this very address lays the matter open, and will, I hope, make it the subject of conversation, and then it will soon be known, whether it be like to succeed. We shall know too, should there be any difficulties, where they lie; and then, reasonable expedients may be found to remove them.

2. The Presbyterians and Independents departed from the church, making a schism in it. It is therefore reasonable they should make the first advances toward a reunion. I know not how this reason can be evaded but on two grounds; one is justifying the schism: the other is, that the local situation of both parties in this country takes away the imputation of schism. With regard to the first—if the schism made by the first Presbyterians and Independents be justifiable, the matter I have in hand is at an end; for the schism that was justly made may be justly continued.

It is beyond my design to enter into a particular discussion of this subject. I shall therefore only remark, that no schism can be justified but on the score of sinful terms of communion. If the Church of England required sinful terms of communion, to depart from her was right—If her terms of communion were not sinful, to depart from her was needless, and consequently not to be justified. I have formerly heard a good deal said upon this subject of sinful terms of communion, and I know a great deal has been written upon it; and so there has upon the Philosopher's stone. When these sinful terms are pointed out with precision, it will be time enough to attend to them.

The other ground, That the relative situation of the Church and Presbyterians in this country is such, as will take off all imputation of schism from the latter, is, I take it, untenable. It makes the unity of Christ's church

church to depend on local situations and human establishments, with which it has nothing to do. Christ's church is, and can be but one: It may subsist in different countries, under very different circumstances. In one country it may enjoy human establishments—in another it may suffer grievous persecution. The forms of its worship, its rights and ceremonies may vary—But if the different branches of this church hold the true priesthood, government and faith, they are at unity, and can reciprocally communicate with each other, without any reference to their outward situation. But if a body of men depart from the government, priesthood, or faith of the church, and set up in opposition to it, they break the unity of Christ's church, whether the church in the country where they make, or continue the separation, have, or have not, the benefit of a legal establishment.

As such a separation has been made, and is continued by the Presbyterians and others, it is their duty to take the first step towards reconciliation, that so the breach of unity in Christ's church which they have made, may be healed, as speedily and soundly as possible.

3. It is reasonable that the Presbyterians and Independents should make the first overtures to a junction, because the church Episcopal does not stand on such ground as to be able to come forward in the business, without some previous conditions. She supposes that the Presbyterians and Independents have departed from the true government of Christ's church, and are essentially deficient in the matter of ordination. Unless the Presbyterians can be prevailed on to give up this point, all my labour is lost, and my hopes are at an end. It is disagreeable to me to say disagreeable things: but as I heartily wish for the union I have been proposing, and wish also that it may be more than nominal, even an union of heart and spirit, it is necessary this point should come fairly into view: Candour I trust will guide my pen, but plainness of speech must be its companion.

Ordinations among the Presbyterians and Independents, have originated either from presbyters of the church of England, or from the people of their congregations, or from both. If the people have the power of ordination, it must be in consequence of some com-

mission

mission from Christ, because from him all such power must come. Where to find such a commission I know not; and I think I have been a pretty careful reader of the Bible. If it be said that this power of ordination belongs to the congregation collectively, as a body of christians, I ask, whether to the women as well as the men? Whether this power is so peculiar to the congregation collectively, that it ceases if one be absent? or, whether it resides in the majority? Whether this power be so volatile that it evaporates and is lost, as soon as the congregation breaks up? If so, how is it again recovered? Or, does every one carry home a particle of it, and occasionally bring it back to the common stock?

I have sifted and considered this matter every way, and can make nothing of it. *Nil dat qui non habet*—no man can communicate a power to another which he does not possess himself. So that after a man is ordained by the whole congregation, or by any part of it, he is no more a minister of Christ than he was before.

Let us next attend to the ordinations performed by presbyters who were episcopally and regularly ordained. These, I say, have no power to ordain, because they never received any such power; and a man cannot obtain it by nature, nor by accident—he is neither born with it, nor does he pick it up. The English office of ordination of priests is in every folio prayer-book. Let any one examine it, and he will find no power of ordination conveyed in it. How then can he give what he never received? not a whit more than the people: for no man whether he be clergyman or layman, episcopalian or presbyterian, can give what he does not possess. Ordination is the conveying of a commission of which Christ is the fountain: its intention is to make a man a minister of Christ to his church, in that station for which he is intended, and for which the ordination is performed. In the church of England, from which these presbyters of whom we are speaking, came, when the bishop ordains a presbyter, he has no intention of communicating episcopal powers, but directly guards against such a supposition, by designating the office conveyed, and particularizing the duties of it. Nor has the person ordained any pretence for supposing he is to obtain more

than

than the powers of a presbyter. Whence then does he get the power of ordination?

I know what has been said in this case, and what I suppose may be said again, viz. That presbyter and bishop in the New Testament mean the same office; and, therefore, he who is ordained a presbyter, is, of course, ordained a bishop; and consequently must have the power of ordination. And also, that the power which Christ left in his church, to ordain and send ministers, is one only, and cannot be divided, but must be communicated wholly or not at all; and consequently, that every person who is ordained must receive the whole power which Christ gave, and of course the power to ordain others—therefore the presbyters who separated from the church of England must have brought off with them all the power which Christ gave, and consequently the power of ordination, whatever may have been their own expectations, or the bishop's intention, when hands were laid on them.—Let us see how these positions will bear examination.

I have no inclination to dispute about words, or names of office. Let it then be granted that bishop and presbyter in the New Testament were then used as names for the same office—yet it will not follow that the power of ordination belonged to their office. I deny that one instance can be produced from the New Testament, of an ordination performed by those bishops or presbyters. It is the power, not the name of an office, that ought to be the subject of our enquiry. If we look into St. Paul's epistles to Timothy, we shall find three orders in the church of Ephesus—Timothy the superior, bishops or presbyters subject to his superintendence, and the order of deacons. There were bishops or presbyters in it before Timothy was fixed there, as we learn from Acts xx. If those bishops or presbyters had the power of government and ordination in their hands, Why was Timothy set over that church? Was it merely to do that which, according to the Presbyterian plan, those bishops or presbyters could have done just as well without him? And that Timothy was set over that church, no one can doubt who has carefully read the epistles of St. Paul to him.

Upon

Upon supposition that Christ designed but one order of ministers in his church, How came the great St. Paul under the immediate inspiration of the Holy Ghost, to make so violent an alteration in his Master's plan, as he did at Ephesus, and again at Crete? St. Paul had, previously to this event, projected a journey into Spain and the West (Rom. xv. 24.) Hitherto he had kept those churches under his own superintendence. But the time, during which he would necessarily be absent, and the uncertainty whether he should ever return, rendered it highly expedient that he should settle superintendents, with apostolical powers, in those churches which he was to leave, to supply his place, and take that personal charge, which he had thitherto executed. On this occasion, it most probably was, that he settled Timothy at Ephesus, Titus in Crete, Epaphroditus at Philippi, Andronicus and Junia in other churches.—There is therefore, no ground to suppose that those bishops or presbyters mentioned in the New Testament ever had the power of ordination committed to them.

It is not uncommon for words and titles of office to change their signification in living languages. There was a time when the English word *knave*, signified a faithful, diligent servant (from the latin word *gnavus*); what it signifies now every body knows. The word *consul* was once a title of office for the first magistrate in Rome—it now means an agent or officer in foreign parts, to regulate the affairs of the people of his nation. That a change has happened in the application of the word *bishop*, is admitted. Its precise meaning (from Επισκοπος) is *overseer*, *superintendant*, and was sometimes given to those presbyters whom the apostles appointed, under themselves, to oversee or superintend particular congregations, in the same sense in which the word rector, that is governor, is now applied to the superintendent of a parish, under the bishop of the diocese. Such a presbyter is the rector—ruler, bishop, or overseer of the parish to which he is appointed; but with respect to the bishop, he is only a curate, one who takes care for him of that parish, which is a part of the bishop's diocese. With regard to the people, he is their rector, bishop, or superintendent—with regard to the diocesan, he is his

curate. This, I take it, was exactly the case of those elders, presbyters, or bishops at Ephesus. They were the overseers of the flock or congregation to which they had been appointed; but they were St. Paul's curates while he kept the superintendency of that church in his own hands. When Timothy was settled there, they bore the same relation to him which they had before borne to St. Paul; and he bore the same relation to them which St. Paul had formerly done. They were still rectors, overseers, bishops, elders, presbyters—call them which you will—of their several congregations, but they were Timothy's *curates*—that is, they took *care* of that part of his diocese, in which they were appointed to minister—they were the overseers of the people—he was the overseer of those overseers. Let any one read with candour St. Paul's epistles to Timothy, and this will appear to have been the case; especially if he take into the account the history and practice of the church in its early period, which was evidently on this plan.

Persons in this station are, in the prophetic stile of St. John's Revelation, called *Angels*, a word of the same import with apostles; the one coming from Ἀποστέλλω, *to send on a message*; the other from ἀγγέλλω, *to declare or deliver a message*. In the next period, viz. in the time of Ignatius and Polycarp, we find these supreme officers called *bishops* by the ecclesiastical writers; and the term *bishops* never more used to denote the presbyters of the church, so far as I can recollect. About the time then of St. John's death, the use of this word was changed, and from signifying in general an overseer of the church, became appropriated to those who were invested with apostolical authority in the church. The opinion of those is, therefore, the most probable who suppose that, on the death of the original apostles, their successors modestly declined the title by which they had been distinguished, and contented themselves with that of overseers, or bishops. On any other ground, ecclesiastical history is confused and unintelligible. To argue, therefore, from the sameness of title to the sameness of office, shews either want of knowledge, or want of candour. If it be want of candour, nothing, I fear, will ever remedy it—if want of knowledge, the argument will

never again be brought into view. Should a writer affirm confidently that the title of *Imperator* at Rome, in the time of Augustus, implied no more power than it did a few years before, when the army of Cicero saluted him with that title; and should from thence infer that Cicero was as absolute an emperor, as ever Augustus was, he would render himself forever ridiculous: and he would deserve to be so; but not a whit more than those who are forever harping on the word *bishop*, and insisting that, as it has been used in the acts of the apostles to signify the office of a presbyter, it, therefore, could not possibly mean any higher office an hundred years after. Hard pressed in argument, they forever invelope themselves in the obscurity of words—of words too made obscure by themselves, and then think their antagonist can neither see nor hurt them.

Let us now attend to the other position, and see whether it will, unhurt, endure examination, viz. That the power which Christ left in his church, to ordain and send ministers, is one only in such a sense that it cannot be divided, but must be communicated wholly, or not at all; and consequently, that every person who is ordained, must receive the power to ordain others.

From this position it seems to follow, that the whole apostolical power was communicated in every ordination which the apostles performed. For if they must communicate the whole power which Christ gave them, or none at all, then all who were ordained by them received all the power which they possessed, and were apostles equally with themselves; or they received no power whatever by their ordination. That Philip was ordained, and did receive power to preach and baptise, we have the fullest testimony (Acts vi. 6. viii. 6, 16, 35, 38.); and yet he did not receive the full power which the apostles had received from Christ. The power of conferring the Holy Ghost on those who had been baptised, by the laying on of hands, had never been committed to him; but to execute this office, two of the apostles went down from Jerusalem to Samaria, which would have been altogether needless, had Philip possessed the whole apostolical power. The power, therefore, which Christ gave to his apostles to send ministers in his name,

name, is not *one* in this ſenſe, that the whole of it muſt be communicated in ordination, or none at all: For if the ſeven deacons received only part of this power in their ordination, namely, the power of preaching, baptiſing, and aſſiſting at the holy communion and love-feaſts, here was one order of clergy with powers inferior to thoſe of the apoſtles. And where is the abſurdity of ſuppoſing that the elders, preſbyters, or pariſh overſeers at Epheſus, were another order of clergy with powers ſuperior to thoſe of deacons, but inferior to thoſe of the apoſtles? eſpecially as ſuch a ſuppoſition is neceſſary to give conſiſtency to St. Paul's conduct: For if thoſe miniſters at Epheſus had received the full eccleſiaſtical powers which the Apoſtles poſſeſſed, there was not only a manifeſt impropriety, but an abſurdity in fixing Timothy there as chief governor of that church. By parity of reaſon we muſt conclude, that the preſbyters of the Church of England have only ſuch a limited commiſſion as the preſbyters of Epheſus had; and though they are every one rectors, governors, ſuperintendents, elders, preſbyters, overſeers, biſhops if you pleaſe, of their ſeveral pariſhes, which you may, if you will, call their dioceſes, for I diſpute not about names, yet it is in ſubordination to their chief biſhop—their Timothy—to whom, and not to them, the fullneſs of power to govern the church, and conſequently the power of ordination is committed, within their diſtrict, dioceſe, or epiſcopal pariſh.

To ſay that a perſon inveſted with a commiſſion can convey the *whole* power of that commiſſion to another, but cannot convey a *part* of it, is downright nonſenſe, and deſerves no better name—unleſs his principal has reſtrained him in that particular: And if Chriſt has left ſuch a reſtriction, it may, I preſume, be pointed out. Inſtances, in ſupport of what I have ſaid, might be readily produced from civil affairs, but I ſhall wave them, and content myſelf with one from the Preſbyterians in the management of their eccleſiaſtical polity. I believe it is not uncommon for their preſbyteries to licence candidates for the miniſtry to preach, and preſide in the public worſhip of their congregations, by making extempore prayers; that is, they give them power

power to do ſo. But do they give them the full power which they claim to themſelves?—the power of government and of adminiſtering the ſacraments? They, it ſeems, can give a limited commiſſion, extending ſo far, and no further, but they exclude the apoſtles and biſhops from having any ſuch power: This is ſurely uncandid and uncivil.

I conclude, therefore, that the elders, preſbyters, overſeers, biſhops, mentioned in the acts and epiſtles of the apoſtles, unleſs when the apoſtles are denoted by one of thoſe titles, had not the power of government or ordination, but where ſubordinate officers, miniſters of particular congregations, under the controul or direction of an apoſtle, or of one whom an apoſtle had appointed over them, ſuch as were Timothy, Titus, Epaphroditus, Andronicus, Junia and others—That they were eſſentially diſtinct in power and rank, not only from the original apoſtles themſelves, but from thoſe whom they appointed to ſucceed them in the chief government of the churches which they planted; and who, in the next age, obtained the appropriated name of *biſhops*, which name, with the ſupremacy of apoſtolical power, continues to this day, in the dioceſan biſhops of the chriſtian church.

I conclude alſo, that the power which Chriſt left with his apoſtles to ordain and ſend miniſters to preſide over, and officiate in his church, is not *one* in ſuch a ſenſe that they could not communicate ſome portion of it, without communicating the whole; but that they did communicate ſome portion of that power to the deacons, and a greater portion to the preſbyters or elders, making, with themſelves, three diſtinct orders of clergy in the church—That the preſbyters within a certain diſtrict, now called a dioceſe, preſided over their reſpective congregations—the apoſtle or chief biſhop of that diſtrict or dioceſe preſiding over them and the people committed to their care and charge.—That the unity of the church conſiſted in this—that the people of every congregation held communion with their particular overſeer, elder, or preſbyter, in faith, worſhip, diſcipline, and ſacraments—that the overſeers of the ſeveral congregations held communion with each other in the ſame particulars, through

through the medium of their overſeer or chief biſhop, that is, by keeping up communion with him, and ſubmitting to his government.—And that theſe chief biſhops of the churches, or of different dioceſſes, held communion with each other by maintaining, through the operation of the Holy Ghoſt, the ſame apoſtolical government, worſhip, ſacraments, and faith in Chriſt Jeſus, the all-glorious and all-ſufficient head of the church, *from whom the whole body fitly joined together, and compacted by that which every joint ſupplieth, according to the effectual working in the meaſure of every part, maketh increaſe of the body, unto the edifying* (building up) *of itſelf in love* (Eph. iv. 16.)—And my opinion is, that whoever needleſsly breaks this unity by departing from this communion, that is, when he could continue in it without ſinning againſt God, is guilty of ſchiſm, and ought to repent of his wickedneſs, and return to the church of Chriſt from which he has ſtrayed.

I conclude again, that thoſe preſbyters who ſeparated from the church of England did not, and could not bring off with them the apoſtolical power of ordination, becauſe they never had received it. Their ſeparation made them ſchiſmatics, but gave them no new eccleſiaſtical powers.

If, then, neither the whole congregation of the people, nor any part of it, have the power of ordination; nor thoſe preſbyters who ſeparated from the church of England; a junction of both cannot create a power which neither of them had before. *Ex nihilo, nihil fit*—*from nothing, nothing can come*—is an adage which has been true a long time, and probably will continue to be ſo to the end of the world. Whence then comes the power of ordination which the Preſbyterians and Independents claim?

On this ground, therefore, it is reaſonable that they ſhould make the firſt advances to a re-union with the church;—they admit the validity of her orders, and ſhe unhappily cannot return the compliment: And let me aſk the gentlemen for whoſe benefit theſe charitable efforts are principally intended, why, if they can effect a re-union with the church, on reaſonable and liberal terms, and in her boſom do away the odious imputation of

of schism, and obtain valid orders for their ministers, they should not do it? Many of their ministers, as well as people, must have doubts and misgivings of mind concerning their ordinations. It is their misfortune too that those doubts and misgivings are well founded, and leave them no chance of getting rid of them any other way, than by removing the ground on which they stand. They may turn and twist every way; it will only shew the rankling of the wound. They may raise mists, create perplexities, and obscure plain points, and keep controversy alive, in hopes the people will not perceive the dilemma in which they are entangled. But truth will at last break through the gloom, and they must either leave their errors, or their more sensible people will leave them. They may put a bold face on the business, and think to brave it out; and, as they at first assumed the title of presbyters, and the stile of Reverend, so they may in imitation of Dr. Stiles and his brethren of Connecticut, usurp the title of Bishops, and, it may be the stile of Right Reverend (pray who then would be reverend?) it will all end like those plays of children which they call *make believe*. Their doubts and misgivings will continue, and, like a perpetual blister, keep them forever uneasy and wincing. The people will see it and laugh.—They see it already; and the number of those who return to the church is daily increasing. Think me not censorious; my words are the words of truth and candour. They are plain words, it is true, and you may not have been used to them, and therefore they may seem strange. They are the words of benevolence, as well as of truth, and soberly intended to do you good; and I shall be very sorry should impatience or restifness, on your part, prevent their having full effect.

"Do you then," you will ask, "unchurch us all? "Have our congregations no authorised ministers? No "valid sacraments?" I answer, I unchurch nobody. If you were true churches before I wrote, you are so still. If you were not, all the bustle you can make will do you no good—quietness and patience will be the best palliation for your disease—a radical cure can only be effected by your return to the church from which you departed. You ask, "Have we no authorised ministers? no valid sacraments?" To these questions, I fear, I shall return disagreeable answers. You have ministers of the people, I confess; and if I may be allowed to make a supposition (and I have made a good many without any leave at all) I must suppose that such as your ministry is, such are your sacraments.

These, in short, are matters that neither concern me, nor my argument, any further than as they influence my benevolence in your behalf. To be a member of the true church of Christ is a matter of important concern to every body. I have pointed out this true church to you; into it you can enter; and in it you will have, in your own judgment, an authorised ministry, and valid sacraments. I hope you will avail yourselves of this information; and then, and not till then, all your doubts and misgivings will be at an end.

Probably I may also be asked, "Would you have us "abandon the religion of our forefathers?—those pious "and good men, who left all the comforts of their native country, and came over to this then howling "wilderness, for the sake of liberty of conscience?" I answer, I have no inclination to bring any reproach on our forefathers, were it in my power to do so; nor to call in question their piety and goodness: I must however remark, that their departure from the church of England was no proof of either. Nor have I a word to say against liberty of conscience. I pray God to preserve it to us all. That our forefathers were conscientious men, I doubt not; nor do I think it improbable that they came to America to enjoy greater liberty of conscience than they could obtain in England. They had certainly set their hearts on it; at least the principal men and the ministers had done so; for they no sooner obtained in America that liberty of conscience which they sought, than they endeavoured to monopolize it all to themselves; and, with their good will, would not suffer a neighbour to have an atom of it.

With regard to departing from the religion of our forefathers—Did not our forefathers depart from the religion of their forefathers, when they separated from the church of England? And have we not a better right to depart from their religion and return to the church, if there be better reasons for our return, than there were for their departure?

But this is talking altogether in the stile of New-England.—Most of the original settlers to the southward had never separated from the English church. If many of their descendants have done so, it has been owing to the arts and example of the Presbyterians of New-England, and of their new-fangled brethren of Mr. John Wesley's mission*.

The opinion that we must never depart from the religion of our forefathers, has no good foundation. Error sometimes creeps in slily and slowly, and may make great progress before it give any alarm. This was the case with the errors of the church of Rome; and had it been wrong, under any circumstances, to depart from the religion of our forefathers, we must have continued in the errors of Popery to this day. Nay more; on that supposition, Christianity could never have obtained footing in the world. The true line of conduct is to do what is right, and not to continue in error, merely because our forefathers erred in the same way before us.

But, in truth, returning to the Episcopal Church is not giving up the religion of your forefathers—not even of your New-England forefathers. It is only relinquishing those errors which they, through prejudice, most unhappily imbibed. You would give up an ill-founded church government, and an unauthorised ministry and sacraments, and you would obtain a government, ministry, and sacraments, according to the institution of Christ, the example of his holy apostles, and the practice of the primitive church, in its purest period. You would

* The Reverend Mr. John Wesley, the founder and former of the Methodists, as they are called, some years ago published a little pamphlet of reasons why the Methodists should not separate from the Church of England: yet in his dotage, being 82 years of age, a certain Dr. Coke prevailed on him to confer the Episcopal character on him the said Coke. This was done privately at Bristol.—*Quere*—What becomes of Mr. Wesley's reasons against a separation from the Church of England? Where did Mr. W. get his power of ordination? Is Dr. Coke more a Bishop now than he was before Mr. W. laid hands on him? Yes, say the Methodists; Mr. W. is a very good man, and God has blessed his ministry with many conversions, therefore a good man has a right to do *evil*.—God defend us!

would give up an unjustifiable separation, and heal a breach, which the intemperate zeal of your forefathers made in the unity of Christ's church. You would get rid of extempore prayers in public worship, which to many of you are a real source of uneasiness and discontent; and you would have your public devotions regulated by a form composed by the joint efforts of men of ability and prudence. You would silence those disputes between you and the Episcopal church, which must otherwise forever remain, and would thereby greatly promote the union, peace, and social happiness of the country in which we live.

Let me now ask, why the attempt should not be made? Whether it shall or shall not be made now lies with you. I have made the opening; and though I have written this address unauthorised by any public body, or particular cognizance of private friends—merely as a volunteer in what I suppose a good cause—the peace and union of the country—the unity and prosperity of the church of the blessed Redeemer—and the eternal felicity of us all—yet I *do* know that the union I have proposed would give the highest pleasure to the members of the Episcopal church—that a great majority of them, especially of those of weight and influence, would rejoice in the prospect of its taking effect, and would glory in helping to accomplish it.

Though my partiality for the church of England and her form of public worship must be evident from what I have written, I am not so enthusiastically attached to it, as to suppose no other form can be proper for public worship, or acceptable to God. Some things in it might probably be changed so as to be better adapted to the state of this country; and these alterations—I mean not those only which its political situation requires—it is hoped have been prudently and cautiously made by the late general convention of the Episcopal Church at Philadelphia. If they have used their power discreetly, the church and country will be under great obligations to them. If they have made many needless alterations, much mischief is to be dreaded. But a good man will hope for the best event in so important a concern; and I cannot help indulging an expectation that you, gentlemen,

will attend to their book of common-prayer, which, I understand, is now in the press, with the eye of candour, and see whether you could not with a good conscience adopt the use of it in your public worship. If you could, one great difficulty would be over. What gives me the more hope is the declaration which some of your ministers are said to have made, viz. That they could read the liturgy of the church of England in their assemblies, and would be willing to do so, one half of the day, if the congregation desired it. That many of your laity do decidedly prefer the liturgy of the church of England to extempore prayers, I know assuredly, for I have heard them declare it. These are certainly encouraging circumstances, and would justify some prudent attempts to introduce that, or a similar liturgy, into your public worship. And though uniformity in public worship would be much preferable to a diversity of liturgies in the same country, as it would be a greater security to the unity and peace of the church, and to the brotherly-love and affection of its members; yet, any liturgy, in which a due regard was paid to the analogy of the christian faith, and the approved practices and usages of the primitive church, would be much better than extempore prayer, where every thing is left to the prudence and judgment of the minister. I see not however why christians should break unity on account of diversity of modes of worship.

It would be a great satisfaction to me to be able to join in worship and communion with all christians with whom I have intercourse; and I would do so occasionally with you, gentlemen, notwithstanding your extempore prayers, as much as I am attached to forms, were it not for two considerations; the one is, that I should thereby depart from the unity of Christ's Church, and become an abettor of an unjustifiable separation from a true branch of it. The other is, the doubts I have of the validity of the ordination of your ministers, and consequently of the sacraments they dispense. These are serious points, and the serious consideration of them can do you no harm. It was to bring you to this serious consideration this address was written—It was the design too of some expressions in it which to you may appear harsh.

harsh. I repeat it, they are the words of truth and benevolence. I repeat also, that truth fears no inquiry; and I add, that the church to which I belong will endure the most exact scrutiny—try it who will.

I do not flatter myself that this address will pass without public animadversions. As I do not wish for controversy, so neither have I made any resolution to avoid it, when the occasion calls for it. I am, however, so confident of the ground on which I stand, that if, evasions are avoided, and the merits of the cause only brought into view, the controversy, I am sure, will be very short.

It may be enquired, Why this address is particularly directed to you, gentlemen, of the Presbyterian and Independent persuasions, and not to all in general who differ from the Episcopal Church? The reason is, that as the points of difference between you and the Episcopal Church were fewer, I thought it would be best to make the first essay where I have made it; trusting that your candid and favourable acceptance of it would be such, as should encourage me to make my efforts more extensive: And I do hope my expectations will not be entirely disappointed, but that your good example will influence all denominations of christians to think more seriously of the great duty of christian unity, for the sake of both their temporal and eternal interest.

God speed the happy time, when all who profess and call themselves christians, may be led into the way of truth, hold the faith in unity of spirit, worship him in the bond of peace, and live together in righteousness of life. *Amen.*

F I N I S.

A

DISCOURSE,

DELIVERED IN

ST. *JOHN's* CHURCH,

IN

PORTSMOUTH, *NEWHAMPSHIRE*,

At the conferring the Order of PRIESTHOOD on

The REV. ROBERT FOWLE, A. M.

of *HOLDERNESS*,

On the FESTIVAL of ST. *PETER*, 1791.

By the Right Rev: SAMUEL SEABURY, D. D.
BISHOP of CONNECTICUT.

Am I therefore become your enemy, because I tell you the truth?—GAL. iv, 16.

——the devil——is a liar, and the father of it.—St. JOHN, viii. 44.

——the Church of the living God, the pillar and ground of the truth.—1. TIM. iii. 15.

PRINTED AT *BOSTON*,
BY ISAIAH THOMAS AND EBENEZER T. ANDREWS,
FAUST's STATUE, No. 45, NEWBURY STREET.
For GEORGE JERRY OSBORNE, jun. Printer, in *Portsmouth*.
MDCCXCI.

ADVERTISEMENT.

THE misrepresentation of a passage in the following Sermon, and the publick abuse of the author, are the reasons of its publication. As far as it goes, it contains his deliberate sentiments on the subject, which he has no disposition to retract. He has expressed them freely, *because he thought it his duty; and because in a* free *country, he supposed he had a right to do so. And he still hopes he has as undoubted a privilege to explain and establish the Episcopacy of the Church, as others claim to revile and destroy it. Should any one be disposed to nibble at particular sentiments and expressions, he is heartily welcome: The principles, he flatters himself, will abide the trial of reason and scripture. Nonsense, he knows, will have its paroxysms, and that they will sometimes be violently abusive, especially when the secrecy of a newspaper can effectually conceal an author in venting his ignorance and malice. The blessed Redeemer was reviled as a drunkard—the holy Baptist as a demoniack—St. Paul as a babbler—They were defamed—made as the filth of the world—the off-scouring of all things—and by whom? In such company it is the author's highest honour to be found, suffering reproach as they did in the cause of truth.*

A DISCOURSE, &c.

St. MATT. XXVIII. 18, 19, 20.

JESUS CAME, AND SPAKE UNTO THEM, SAYING, ALL POWER IS GIVEN UNTO ME IN HEAVEN AND IN EARTH. GO YE, THEREFORE, AND TEACH ALL NATIONS, BAPTIZING THEM IN THE NAME OF THE FATHER, AND OF THE SON, AND OF THE HOLY GHOST: TEACHING THEM TO OBSERVE ALL THINGS WHATSOEVER I HAVE COMMANDED YOU: AND, LO, I AM WITH YOU ALWAY, EVEN UNTO THE END OF THE WORLD. *AMEN.*

HAVING been engaged in the ſolemn ſervice of conferring the order of Prieſthood, and thereby ſending another labourer into GOD's harveſt, to gather men into his church, and prepare them for future happineſs in his eternal kingdom, I think it my duty to call your attention to the commiſſion which our SAVIOUR gave to his Apoſtles juſt before his aſcenſion; becauſe that commiſſion, being the foundation of all authority which ever did, or can ſubſiſt in his Church, it is a matter of importance to us rightly to underſtand it, and conform our practice to it.

IN a country where religious opinions and profeſſions are ſo various, and in an aſſembly ſo large as this to which I now addreſs myſelf, it cannot be ſuppoſed that a diſcourſe on this ſubject can be equally acceptable to every one—ſome will condemn what others may approve. The boaſt of the preſent age, and particularly of this country, is liberality of ſentiment, and candour to thoſe who differ from us. Permit me then to avail myſelf of theſe diſpoſitions; and to hope, that while I endeavour, in truth and ſincerity, to explain the commiſſion which CHRIST gave his Apoſtles, as I underſtand it, I ſhall eſcape the cenſure of thoſe who differ from me in opinion, ſeeing I take no greater privilege in diſſenting from them than they do from me.

HUMBLY truſting in the grace of GOD's holy Spirit to preſerve me from all error in doctrine, and intemperance in expreſſion, I now apply myſelf to the buſineſs before me.

ALL power, ſaid our REDEEMER, *is given to me in heaven and in earth. Go ye, therefore, and teach all nations, baptizing them in the name of the Father, and of the Son, and of the Holy Ghoſt: Teaching them to obſerve all things whatſoever I have commanded you: And, lo, I am with you alway, even unto the end of the world.*

HERE a power is claimed by CHRIST, an authority is delegated to his apoſtles, a duty is enjoined on them, and a promiſe of ſupport is annexed

to it. The power claimed by CHRIST is unlimited—*all power is given to me in heaven and in earth.* As CHRIST is the ſon of GOD, this plenitude of power is inherent in him by his divine nature, and was ſo from eternity. As he is the ſon of man, and the mediator of the new covenant between GOD and man, this power was conferred on him by the ALMIGHTY FATHER.

The power, therefore, which CHRIST poſſeſſes in heaven, comprehends the power of ſending the Holy Ghoſt, of commanding the ſervice of the holy Angels, and all the hoſt of heaven, and of giving heaven itſelf to all who believe in him and obey him. His power on earth includes authority to gather his Church out of the nations, to rule and govern it by his will, to protect it by his might, to ſanctify it by his Spirit. This privilege CHRIST obtained by his reſurrection and aſcenſion.

The great end of CHRIST's coming into the world was to make atonement for ſin, and, through that atonement, to put man under a new covenant, even the covenant of grace and mercy, becauſe he was become incapable of fulfiling the original covenant of perfect obedience, by reaſon of the apoſtacy of human nature from GOD. CHRIST, therefore, inſtituted his Church to be a holy ſociety, conſiſting, in every age, of all thoſe who, through faith in him, and dependence on his atonement, ſhould renounce the apoſtacy of human nature, and ſhould live in

obedience to the laws and conditions of the new covenant of grace and mercy, which accepted of repentance instead of innocence, of earnest endeavours after holiness instead of that which is perfect, and of unfeigned obedience instead of that which is unsinning.

THOUGH CHRIST'S Church is not *of this world*, but is taken out of the world, and separated from it, and therefore, is not to be governed by worldly policy, but by the laws of CHRIST; its members not to live by worldly maxims and principles, but by the rules and directions of the Gospel; not by the spirit of the world, but by the spirit of GOD; yet as it is made up of members, collected out of the nations of the world, and brought into it by conversion from the service of sin to the service of GOD, it must, at least, for a time and in part, viz. while this life continues, be in the world.

THE instituted means of conversion was the *preaching* of the Apostles, and of those who were commissioned by them—*Go ye and teach all nations*, that is, preach the Gospel to all nations: Or, as St. Mark expresses it, *Go ye into all the world, and preach the Gospel to every creature*—to all who will hear you.

THE appointed mode, or instrument of admission into the Church upon their conversion, was *Baptism*—*Baptizing them in the name of the Father, and of the Son, and of the Holy Ghost.*

THE rule of life to those who were converted to the faith, and baptized into the Church, was the *Commandments of* CHRIST—*teaching them to observe all things whatsoever I have commanded you.*

THE end of their faith and obedience, as we learn from St. Mark, was *eternal life*—*He that believeth and is baptized shall be saved.*

THE support the Apostles and their successors were to receive in the execution of their commission, was the *presence of* CHRIST—*Lo, I am with you alway, even unto the end of the world.*

HOLY Scripture informs us that CHRIST purchased this Church by his death; that it is made subject to his authority by him who hath put all things under his feet; that it is animated and sanctified by his spirit. On all these accounts, then, it must be his Church, and his only; and no man can have a right to interfere in its government or discipline, but by commission from him; because he is its head and king, its proprietor and supreme governor.

THAT he did give a commission, or delegated a power to his Apostles to govern his Church under him, when he said to them, *All power is given to me in Heaven and in earth*, &c. has been already observed, and further appears from St. John, *As my Father hath sent me, even so send I you.* Let us then see what this commission empowered and required them

to do, and then we shall be able to form a judgment of its extent and limitation—whether it was given to the Apostles in such a manner as to exclude all others, except those to whom they communicated it according to the will of CHRIST; or whether it be left common to all men, so that every one who chooses may validly interfere in its government and offices?

BY their commission, the Apostles were empowered and commanded to preach the Gospel to all nations. To them our SAVIOUR'S words are particularly directed; and from comparing together the accounts which St. Matthew and St. Mark have given us of this transaction, it appears that none were present but the eleven Apostles: to them, therefore, the commission must be restrained. By a former commission, they had been sent to preach to the lost sheep of the house of Israel, but were forbidden to go into other nations. Here their commission was enlarged, and made to extend to all the nations of the world.

THAT GOD originally intended, that the blessings of redemption through MESSIAH should extend to all nations, appears from the promise made to Abraham, that in his seed all the families of the earth should be blessed. It was, therefore, necessary that the knowledge of redemption through him should be preached to all nations, that they might believe in him, and in his Church obtain salvation through

his mediation: but how ſhould they *believe* in him of whom they have not *heard?* *Without faith*, ſaid an Apoſtle, *it is impoſſible to pleaſe* God. He ſaith, too, that *faith cometh by hearing, and hearing by the word of* God. His argument proceeds in this manner—*Whoſoever ſhall call upon the name of the* Lord *ſhall be ſaved.* They cannot *call* upon him in whom they have not *believed*: They cannot *believe* in him of whom they have not *heard*: They cannot *hear* without a *preacher*: They cannot *preach* except they be *ſent.* So that there can be no faith in God, but what is founded on ſome declaration which God hath made. But how ſhall we know what God hath declared except ſome one inform us? And who can inform us except they whom God hath commiſſioned to do ſo? He whom God hath ſent, can act in the name of God, and make known to us the will of God in thoſe particulars for which God hath ſent him. But ſhould one come without being ſent of God, though what he ſhould ſay might be reaſonable and true, our belief of it would not be faith in God, becauſe not founded on his authority. The neceſſity, therefore, of a commiſſion from God to preach his word, and make known his will, that we may believe in him and obey him, is evidently apparent.

Another power, which the Apoſtles received by their commiſſion, was that of admitting, perſons into Christ's Church by baptiſm. The Church being Christ's, he only can have power to appoint

its government and officers: he only can preſcribe the mode of receiving members into it, becauſe he only is its king and head. No man, therefore, can have authority to receive perſons into Christ's *family*—his *kingdom*, and make them members of his *body*—(for by all theſe titles is his Church diſtinguiſhed)—but by commiſſion from him, and in the way which he hath commanded. Suppoſe a man takes upon himſelf to make members of Christ's Church, by ſome other mode than Baptiſm; Do they, in conſequence, become members of it? Or ſuppoſe he baptizes with water, in the name of the Father, and of the Son, and of the Holy Ghost; Is the Baptiſm he adminiſters, Christ's Baptiſm, when he has no authority from Christ to adminiſter it? Baptiſm is a covenant between God, and the party baptized. It includes engagements on both ſides. The party baptized acts for himſelf, or his ſureties, who are his repreſentatives, act for him. God's miniſter is his repreſentative, and acts in his name, by virtue of the authority he has received from Jesus Christ, the mediator of the Covenant. The valid adminiſtration of Baptiſm, therefore, depends on a valid commiſſion from Christ.

The other power, which the Apoſtles received by their commiſſion was, to inſtruct thoſe who had been baptized, and thereby admitted into the Church of Christ, in the directions and commands which he had given for the regulation of their con-

duct, that they might live ſuitably to the ſolemn engagements into which they had entered. They were to *teach them all things whatſoever* Christ *had commanded.*

The exerciſe of this power conſiſted in their declaring and explaining the principles and doctrines of Chriſtianity; in their inculcating and enforcing the practice of virtue and holineſs; and in their adminiſtering, according to Christ's will, the ſacraments and diſcipline of his Church.

To convey theſe powers, in the whole, or in part, is the deſign of Ordination; which is no more than the communicating ſuch a portion of Christ's commiſſion, as that order of the Clergy requires, to which the perſon ordained is appointed.

That our Lord intended the Apoſtolic office ſhould continue to the end of the world, is plain from the text, *Lo, I am with you alway, even unto the end of the world.* He knew the Apoſtles were not to live to the end of the world, and had warned them to expect, not only perſecution, on account of their preaching the Goſpel, but death alſo. Christ's promiſe, therefore, to be with his Apoſtles to the end of the world, was not only perſonally to them, but included their ſucceſſors alſo—all who ſhould hold their commiſſion to the end of the world: And indeed, may be ſaid to have been made rather to their commiſſion, than to their perſons; for it was only in the diſcharge of the duties of their

commiſſion, that they were the objects of the promiſe.

If, then, the Apoſtolical commiſſion ceaſed with the lives of the firſt Apoſtles, as ſome have taught, the promiſe of CHRIST, *Lo, I am with you alway, even unto the end of the world*, has failed; for the Apoſtles have been long dead, and the end of the world is not yet come; Then, too, there is no authority from CHRIST ſubſiſting in the Church; and of conſequence, CHRIST has no Church: The gates of Hell have prevailed againſt it, and it is extinct. For a Church, in which CHRIST has no authority, cannot be his Church: It may be the Pope's Church, or Luther's Church, or Calvin's Church, or Weſley's Church—his Church, whoever he was, who inſtituted its government and miniſtry: But CHRIST's Church it cannot be, unleſs it be founded on his authority, and governed by his commiſſion. If, now, it be abſurd to ſay that CHRIST has no Church in the world, it is abſurd to ſay, that the Apoſtolical commiſſion ceaſed with the lives of the firſt Apoſtles; for if that commiſſion ceaſed, the Church founded under it ceaſed of courſe.

TAKING it then for an eſtabliſhed point, that the Apoſtolical commiſſion was to continue to the end of the world, it will follow that the government of the Church is, at leaſt ought to be, the ſame now, it was in the time of the Apoſtles, after they had ſettled it according to the will of CHRIST, and by virtue of

his commiſſion: No human authority can have power to alter it; and in whatever degree it has been any where altered, in the ſame degree it ceaſes to be the Church of CHRIST, and becomes a Church of human invention. For, the Apoſtles being divinely inſpired, and acting under the immediate direction of the HOLY GHOST, in all things neceſſary to the eſtabliſhment of the Church according to the will of CHRIST, none of their ſucceſſors could have authority to change the government they had eſtabliſhed, unleſs they could plead the authority of CHRIST for the change, with as much certainty as the firſt Apoſtles could for the original eſtabliſhment, and could give the ſame proof of divine inſpiration as thoſe Apoſtles had given. The power, therefore, of their ſucceſſors could go no further than to the adminiſtration of the government the Apoſtles had inſtituted:—The doctrines, ſacraments, government, and diſcipline of the Church were the *depoſitum*, the ſacred truſt committed to them, which they were to guard and adminiſter, not to corrupt, or change.

NOTWITHSTANDING the different opinions which have been entertained, and the many altercations which have in conſequence enſued, it ſtill remains a poſition capable of ſolid proof, that the government and offices of the Church were, in the time of the firſt Apoſtles, adminiſtered by three orders of Clergy in ſubordinate degrees. The Apoſtles, by CHRIST's appointment, held the higheſt ſtation, and, under

him, were the ſource of all eccleſiaſtical power. Subordinate to them were the Preſbyters, ſometimes called Biſhops: While the Deacons ſtood in the loweſt rank, and were properly the aſſiſtants of the higher Clergy in the adminiſtration of their office.

THAT theſe three orders were in the Church, in the time of many of the firſt Apoſtles, has never been denied by the moſt zealous oppoſers of Epiſcopal government that I can recollect. They indeed ſay, that the apoſtolic office was temporary, and ceaſed at the death of the original Apoſtles. But it has been proved, that this opinion has no foundation to ſtand upon; becauſe if it be admitted, it will follow that CHRIST's promiſe, *Lo, I am with you alway, even unto the end of the world*, has failed. But if it be impious to ſay ſo, it is nonſenſe to ſay that the apoſtolical office has ceaſed.

WITH regard to *Preſbyters* there is no diſpute, unleſs it be about the names by which they are denoted. That Preſbyter and Biſhop are in ſeveral inſtances uſed in the New Teſtament, to expreſs the ſame office or degree of Clergy, is readily granted. But this conceſſion, if our opponents chooſe to conſider it as one, hurts not our argument, nor helps theirs. Suppoſe both terms to denote one and the ſame office, you muſt, at the ſame time, ſuppoſe the office denoted by thoſe terms to have been in the Church, or it could not have been denoted by any

terms at all. Now, if there were such officers in the Church in the times of the Apostles, as were stiled Presbyters or Bishops, it is easy to prove that they were subordinate, not only to the original Apostles, St. Peter, St. Paul, &c. but also to those who were ordained Apostles by them, St. Timothy and St. Titus. Should any one doubt the fact, let him read St. Paul's Epistles to Timothy and to Titus, and then let him doubt if he can. So that whether we can give a decided reason for the appropriation of the name of Bishop to the successors of the Apostles, or point out the precise time when it happened, or not, our argument is unimpaired, while it can be proved, that those Presbyters or Bishops were but secondary officers in the Church, and did not fill the highest seats.

With regard to the Deacons, the enemies of Episcopacy have reduced that order down to be of no degree of Clergy at all. They have some persons, it is true, whom they stile Deacons, who are chosen by a plurality of lay voices, and enter on their office without even the pretence of an ordination. Whereas in the apostolical times, their title to be considered as an order of the Clergy is incontestible. They were ordained to their office by the laying on of the hands of the Apostles: And besides their ministration at the holy communion and love feasts, and their superintending the charitable funds of the Church, they preached and baptized—witness St. Stephen and St. Philip.

Another proof of the Deacons being an order of Clergy may be taken from St. Paul's first Epistle to Timothy, where they are mentioned in such terms, and such directions are given concerning them, as can comport with no order of laymen.

If then it was necessary the Deacons should have those powers in the time of the Apostles, why is it not necessary they should have the same powers now? And if ordination, by the hands of the Apostles, was then necessary to confer those powers, why is not ordination, by the hands of those who succeed to the Apostles in conveying Christ's commission, now necessary to communicate the same powers?

It has, I trust, been proved, that there were, in the time of the Apostles, three orders of Clergy in the Church, by their institution under the immediate inspiration and direction of the Holy Ghost. That they, who have departed from the Episcopal government of the Church, have but one order, needs no proof—That there *ought* to be but one order is the ground of their system. However, therefore, it may be with the Episcopal Church, they who reject Episcopacy (to say nothing of the invalidity of Presbyterian ordination) have not that Church government, which the first Apostles settled and left in the Church.

Thus it appears to have been the intention of Christ, when he commissioned his Apostles to preach the Gospel to all nations, that their commission should continue to the end of the world.

It appears also, that the Apostles, by virtue of that commission, and under the inspiration and direction of the Holy Ghost, did leave in the Church three orders of Clergy, then stiled Apostles, Presbyters, or Bishops, and Deacons; now called Bishops, Presbyters or Priests, and Deacons. Our duty, therefore, requires that we abide by that Church government which they instituted according to the will of Christ; because no power on earth has authority to change it; because too, if we do change it, and substitute another government in its stead, we have no warranted claim to the privileges and blessings which Christ has annexed to it.

The duties, which belong to the office of Presbyters in the Church of Christ, have been particularly specified, and the obligations they are under to fidelity and diligence in the discharge of those duties, have been strongly enforced in the solemn service which has been before you. It is to be hoped, that all who enter into this holy order, will ever remember the awful engagements they are under, to execute their office in the fear of God, to his glory, and the edification of his Church; knowing that they must give account to God of their conduct, both as Clergymen and Christians. For their encouragement let them remember, that the *Presbyters who rule well* that part of the Church which is committed to their charge, and *labour* in

the preaching of *the word and doctrine, are worthy of double honour*, and ſhall receive from GOD a crown of glory, in the day when he ſhall judge the world by JESUS CHRIST.

BUT, however honoured by their commiſſion, the Miniſters of CHRIST have *their treaſure in earthen veſſels*, and are ſubject to the infirmities, paſſions, and temptations of other men. It is therefore our duty to pray for them, that every one of them in his vocation and miniſtry, may truly and acceptably ſerve GOD through JESUS CHRIST. It is alſo our duty to treat them with candour and reſpect, if not on their own account, yet on his, whoſe Miniſters they are—to cover their imperfections and miſconduct with the veil of charity, eſpecially when no good is likely to accrue to the Church of GOD by expoſing them—to miniſter cheerfully to their neceſſities—to ſupport them in their duty by our influence, and eſpecially by our punctual and devout attendance on all the ſacred offices of our holy religion.

PERMIT me now to cloſe this diſcourſe by an application of the latter part of the text, taken principally from the writings of a divine of great piety and conſiderable eſtimation*—*Lo, I am with you alway, even unto the end of the world*—"I am and will be with you and your ſucceſſors, lawfully called by my power

* Burkitt, whoſe obſervations on the text, the author begs leave to recommend to all pious people.

power and authority, by the bleſſing and aſſiſtance of my Spirit: I will be with you to uphold 'and perpetuate' mine own ordinance; to protect, encourage, and reward you, and all your ſucceſſors in the faithful diſcharge of your truſt: And this not for a day, a year, or an age, but to the end and conſummation of all ages."

"THE miniſtry of the word, and adminiſtration of the ſacraments, are," therefore, "a ſtanding ordinance in the Chriſtian Church throughout all ages:" Conſequently there muſt be a continued ſucceſſion of ordinations to ſet men apart for ſo ſacred a ſervice.

FROM the text it alſo appears, "That all the faithful miniſters of CHRIST, in what part of the world ſoever GOD ſhall caſt their lot, and in what time ſoever they ſhall happen to live, may comfortably expect CHRIST's gracious preſence with their perſons, and his bleſſing on their endeavours," to extend the knowledge and means of ſalvation through him, among all nations; on their readineſs to receive all who ſhall be duly qualified, into his Church, by holy Baptiſm; and on their fidelity and diligence in inſtructing thoſe who are baptized, to obſerve all things whatſoever CHRIST hath commanded, and to live in all holineſs and righteouſneſs of life. To ſuch miniſters, duly called, and ſent according to CHRIST's appointment, the promiſe of the text belongs—To them CHRIST ſaith, *Lo,*

I am with you; I am alway with you; and to the end of the world. I will be with you.

GLORY be to the great REDEEMER, for this his gracious promiſe:—May it inſpire all, to whom the ſacred myſteries of our holy religion are committed, with diligence and zeal in his ſervice, and with ſuch reſolution and courage, that they may think "No labour too great; no ſervice too much; no ſuffering too ſevere; ſo that they may finiſh their courſe with joy, and fulfil the miniſtry in which they are engaged."

So be it, heavenly Father, for his ſake, to whom thou haſt given all power in heaven and in earth—That we obeying thy will in all things, may be partakers of thy heavenly treaſure. To Thee, O Father, to thy CHRIST, our SAVIOUR, to thy HOLY GHOST, the Sanctifier of the Faithful, be honour and glory, now and forever.—AMEN.

F I N I S.

[This tract ends with an "Extract from the London Review and Literary Journal ..." which appears on the next page.]

A DISCOURSE

DELIVERED BEFORE THE

TRIENNIAL CONVENTION

OF THE

Proteſtant Epiſcopal Church

IN THE

UNITED STATES OF AMERICA,

IN TRINITY-CHURCH,

NEW-YORK,

ON THE TWELFTH DAY OF SEPTEMBER, ONE THOUSAND SEVEN HUNDRED AND NINETY-TWO.

By SAMUEL SEABURY, D. D.

Biſhop of Connecticut *and* Rhode-Iſland.

NEW-YORK:

PRINTED BY *HUGH GAINE*, AT THE BIBLE, IN HANOVER-SQUARE,

—1792.—

In the Houſe of Clerical and Lay Deputies of the Proteſtant Epiſcopal Church in the United States of America, Wedneſday September 12, 1792.

RESOLVED UNANIMOUSLY, That the Thanks of this Houſe be given to the Right Reverend Dr. SEABURY, for his Sermon delivered this Day in Trinity-Church ; and that the Rev. Dr. *Beach* and *Robert Andrews*, Eſquire, be appointed to preſent the Thanks of this Houſe, and to requeſt a Copy of the Sermon, for Publication.

Extract from the Minutes,

J. BISSETT. *Sec'ry.*

In the Houſe of Biſhops, Saturday, September 15th, 1792.

RESOLVED, That this Houſe concur with the Houſe of Clerical and Lay Deputies, in thanking the Right Rev. Biſhop SEABURY, for his Sermon delivered at the Opening of the Convention ; and in requeſting a Copy of the ſame to be printed.

Extract from the Minutes,

L. CUTTING, *Sec'ry.*

Extract from the London Review, and Literary Journal, for Feb. 1793.

THE elegance of ſtile, and energy of argument, in this diſcourſe, are as pleaſing as the candor and liberality of the preacher ; and, we doubt not of its ſalutary and healing effects in New-England, where religious opinions and profeſſions abound, and have multiplied ſince 1620, in defiance of the ancient pious puritans, who ſettled that country under a genus of Epiſcopacy reſembling the hierarchy of the Church of England, when Biſhops were not peers of the realm. The learned Biſhop will eſcape the cenſure of every candid perſon that may differ in opinion with him, ſeeing he has taken no greater privilege in diſſenting from modern puritans, than they have taken in diſſenting from the Biſhop and ancient puritans.—Each of the ſubjects the Biſhop has forcibly illuſtrated in a manner that every admirer of revelation muſt feel to be of importance to the Chriſtian ſyſtem, and thoſe who yield not their aſſent to the truths, will not be able to overthrow the facts alledged for their ſupport.

TO THE

GENERAL CONVENTION

OF THE

PROTESTANT EPISCOPAL CHURCH

IN THE

UNITED STATES OF AMERICA;

THE FOLLOWING

DISCOURSE

IS RESPECTFULLY INSCRIBED,

BY THEIR VERY AFFECTIONATE

AND HUMBLE SERVANT,

THE AUTHOR.

NEW-YORK, *September 15th*, 1792.

A SERMON, &c.

COLOSS. iii. 14.

And above all these things put on Charity, which is the bond of perfectness.

THAT GOD created man to make him partaker of his own immortality, in blessedness and glory for ever, will, I presume, be generally acknowledged by Christian people. In wisdom He made all his works, and therefore must have had some end in view in all that he did, and must have used means perfectly adapted to accomplish it.

No creature can contribute to the happiness of God, because he is all-sufficient, and needeth nothing. The happiness of man must, then, have been the end God had in view, when he brought him into being; and, that his intention was this happiness should continue forever, appears from the manner of his creation. Why, otherwise, was he made in the image of God, and endued with the principles of thinking and willing, which do not seem to have been created, but derived from an eternal source?

THE wisdom of Solomon hath told us, that "God made not death, neither hath pleasure in

"the destruction of the living;" and that, "through envy of the devil came death into the "world, and they that do hold of his side do "find it." Accordingly we read in the book of Genesis, that "God formed man of the dust of "the ground, and breathed into his nostrils the "breath of life, and man became a living soul." Formed of the elements of the world, which are miscible and divisible, the body of man, though animated by an immortal soul, could not, in its own nature, be immortal, but liable to dissolution from the separation of the elements of which it was made. Immortality of body, therefore, man was to obtain through obedience to him who is the Lord and Giver of life, and "who only hath immortality." As the test of his obedience, the tree of knowledge grew in the paradise of God: As the means of immortality, the tree of life also, in the midst of the garden. Of the former, Adam was forbidden to eat, that his obedience and submission to God might appear, and grow, and be confirmed beyond the danger of defection. But of the tree of life, in common with the other trees of the garden, he was freely permitted to eat, that his present life might be sustained by food proper for it, and that he might obtain that immortality for which his Creator designed him, when he should see proper to remove him from the earthly paradise to his own heavenly kingdom. Through the temptation of the devil, he fell from this state of his probation, by eating of the tree of knowledge, of which God had said to him, *Thou shalt not eat of it*; and, through his disobedience, he

loſt, with his right to the tree of life, his title to immortality. His body was left to the natural courſe of diſſolution, according to the tendency of the elementary principles of the world out of which it had been taken. The uſe of the tree of life was interdicted to him, and guarded againſt his approach, he being now no longer fit to eat of it. Through his diſobedience he was defiled with ſin, and loſt the preſence of the Divine Spirit which was the pledge of his immortality, and on which depended the image of God in him.

THOUGH fallen, his Creator, infinite in goodneſs and mercy, forſook him not. The Son of God, who is himſelf *God bleſſed forever*, became his Redeemer, and undertook to bear the penalty of his tranſgreſſion; to renew him in holineſs and in the image of God, by reſtoring to him the preſence and influence of the Bleſſed Spirit, and to make him again capable of immortality, by raiſing his dead body from the grave at the laſt day, when he, with all thoſe who deſcend from him, ſhall be judged concerning the things done in the body, and they who ſhall be found worthy, ſhall be admitted into the everlaſting kingdom of their Creator.

GOD ſaid, *The ſeed of the woman ſhall bruiſe the head of the ſerpent.* The words of God are the words of power. Human nature was thereby put into a new ſtate of probation, every individual for himſelf, that every one might, through the Redeemer, obtain that eternal life

which every one was made capable of acquiring. In various times, this Adorable Perſon appeared unto men, and in various manners ſpake unto them by himſelf, and by holy Prophets and Meſſengers, to make known to them the Divine Will, and to inſtruct them in things neceſſary to their ſalvation; till, in the fullneſs of time, when every thing was prepared according to the wiſdom and good pleaſure of God, He appeared in human nature, being, by the operation of the Holy Ghoſt, born of the ever-bleſſed Virgin Mary, thereby becoming man—God and man united making one Chriſt. In this nature he lived many years, yielding a perfect and abſolute obedience to the law of God; ſetting a complete example of goodneſs and virtue in his own moſt holy life; proving the reality of his divine nature by the moſt aſtoniſhing miracles; inſtructing all who would receive his doctrines in the will of God and the duty of man; promiſing to thoſe who believed in him and obeyed him, a happy reſurrection from death, and a glorious immortality in the world to come; and, at laſt, offering up his human nature to God, a ſacrifice of atonement for the ſin of the world, which ſacrifice was ſoon after ſlain on the croſs by the hands of cruel and unthinking men; and on the third day he roſe to life again, and, forty days after, aſcended into heaven, to *the Right hand of the throne of God.*

WHILE this Divine Perſon was in the world, he gave directions, and enacted laws, concerning the conduct of thoſe who ſhould believe in

him, that they might obtain the full benefit of the redemption he had wrought. That theſe directions and laws might be exactly obeyed, He inſtituted his Church, to be a ſociety holy to himſelf, and appointed its government, and miniſtry, and doctrines, and ſacraments—bleſſing it with promiſes, and guarding it with threatenings; and, after his Aſcenſion, ſending his Holy Spirit to be its animating principle, and perfect director. Into this Church, which is alſo called his *body*, his *family*, his *kingdom*, he commanded all who ſhould believe in him to enter by Baptiſm; that, being called out from this wicked world, which is *enmity againſt God*, they might be regenerated, *born again*, or *born from above* by the operation of the Holy Ghoſt, and under his influence, might believe and do all thoſe things which he had commanded, and in which they were to be inſtructed in his Church, that they might, through him, attain the reſurrection of the juſt, and eternal life in heaven.

THIS Church is to continue in this world as long as this world continues, and in heaven forever; accordingly he promiſed, that *the gates of hell ſhould not prevail againſt it.* Chriſt laid the firſt Foundation of it; and on that foundation his apoſtles built according to his direction, and under the inſpiration of the Holy Ghoſt; therefore are Chriſtians ſaid to be "*built upon the* "*foundation of the Apoſtles and Prophets, Jeſus* "*Chriſt himſelf being the chief corner ſtone.*" He ordained its government and Miniſters; He eſtabliſhed its doctrines and faith; He preſcribed

the manners of its members; and he instituted its sacraments. Where these are in their purity, there is the Church of Christ in all the perfection which it can have in this world. Where these are wanting, there the Church is not. And in the same degree in which they are any where wanting, is the Church mutilated and imperfect.

EVERY thing must be kept together by some principle or band of union. All material bodies —the earth which we inhabit—the system to which it belongs—are, according to the received philosophy, kept together and moved by the law of gravitation or attraction, impressed on them by their Almighty Creator, and not arising from their own nature independent on him; for so, I trust, the Philosophers mean. By this law every thing keeps its place, and duly performs its appointed office, without interference or confusion. What *Attraction* is in the material, *Love* is in the moral world. And Love our Saviour hath declared to be the principle of union and motion in his church; that is, the principle which binds its members together in one holy society, and which is the spring and director of all their actions.

WHEN we consider what the love of their country, their children, their families, their neighbours, their particular connections and friends hath, under a variety of circumstances, excited and enabled men to accomplish, we shall not be surprised to find this principle made the grand cement and band of the Christian Church: Especially if we consider also, that it was from

the overflowing of divine love, that the Father gave his only-begotten Son; and that from the same love the Son of God came to be the Redeemer of the lost race of men. For, how is it possible that they should not love one another who are redeemed by the love of God—who live in the sense of that love, and, through it, hope finally to be saved? If God so loved us as to give his Son for our redemption, we, who are redeemed by his love, ought, most assuredly, to love one another.

ON this view of love, as the cement and band of the Christian Church, the holy Apostle hath said in the Text, "*Above all these things put on* "*Charity, which is the bond of perfectness.*" He had exhorted the Colossians to constancy in their Christian profession, "*being knit together in love;*" and assures them, that their "*order and the sted-*"*fastness of their faith in Christ*" were a source of joy to him, though absent from them. He urgeth them in these affectionate words, "*As* "*ye have received Christ Jesus the Lord, walk ye* "*in him; rooted and built up in him, and stablished* "*in the faith, as ye have been taught.*" He cautioneth them against philosophy, and the vain traditions of men, such as the worshipping of angels, and submission to the law of Moses, lest they should be spoiled thereby, and drawn away from Christ, in whom they were complete, who is the head of all principality and power; in whom they were circumcised with the circumcision not made with hands, by being buried with him in baptism, and risen with him through the faith of

the operation of God who had raised him from the dead. In the third Chapter, he considers them as being risen with Christ, and exhorts them to *set their affections on things above, and not on things on the earth;* to *mortify their members which are on the earth, fornication, uncleanness, inordinate affection, evil concupiscence, and covetousness; to put away anger, wrath, malice, blasphemy, filthy communication; not to lie one to another, seeing they had put off the old man*—the body of the sins of the flesh—*and had put on the new man, which is renewed in knowledge after the image of him that created him. Put on therefore,* saith he, *as the elect of God, holy and beloved, bowels of mercies, kindness, humbleness of mind, meekness, long-suffering, forbearing one another, and forgiving one another, if any man have a quarrel* (a complaint) *against any: Even as Christ forgave you, so also do ye.* "*And above all these things* "*put on Charity, which is the bond of perfectness.*"

IF now the graces and virtues enumerated by the Apostle can subsist without Charity, as plainly appears from his discourse; then Charity, in the sense here used by him, must mean something more than simply love and affection, something more than *bowels of mercies, kindness, humbleness of mind, meekness, long-suffering, forbearing and forgiving one another.*—Above all these, Charity must be put on—to them all it must be superadded; and therefore they may subsist without it.

THIS Charity is called the *bond of perfectness*. The use of a bond is to hold things together which

would otherwise fall asunder. The *bond of perfectness* must, therefore, mean a *perfect bond*, or a bond by which the things held together are made perfect or complete. The perfection of the Christian Church, all other things being as they should be, consists in its unity. Of this unity, Charity is the bond, by which Christians are kept together in one society, and not suffered to part asunder. To this interpretation the verse following the text perfectly accords, "*And let the peace of God rule in your hearts, to* "*which* (peace) *ye are also called in one body*"—the Church of Christ. *There is*, saith this Apostle to the Ephesians "*one body*"—the Church of Christ; "*one Spirit*"—even the Holy Spirit of God, by which that body is governed and sanctified; "*one hope of your calling*,"—the hope of eternal life with God; "*one Lord*," Jesus Christ, the Head of the Church; "*one faith*," which the Church is to keep, seeing she is the pillar and ground of the truth; "*one baptism*"—by which we are admitted into the Church through the one faith; "*one God and Father of all*, who is" the Fountain of the divinity, Almighty, without origin—"*above all, and through all, and in you* "*all*."

SHOULD this point be supposed to want confirmation, it will be readily found by looking to what the author of the Text hath said in his first Epistle to the Corinthians. One principal design of that Epistle was to prevent schisms in the Church, and to bring those back to the unity of the Church who had fallen from it. Their di-

visions arose from their propensity to prefer some Ministers before others, on account of the superiority of the gifts which they possessed. This point the apostle considereth in the 12th, 13th, and 14th chapters. He tells them, that as the gifts of the Spirit were various, they were given to different men for the greater profit of the Church, not for their own aggrandizement and honour. And that for all the members of the Church to have the same gifts, would be as absurd and useless, as for all the members in the human body to have the save office. That God had "*set some in the Church, Apostles, Prophets*, "*Teachers,—miracles, gifts of healing, helps, go*-"*vernments, diversities of tongues*;" that, in the exercise of those offices and gifts, the Church might be supplied on all occasions, and might be built up in holiness and unity, according to the will and good pleasure of God: That as there could be no ground to look abroad for any thing necessary for the good of the Church, or for the spiritual benefit of any of its members, so they who possessed these offices and gifts were to consider them as intended and bestowed for the good of the whole; that therefore they ought to cooperate together in unity, as members of the same body, having no separate interest, but all contributing to the same end—the common benefit and advantage of the Church: That the people too who were under them in the Lord, should consider these offices and gifts as the endowments and manifestations of the one Holy Spirit of God for their benefit; and should reverence and submit to them, as the means of their

growth in grace, and in all heavenly virtues, and not to make them the occasions of schisms and party divisions in the Church, by preferring some Ministers on account of the great gifts they possessed, and despising others as persons of low and mean attainments.

NOR does the Apostle undervalue these gifts, and thereby endeavour to take off the attention of the Corinthians from them. He only cautions them against making divisions in the Church by preferring some Ministers to others, because they supposed they held the most eminent gifts, and were therefore most highly in favour with God. —He considers all those gifts to be divers manifestations of the presence and power of the same Holy Spirit, and therefore to be good in themselves, and most earnestly to be desired; but yet not for their own sake, or for the sake of the honour and influence that attended them, but for the common good of the Church. "*Covet earnest*-"*ly*," saith he, "*the best gifts, and yet shew I un*-"*to you a more excellent way*." A more excellent way than what?—A more excellent way than coveting earnestly the best gifts, on account of which they were ready to fall into animosities and schisms. And that way was *Charity*—that charity which is the bond of perfectness—which preserves the peace and unity of the Church under all possible circumstances.

THIS Charity he prefers before all other gifts and graces; before the most eloquent and popular preaching, even the speaking with the

tongues of men and of angels; before the gift of prophecy; before the understanding of all mysteries, and all knowledge; before that faith which could remove mountains; before liberality to the poor, even to the expenditure of all a man possessed; before martyrdom at the stake for the religion of Christ—All these, he saith, without Charity, are nothing, and shall profit a man nothing.

He then entereth on an enumeration of the qualities and properties of Charity, every one of which is directly contrary to their practice, who, on any account, make divisions and discords in Christ's Church. Such people never *suffer long* what they dislike, however good it may be in itself; nor endure Ministers whom they disapprove, however worthy their characters may be: They are so far from being *kind*, that they generally prosecute their opposition with great ill-will and resentment: They *envy* those who are above them in station and abilities, and whom they can reach in no other way: They *vaunt* of their own gifts, and perfections, and holiness, and are *puffed up* with pride and self-conceit, so as to *behave* themselves *unseemly* and undutifully to those whom God hath set over them in the Church, whom they ought to honour, and to whose judgment, at least in things lawful, or dubious, or indifferent, they are in duty bound to submit: They *seek* their *own* honour, and the interest of their party in every thing, which, in their account, is always the honour of God, and the interest of the true religion: With those who

accord not with them, they are *easily provoked*, not only to *think*, but to *speak evil* of them, by raising or propagating reports of their principles and conduct, which, if not directly false, are yet uncandid, and unfair, and therefore dishonest. If, through human infirmity, or great provocation, or violent and sudden temptation, a person of whom they have not a good opinion should fall into any grievous crime, they rejoice at it, and spread the report, and exaggerate the circumstances; thereby shewing that they do *rejoice in iniquity*, and not *in the truth*; because they think the iniquity of others is a foil to their greater holiness, and makes it appear the more conspicuous to the world. Instead of *bearing all things* from those who do not adopt their principles and particular mode, but are disposed to live in unity with the Church, and in the bond of peace to serve God, and work out their salvation, they will bear nothing which contradicts their views and practice—they will *believe* nothing good of them, and *hope* nothing good from them:—And all this because they want that Charity which is the *bond of perfectness*—the principle of unity in the Christian Church.

For the truth of these remarks I can boldly appeal to history and observation, as far, at least, as our own Church is concerned. And in order to strengthen the remark, that the want of Charity, and of its necessary attendants, humility and meekness, have been the occasion of all the schisms and separations from the Church, let it be remembered, that they have been generally

made by people of otherwise good characters, many of them of ingenuity and abilities—great professors of honesty of heart and of upright intentions—of most remarkable tender consciences, except where the peace and unity of the Church were concerned, and there they do not seem to have had any conscience at all, but to have regarded their own opinions and notions as constituting *the Church*, and their principles as *the cause of God*; and if the peace and unity of the Church were lost in pursuing them, they were lost in a good cause—in fighting the battles of the Lord. In short, they seem to have thought that peace and unity were of no consideration when they came in competition with their schemes and opinions; and, through the want of Charity and its concomitant virtues, humility and meekness, they treated them as matters of no estimation.

St. Paul concludes his discourse on Charity with again preferring it to all other gifts and graces—to prophesies, speaking with tongues, great knowledge, faith, and hope; because these are all imperfect in this life, and shall all fail with it; but Charity, which unites us to God's Church; and, through the Church, to God himself, who is Love, shall endure forever, and form the basis of happiness in heaven.

Nor did what this holy Apostle wrote to the Corinthians on this subject, drop from his pen as it were by accident, and to serve a present emergency. The same doctrine will be found

in various parts of his other Epiſtles. The time will not permit me to cite them; but I cannot omit to call the attention of every one who wiſhes for further ſatisfaction on this ſubject, to the fourth, and part of the fifth Chapter of his Epiſtle to the Epheſians, written, according to the Chronology of our Bible, five years after his firſt Epiſtle to the Corinthians—There he will find the ſame doctrine delivered, and in very ſimilar expreſſions.

THE ground from which this eminent Saint took his ſentiments on this ſubject is the very nature of our holy Religion, and the earneſt and importunate prayer which, in the true ſpirit of it, was made to the Almighty Father by our great High Prieſt, for his apoſtles and whole Church, when he inſtituted the Holy Euchariſt, and offered up his moſt ſacred Body and Blood, under the ſymbols of bread and wine, a ſacrifice of atonement to God for the ſin of the world. After having prayed for his Apoſtles, he ſaith, "*Neither pray I for theſe alone, but for them alſo* "*which ſhall believe on me through their word:* "*That they all may be one, as thou, Father, art* "*in me, and I in thee; that they alſo may be one* "*in us:——And the glory which thou gaveſt me,* "*I have given them; that they may be one, even* "*as we are one: I in them, and thou in me, that* "*they may be made perfect in one, and that the* "*world may know that thou haſt ſent me,*" that is by their loving one another, "*and haſt loved* "*them, as thou haſt loved me.*" Here the union between the Father and Chriſt—(I ſpeak

of his human nature)—between Them and the Apoſtles and believers; and between the Apoſtles and believers themſelves, is made to conſiſt in Love, ſpringing from the love of God towards us. And *if God ſo loved us*, this ſame Apoſtle hath taught us, *we ought alſo to love one another*. By Love, then, the whole Church of Chriſt is united together, and makes one body, one holy ſociety, one family, one kingdom. Hence, therefore, it will follow, that thoſe Chriſtians who are without love, have no real unity with Chriſt's Church. And again, that they, who break their union with Chriſt's Church, are deſtitute of that love which ſpringeth from a due ſenſe of the love of God, which gave Chriſt to be the Redeemer of the world.

IT has been already obſerved, that the Church of Chriſt is diſtinguiſhed by its government, its miniſtry or prieſthood, its doctrines or faith, its diſcipline or the manners of its members, and its ſacraments; becauſe they make it to be what it is—the *Church of Chriſt*. Having theſe marks, it may be eaſily found by thoſe who with unprejudiced minds ſeek for it. They make it like the light of heaven ſhining in the darkneſs of this world, which all may ſee who have eyes, and to which all will repair who love not the darkneſs of party, and ſyſtem, and error, more than the light of divine truth. Like *a city ſet on a hill*, it will attract the obſervation of all men; and they, who truſt in the ſtrength of the Lord Jehovah, will enter into it for protection and ſafety.

MUCH then does it concern all who profeſs Chriſt's holy Religion to maintain and cultivate that Charity which is the bond of perfectneſs; that, in the bond of peace and righteouſneſs of life, they may preſerve the unity of the *one Spirit* of God, in the *one Church* of Chriſt. Much alſo does it concern the Rulers and Governors to whom Chriſt hath committed his Church, to preſerve its government and miniſtry pure and uncorrupted; to retain and adminiſter its ſacraments in their ſimplicity, according to their true nature, as the holy ſcriptures, explained by the practice of the firſt Chriſtians, have taught and directed. All they, indeed, whom God, in his providence, ſhall call to the care and regulation of his Church, even of its external affairs—its peace, and honour, and proſperity in this world—ought duly to conſider the ſolemn and important buſineſs in which they engage, and carefully to maintain in full vigour and energy, the government, prieſthood, faith, ſacraments, and Chriſtian virtue, which their Lord and Maſter hath made ſo eſſential to their holy Religion. Greatly alſo does it concern all Chriſtian people, of all orders and degrees, to ſubmit to the government, to reverence the prieſthood, to preſerve the faith, to communicate in the ſacraments, and to live in that holy and obedient diſpoſition toward God, which Chriſt hath enjoined, and requires of them—Becauſe all theſe things are appointed for their benefit, to make plain to them the way of truth which leadeth to everlaſting life, and which God hath ordained for them to walk in, that they may be conformed to

the image of his Son. Wilful corruption in any of theſe points is wilful departure from the appointment of God—The conſequence needs not be told. They who depart from them, through ignorance, careleſsneſs, prejudice, intereſt, or party, do yet depart from the appointment of God, and are ſubject to his judgment: And he will judge them—in mercy, I hope, for he knoweth the ſecrets of all hearts, and what allowances to make for unavoidable ignorance, weakneſs of mind, and miſtakes of conſcience. His ſervants they are, and to him their Maſter they ſtand or fall.

THERE are two extremes into which men are apt to run in the management of the affairs of the Church. One is, to depreſs the government, and prieſthood, and lay them open to all claimants; to relax the doctrines and faith, according to the prevailing tenets of philoſophy and metaphyſics; and, I may add, according to the faſhionable ſyſtem of divinity—to explain away the ſacraments, till they become merely empty and vain ſhadows, without ſubſtance or reality—to weaken the obligations of holineſs which Chriſtianity lays on us; thereby encouraging people to reſt in decency of manners, according to the mode of the times, without regarding that ſelf-denial which reſtrains all tendencies to evil, or that mortification which ſubdues and keeps under the unruly appetites and deſires of body and mind. This conduct is utterly inconſiſtent with the proſperity of our holy Religion, and muſt be carefully avoided, leſt we make ſhip-

wreck of faith and a good conſcience, and betray the Church into a corruption of that truth, of which God hath made her the pillar and ground.

THE other extreme, to which I adverted, is the ſetting of the terms of admiſſion and continuance in the Church higher, and making them more rigid, than Chriſt and his Apoſtles have ſet and made them; thereby excluding perſons from the unity and communion of the Church, who by a fair and candid conſtruction of the rules given in Scripture have a right to be admitted to the fellowſhip and all the privileges of Chriſt's Religion. Thoſe Chriſtian profeſſors who inſiſt on having a pure Church in this world, and who, to obtain their point, have formed narrow and rigid and very particular rules for the faith and practice of their members—who admit into, and reject from their communion by a vote of their church members, not always making due allowance for the weakneſs of human nature, the violence of ſudden and unexpected temptation, or the nature of things indifferent, which a good Chriſtian may do or forbear without wounding his integrity, are on this ground to be condemned. They forget that Chriſt hath compared his Church in this world to a *net* caſt into the ſea, which encloſeth fiſhes good and bad:—to a *field*, in which tares grow with the wheat—That to ſeparate the good from the bad is the property of God only; becauſe he only knoweth the heart, and hath ability to make the diſtinction; And, that he hath reſerved this ſeparation to the judgment of the laſt day, when it will be effectually

made.—They conſider not, that the affairs of the bad and good are intimately mingled together in this world, and have abſolute dependence on each other, even as the roots of the tares are mixed and tangled with the wheat, ſo that it exceeds all human prudence to root out the former, without injuring the latter. They muſt grow together till the judgment of God ſhall decide upon them. Then ſhall Chriſt *preſent*, that is, take *it to himſelf a glorious Church, not having ſpot or wrinkle, or any ſuch thing; but holy and without blemiſh.*

BE it our care, Reverend and Honoured Brethren, to avoid both theſe extremes; that the Church of Chriſt be not injured by our negligence and remiſſneſs, on the one hand; nor by our rigidneſs and obſtinacy, on the other. But that, following the line which the ſcriptures of God have marked out for us, we may, under the conduct of the Holy and bleſſed Spirit, walk in the light of divine truth, and do all thoſe things which our duty and the intereſt of the Church of the Redemer ſhall require.

SHOULD any difficulty or uncertainty ariſe in the interpretation of ſcripture, it will be our part to look for aid, not to philoſophy, nor to metaphyſics, nor to any faſhionable ſcheme of divinity which may catch the attention, and beguile the judgment of ſuperficial and unſtable minds; but, to the practice of the Church in its firſt periods, before human inventions, and the luſt of power, and attachment to worldly in-

tereſt and honour had corrupted the faith and perverted the practice of Chriſtian men. The time would fail me to enumerate the advantages which ſpring from this conduct. One circumſtance, however, I muſt beg leave to mention; namely, that the firſt Chriſtians underſtood the language in which the New Teſtament was written; of many of them it was the mother tongue. The particular cuſtoms to which the Scriptures allude were familiar to them. They had ſeen and converſed, if not with the Apoſtles themſelves, yet, with Apoſtolic men, their ſucceſſors in the government of the Church, and in the preſervation of its faith. They could not, therefore, be ignorant of the doctrines and practice of the Apoſtles, nor of thoſe traditions which they had delivered to the Churches, not only by their *writings*, but by their *word*. In their time too Chriſtianity was in its infancy—the bleſſings which it proclaimed, the threats which it denounced, the hopes which it inſpired, were new to the world, and muſt, in a very extraordinary manner, have affected the minds of thoſe who honeſtly embraced it, and have kept them free from error and deluſion. They had, of courſe, the beſt opportunity to underſtand the minds of the Apoſtles concerning the government, and doctrines, and ſacraments of the Church; and they were ſecured, as far as human nature can be ſecured, againſt all temptations to betray or corrupt them.

THE beſt guard againſt the extremes which have been mentioned, and againſt every other

improper conduct in Chriſt's Church, is that *Charity* which is the *bond of perfectneſs*. Permit me, then, Reverend and Reſpected Brethren, to addreſs to you one ſhort ſentence of the holy author of the Text, *Follow after Charity*. The love of God, and of Chriſt, of his Church and members, will conſtrain the heart poſſeſſed by it to abide in the unity of the Church, to ſubmit to its government and miniſtry, and to hold its faith and ſacraments in their full energy and primitive ſimplicity—To be kind and tender hearted to all who, in the unity of the Spirit, keep the bond of peace, and walk in righteouſneſs of life; and to live in peace and unity with them. To thoſe who are without the Church, or who live wickedly in it, or who depart from its unity, it will ſtill extend its heavenly influence, as opportunity ſhall offer, endeavouring, in humility and meekneſs, to reclaim them from error in principle, and from wickedneſs of life; by holding up to them the light of divine truth, and explaining in love the principles of that unity of faith, and worſhip of the Son of God, in which all who profeſs to be his diſciples ought to live; truſting in the grace and mercy of God, that they will be reclaimed from error and wickedneſs, and brought into his holy Church and *walk worthy of the vocation wherewith they are called*, till they *come in the unity of the faith, and of the knowledge of the Son of God, unto perfect men, unto the meaſure of the ſtature of the fullneſs of Chriſt*.

TO this conduct the words of the Apoſtle immediately after the Text ought to impel us all:

And let the peace of God rule in your hearts, to the which ye are alſo called in one body; and be ye thankful—More than intimating, that without that Charity which is the bond of perfectneſs, our hearts are not prepared to receive, and to be guided by that peace of God to which we are called in his holy Church. How can he, who is not in unity with Chriſt's Church, be at peace with God whoſe Church it is; and who, being *love*, is the *author of Peace and lover of Concord?* How can he *be thankful* to God for having called him into his Church, received him to peace with himſelf, conferred on him ineſtimable privileges and precious promiſes, who ſtudies not to be at peace with his brethren, who are equally the children of God, and heirs of the ſame heavenly hopes with himſelf?

ABOVE all things, therefore, Reverend and Beloved Brethren, let us beg of God, from whom every good gift cometh, the aid of his moſt Holy Spirit, to illuminate our minds with the light of divine truth, to baniſh from them all partial and intereſted views and prejudices, to inſpire our hearts with the love of his holy name, and to pour into them that moſt excellent gift of Charity, the very *bond of peace and of all virtue, without which, whoſoever liveth is counted dead before him*. Grant this, heavenly Father, to every one of us, for thy Son Jeſus Chriſt's ſake: to whom, with thee and the Holy Ghoſt, be aſcribed honour and glory, majeſty and dominion, as it was in the beginning, is now, and ever ſhall be; world without end. *Amen*.

AN ADDRESS

FROM

JOHN BOWDEN, A. M.

TO

The Members of the Epiſcopal Church

IN

STRATFORD.

TO WHICH IS ADDED,

A LETTER

To the Rev'd Mr. James Sayre.

Pacem quærere debet & ſequi filius, a diſſentionis malo continere linguam ſuam debet, qui novit & diligit vinculum caritatis.
St. Cyprian de unitate eccleſiæ. Page 119.

He who would be one of the children of peace, ſhould ſeek and follow after it: He who is acquainted with the bond of charity, and is deſirous of maintaining it, ſhould refrain his tongue from the miſchiefs of contention.
St. Cyprian, Unity of the Church.

If, in this eſſay, we have offered any thing contrary to reaſon and chriſtianity (which always coincide) or any thing but what chriſtianity and reaſon plainly dictate; we deſire no other favor from thoſe, who underſtand both better than we do, than to make it plain to the world and to us, that what we have offered, is inconſiſtent with the principles of either.
But if, on the contrary, we have ſpoken only the words of truth and ſoberneſs, according to the principles of reaſon and the goſpel; and if upon examination, and applying to conſcience, it cannot be denied but we have done both, then the ſingle queſtion remaining will be, whether our requeſt ſhould be granted? Or if not, whether the goſpel and reaſon are of any farther uſe in an affair of this nature, than to ſhew men that truth, which they are not permitted to follow.
Candid diſquiſitions, p. 17, 18.

NEW-HAVEN: PRINTED BY T. AND S. GREEN.

Brethren,

IT gives me real concern to perceive, that the oppoſition to the *Proceedings of the General Convention*, held at Philadelphia in the year 1789, ſtill continues in the church of Stratford. So unreaſonable is this oppoſition in its principle, and ſo injurious in its effects, that I cannot refrain any longer from addreſſing you upon the ſubject. Take, I beſeech you, what I ſhall ſay, in good part. I do not mean to *offend*, but to *inform*. Excuſe the word *inform*—I do not uſe it from vanity, but from a conviction, that you do not view the ſubject in its true light—that you are not acquainted with the principles, and reaſonings, and facts, by which, the conduct of the biſhop and clergy of this *State*, in adopting the proceedings of the convention, may be triumphantly vindicated. You ought indeed to have preſumed, that they acted upon the beſt reaſons, and from the pureſt motives; for, let me ſay it, no body of clergy have ever given more clear and uniform proofs of their zeal for the church, than the clergy of Connecticut. I know them well—they are excellent men;—too honeſt to ſacrifice the church to any worldly motive whatſoever; and too well acquainted with its conſtitution, to be led into an error, unwittingly. You, I fear, have had them and their conduct held up in a very different light. God forgive thoſe who have done them this wrong!

The reaſons, which I have heard aſſigned for your not uniting with the *Proteſtant Epiſcopal Church* are, 1ſt. You do not approve of the alterations, nor indeed of any alterations in the liturgy. 2dly. You conſider the introduction of lay-men into an eccleſiaſtical council,

council, as inconsistent with the true principles of the christian church. And 3dly, by these innovations, (as you deem them) the church in this country has departed from the Church of England.—This, I believe, is a just statement of your objections—expressed, too, in as strong terms as you can wish. I will now fairly and fully, without evading any thing, take these objections into consideration; and I cannot but flatter myself, that the result of our investigation will be, by no means, favorable to your conduct.

Your first objection lies against the alterations, or against any alterations in the liturgy. In answer to this particular, I would observe,—That a number of learned, sensible, and judicious divines, aided by several laymen of abilities, all anxious to put the church in this country upon the best footing, deemed it expedient to make a few alterations in the liturgy of the church of England. These alterations are in general, the same that many of her best friends and most illustrious divines have pointed out. Kennet, Wake, Tillotson, Tennison, Stillingfleet, Sherlock, Burnet, Prideaux, Wetenhall, Whitby and several others, ‡ *recommended*, and had it been in their power, would have *made*, the alterations with which, you are finding fault. And, at this day, were it in the power of the *English Convocation*, that venerable body would pursue the same conduct. The deviations from the old book, are but few —so few, that I am persuaded, if the generality of church-men had no book in their hand during divine service, they would hardly perceive the difference. A few obsolete expressions are expunged—a few grammatical improprieties are corrected—a few repetitions are

‡ See proposals for amendments and improvements made in 1688 by the Lord Keeper, Bridgman, Lord Chief Justice Hale, Bishop Wilkins, Dr. Burton, &c. See also extracts from the proceedings of the Bishops and other divines at Westminster in 1641.

are omitted, and several fine prayers, and two excellent occasional offices are added. The congregations throughout the states are pleased, and have almost universally adopted the book. Even at first there was but little opposition; and *that little* has been daily declining, and is now almost extinguished:† The united voice of Episcopalians thro'out the continent, proclaim, *The Prayer-book of the Protestant Episcopal Church*, to be a pure, correct, and elegant form of devotion.

But it may be asked, "What necessity was there for any alterations? Was not the old book good enough? It was deemed so formerly, why should it not be deemed so now"? I answer, The old book is undoubtedly, an excellent one. It has been admired by the best judges of composition, the English nation hath ever produced.* It breathes a spirit of piety, and contains a profusion of beauties, which, no other liturgy does. But nevertheless, it is acknowledged by its best friends, that it is not intirely free from faults. Like a grand and venerable edifice, it challenges the admiration of beholders, yet discovers to a critical eye, a few defects and blemishes. These defects are not of a material nature, and, therefore, may be very well used. Before the separation of this country from Great-

† There are but two congregations in the United States that I have heard of, which prefer the old book---those of Stratford and Stamford; but the latter abhors the most distant idea of a separation.

* Sir Richard Steele in his Tatler, No. 56, p. 100, says, "It is the most proper form of words that were ever extant in any nation or language, to speak our own wants, or his power from whom we ask relief."---Dean Swift (whose judgment no man will dispute) in his letter to the Lord Treasurer Oxford, thus speaks, "As to the greatest part of our liturgy, there seem to be in it as great strains of true sublime eloquence, as are any where to be found in our language; which every man of good taste will observe in the communion service, *that* of burial, and other parts."---Bp. Newton, in his works, Vol. 4th, p. 227, 229, observes of the liturgy, "In the main, it is a most excellent service, but we must not look for perfection in any human composition. Some things perhaps might be changed for the better, some repetitions avoided, some phrases and expressions amended."---This was exactly the sentiment upon which, the *general convention* acted.

Great-Britain, there was no avoiding the uſe of them; but now that the church is independent, the neceſſity ceaſes. The clergy and laity have availed themſelves of this liberty, and I think, have uſed it with modera- tion, judgment and diſcretion. That they had a right to act for themſelves, cannot be denied—to deny it, would involve this abſurdity, That an independent church, does not poſſeſs a power to take ſuch meaſures, as ſhe deems proper to promote her own intereſts. The right being undeniable, the ſenſe of the majority muſt prevail. This is an acknowledged principle, both in church and ſtate; not to admit it, would diſſolve every free government upon the face of the earth.

On this head, I appeal to impartiality and candor, whether any thing more need be ſaid. Taking it for granted, that the reſult of ſuch an appeal, would not be unfavorable, I ſhall cloſe this point, with putting into the mouth of the biſhops, preſbyters and laity, met in general convention at Philadelphia, the apology, which, the rulers of the church of England made for themſelves, at the laſt review of the book of common-prayer—"Our general aim in this undertaking, was not to gratify this or that party, in any of their unreaſonable demands; but to do that which to our beſt underſtandings, we conceived might moſt tend to the preſervation of peace and unity in the church—the procuring of reverence and exciting of piety and devotion in the public worſhip of God; and the cutting off occaſion, from them that ſeek occaſion of cavil or quarrel againſt the liturgy of the church. And having thus endeavored to diſcharge our duties in this weighty affair, as in the ſight of God, and to prove our ſincerity therein (ſo far as lay in us) to the conſciences of all men, although we know it impoſſible (in ſuch variety of apprehenſions, humors and intereſts as are in the world) to pleaſe all; nor can expect that

men

men of factious, peeviſh and perverſe ſpirits, ſhould be ſatisfied with any thing that can be done in this kind by any other than themſelves; yet we have good hope, that what we have with great diligence examined and approved, will be alſo well accepted, by all ſober, peaceable and truly conſcienſcious ſons of the church."

This, their pious wiſh has been amply gratified. The trueſt—the moſt zealous ſons of the church, have approved and accepted the book of common prayer, with the alterations and amendments; by which, they have ſhewn that they are not only free from the prejudice, which, education and long habit are apt to create, but alſo, that they are not "factious, peeviſh and perverſe ſpirits, and are well ſatisfied with what has been done by others than themſelves."

But, perhaps, you will ſay, "We alſo could uſe the new prayer book as well as others, were it not for the authority, by which, the book is ſit forth. Lay-men, we conceive, have no right to ſet in convention with the clergy, to form a liturgy and canons. It is an encroachment upon the prieſtly authority—a wreſting from the rulers of the church, the Keys of the Kingdom of heaven—in ſhort, a ſubverſion of all order and authority in the church of Chriſt."

Theſe, my brethren, are ſtrong expreſſions; but no ſtronger than you are uſed to hear. I do not, however, deſpair of making it very evident, that they are words without meaning—that the caſe is intirely miſconceived;—and that, by condemning the influence of the laity in the epiſcopal church in this country, you alſo paſs condemnation upon the Church of England.

If the laity have no right to ſit in convention with the clergy, they muſt be excluded, either by reaſon, or by revelation. But is it unreaſonable, that lay-men ſhould have a voice in forming the prayers, which they are to offer to Almighty God, and the laws, by which,

they

they are to be governed? surely, you cannot say, it is unreasonable. Who has a right to force prayers *upon* them? To say, *thus* shall you address your Maker, and no otherwise? Who has a right to make laws *for* them?—to declare, *thus* shall you act, for it is our will and pleasure, that you should?—Certainly, this is not the language—these are not the dictates of reason. On the contrary, reason declares (and your conduct my Brethren puts the matter beyond debate†) that, in the last resort, the laity must be consulted. Let the prayers be ever so good, and the canons ever so judicious, the laity must be asked, whether they will receive them. There is no authority in this country, which can say,—You shall submit. Now, where is the difference between their having a negative *in* and their having it, *out* of convention? If they can reject in the one situation, why not in the other? yes, you may say, "We acknowledge, that at last, they *have*, and *must* have, a negative upon the proceedings of the clergy, but we think that they ought not to make a constituent part of a convention—mingle in the debates, and prevent the clergy from doing what they would wish." But, I beseech you where is the difference, if they can, *at last*, prevent the clergy from doing what they would wish? Evident it is, that they have no more power in the one case, than in the other. *Out* as well as *in* convention, they can give their opinion—they can insist upon alterations and amendments—they can finally reject. Turn the matter which way you will—view it in every point of light, and you will find, that it does not amount to so much as spliting of hairs, to allow them a negative in the last resort, and yet exclude them from an ecclesiastical council, where, they have not one degree more authority.

Now,

† Is it not surprizing, that the people of Stratford do not see, that by rejecting the new Prayer Book, &c. they are exercising the very power they are condemning? This is not the first instance where error has made men inconsistent.

Now, if reason does not exclude them, but on the contrary pleads for them, it cannot be supposed that revelation excludes them; for reason and revelation are never at variance. And, upon examination, we shall find this to be the case.

In order to determine this point, it will be necessary to recite the commission, which, Christ gave to his apostles. This commission was given at different times. Once in these words.—†"And Jesus came and spake unto them saying, All power is given unto me in heaven and in earth. Go ye therefore and teach all nations, baptizing them in the name of the Father and of the Son and of the Holy Ghost. Teaching them to observe all things whatsover I have commanded you: And lo, I am with you alway, even unto the end of the world." The other time in these words,‡ "Then said Jesus to them again, peace be unto you. As my Father hath sent me, even so send I you. And when he had said this, he breathed on them, and saith unto them, Receive ye the Holy Ghost. Whose soever sins ye remit, they are remitted unto them, and whose soever sins ye retain, they are retained." These, are the only sources of ministerial authority, in the church of Christ. Now the question is, what is implied in these commissions? By answering this question, we shall be able to determine, whether the laity are excluded from an ecclesiastical convention.

In the commission recorded by St. Matt. is implied authority to preach the gospel—"Go ye therefore and teach all nations:"—To baptize into the christian church—"baptizing them in the name of the Father and of the Son and of the Holy Ghost;" and by parity of reason, the other sacrament.—In the commission recorded by St. John is implied, authority to communicate the same power to others, which, Christ had

B com-

† St. Matt. 28—18, 19, 20. ‡ St. John 20—21, 22, 23.

communicated to them.—"As my Father hath sent me, even so send I you." His Father sent him with power so send others. His apostles therefore must have had the same power, otherwise they were not sent as Christ's Father sent him; nor could his promise to them in St. Matt. have been fulfilled—"Lo! I am with you always, even unto the end of the world."—Not with their persons, for *they* could not continue, but with their commission, *unto the end of the world*: Their commission must, therefore, be communicated by successive ordinations, *to the end of the world*. This commission also implies what is usually styled, "the power of the keys," that is, receiving into the church (which is called the Kingdom of heaven‖) by baptism, and excluding from it, by withholding the sacrament of the Lord's supper—the former expressed by "remitting of sins;" for baptism is administered for the remission of sins.†—The latter, by "retaining of sins;" for whosoever is duly and justly excluded from the communion of the church, is in a state of condemnation.—To give the whole ministerial authority in one view:—The commission implies, power to preach the gospel; to administer the sacraments of baptism and the Lord's supper, and to ordain the various orders of the clergy. This is the whole of the spiritual authority, left by Christ to his church—all besides is of a secular or temporal nature; that is, may be exercised without any commission. It requires no commission to make prayers and canons for the church, no more than it does for an individual to make a prayer for himself; For what are the prayers of the church, but the prayers of every individual both clergy and laity. All use them, why therefore should not all concur in framing them? All are governed by the Canons or Laws of the Church, why therefore should not all have a voice in

‖ Acts 2--38.
† St. Matt. 3. 2--13 c--33v--44v--52v. and various other places.

in making them? None, as appears by the commission, have a right to preach Christ's gospel, nor to administer Christ's sacraments, nor to ordain Christ's ministers, but those, to whom Christ has given authority: but every christian has a right to pray to Almighty God, and therefore, a right to *make* his prayers. If an exclusion of the laity had been designed by our Savior, the commission would either expresly, or by fair implication, exclude them; or there would be some intimation of it; in some other parts of scripture; but as neither is the case, what are we to infer but that Christ has left it to his church, to determine the matter upon principles of reason and convenience and expediency.

And as reason and revelation, do not forbid the interference of the laity in ecclesiastical affairs, where those affairs are not of a purely spiritual nature, neither does the church of England.* The inuflence of the laity in that church, is much greater than in ours. With them, as with us, the liturgy and canons could not be used, till they had the sanction of the people; or what is the same thing in Great-Britain, the sanction of the parliament. In this particular, both churches are equal; but in what follows, you will find the difference much in our favor.

In the Church of England, the exercise of ecclesiastical discipline, is too much restrained by the prerogative of the Crown. For although, every act of excommunication must originate in the bishop's court, yet an appeal may be made to the King in chancery, where the sentence of the spiritual judge may be annulled.† But with us, there lies no appeal from the bishop to the laity, but the sentence of the former is, as it ought to be, decisive.‖

A

* In 1640, A Committee was appointed consisting of ten Bishops and ten Earls to re-examine the Common Prayer--(candid disquisitions p. 245)
† Blackstone's Comment. vol. 1. p. 84 and 280 duod. edit.
‖ This is the case in Connecticut. How it is in the other states, I do not know.

A second instance, which proves the influence of the laity in the church of England, to be greater than in our church, is, That the King is considered by the laws of England, as the *supreme governor* of the national church. In virtue of this authority, he convenes prorogues, restrains, regulates and dissolves all ecclesiastical synods, or convocations.—Blackstone p. 278, 279.

This puts the well-being of the church, too much in the power of a lay-man.‖ For if abuses were ever so great—if corruptions affecting the very vitals of the church were to take place, the bishops and their clergy could not meet to apply a remedy. If, in defiance of the royal prerogative, they *were* to meet, their proceedings could not be carried into effect, as the church and state are so closely connected, that nothing can become a law of the *former*, till it has the sanction of the *latter*. Many able pens have wrote and proved to a demonstration, that this state of things, is inconsistent with the true and genuine principles of the christian church; but their labor has been in vain—so long as the church and state are connected, in all probability this evil will continue.—Here we have a manifest superiority—Our conventions can meet when they please—the rulers of the states claiming no authority to restrain them.*

A third instance of the power of the laity in England is, That the parliament, without the concurrence of the clergy, can alter the established religion, as was done in a variety of instances, in the reign of Henry 8th and his three children.—Blackstone. p. 161.

About

‖ "No society can subsist without meeting and consulting of their affairs, and giving orders, as occasion shall require: If one society cannot meet or converse together without the leave and licence of the other society; nor treat or enact any thing relating to their own society, without the leave and authority of the other; then that society subsists upon the mere will and pleasure of the other." Leslie's Works, Vol. 1. p. 608.

* In the kingdom of Sweden, the King leaves the church intirely free, as to the choice of her bishops, and all other ecclesiastical matters whatsoever. He intermeddles not at all. Ibid.

About twenty years since, (my memory will not furnish me with the exact time) a bill was introduced into parliament, to abolish the 39 articles. The bill did not pass; but *that* did not proceed from any idea of incompetency in the parliament. Nor were the clergy, as a body, consulted upon the business; for the convocation did not meet at the time ‡; nor could they with their utmost efforts, if they had made any, have prevented the design from being carried into effect. Even the bishops in the upper house, could not have hindred its passing the lords; for although in common style, they are distinguished from the temporal lords, yet they are not in effect, a distinct branch of that house. A majority of votes, although all the bishops should be in opposition, carries every point. Blackstone of Parliament.

A 4th instance which shews the superiority of our church to that of England, is, That the English clergy have it not in their power to choose their bishops. The king has the nomination to all vacant *sees*, and if the dean and chapter, do not elect the person nominated by the king, they are liable to the penalty of a præmunire.† B. p. 380.

From these particulars, it appears beyond all contradiction, that lay-men in the church of England, have more authority than with us; and that the bishops and clergy have less. The general opinion in this country has been, that the English bishops have too much authority. But it is no such thing: They have not.

‡ I believe, the convocation has not been suffered to meet for the last 50 or 60 years.

† This was not always the case in the church of England. There is a record in the hospital at Ledbury in Herefordshire, which mentions, that Hugh Foliot, bishop of Hereford, the founder of that hospital, was elected by the presbyters of the cathedral church of Hereford in October 1219, without letters from the King, written to the prejudice of there free election. And for a length of time after that period, the *conge d'eslire* was no more than a request to the clergy---the King besought them to lend a favorable and benign ear to his petition---ut huic petitioni me a favorem prebeant benignum. Leslie vol. 1. p. 628.

not, what is clearly and undeniably implyed in their office. Surely, I need not give any further proofs. One more, however, I will give. Bishop Newton, in his life written by himself, has these words, "The power of bishops is thought to be something, and it is really nothing."‖ But with us, their authority is very considerable, altho' it is not what it ought to be. In this state, the bishop has a negative upon the determinations of his clergy as the bishops of the primitive church had. How it is in the other states, I do not know; but if they have acted upon true episcopal principles, they have given their bishops the same power.§

These instances, I think clearly evince, (as has already been observed) that the influence of the laity in the church of England, is much greater, while the authority of the bishops and clergy, is much less, than in our church. Yet, you, my Brethren will not unite with us, because of lay-influence—you will not use the new Prayer Book, because it is set forth by the authority of both clergy and laity.—Strange inconsistency! Every time you go to church, you approve by your conduct, what you are daily condemning with your lips. You use a form of prayer, that was set forth by the authority of the laity, as well as of the clergy. See the 34th article, which delares, that the ceremonies and forms of worship, were ordained both by ecclesiastical and civil authority; for *that* is the meaning of the words, *ordained and approved ly common authority*, as is evident from the following part of the article, wherein a violation of these ceremonies, is called as well

‖ Posthumous works, vol. 1, p. 128.

§ It is to be hoped, that the next general convention will place the bishops upon their proper ground, that is, give them an absolute negative. As the chief ministers in Christ's church, to whom, he principally looks for the purity of the faith, and the due exercise of discipline in their respective districts, they ought to have this power. They cannot otherwise be answerable to the great Head of the church. And that they are answerable, will appear very evident from St. Paul's epistle to Timothy, and the 2d and 3d Chapters of the Revelations; and this was the universal sentiments of the primitive fathers.

well *offending against the common order of the church, as hurting the authority of the civil magistrate.* Nor were this, and the other acts of parliament respecting the church, passed, merely to countenance and aid her in her decisions, but they are acts of authority, implying *a negative*, upon all her determinations—acts, whose language is, You shall not so much as meet to regulate your own affairs without our permission; and when you have obtained it, your decisions shall have no force, till we give it to them.—Pray, have the laity in our church, more authority than this?

But perhaps, you will say (for distinctions without any difference must be made, when answers cannot be given) "this authority of the laity in the church of England is mere usurpation—it never was granted, nor is it now acknowledged to be legal by the clergy. They indeed submit to it; but it is submission by force."—It is of no consequence to the argument in hand, whether the laity in England obtained their authority by usurpation, or by compact:‡ The origin of their power I have nothing to do with: The facts are as I have stated them; whoever therefore, is a member of the church of England, is the *subject* of lay-authority—whoever uses the common Prayer Book does it, at least, as much upon the authority of the laity, as of the clergy.—Now, my Brethren, What more is required of you by the *Protestant Episcopal Church*?

"All this *may be*, but still we choose to adhere to the church of England; because we were born and educated

‡ The Rev. Mr. White, in his masterly defence of the church of England against the objections of the *dissenting Gentleman*, observes, "As the state by its terms of alliance with the church, has undertaken to protect it, it is not fit that the church should make, either in doctrine, discipline or worship, any essential determinations or alterations, and impose them upon the people without the approbation and concurrence of the state. For then the state would be engaged to protect what it does not perhaps approve---to protect a society quite different from that, the protection of which, by the original convention was undertaken for." If this is the case, there is an end of the above distinction. See also Bp. Warburton's Alliance of church and state; and a consecration Sermon by A. Bp. Synge.

educated in that church; and because we believe her to to be the best church in the world."—If you *could* adhere to the church of England, I am very certain, that the clergy would have no objection to it; for they themselves *would*, if they *could*. But this is impossible: The church of England *does* not—*cannot* exist in this country. By making this appear, you will, I think, be deprived of every shadow of a plea for your present conduct.

It is an essential principle in politics, That the government of an empire, extends to all its parts. Some particular parts, from situation, from distance, from the terms of original settlement, or from other causes, may be favored with privileges, or exemptions in some cases; but the fundamental laws of the government and its authority, must be co-extensive with the empire itself; and any part which ceases to be subject to that authority, ceases to be a part of that empire. Thus it is with the United States of America, in regard to Great-Britain.—In like manner, the laws and government of a church, must extend to all the parts of that church. Particular privileges, or exemptions, may take place in this, as in the former instance. But when any branch of a church ceases, in the last resort, to be subject to the authority of that church, that branch immediately becomes independent. This was the case of the episcopal church in this country, at the treaty of peace. The laws and government of the church of England do not extend here;—the English bishops do not claim any authority here; but if they did, they could exercise none. Now, it would be an absurdity to say, that our church is a part of the church of England, when her laws and government do not extend to *us*—as great an absurdity as to say, that the United States are a part of the British empire, when its laws and government do not extend to *them*. The same

reason which makes the state independent, makes the church also, viz. A freedom from dominion. If this is not so, it will be impossible to form an idea of any government whatsoever.

"But may we not say, That we are of the church of England, because we use the liturgy of that church?" I answer 1st, You do not use the liturgy of that church. You omit part of it—the prayers for the king and royal family and parliament and nobility are omitted—the service for the 1st of January, the 29th of May, the 25th of October and the 5th of November, are all omitted. The *Canons* of the church also, you do not observe; for the greater part is not applicable to your situation; nor are several of the articles. It will be no answer to say, That you are obliged to do so. This, on the contrary, confirms the position, That you are not of the church of England, because you cannot possibly comply with her laws and obey her government.

But 2ndly. If you *were* to use the *common prayer* just as it stands without a tittle of alteration, *that* would not make you of the church of England. The principle of union, does not consist in the use of the same liturgy, but in a subjection to the same laws and government. Were the different dioceses in England to use different liturgies,§ they would still be members of the national church. On the contrary, although they use the same liturgy, if they were not subject to the same laws and government, they would be so many distinct, independent churches. The church of Russia (if I am not mistaken) uses the same liturgy with the Greek Church; but does not acknowledge any subjection to the patriarch of Constantinople. The analogy between them is very great; but still they are distinct churches.

C 3dly.

§ That was the case in a great measure formerly.---In the preface to the book of common prayer are these words,---"And whereas heretofore there hath been great diversity in saying (that is praying) and singing in churches within this realm---some following Salisbury use, some Hereford use, and some the use of Bangor, some of York, some of Lincoln; now from henceforth all the whole realm shall have but one use."

3dly. The church in Stratford, can have no pretentions to the title of the church of England. That church is under the immediate inspection of bishops; but you my Brethren, are not under the inspection of any bishop upon earth. You are indeed, in the orders of your minister, *episcopal*, but in your government (if you have any) you are congregational. Thus, in order to avoid lay-authority, you exert it in a high degree—In order to shew yourselves staunch churchmen, you become almost Independents; for you have to take but one step more to be *complete*, and that is, to ordain your next minister by the imposition of your own hands.

4thly. In your conduct towards the Protestant Episcopal Church, you act in direct opposition to the rulers of the church of England. They, both civil and ecclesiastical, have acknowledged our right to act for ourselves—the English Bishops have made no objections to lay representation—have found no fault with the alterations in the Prayer Book; but on the contrary, have declared by their consecrating bishops for us, that they consider ours as a sister-church—apostolical in every material part of her constitution, and pure in her doctrines and worship. If you have no respect for the wisdom of the bishops and clergy and laity, who sat in convention at Philadelphia—if you think, that you are better acquainted with the constitution of the church of Christ, than they are—at least, pay a little respect to the opinion of the rulers of the church of England. Do not by your conduct, tell *them*, as you have told *us*, " that you think yourselves wiser than they are, nor condemn *them* for holding ecclesiastical communion with *us*, by your refusing to do so. Be at least consistent—either condemn us both, or favor us both with your approbation; for to common apprehensions, it cannot appear any great proof of wisdom to approve of them, and condemn us, while *we* and *they* hold communion.

Thus,

Thus, I think, it appears very evident, that you *are* not, because you *cannot* be of the church of England; and as you *were* a part of the Church of Connecticut, but do not now acknowledge yourselves to be so, (as your whole conduct evinces) it follows, that you are in a state of schism—separated from your bishop, to whom you *once* paid, and *now* owe canonical obedience. Whether this is a sin or not, we shall proceed to inquire.

It is acknowledged by all protestant writers, that every schism is not sinful. When the terms of communion required by a church, are plainly contrary to the law of God, it becomes a duty to separate from that church. Upon this ground, the separation of the protestants from the church of Rome, is justified. But what sinful terms of communion, are required of you, my Brethren? You acknowledge, that there is nothing in the new-prayer book, but what a good christian may use. Is it then sinful, to allow laymen to concur in making the prayers which they are to use, and the canons, by which, they are to be governed? If it is, point out the law transgressed thereby; for " Sin is a transgression of the law, and where there is no law, there is no transgression." If Christ, or his apostles have forbidden it, you are right; or, if laymen are evidently excluded by the spiritual commission, you are right; but it has been shewn, beyond all reasonable contradiction, that neither the one, nor the other is the truth. What then is your situation? I must speak the conviction of my mind.—You are in a state of sinful schism. You have, without any cause, separated, if not *in words*, certainly *in deed*, from your bishop. How great a sin this is, the scripture and all antiquity will inform you. Schism is in the church, what rebellion is in the state—an opposition to lawful authority, which ever *has* been, and ever *will*

be

be a ſource of contention, hatred, malice, tumult, wars and bloodſhed. Well then might our Savior, when he was about to be crucified, pray to his heavenly Father, not for the apoſtles alone, but for them alſo that ſhould believe in him through their word. "That they all may be one, as thou Father art in me, and I in thee, that they alſo may be one in us, that the world may believe that thou haſt ſent me."† Well might St. Paul warn the Epheſian converts, to keep the "unity of the Spirit in the bond of peace. One body and one Spirit, even as you are called in one hope of your calling—one Lord, one faith one baptiſm, one God and Father of all."‖ And how pathetically does the ſame apoſtle exhort again to the ſame thing, by all the endearments, which, chriſtianity affords? "If there be therefore any conſolation in Chriſt, if any comfort of love, if any fellowſhip of the Spirit, if any bowels and mercies; fulfil ye my joy, that ye be like minded, having the ſame love, being of one accord, of one mind."¶ Again: "Now I beſeech you, Brethren, by the name of our Lord Jeſus Chriſt, that ye all ſpeak the ſame thing, and that there be no diviſions among you, but that ye be perfectly joined together in the ſame mind, and in the ſame judgment."§ And how vehemently do the ancient fathers cenſure ſchiſmatics, and exhort to unity and brotherly love. Hear Ignatius, the diſciple and intimate friend of St. John. In his Epiſtle to the Magneſians, he exhorts both preſbyters and deacons and lay-men to "reverence their biſhop and to do all things in godly peace and concord—their biſhop preſiding in the place of God—the preſbyters as the council of apoſtles, and the deacons as the miniſters of Chriſt." In his epiſtle to the Trallians, he exhorts, "Let nothing by any means be done without the biſhop---ſubject yourſelves to the college of preſbyters---let all of you reverence the deacons;

† John 17--21. ‖ Epheſians 4 c. 3, 5, 6 v.
¶ Philipians 2 c. 1, 2 v. § 1 Cor. 1 c. 10 v.

deacons; without theſe no church is named." Afterwards, having cautioned them to beware of hereſies and hereticks, he adds, "And ſo ye will, whilſt ye are not puffed up, and are not ſeparated from God, Jeſus Chriſt, nor from the biſhop. He that is within the altar is pure: But whoever does any thing without the biſhop, his conſcience is defiled." In his epiſtle to the Philadelphians, having cautioned them againſt diviſions, he adds, "Whoever belongs to God and Jeſus Chriſt, is with the biſhop; and they, who repent and return to the unity of the church, ſhall be God's.—Be not deceived my Brethren, if any man follows one who divides the church, he ſhall not inherit the Kingdom of God." Again, "When I was with you, I cried out and ſpoke with a loud voice—Adhere to the biſhop, the college of preſbyters and the deacons; which ſome have thought to be ſaid by me, from my foreſight of the ſeparation, which hath happened ſince that time. And he for whoſe ſake I am in bonds, is my witneſs, that I know it, not from men, but the Spirit proclaimed theſe things ſaying—do nothing without the biſhop—keep your bodies as the temple of God—love unity, fly diviſions." A little afterwards he adds, "That God would forgive the ſchiſmatics, provided they repented and returned to the unity of God, and the council of the biſhop."

It is needleſs to give you any more quotations. A volume of teſtimonies to the ſame purpoſe, might be produced from the primitive writers. They all breathed the ſame ſpirit, and ſpoke the ſame language. And will you, my Brethren, proceed in an error of ſuch pernicious conſequence? God forbid! Many of you, I ſincerely believe, have been brought into your preſent ſituation, without knowing whether you were led. But the caſe has been now fairly and fully ſtated. Conſider it, I beſeech you, as in the fear of God. Take no ſtep, that will finally and irrevocably ſeparate you, from

from the *Proteſtant Epiſcopal Church.* Seriouſly conſider the guilt and the conſequences of ſuch a meaſure. The guilt has been juſt demonſtrated, and I will now conclude this addreſs, with pointing out the conſequences.

1ſt. You will become the determined enemies and oppoſers of the church in this country, and the church of you. This will of courſe produce hatred, variance, and a perpetual ſcene of diſpute and contention. Read the hiſtory of the Arians, Novatians, Neſtorians, Monothelites, Donatiſts, and others among the ancients; and of the various ſects of diſſenters from the church of England among the moderns, and tremble at the effects of ſchiſm.—For my own particular, when I caſt my eyes upon the page of hiſtory, and obſerve the horrible conſequences of this ſin, I cannot but ſubſcribe to the opinion of St. Cyprian, that "even martyrdom will not expiate a crime of ſo deep a dye." Men may if they pleaſe plead honeſty and good intention in excuſe—the ſame plea I ſuppoſe might have been made by Guy Faux when he was laying a train to blow up the Britiſh parliament, and by Queen Mary when ſhe was butchering the proteſtants. Honeſty will not reſtore peace to the church, when her peace is broken, nor good intention heal diviſions, when diviſions are made. Honeſty hath tranſgreſſed the great law of chriſtian unity, and brought miſchief and miſery upon the church; and we know who hath ſaid, Woe unto that man by whom the miſchief cometh.†

2ndly. You muſt become a *congregational* ſociety; otherwiſe, it will be impoſſible to provide a ſucceſſion of

† If we examine eccleſiaſtical hiſtory, we ſhall find, that theſe honeſt, good men (as they are called) have been the authors of almoſt all the miſchiefs which the Church of Chriſt has ſuffered, in every age. The honeſty of Novatian, in the 3d century, produced a miſerable ſchiſm in the church--the honeſty of the enthuſiaſtic Baptiſts, filled Germany with confuſion and bloodſhed in the 16th century---the honeſty of the various ſects of diſſenters in the laſt century in England, almoſt extinguiſhed the proteſtant religion. Whenever I hear of a ſchiſm, I take it for granted, that very honeſt, good ſort of men, are at the head of it.

of miniſters. No clergyman in the United States, who has any reputation, will accept a call to be your paſtor; for their is not one, I am ſatisfied, who approves of your conduct. And as to the idea which ſome entertain, that a clergyman may be obtained from England, it is hard to conceive, how that idea could have entered into any man's mind. Can you make it worth the while of an Engliſh clergyman, to croſs the water to be your rector? You know, you cannot. "But perhaps the ſociety for propagating the goſpel, or the Britiſh government will aſſiſt us." The *former*, have more miſſions of their own to ſupport, than they can well bear. But if they had not, their charter precludes them from maintaining miſſionaries in foreign dominions, and *that* they declared was the reaſon of their withdrawing their bounty from this country. And as to the Britiſh government, you may either uſe the old book, or the new book, or the maſs-book, or the Turkiſh alcoran, for any thing they care about you.—Some people, my Brethren, delight in viſions; but they are not viſions of the Lord, but of folly and deluſion.

Laſtly. Your congregation, in time, will melt away—Some will not join in ſuch extravagancies, but leave you, and others will ſettle in total indifference, or become Deiſts and deſpiſers of all religion. And thus if cauſes produce their natural effects, will end the epiſcopal church in Stratford.

I have now, my Brethren, fully and faithfully laid before you, your true ſituation. As I have no motive in addreſſing you, but your good, and the good of the church, take kindly, I entreat you, what I have ſaid, and weigh it ſeriouſly and conſcientiouſly. And the reſult will be, I have good hope, that you will return from whence you are fallen, and that uniting your hearts and your endeavors with us, you will ſtrive earneſtly to promote the peace and honor and happineſs of the *Proteſtant Epiſcopal Church in America.*

TO THE READER.

THE foregoing address was written four months ago, and would have been then published, had not some of the clergy thought (from the accounts they had received) that Mr. Sayer would certainly quit Stratford; and then, the people would, no doubt, return to their duty. I was of a different opinion; but I submitted to the judgment of others. What has now brought the address *to light (at least sooner than it would have been) is the following circumstance.—A short time since, I dropped out of my pocket a letter from Bishop Seabury addressed to me, which was picked up and put into the hands of Mr. Sayre. This letter, (in which, the* address *happened to be mentioned) Mr. Sayre was so* gentlemanly *as to read in the publick Church to his Congregation. The matter being now known, I got a Gentleman to read the* address *to the Congregation on Sunday the 4th inst.—the day appointed for determining the question, Whether they would unite with the Protestant Episcopal Church or not. Notwithstanding the arguments contained in the* address, *They voted to continue in the old way.---A small specimen of the methods used to lead this congregation into their present unhappy situation, is, with the utmost fidelity, exhibited to the public view, in the following letter to the Rev'd Mr. Sayre. The spirit also of that gentleman, and his disregard to the peace and unity and authority of the church, are specified with the strictest regard to truth.*

J. Bowden.

Stratford, March 13th, 1792.

Rev'd Sir,

IT gives me no little uneasiness, that I am by my situation and an unforeseen concurrence of circumstances, unavoidably led into a public controversy; yet it affords me some comfort to think, that those who know my disposition, and the unhappy state of things in this church, will be convinced that it is not of my seeking; but that the obligation which every Clergyman is under, to oppose error and schism when persevered in with obstinacy, is the only motive that induces me at this time to address you. This controversy, seems naturally to fall upon me, from being upon the spot, where I have seen with my own eyes, and heard with my own ears, with what spirit and in what manner, you have conducted yourself in this affair. Shocking indeed has been your behavior: insomuch that, for the honor of christianity, I could wish it were prudent to pass it over in silence. But I am fully convinced that it is not prudent—that the good of the church and the honor of the clergy, render it highly expedient that I should hold you up, in your true colors, to the public view.

I set out in this business with this great advantage—It is well known in Stratford, and by many who do not live here, that I did not come to this place with any prejudices against you; but on the contrary, with those sentiments of regard for you, which a long intimacy would naturally cherish. Nay, you yourself know, that to enjoy the society of your family, was my principal reason for coming here. I knew indeed before I returned from the West-Indies, that you did not like the alterations in the prayer-book, nor some things in the constitution of the church: but it never entered into my mind, that you could have

gone to ſuch an extravagant length, as to break off all eccleſiaſtical communion with your brethren, and to have formed a plan to ſeparate this church from the dioceſe. I had been here but a few days, when I perceived what a miſtake I had made; but there was no retracting. I therefore determined to conduct myſelf in ſuch a manner, that you ſhould not have ſo much as a ſhadow to catch at. We had frequent and lone debates, and for ſome time, they were friendly enough. Theſe debates however, were always commenced by yourſelf; I was really forced into them; for you well know, that I could not when I firſt returned, ſpeak but with great difficulty. Yet you have harraſſed me with the ſubject beyond all bearing; of which, I ſeveral times complained to a particular friend of yours. Oft times have I ſat ſilent in your own houſe, without ſaying a word—not becauſe I was at a loſs what to ſay, but becauſe I was weared out, and was very unable to ſpeak. All this while I went to church, and the ſecond Sunday after my arrival, at your requeſt, aſſiſted you at the communion. But before the next communion, you told me plainly, in the houſe of the Rev'd Mr. Clarke, his father being preſent, that you ſhould not conſider me any longer as a brother, if I perſevered in my ſentiments. [This was high and dictatorial enough!] If I remember right, I laughed at you; for I could not really conceive, that you poſſeſſed ſuch a wretched, narrow ſoul, as to threaten in earneſt to break off all eccleſiaſtical communion, and all friendſhip with me, becauſe I happened not to think as you did—in matters too, which, if they are even wrong, are no ways material. I ſtill continued to go to church, and as I was not able to officiate, *that* was the reaſon, which, in the ſimplicity of my heart, I gave when aſked, why I did not preach. But the next communion ſhewed, that my weakneſs was not the reaſon of your never expreſſing a wiſh, that

that I would make a trial to deliver a ſhort ſermon, or take ſome part of the ſervice. For (hear it reader with aſtoniſhment!) I was not aſked to aſſiſt you in delivering the elements, but was obliged to receive it myſelf, out ſide of the rails, with the laity. I believe, moſt clergymen would not have ſubmitted to this groſs inſult, but would have taken their hat, and gone out of the church. I ſuppreſſed all improper emotions upon ſo ſolemn an occaſion, and received the ſacred elements, I can truly ſay, with charity for you and all mankind. After this, I believe every man living would ſay, that I ſhould have done right, never to have put my foot in the church again. Yet I continued to go, and even a ſecond time to receive the *ſacred ſymbols* in the ſame humiliating ſituation. This ſecond inſult determined me, but without any bitterneſs againſt you, never to put it in your power to treat me ſo again. I accordingly withdrew myſelf intirely from your communion, and by degrees from your church. Still, however, I went as uſual to your houſe, even after you had almoſt ceaſed coming to mine; till at length, ſhewing me in the plaineſt manner, that you did not deſire my company, I ſpared you the pain of all further viſits from me.—This Sir, is ſuch a faithful ſtate of facts, that I believe you will not venture to deny it. If you ſhould, I have evidence ſufficient, even among your friends, to confirm evey part of it.

I will make no comments upon theſe tranſactions; but will leave the reader of this letter, to form ſuch an opinion of this part of your conduct, as he may think proper.

Upon my firſt arrival at Stratford, ſome perſons expreſſed great ſatiſfaction at it,—as they thought I was the moſt likely perſon, from the friendſhip ſubſiſting between you and me, to convince you of the unhappy miſtake you had fallen into; or at leaſt, to moderate the violence, with which you conducted your oppoſition.

tion. I always replied, that I had but little hope of it; for I knew the obstinacy of your temper too well, to expect that you would yield to any point that you had once determined. I was very right in my opinion; for instead of moderating, my speaking to you, made you more violent. You really became so heated, and went so far beyond the bounds of all decency, in railing both from the pulpit, and on other occasions, against the protestant Episcopal Church, and against Bishop Seabury and his clergy in particular, that I really entertained serious apprehensions that you would lose your senses. I was not single in this apprehension—Others expressed the same fears to me. This *you* represented as zeal for the glorious cause of Christ, and I suppose some of your admirers took it for the same thing; but I never knew that a pure and genuine zeal for Christ, made men furious—made them railers, slanderers, and gross misrepresenters of truth and facts. I speak not rashly, but with the utmost soberness, and in the fear of that God, to whom I must give an account for every assertion in this letter.—You have said more than once, that the clergy of Connecticut were Judases—nay worse than Judas, for *he* got something for betraying his Master, but *they* got nothing. That is, in plain English, they are scoundrels and villains; for a man who betrays any temporal trust committed to him, is a villain—much more the man who betrays the sacred cause of Jesus Christ. At the head of this list of villains, stands bishop Seabury—the most conspicuous figure in the groupe. It is really enough to irritate the utmost meekness, to hear what torrents of abuse, you have poured out against that venerable prelate. You have represented him as an enemy to truth and religion—a man of no principle, who can be of any religion just as it suits him*—

a

* You told a clergyman, from whom I had it, that you expected *that great corpus* (meaning the bishop) would turn universalist yet. Good heaven! what rancour is this!

a Roman catholic, who is now striving with all his might, to introduce *transubstantiation* and *purgatory* into the church, in which design, he is aided and abetted by his clergy.—To be short—you have declared that the bishop and his clergy have subverted the church of Christ. (This I heard you utter from the pulpit.)

With a man, who has thus gone far beyond all decency, every soberminded person will think I am very idle in attempting to reason. Were you alone concerned, I should think so too. But as some, who have been led by you into the same fatal error, but who are well-meaning men, may, perhaps, if not at present, while their passions are warm, yet in some future day, when they shall become cool, be disposed to hear what may be said on the other side of the question; for their sakes, but much more to vindicate the clergy from your foul aspersions, I shall give the most irrefragable proofs of gross misrepresentation, as I have given above, of scandalous abuse.

You have been endeavoring for several weeks past, both from the pulpit and in private, to impress your people with an idea, that Bishop Seabury intends, by means of the *Scotch Catechism*, which has been lately re-published, to introduce into his diocese, the Romish doctrines of *transubstantiation and purgatory*. Now one would suppose, from the vehemence, with which, you have been insisting upon this point for so long a time, that you had some strong ground for your assertion, and that the Catechism did *plainly* and *professedly* teach these doctrines. Yet so far is this from being the case, that I do assert, (and will immediately give the proof) that there is not so much as a shadow to justify you in this shameless misrepresentation.

Every body knows, what transubstantiation means. When the priest consecrates the bread and wine, they, (in the opinion of the Romish church) immediately become the natural body and blood of Christ. Now what does the Scotch catechism say?—Question,—

" Does

"Does he (the priest) then do as Christ did? Answer. Yes; he takes bread into his hands, and breaks it. Q. What does that broken bread represent? A. The dead body of Christ pierced upon the cross. Q. What does he take into his hands besides? A. The cup of wine and water.* Q. What does that represent? A. The blood and water that flowed from the dead body of Christ upon the cross. [Observe, reader, the bread and wine *represent* the body and blood of Christ, but are not the things *represented* as transubstantiation absurdly implies.] Q. What does he do afterwards? A. He repeats our Savior's powerful words, This is my body, This is my blood, over the bread and cup. Q. What is the effect of these words? A. By them the bread and cup are made (not the *natural* body and blood of Christ as the church of Rome asserts, and as you want to have it believed; but as the catechism declares) authorative representations, or symbols of Christ's crucified body, and of his blood that was shed." Again, Q. "Do the bread and wine remain after consecration? A. Yes; they are not destroyed, but sanctified. Q. But are they not changed? A. Yes; in their qualities, but not in their substance. Q. Are they not made the body and blood of Christ? A. Yes; but the sacramental body and blood of Christ, not the natural." Q. Are they then bread and wine, and the body and blood of Christ at the same time? A. Yes; but not in the same manner. Q. How so? A. They are bread and wine by nature, the body and blood of Christ in mystery and signification. Q. How again? A. They are bread and wine to our senses, the body and blood of Christ to our understanding and faith. Q. And again? A. They are bread and wine in themselves, the body and blood of Christ in power and effect."—Thus, we have the most express and pointed testimony (at least as much so) against

* The Scotch, in conformity to the primitive church, mixes a little water with the wine; because our Savior consecrated the cup of blessing; which (say the Jews) was always mixed with water.

gainst the doctrine of *transubstantiation*, that is to be found in any system of divinity whatsoever.†—O Sir, Sir! What shall I say to you upon this occasion? If I could find any, the least circumstance to palliate your conduct, it should be readily admitted. But I can find none, Charity herself, which hopeth all things, can offer nothing in your favor.

Of a piece with this, is the other point relating to purgatory.—Purgatory, you well know, Sir, is a place of punishment, where, those who are not desperately wicked, are, according to the church of Rome, purified from their sins, and thereby made meet for heavenly happiness. But there is not in the Scotch catechism, a single expression that looks that way. The Scotch church believes as the whole primitive church *did*,‡ and as many modern divines *do*, That the happiness of the souls of departed saints, will not be perfect till the day of judgment, when soul and body being reunited, the righteous will receive their consummation and bliss in God's everlasting kingdom. Till *then* the souls of the righteous are happy in paradise, (or that part of *hades* appropriated to them) but not consummately so. The advocates for this opinion say very

† If the Scotch church teaches transubstantiation, the Protestant Episcopal Church in this county does so too. For the prayer of oblation in the new prayer book, was taken from the Scotch Communion Office.

‡ Clemens Rom. 1st ep. Corints. Justin Martyr. Dialogue against Trypho. p. 223. Ireneus adv. heres. c. 64 on St. Luke 16. also in his 5th book Chapr. 5. Tertulian de anima Chapr. 54. Against Marcion c. 34. Clemens Alex. Liber---Quis dives salutem consequi possit, Oxon 1683 p. 118. Origen 7th Homily upon Leviticus---26th Hom. upon Numbers St. Cyprian ep. 34th. Lactantius, Divine Inst. Lib. 7th c. 21st. Hilary Pictavien upon the 2nd Psalm. Gregory Nyssen. Lib. de hominis opificio ch. 22. Gregory Nasian. in laudem Casarii fratris Oratio. Basil the Great, upon Psalm 15th. Macarius Ægypt. Homily 22d. St. Ambrose de bone mortis Chap. 10th & C. 11th. St. Augustine Lib. 9. C. 3. and upon Psalm 36th and in other places. Aurelius Cassiodorus, de anima Chap. 19.---I presume this is sufficient to shew what the sense of the church was for the first 400 years after Christ.---I will now mention some distinguished modern Divines.---Calvin's Institutions, Chap. 25, Sect. 6. Bishops Bilson, Forbes, Taylor and Bull.---Mead, Perkins, Hammond, Thorndike, Sherlock (the father) Wall, Hicks, and many other illustrious divines of the church of England.---If Mr. Sayre did not know all this, he should have informed himself better---if he *did* know it, he should have been more *modest* than to accuse the brightest lights of the Christian Church both in ancient and modern times, of popery.

ry justly, that *the man* cannot be perfectly happy, till the soul and body are reunited ; for the body is as much a part of the man as the soul, altho' it is the inferior part. They observe also, that, by this sentiment, they avoid, on the one hand, the doctrine of two judgments, which has not the least countenance from scripture—(on the contrary, the scripture uniformly speaks of only one general judgment)—on the other hand, the uncomfortable doctrine of the sleep of the soul, into which some have run to avoid two judgments. The righteous, being in this imperfect state, the Scotch catechism asserts that it is the duty of christians upon earth, to pray that the departed saints in paradise, may be embraced by God's mercy at the last judgment, and *then* receive their consummation and bliss both in body and soul.† This is evidently the doctrine of the church of England; and you, Sir, never use her burial office without expressing that idea. Thus we pray—"that we, with all those that are departed in the true faith of thy holy name, may have our perfect consummation and bliss, both in body and soul, in thine eternal and everlasting glory, through Jesus Christ our Lord." Here, it is evident, that the departed saints are supposed not to have their perfect consummation and bliss as yet : and therefore, we pray

† S. Cat. Question. Does the communion of saints extend to the other world? A. Yes; the church upon earth, and the church in paradise communicate together, by mutually praying for each other. Q. Need we apply to the saints in paradise for their prayers? A. No; they know our dangerous condition here, and their charity wants not to be desired to recommend us to God. Q. Are there not likewise other reasons for our not desiring their prayers? A. Yes, there are several reasons; and in particular, we are not sure that they could hear us, were we thus to address ourselves unto them. Q. Why do we pray for them? A. Because their present condition is imperfect, and therefore capable of improvement, and because they are to be judged at the last day, and will then stand in need of mercy.

Altho' it is not my business to prove, that the saints in paradise will enjoy but an imperfect state of happiness, till the general judgment, yet to satisfy the reader I beg leave to refer him to a few texts of scripture. Rev. 20, 12. Matt. 7, 22, 23---8 c. 29 v. 13 c. from 24 to 31st v. John 12. 48. 14 c. 2, 3, 19, 20 v. Rom. 2. 16. Cor. 2nd ep. 5, 10. compared with Rom. 14 c. 10, 11, 12. Philip. 2. 16. Colos. 3. 3, 4 v. 1 Thes. 5. 23. 2 Tim. 1. 16, 17, 18. and Tim. 4. 7, 8. Heb. 11---39, 40. 1 Peter 1. 3, 4, 5, 7, 9, 13. 2 Peter 2. 9. Rev. 6. 9, 10, 11.

pray for *theirs* as well as for *our own*. Nay Sir, You never use the Lord's prayer, that you do not pray for the departed saints in paradise---"Thy kingdom come," implies not only, that the gospel of Christ may be extended *to* and embraced *by* all the nations of this world, but also, and perhaps principally, that the souls now in paradise, together with those who shall be alive, when the last trumpet shall sound, may be adorned with celestial and incorruptible bodies, and being presented before the throne of God and the Lamb, may be acquitted before the assembled hosts of heaven and earth, in these heart delighting words, "Come ye blessed of my Father, inherit the kingdom prepared for you from the foundation of the world." For this glorious period---for this consummation of bliss both in body and soul, the Scotch catechism says we *ought* to pray, the Church of England does *actually* pray, and also every Christian when he uses the Lord's prayer—And is this, Sir, the doctrine of purgatory?—Shame flush the cheek of that man who could from the sacred pulpit abuse a congregation with so gross a misrepresentation!

There is but one more instance of your misrepresentation among many I could name, that I shall take notice of.—You have represented the part Bishop Seabury acted at Philadelphia, as inconsistent with his former declarations; and you quote a *charge* delivered by him to his clergy at *Derby*. Unfortunately, I have not the *charge* by me; but I well remember the substance of what he said upon the point before us; for I have read it several times since. He declared, that the first *General Convention* which sat at Philadelphia, was not episcopal, but presbyterian; that therefore the prayer book and constitution which *that convention* formed, could not be received by any true Episcopalian—that the government of the Church was a fixed thing—that bishops were essential to that government, and that no power on earth had a right, in this

E particular,

particular, to alter it.—Now, reader, admire the candor and fairness of Mr Sayre!—In the *first general convention*, there were no Bishops, but the first new-prayer-book and constitution of an episcopal church, were formed by presbyters and lay-men—this was genuine presbyterian government, to which neither Bishop Seabury nor his presbyters would have submitted on any consideration. In the *last general convention*, which, the Bishop himself attended, there was an house of Bishops; the convention therefore, was episcopal. It was before this last convention, that the Bishop delivered his *charge* at Derby. And thus, *the single circumstance of time*, sets the Bishop at perfect consistency with himself, and shews that he has not deviated a tittle from his former principles.—And as to his saying, that the government of the church is unalterable, he evidently means, in the point of episcopacy, which he considers as essential to it; but not in those indifferent matters which must ever be regulated by the circumstances of time and place, and a variety of other considerations. These, in their nature, *are* alterable; and it is only *in these*, that the episcopal church in this country *has* altered. She would have shewn neither sense nor prudence, if she had not done so; and yet, what a dreadful outcry have you made, even to the loss of peace and unity, and charity, against a few, circumstantial deviations, which, every principle of reason and expediency pointed out.—Many are the instances of wretched bigotry, which ecclesiastical history affords us; but I cannot, at present, recollect one to be compared with this. I have ever considered bigotry, as unworthy of a rational being, and utterly inconsistent with the exalted principles of Christianity. It contracts and debases the human heart, and leaves no room for the noble principles of liberality and candor, to dilate and play. Bigotry is a determined enemy to truth, as it restrains private judgment,—confines our regards

regards to a party, and by limiting moderation and mutual good will, tears up charity by the roots. It is, in short, the very essence of popery (of which, you affect to be so dreadfully afraid*) and often times carries those who are governed by it, into the bosom of that corrupt church.—May God preserve all sincere Christians from its baneful influence!

Before I conclude this letter, I must produce a quotation from your "candid narrative" of the proceedings at New-Port—not to shew that you are a roman catholic, but that there is ten times more the *appearance* of it, from that quotation than there is of Bishop Seabury's being one, from the Scotch Catechism. In the 1st and 2nd pages, you write thus, "In a sermon which I preached in Trinity Church on the 30th of March 1788, upon these words (Matt. 5. 30.) For I say

* Mr. Sayre seems, at present, to be at a loss to determine, whether the popish or mahometan religion will prevail in this country. On Sunday the 4th of this month, (the fatal day when this congregation voted that they *would continue in the old way*) Mr. Sayre, after having very earnestly exhorted them to beware of popery, told them that he must also warn them against another religion, mahometanism, which, he apprehended, the *free-masons* were about to introduce.---Numerous are the visions of that gentleman. He told a person of note in his church, from whom I had it, That he (Mr. Sayre) conceived himself to be one of the *witnesses* spoken of in the Revelations.---I have heard him say, that he was convinced the 2d apocryphal book of Esdras was an inspired book; and in a conversation upon the subject with a gentleman in this place, he observed, that he could perceive in Esdras, a prophecy of the late defeat of the continental army by the Indians.---He has often from the pulpit, (once I heard him myself) as well as in private conversation, declared, that he believed some dreadful event would soon befal the church in this country. Several other things of this kind have I heard *of* him; but as I cannot recollect authorities, I do not choose to mention them; yet I have no doubt of the truth of them, as they perfectly agree with "the gloomy habit of his soul."

A person of such a visionary turn, must of necessity, be an unstable man. Violent church of England man as he is *now*, insomuch that he cannot bear the least deviation from her, it is but a few years since, that he told me, he did not know but he should join the Moravians. [What a blessing would he have been to that peaceful people!]---*Now* he will not bear of any defects in the church of England---*formerly* he used to complain bitterly, that she had no discipline.---*Now* he is such a high Episcopalian, that he cannot bear to have laymen sit in an ecclesiastical convention, to concur with the clergy in forming prayers, which, the laity are to use, and *canons*, by which, they are to be governed; but a few years since, he was so much a presbyterian, that he declared to a lady in New-York, that there was not "twenty big apples difference between episcopal and presbyterian ordination."---Quo teneam vultus mutantem Protea nodo?

I ſay unto you, that, except your righteouſneſs ſhall exceed the righteouſneſs of the Scribes and Phariſees, ye ſhall in no caſe enter into the Kingdom of heaven." I took occaſion, when I came to treat of the laſt words of the text, *the Kingdom of heaven*, to ſay thus—For my own part, if I did not firmly believe, that the Church was the Kingdom of heaven—that a miniſter lawfully ordained by a biſhop, hands the forgiveneſs of ſins and eternal life from his maſter, who is both in heaven and upon earth, to every fit ſubject of baptiſm, when he baptizes that ſubject—that ſuch a miniſter has power to bind and loſe on earth; that is to forgive ſins or to retain them—to adminiſter a full pardon of ſins in abſolution, to the really penitent and believing—and that his regular exerciſe of the diſcipline of the Church, in admitting to the holy ſupper and excluding from it, was, to all intents, an admiſſion into the real and true kingdom of heaven, and an excluſion from it—I ſhould hold myſelf obliged, as an honeſt man, to tell my people, that they acted like blind and ignorant enthuſiaſts in building and conſecrating a Church and retaining a miniſter—that all the tranſactions in church, were only a more ſolemn ſort of theatrical exhibition, &c."

When you were told that ſome perſons, from that diſcourſe charged you with advancing the tenets of the Church of Rome, concerning abſolution, you tell us, —"I wondered that ſuch guarded expreſſions upon the ſubject had been ſo miſunderſtood." How much more may every mortal wonder, how you could ſee *tranſubſtantiation* and *purgatory*, where there is not the ſmalleſt appearance of theſe doctrines, but on the contrary where they are, in the cleareſt and moſt expreſs manner oppoſed.—Good God! what is man when under the influence of reſentment and paſſion! How incapable is he of forming a fair and juſt judgment!—He

He can ſee nothing as he ought---all is darkneſs before him.*

There is but one thing more that I ſhall attend to, and *that* reſpects myſelf. I have been informed that you have ſaid, That my view in oppoſing you, is, to get poſſeſſion of this church.§ I will not heſitate to declare, that you have not the ſlighteſt conviction of my being actuated by ſuch a vile motive; however convenient you may find it, to throw out ſuch an idea among your adherents. For, in the firſt place you know very well, that I made up my mind upon the ſubject, of the proceedings of the *general convention* at a time, when I did not know, that I ſhould ever return to this country. 2. Altho' my voice is better than it was, yet it is very far from being equal to the publick duties of a church. But 3dly, If it was equal to thoſe duties in this church, (which is not a ſmall one, and difficult I am told to ſpeak in) it muſt *be ſo* to moſt churches on the continent. Now it cannot be ſuppoſed, that I ſhould be ſatisfied with a congregation, which affords the miniſter but 40, or 50 pounds a year at the moſt. It certainly does not imply the leaſt degree of vanity in me to ſay, that when I am able to officiate, I ſhall find no difficulty in getting a much better living than *this*. But 4thly, If I was perfectly able to officiate, and diſpoſed to put up with ſo ſmall a ſalary, it muſt be evident to common ſenſe, that my oppoſition to *you*, would prejudice your friends againſt me: They therefore, would not concur in calling me to

* Another inſtance of this wretched blindneſs appears from Mr. Sayre's ſaying (page 17) "I wiſh Mr. Bours would aſk himſelf, what is worſe than rebellion againſt the church." Mr. Sayre and Mr. Bours had a quarrel---Mr. B. therefore, rebelled againſt the church, which, in Mr. Sayer's opinion (page 17) is as bad as murder. But Mr. Sayre oppoſes the authority, not only of his own biſhop, but of the whole epiſcopal church, in the United States; yet *he* is pure from the ſin of ſchiſm and rebellion.

§ Such alſo were your candor and charity towards the Rev. Mr. Smith, who happened to ſucceed you at Newport. Of this I can give full proof.---From the ſame Chriſtian temper, proceeded your treatment of the Rev. Mr. Neſbit, becauſe he *preſumed* to viſit a church which you had left.

to be the minister of this Church. But 5thly, If this unlikely thing should be supposed to take place, a regard for my reputation, would prevent me from accepting the call; otherwise you would have some color of reason, that I was actuated by the motive you have suggested.—Lastly, You are too well acquainted with me to believe, that I would be guilty of a dishonorable action. You may, possibly, think me a weak and foolish man—or a man too much under the influence of others; but I defy you ever to think me a mean man.

I have now Sir, freely delivered my mind upon your conduct in this unhappy affair. I have spoken plainly; for I could not otherwise have done you justice. Yet I have spoken with the strictest regard to truth, and have asserted nothing, but from my own knowledge, or from the information of men of veracity. If I have said any thing that is not true, or misrepresented any thing, you have it in your power to point it out. The press is open to you as well as to me; and you have now a powerful call and fair opportunity to vindicate yourself at the bar of the publick. I am curious to know, what a man can say for himself, who opposes the sense and authority of the whole episcopal church in America—who has led a congregation into a separation that must in a few years, end in their ruin—who has in a variety of instances, most shamefully misrepresented—who has treated his brethren with the utmost contempt, and poured upon them the most profuse abuse.—You have I know, Sir, an excellent talent at coloring; but whether your colors will be fit for the public eye, on this occasion the trial alone can determine.

I cannot conclude this letter better, than by heartily praying, that you may no longer spend your time and your abilities, in the circulation of error. I am not ignorant, that you possess a considerable share of understanding;

standing; but what is understanding when employed, as you have done yours. No less just than ingenious, is the remark of an excellent writer. "The riches of the mind like those of fortune, may be employed so perversely, as to become a nuisance and pest, instead of an ornament and support to society." ‡ ||

I am,

Sir,

Your humble Servant,

JOHN BOWDEN.

‡ Dialogues of the dead, p. 297.

|| Would to God, that Mr. Sayre and those who countenance him, would endeavor to imbibe the amiable spirit, which our excellent reformers breathe in their homily on *contention*.---The following words deserve to be engraven upon every heart. "He that is faulty, let him rather amend, than defend that, which he hath spoken amiss; lest he fall by contention, from a foolish error, into an obstinate heresy. For it is better to give place meekly, than to win the victory with the breach of charity; which chanceth, when every man will defend his opinion obstinately.---The Wisdom that cometh from above, from the Spirit of God, is chaste and pure, corrupted with no evil affections: It is quiet, meek and peaceable, abhorring all desire of contention.---For there shall never be an end of striving and contention, if we contend who shall be master---if we shall heap error upon error, if we continue to defend that obstinately, which was spoken unadvisedly."---May all the genuine sons of the church pay a dutiful regard to this kind admonition of their mother! Then peace and charity will be restored, and discord and contention will be forever extinguished!

A

DISCOURSE

DELIVERED IN

ST. JAMES' CHURCH,

IN NEW-LONDON,

On Tuesday the 23d of December, 1794

BEFORE AN ASSEMBLY OF

FREE AND ACCEPTED MASONS,

CONVENED FOR THE PURPOSE OF INSTALLING

A LODGE IN THAT CITY.

BY SAMUEL SEABURY, D. D.
BISHOP OF CONNECTICUT AND RHODE-ISLAND.

NEW-LONDON:
PRINTED BY BROTHER SAMUEL GREEN,
M, DCC, XCV.

UNION-LODGE, *New-London*, Dec. 23, 1794.

VOTED unanimously, That Brothers *William Richards*, *Elias Perkins*, and *Robert Allyn*, be appointed a Committee to wait on our Right Rev. Brother BISHOP SEABURY, with the Thanks of this Lodge for his Sermon delivered to the Brethren this day; and to request a copy of the same for the Press.

Extract from the Records,

Attest. S. GREEN, Sec'y.

TO THE

ANCIENT AND HONORABLE FRATERNITY OF

FREE AND ACCEPTED MASONS,

THE FOLLOWING

DISCOURSE

IS RESPECTFULLY INSCRIBED,

BY THEIR AFFECTIONATE BROTHER

AND HUMBLE SERVANT,

THE AUTHOR.

NEW-LONDON,

Jan. 2, 1795.

A DISCOURSE, &c.

Worthy and honored Friends and Brothers,

GREAT is the pleaſure with which I embrace the opportunity that your kind invitation has given me of addreſſing myſelf to you this day—a day which, I truſt, will ever be joyfully remembered by you all;—a day in which, by the Inſtallation of the Maſter and other Officers of a Lodge of Maſons in this city, the influence of that venerable fraternity will be extended, and the bands of mutual love and good-will ſtrengthened among them;—A day in which the preſence of ſo many Brothers from the neighboring

neighboring Lodges met together to cultivate the principles of mutual love, and ſpread its happy influence, muſt cheer the heart and exhilarate the ſpirits of every humane man.

BOTH as a Miniſter of that Goſpel which proclaimeth peace and good-will to mankind, and as one of the common brotherhood of men, I feel myſelf deeply intereſted in the honor, proſperity, and happineſs of every Society, whoſe object is the peace, order, and welfare of the human race; and whoſe aim is the eſtabliſhment and cultivation of unity, brotherly love, and benevolence among its ſeveral branches.

THIS is the profeſſed deſign of your ſociety. It conſiders the helpleſsneſs of the infantine ſtate of man, the wants and neceſſities of his mature age, the numberleſs evils attendant on his declining years, as ſo many proofs that "it is not good for man to be alone"—that in a ſolitary, unconnected ſtate, *He could not ſubſiſt*, or could not ſubſiſt with ſafety and ſatisfaction to himſelf.

ANOTHER

ANOTHER proof that man was made for ſociety ariſes from the tender feelings of which his heart is ſuſceptible; of which, indeed, without violence and often repeated efforts it cannot be diveſted; from the ſympathetic anguiſh which riſes in it at the diſtreſſes of others; from the thrillings of joy and gladneſs with which it is delighted by the proſpect of human happineſs; from the ſoft emotions and extacy of pleaſure which ſpring from the reciprocal offices of friendſhip and love.—Theſe all proclaim that God intended man for ſociety—that every individual of the human race ſhould be a help and comfort to every other.

To give full energy to theſe happy principles of human nature, and carry them to their utmoſt effect, to cultivate natural knowledge and acquired arts, and to diſſeminate their principles and improvements for the comfort and benefit of man, as well as to harmonize the ſoul, and bring the tender affections of his nature into action, is the profeſſed purpoſe of the Maſonic inſtitution. It commences its origin from the origin of man,

becauſe

because, from his origin, man hath ever wanted the advantage of knowledge, and arts, and humane affections to ensure and make perfect the happiness of social life. Through various forms and degrees of refinement it hath hitherto subsisted in the world, sometimes clouded in obscurity, and sometimes shining in splendor; now distressed by persecution and oppression, then cherished by the favor of the world and the countenance of great men and princes. The former state arose from the ignorance and the prejudices of narrow-minded men, the latter from the improvement of the human mind by knowledge and liberality of sentiment.

But whatever was its outward condition in the world, whether persecuted or cherished, Masonry was still the same; still it labored to promote the peace and harmony of the world, by cultivating the principles of benevolence and love; still it sought the happiness of men, by advancing the knowledge of Architecture, Agriculture, Manufactures, and Commerce; still it endeavored to promote the prosperity of social life, by restraining the tempers and enlivening the affections which

could either retard or advance it. Human happiness was its object, and that object it kept ever in view. Through evil report and good, it still pursued it. Though sometimes disappointed of its aim, it renewed its attempts: Though baffled by human infirmity, and possibly by the fault and ill conduct of particular members, it pursued its point, it repeated its efforts, its object was still before it, still the end of its warmest wishes, of its most zealous endeavors.

Exactly does the Masonic institution in this respect, coincide with the morality of that holy religion, to the profession of which the mercy of God hath called us. To establish this assertion, I recommend to your attention the exhortation of St. Paul, which I purpose for the subject of my present discourse. It is recorded in

HEB. XIII. 1.

Let brotherly love continue.

I have the rather chosen this text because it will give me the opportunity of contributing my endeavors to promote the good purposes of your Society and the end of this day's

solemnity, by enforcing the precepts and spirit of that amiable and divine Religion which we profess, respecting brotherly love and benevolence—a principle which, did it engage the hearts and regulate the actions of men, would calm all their discordant passions and partial views, and bind them together, as strong cement binds together the materials of a building, which without it would part and fall asunder.

This religion, I trust, is not only ours by profession, but by its being the ruling principle in our hearts; and that it will bring every thought and design, every temper and passion in obedience to its divine precepts. Its importance demands our utmost attention; and that attention will convince us that Christianity furnishes mankind with the best philosophy, and most perfect institutions of life; that it contains not only the best system of moral duties that is extant, but, in truth, the only system that is fully adapted to the nature and condition of man in this world; being exactly squared to his circumstances, and levelled to his capacity; laying the sure foundation for his happiness; tending to raise

his powers and faculties to their highest perfection, to cement together the whole brotherhood of men, and build them up an edifice of love, supported by the two grand pillars of virtue and holiness, the light and strength of the world.

THE precepts of this religion which enjoin love and charity are very numerous, and expressed in the strongest and plainest terms: And reason, as well as experience, evinces the necessity of these precepts, to procure and preserve the happiness of the human species. Born in weakness and ignorance, entirely dependant on the care and protection of others; how soon must man fall a prey to those numberless evils which surround him, did not the tenderness of love, and sympathy of affection prevent it? And as he grows up to more mature age, he still continues indebted to the same amiable principles for almost all his enjoyments. Bodily strength comes too late to protect him against injuries, and experience comes too late to point out the road to happiness. He must depend on the protection and instruction of others; and nothing but love and affection can excite others to afford this

this protection, or give this instruction. And in his best estate, when bodily strength is perfected; when reason has come to maturity, and instruction and experience supply their utmost help, the greater part of his happiness must arise from the affectionate and social tendencies of his nature.

LOOK at the malignant and baneful passions and tempers with which his nature is now unhappily debased, and you will be immediately convinced of the truth of what I have said. Malice, and revenge, and ill-nature carry their own torment with them.—They *may*, and they probably *will*, vex, and and fret and torment those against whom they are exerted: But, at the same time, they *must* torment the bosom which indulges them; and, while they prevail, render it incapable of any rational enjoyment. To have mentioned this matter is enough: It carries its own evidence along with it, and needs no elaborate proof to convince us of its reality. We know that ill-nature and malice make those who indulge them miserable in themselves, and odious to all around them. And we know that the benign and social propensities of our nature

nature give pleasure in their exercise, and ensure happiness wherever they are practised.

IN this view, then, as well as in all other views, the Christian Religion deserves our best regards. It teaches us to consider mankind as one common brotherhood—the children of the same parent, and members of the same family—allied to each other by partaking of the same nature, and being subject to the same necessities and infirmities: And it directs us to seek and promote their happiness by all the means that shall be in our power; to comfort the afflicted, to protect the weak, to relieve the oppressed, to support the indigent, to instruct the ignorant, to administer, in short, to the various necessities of mankind, as God shall bless us with ability and opportunity.—It forbids all malevolent designs and intentions, as well as the open and avowed acts of malice; and it carries the principle of love and charity so high, as to require the forgiveness of real injuries, and the suppression of even our just anger.

ALL the writers of the New Testament, however

however they may vary in the enumeration of the other virtues, and in the encomiums they bestow upon them, are unanimous in giving this of brotherly love the preference; making it pre-eminent in its station, in its influence, and excellency above them all.

THE adorable Jesus, the great lover of men, declares that command of God, which enjoins us to love our neighbor as ourselves, to be equal to that great command which requires us to love the Lord our God with all our hearts; and says, that on these two commandments, the love of God and man, all the Law and the Prophets do hang: Thereby more than intimating to us, that the foundation of all *moral* precepts, lies in this love of God and man; and that nothing in morality has any virtue or real excellency in it, but as it is deducible from, or may be referred to one or other of these principles.

ST. James calls this law which commands the love of our neighbor, the *Royal Law*; thereby declaring its excellency and pre-eminence: And assures us that the whole train of social duties is fulfilled by fulfilling this law, *Thou shalt love thy neighbor as thyself*.

ST. Paul represents Love to others as a debt which, though due to all, can never be paid so as to cancel its obligation, and declares, in expressions similar to those of St. James, that the whole law, or obligation of duty, which one man owes to another, is fulfilled by observing this one precept, *Thou shalt love thy neighbor as thyself*. And in the conclusion of his epistle to the Hebrews, the strong sense he had of it returns upon his mind with such force, that he could not help mentioning it, as necessary to complete the Christian character, *Let brotherly love continue*. He saith nothing of the commencement of it. It already subsisted among Christians. Christians they could not be without it—it was woven into their religion, and made a part of it. Their duty, therefore, required them to nourish it, to support and maintain it, to regulate their hearts and actions by it, to pursue it through all its branches, and follow wherever it led them. It was one of the fruits of the Spirit of God, and at no rate to be neglected.

FROM the Spirit of God it hath descended and become the professed principle of the Masonic

sonic fraternity: For wherever the principle of brotherly love is, wherever it resides and governs the passions and actions of men, there is the Spirit of God; for *God is love*; and "there is none good but one, that is God."

BE this love then the Line which directs your conduct, the Square by which to form the rectitude of your principles and actions, the Plummet to try their uprightness, the Level to ascertain their conformity to the Almighty Architect; and let its Compass embrace the whole human race. Love hath ever distinguished your fraternity: Let, therefore, brotherly love continue. It will give reputation to your Society, stability to the Lodge this day installed, and make it an ornament to the city in which we live. Love to others, a desire to promote their happiness will ensure respect. Real worth alone can acquire real dignity, and propriety of conduct only can secure respect, either to individuals, or to bodies of men.

I HAVE thought it needless to take up your time in explaining what is meant by *brotherly love*. The feelings of your own hearts will do that

that better than the most elaborate descripti-on. Let us only remember that *every* man is our brother, being all the children of the same common parent, God Almighty, and the extent of the duty will be immediately perceived. Only consider the common wants and necessities of this brotherhood—that its happiness can no otherwise be promoted, and the variety of evils to which it is exposed no otherwise prevented than by loving one another, and the reasonableness of the duty will be clearly seen. Only reflect, that to love one another, to delight in doing good to all, to cultivate the tender, benign, and social propensities of our nature, is the command of our Creator, and the obligation of the duty will be strongly felt. Only recollect, that God hath declared him who hateth his brother to be a murderer, and that he must have his portion with apostate spirits—that He, God himself is the essence of love; and that he who loves his brother resembles his Creator, and shall enjoy everlasting felicity with him in heaven, and the motives to the practice of the duty will be too forcible for an ingenuous mind to resist.

How unhappy is it for the world that unthinking man attends so little to these considerations! How much of the misery which man endures, how many of the evils under which he constantly groans, might be prevented by cultivating this amiable, this divine quality! Look at the calamities that overspread the earth—What we call the evils of nature, sickness and accidents, storms and tempests, thunder and earthquakes, bear no proportion to those evils which the malevolent and baneful passions of men bring on it. War alone hath done more mischief, hath destroyed more of the human race, hath brought more misery into the world, than all of them together. And whence come wars and fightings among men? come they not from their unbridled lusts and malignant passions? How dreadful is the situation! how melancholy the prospect, when brotherhoods of men arm themselves for mutual destruction!

To have mentioned this horrible state of human depravity is enough to expose its enormity. With pleasure I turn from such a theme, to the contemplation of the amiable

qualities of affection and benevolence, which first founded that brotherhood to which I have, this day, the pleasure of addressing myself; and which hath cemented it together, and built it up, an edifice of love, a temple of unity and concord. May God prosper their endeavors to extend the blessings of peace, friendship, love, and knowledge through the world!

In cultivating this principle you are engaged; a principle on which human happiness must be built. Of this happiness the foundation was laid by God his Creator, when he gave man those tender, benign, and social feelings which are the greatest ornament and highest perfection of his nature. To rear the fair fabrick to this perfection; to bring to maturity that seed of salvation which was sown in the hearts of all men, when God said, *The seed of the woman shall bruise the head of the serpent*, was the end the Son of God, the adorable Savior of men, had in view, when he took our nature upon him. He therefore went about doing good, cultivating the tender propensities of that nature he had assum-

ed, calling into action all the amities and charities of the human heart, enforcing them by his precepts, and confirming them by his example; making it the very mark and essential characteristic of his disciples, that they should *love one another*.

To further this blessed disposition, and give it its utmost efficacy, is your professed design; and as, I trust, it has the warmest wishes of your hearts, I trust, also, it will have the utmost exertions of your abilities to bring it to perfection. In this business you are workers together with God, and fellow-laborers with Christ and his apostles, and with all good men.

Permit me then with the affection of a brother who earnestly wishes your prosperity, as well as with the authority of a minister of the Gospel of peace and good-will to men, whose greatest glory it is to recommend that Gospel to men, and make it effectual to their salvation, to put you in mind of your obligations in this respect, and earnestly to exhort you, not to be weary in doing good, but to *let brotherly love continue*, and mark all your conversation as Christians, as well as Masons.

The evil propensities of wicked men will, it is true, rise up in opposition; and the malignant passions of human nature will counteract the benevolent design of your holy religion, as well as of your particular institution. But these, by their contrariety, will only add to the splendor of your glory, and make the virtue of your conduct the more conspicuous, while you strive to bring order and peace out of confusion and discord, and to make friendship and love triumphant over enmity and malice.

Recollect, therefore, that all the words and actions of men,—the whole tenor and particulars of their lives—are noted by God who made them, and will by him be brought into judgment. Not only so; but their open conduct is viewed and scanned, and judged by their fellow-men; and that they will esteem or disregard the particular Society to which they belong, not only according to the worth of its institutions and regulations, but also according to the conduct of those who are members of it. Of the institutions of Masonry, it may, I assure myself, be justly asserted,

ted, that they are calculated to promote the happiness of the world. Let then the conduct of Masons be answerable to them. Let the force of their good institutions appear in their deportment. Let truth and justice, sobriety and modesty, courtesy and affability, liberality and candor, affection and love, benevolence and charity mark their whole conduct, and shew to the world, that they are the faithful servants of the merciful Savior of men, united by particular badges and institutions, to do good to mankind by promoting their happiness. Then shall their fellow-men regard and respect them: God will look with favor upon them and bless them: This temporary life will be closed in the satisfaction of having done good in their generation, and the merit of their Redeemer will carry them to the eternal kingdom of peace and love.

Keep, therefore, Brethren, the lamp of brotherly love burning bright in your hearts, square all your actions by the eternal rules of equity and just proportion; measure your designs by analogy with that ratio which the lip of truth hath given you, "Whatsoever ye would

THE

BLESSING OF PEACE:

A

SERMON

PREACHED AT NORWICH,

ON THE

Continental Thanksgiving,

February 19, 1795.

Published at the Request of a Number who heard it.

By JOHN TYLER, A. M.

RECTOR OF CHRIST'S CHURCH, NORWICH.

NORWICH:
PRINTED BY JOHN TRUMBULL,
M,DCC,XCV.

would that others ſhould do to you, do ye e-ven ſo to them;" circumſcribe all your deſires by the compaſs of duty, and level them by patience to your circumſtances: So ſhall the Lodges of the craft riſe in order, beauty, and ſtrength, cemented by the Spirit of the Almighty Architect of nature, who always worketh in and by Love—Jehovah—Trinity of Perſons, in Unity of Eſſence: To whom be aſcribed, by men and by angels—by every creature his hand hath formed—Glory, Honor, Dominion, Praiſe, Thankſgiving, now and forever.

AMEN.

THE BLESSING OF PEACE, &c.

PSALM, XXIX, 11.

—*The Lord will bless his People with Peace.*

WE are met together, to make grateful Acknowledgements to the supreme Governor of the World, for a Number of distinguishing Mercies, which we are favored with, as a Nation. In particular for * 'our Exemption hitherto from foreign War—for an increasing Prospect of the Continuance of that Exemption—*for* the great Degree of internal Tranquility we have *of late years* enjoyed—*for* the recent Confirmation of that Tranquility, by the Suppression of an Insurrection, which so wantonly threatened it—*for* the happy Course of our public Affairs in general—*and for* the unexampled Prosperity of *most* Classes of our Citizens—*all* which peculiarly mark our Situation, with Indications of the divine Beneficence towards us.' And when we continually hear of the Calamities, which sorely afflict most of the Nations of Europe, the present peaceful Condition of the United States in general, affords us much Consolation.—'In such a State of Things it is, in an especial Manner our Duty as a People, with devout Reverence and affectionate Gratitude, to acknowledge our many and great Obligations to ALMIGHTY GOD, and to implore him to continue and confirm the blessings we experience.'

AND it is to be hoped, that under the divine Influence, Instructions from the Pulpit, may serve in some good Degree, to excite a more lively and vigorous Gratitude, than would otherwise exist among us, for Benefits so visible and so important. And that I may be so happy

* Proclamation.

happy, on my Part, as to contribute Something, to fix in our Hearts, a more durable sense, of the Favors, which we acknowledge; and, which is the End of all well-meaning Instruction in this Case, inculcate such Behaviour, as will have a most efficacious Tendency, to secure and improve the public Happiness we enjoy:—Therefore, at present, I will set before you,

I. The Blessing of Peace.

II. Consider it as the Gift of GOD.

III. Put you in Mind, that only they, who as a People, in general acknowledge God by their Conduct, have any just Reason to expect the Blessing of Peace.—— But I will set before you,

I. THE Blessing of Peace.——* An Author of Distinction, has observed to this Effect, that from the harmless Appearance of man's Body—from the social Disposition of his Mind—from the Tenderness of his Affections, especially when moved to Compassion—from the Power he has of reflecting—from the Necessity he is under of Assistance, in his various Wants—and from the very benevolent Rules of Life, expresly given him by divine Revelation, Man appears to have been at first formed, for a sweetly social and perfectly inoffensive Creature. And the originally natural State of each Being, must certainly be the most happy State for each. And, as Man was evidently first formed, a benevolently social, peaceable and inoffensive Creature; so every Departure, by his sad Fall, from the original Design of his Formation, must be his Misery. And every Approach towards the first Design of his Formation, must also be an Approach towards his genuine Happiness. And since Man was originally made a peaceable, benevolent Creature; so Peace and Benevolence must be essential to his Happiness.

AND the Happiness of Peace, is like the Happiness of Health: it spreads itself through the Body of a Nation; as the Happiness of Health does through the animal Constitution;

* A. Bp. Secker.

stitution; and furnishes Pleasure and Vigor to each Part, without being, in general distinctly perceived by one, more than another. And however it happens, we are always too apt to become insensible of the great Happiness, both of Peace and Health, till the Loss of them for a Time, renews our Estimation of their Value: and even that Experience of their Loss, does not usually when past, preserve a due Esteem of them, very long in our Memory. Therefore to make our Minds sensibly relish the blessing of Peace, we must endeavour to recollect the Miseries and Horrors of War: for both Peace and War, strike our Minds most forcibly, in a contrasted View.

BUT most People attend very little more, to the Miseries of War, than they immediately feel them. And many seem to feel only the Expence: which is indeed a sore Evil: and the Expence of our late national War, is still a heavy Burden upon us. The lower Order of People are, in a Degree, straitened by it, in their Enjoyment of the common Necessaries and Comforts of Life; and the Public, under a Load of Debt, must find many Embarrasments attending it's due Exertions, even for it's own necessary Defence, when future Occasions require them.

YET, however considerable, the Evils may be, arising from the Expences of War; there are other Evils, some of which are much more distressing, to a compassionate Mind, and which ought to have the first Place in our Thoughts, such as the various and continual Hardships, which must be endur'd by great Numbers of our Fellow-Creatures, while exposing themselves in Defence of others, through the Course of a national War—The Loss of many Thousands of Lives, in Battle and by Sickness—the piercing Grief of a vast Number of Relations and Friends—the Miseries of a Multitude of destitute Families; Part of these, our Fellow-Citizens; not a few of them, perhaps very dear to some of us—the Rest indeed called Enemies: but it may be, few of them much in Fault for that Enmity, however much their Rulers are: and

and all of them, in Truth, our Brethren by Nature; of the same Blood, and perhaps most of them, in Essentials, of the same Faith.

AND furthermore, War not only weakens and distresses a Country, in these several Respects; but also takes away the Freedom of Commerce—retards useful Knowledge—prevents beneficial Improvements—diverts the public Attention from many domestic Concerns—furnishes Occasions for a Variety of Abuses, Frauds, and mischievous Speculations—obstructs the Remedy of Inconveniences in the Government, 'till they become inveterate and difficult to cure—in Short, War disorders, and in many Respects unhinges, the regular System of civil Affairs. And what is a Consideration not a little alarming, while Hostilities continue, who can tell how they may end?

BUT still, War is no less productive of Wickedness, than of Terror and Calamity. Whenever Hostilities commence; one Side, at least, must have been guilty of grievous Violations of Humanity and Justice—of violating also, in all Probability, solemn Treaties. And all this perhaps for no better Reasons, than little base Resentments—groundless or distant Fears—unwarrantable Desires of gaining unnecessary Advantages, over a neighbouring Nation—restless Pride and Ambition—false Schemes of Glory—or mere Wantonness of Power. To such horrid Idols as these, whole Armies are deliberately sacrified—whole Countries ravaged and plundered, and whole Nations greatly impoverished and distressed: though every Suffering, produced by such Motives, is a detestable Crime; and every Death, thus caused, a Murder, chargeable somewhere. Nor will that Side, which was at first the most innocent, fail in the Progress of Hostilities, to be guilty of many shocking Transgressions, Barbarities, and Cruelties, in common with the other. By the fierce Contentions of War, the main Body of a Nation, are too apt to become uncharitable, unpitying, implacable, and regardless of the Miseries of others: and of Course, the Soldiery will be prone to Cruelty, Rapaciousness, great Profaneness, Lewdness, and Intemperance: and but barely to mention, that when they have once changed the common Business of Life for that of War, a large Proportion of those poor, worn-out People, will be in great Danger, of never settling to their former honest, sober, and useful Employments again.

To the worldly-minded or inconsiderate, some of these Things, may seem but mere Trifles. But to every well-disposed, or only prudent Person, they will appear very great Mischiefs: and every truly benevolent and pious Heart will seriously lament, that so much Cruelty and Misery are introduced; and all the generous Sweetness of human Society more or less imbittered, with these mournful Evils; and that *The worthy Name, by which we are called, is blasphemed among the Nations*, by Means of the crying Sins, and particularly by the Enmities, of those who profess the Gospel of Peace; instead of that benevolent and peaceable Religion's procuring, the *Glory to God, Peace on Earth, and Good-will among Men*, which the celestial Messengers proclaimed at the Saviour's Birth.

BUT still, this dreadful Evil of War, pregnant with such a Variety of Mischiefs, becomes, through the Pride, Folly, and Perverseness of Men, sometimes unavoidable. It must certainly be the Will, of the common Father and Benefactor of all, that civil Societies or Nations, as well as Individuals, should be restrained from committing material Injuries, and from offering gross Affronts or Abuses to each other, except when great Purposes of his Providence, are to be answered by a Permission of them: otherwise, very destructive Abuses would, considering the Depravity of Man, be almost perpetually committed.—When one Nation injures another, offering high and provoking Abuse, amicable Methods, most certainly are to be first tried, for a Redress of Injuries, and for a Restoration of national Tranquility.

WE

WE have lately had Experience of such a Case—We have received gross and provoking national Injuries and Abuses—Instead of precipitate Revenge, and hasty Reprisals, the beneficent Ruler of the World, inspired our national Council with the Wisdom to try prudent, and amicable Methods for Redress, in the first Place: and according to the latest and best Information, we have been able to obtain, the same beneficent Being, who inspir'd our national Council with Wisdom, has, or we have Reason to expect, will, bless their prudent Endeavors with Success: which is one material Subject of Praise and Thanksgiving this Day. Therefore, my Brethren, we have Reason to be very thankful to God, for the good Prospect before us, of the Continuance of the richest of temporal Blessings, that of national Peace and Tranquility; instead of the Horrors of War—that our God, in the Abundance of his Mercy, is so kind to a back-sliding People, and by far too forgetful of him, as to prevent so much Guilt and Misery, as seem to be the natural, and almost necessary Attendents on War: under the pressing Distresses of which, so many Nations are now groaning.—And it can never be justifiable to refuse any equitable, or even tolerable Conditions, of avoiding so great a Calamity. If some well-meaning Persons have thought otherwise, Diversity of Opinions are ever to be expected in such Matters: and if any are mistaken, or so perverse, as to wish Ill to our happy Constitution, or are sorry, or angry that we were not involved in a foreign War; we have the more Reason to be glad and thankful, for the increasing Prospect, of the Continuance of our Exemption from foreign War, and for the recent Confirmation of our national Tranquility, by the Suppression of an Insurrection, which threatened the Stability of our Government.—Therefore, let us proceed,

II. To consider Peace, as the Gift of God.—This will require but little said to prove it: but needs a far more serious and practical Consideration, than we are commonly disposed to allow it.---Every Enjoyment we have,

have, is the Effect of God's Bounty : and every Suffering we endure, either directly or indirectly, of his inflicting. The Connexions of all things, were by him originally appointed : and the whole Series of Causes and Effects, are continually under his Superintendence. In every Generation, he brings forth upon the Theatre of the World, such Persons to act their various Parts, generally according to their own free Choice, as he foresees will accomplish, sometimes by their rare Abilities and benevolent Dispositions, and sometimes by the Contrary, his wise and holy Designs of Mercy or of Judgment. And the benign Influence of this providential Arrangement, on the Preservation of our present Tranquility, may have been, and I doubt not has been exceedingly great. He, who is the Head, of the executive Department of our Government, seems to have been designed, by the great Disposer of all Events, for very great and noble Purposes—to be a rare Blessing to this Land. And perhaps the Benefits of his wise, disinterested, and benificent Influence, may yet extend to those important Objects of divine Goodness, of which we at present, have but very imperfect Ideas—His Influence may be no inconsiderable Mean, of preparing this Country, to be in future a happy and important—a more and more safe and propitious Asylum, for the Unfortunate and Aflicted of many Nations, *When God shall* even yet, in a more peculiar Manner *arise, to shake terribly the Earth.*

But, let the Qualifications, Tempers, or Designs of Men be what they will ; the great and invisible Superintendent above, can, totally unperceived, even by themselves, inspire them with Thoughts, which will efficaciously excite them to, or withhold them from particular Designs, or divert their Attention, from one Object to another, just as he pleases.—And besides all this, the whole Frame of inanimate Nature, as it was at first produced by him, so it is also at all Times under his immediate Influence ; and actuated and directed by him : and he could, in it's original Formation, adapt it's most natural Effects to his Purposes : or can now, by very

slight

slight Changes, in the minutest Parts of it, totally unperceived by us, or through the Mediums of fair Weather, Winds, or Storms—healthy or unhealthy, fruitful or unfruitful Seasons—the sound Health, or Sickness, or Deaths of certain Individuals—a vigorous or depressed State of Nerves, in some one Person, at a critical Time—and by innumerable other Methods, unthought of by us, with perfect Ease, occasion, obstruct, or alter, to almost any Degree, the most important of worldly Events.—And in Addition to this, we ought to consider, that the same wise and beneficent Motives, which were Reasons in the great all-creating Mind, for making the World ; must certainly be sufficient Reasons for his strict Attention to the Concerns of it. And the Attention of a Mind, infinitely intelligent, wise, & powerful, must necessarily infer the accurate Regulation of every Thing, even of the most minute Particulars. But Matters of such important Consequences, as those of Peace and War among the Nations, cannot fail of occupying an especial Place, in the grand and unfathomable Scheme of divine Providence.

To these Deductions of Reason, the peculiar Changes in human Affairs of late Years, have been Means directly calculated to turn our Attention. And Passages in the holy Scriptures, in Confirmation of them, are to be found in great Numbers ; as where the Almighty says, by his Prophets, *The Heart of Kings is in the Hand of Jehovah, as the Rivulets of Water : he turneth it whithersoever he will.—I form the Light, and create Darkness : I make Peace, and create Evil : I Jehovah do all these Things.*—To those who put their Trust in his Loving kindness, he says, *Jehovah is thy Keeper, the Lord is thy Defence upon thy right Hand.* And on the Contrary, he says, *Shall there be Evil,* i. e. Calamity, *in the City, and Jehovah hath not done it ?*

'Frequently indeed,' says a very great and pious Author,* 'we perceive no Marks of the Interposition of God

God in what passes. But we are both inadvertent and short-sighted : ignorant, not only of the secret Springs, and material Circumstances of many human Actions ; but yet more, beyond Comparison, of principal Purposes in the divine Administration. Yet this however we know, that he is incessantly conducting the Affairs of the present World, towards a full Display of his Wisdom, Justice and Goodness in the next : though often by steps invisible to our eyes, and improbable to our Imaginations. *For his Judgments are unsearchable, and his Ways past finding out.*'

In every Thing therefore, we should confide in the Wisdom of divine Providence ; but in many Cases we may evidently perceive it : and I think plainly in our own Case, as a Nation ; for both civil and religious Liberty have been preserved to us, in the Midst of various Dangers : and the Quiet and Safety, naturally attending on national Peace, have been, in a great Measure, our Lot, though strongly tempted to hazard them, by Dangerous Pursuits and Enterprises ; and whilst all the great Nations, with whom we are most conversant, and several others, are struggling under the severest Calamities of War. And he, whose Beneficence has bestowed these Blessings of Peace and Safety upon us, in the most critical Times ; is daily increasing our Prospect of their Continuance ; from whom, 'Every Day's Peace, as well as every Day's Bread, is a new Gift.'

Most certainly then, we have abundant Reason, not only for Joy ; but also for the sincerest Praises—for the most devout Thankfulness—and for the most grateful Acknowledgments, to the infinite Source of all our Blessings. But if, instead of this, our Prosperity should make us so arrogant as a People, that we should in Effect, ungratefully disown, or carelesly forget the Author of all our Happiness ; what is more probable than that, for our Correction, we may be left to undermine and destroy our own Prosperity, by vain Speculations, imprudent and unfortunate Enterprises, and by very delusive Pursuits ?

Too

* A. Bp. Secker : to whom the Writer is indebted for several of the best Ideas in this Discourse.

Too many perhaps will think, that they have fully discharged their Consciences, towards their great Benefactor, with Respect to the invaluable Blessings we are contemplating, by giving their Attendance on the present religious Solemnity. But outward Acknowledgments only, are to God no more than vain Show, Amusement, Ostentation, and Mockery. And even the inward grateful Sense of our Obligations to God, for his distinguishing Favors, accompanying our outward Acknowledgments, if it speedily dies away, and fails of producing the proper and lasting Fruits of Obedience, to our great Benefactor, is but an imperfect, ineffectual, delusive Homage, which our all-wise Creator cannot accept. *Herein is my Father glorified*, said our blessed Redeemer, *that ye bear much Fruit.* And in this Light we must view, that solemn Warning in the Prophecies of Malachi; *If ye will not hear, and if ye will not lay it to Heart, to give Glory unto my Name, Saith Jehovah of Hosts, I will send a Curse upon you, and I will even curse your Blessings.*

But this rather anticipates my last Head of Discourse, which is to put you in Mind,

III. That only they, who, as a People, in general acknowledge God by their Conduct, owning his Authority by observing his Laws, have any just Right to expect the Blessing of Peace; or that Peace will in Fact operate as a Blessing to them.

The natural Effect or Tendency of sincere Religion, upon Nations, is, to make them industrious, frugal, healthy, rich, populous, public spirited, unanimous, and brave; and at the same Time, prudent, just, friendly, and benevolent. Now these are the very Qualities, which render them dreaded as Enemies—inviting as Confederates—and inoffensive, good, and agreeable as Friends and Neighbours: and, so far as any Thing short of the immediate Interposition of Heaven, can, will secure to them, the Blessing of Peace. But the natural Tendency of Wickedness, is, to make them idle, dissipated, enfeebled; to impoverish, depopulate, to render them mean-spiritedly selfish, disunited, and dispirited; to make them imprudent, injurious, unfriendly, and malevolent; to extinguish their Concern for the common Good, to inflame their selfish Appetites and mischievous Passions; to make the People rash and provoking; and at the same Time, upon the Whole, indolent and despicable.—And, in general, it seems scarce necessary for divine Providence to interpose, otherwise than by the original Constitution of Things, to exalt a People, of good Morals and sincere Piety, to a State of Prosperity, Peace, and Happiness; or to depress and chastise a vicious People; because it seems as though they would do this effectually themselves. But when it is necessary, for the Disposer of all Events to interpose specially, and to do this, we may expect that in due Time, it will be done. For the supreme Controller of Events, will reward what he approves, and punish what he detests. And though his Rewards in this World, are neither perfect, nor exactly proportionable; yet even here, with Respect to Nations, they are real, and often very considerable. The holy Scriptures have proclamed this; and Experience has always confirmed it.

Prosperity or Calamity indeed, according to their Conduct as a People, more equally and constantly attended the Jewish Nation, than others. But though *These Things happened unto them* partly *for our Ensamples; and are written for our Admonition*, to whom these last ages of the world are come; yet the universal Governor, also visited the Heathen for their Abominations; and *Lengthened out their Tranquility*, when they *brake off* the basest of their Vices, *by Righteousness*, or a Return to those Principles of Equity, which their darkened Minds still retained. And when the Books of the New-Testament were written, as Christian States were not then in Existence, no Mention was made of them, either in the Writings of the Evangelists, in the Acts of the Apostles, or in the Epistles; but the Revelations by St.

St. John, prophetically describe, not only Kingdoms, but even much larger Portions of the World, as suffering the most severe Judgments, for their great Abominations. We ought therefore, seriously to attend to what divine Inspiration teaches us, concerning these Things. And the substance of the divine Declarations, respecting this subject is; *If ye be willing and obedient, ye shall eat the Good of the Land. But if ye refuse and rebel, ye shall be devoured with the Sword: for the Mouth of Jehovah hath spoken it.*

What then is our true Character? Are we properly the People of God? Are we duly sensible what this Term means? Instead of vain and presumptuous Systems of rational Religion falsely so called, and framed according to our own Fancies, do we in fact steadfastly believe *The Truth as it is in Jesus—whom God hath set forth to be a Propitiation* for our sins, *through Faith in his Blood?* And, instead of an arbitrary System of Morals, modelled by Custom and Fashion, and relaxed so indulgently, as to set easy upon our corrupt Inclinations, do we in Fact *Deny Ungodliness and worldly Lusts, living soberly, righteously, and godly in this present World, and looking for that blessed Hope, and the glorious Appearance of the great God, and our Saviour Jesus Christ—who gave himself for us, that he might redeem us from all Iniquity, and purify unto himself, a peculiar People, zealous of good Works?*——I hope we may be said in truth, to bear at least some faint Resemblance of this Picture. And perhaps some will be ready to say, by Way of Extenuation of our Faults, that we are not so corrupt as many other nations. But it must be confessed, that we are very far from being what we ought to be. And I am sorry to say, that we seem too fast declining, into the loose opinions, and into that Contempt for Religion, which have in a great Measure overwhelmed, many of the old and corrupted Nations of Christendom: and for which several of them are now suffering severe Correction.

But Indeed, *Sin* alone, which *Is a Reproach to any People,*

People, without any other Scourge, except the natural Consequences which attend it, is sufficent to ruin any Nation completely.——A Disregard of God, and a Contempt of our duty, in Proportion as they prevail among us, must gradually undermine every Blessing we enjoy. And if these Evils should increase to an extreme Degree, they with many other moral Evils, naturally connected with them, must eventually fill our Families with Disorder and various Distresses—put an End to mutual Faith and Confidence—open a Door to all manner of Fraud and Violence—defeat the Administration of Justice—render our happy Constitution ineffectual to it's great Ends, and turn all the Good of it into Evil; 'till we are able to bear, neither our Diseases, nor their Remedies.'

I am sensible, that such Observations as these, may seem comfortless and unsuitable to the present joyful Solemnity: but outward Joy for divine Mercies, without any inward Concern for increasing Unworthiness, and without any fixed Resolutions of a virtuous Improvement, is not only absurd and insolent; but too apt to prove a short-liv'd Mirth. For Praises and Thanksgivings are not seemly, in the Mouths of presumptuous Sinners. Think it not strange, I beseech you, to hear at this Time, not solely the Voice of Joy, though there is a just Occation for it: but remember that *The Fear of the Lord is the Beginning of Wisdom*; and casting it off, must consequently be the Door and Flood-Gate of Folly. For no Motives but religious ones, can, with sufficient Force, either prompt to what is right, or restrain from what is wrong. We evidently have the greatest of Blessings to incline us to be religious; and rational and pious Instructions enough to shew us how to be so.—That Religion ever has been the greatest Security of public Happiness, all Nations have been ready to confess: and when this Tie is broken, no other will hold very long. The holy Scriptures have foretold it—Reason plainly proves it—and the Experience of all Ages confirms it. And instead of encouraging irreligious Discourses; and giving Heed to infidel Books, let us strive to become more and more,

a wise, religious, sober minded, frugal, industrious, honest, benevolent, and united People: for otherwise, we cannot long continue a free one. For neither the Justice of God, nor the Connection of human Affairs, will naturally admit of it.

The Dangers are so constant, and the Sufferings so frequent, to which human Nature is exposed, that behaving wisely under the Apprehension of Dangers, and properly under the Experience of Sufferings, constitute no inconsiderable Part of our Business in the World. And the best Methods we can use, to guard us against Dangers, are of two Sorts; comprehended in worldly Prudence, and religious Wisdom. It is not the Business of this Place, to deliver the Dictates of worldly Prudence; but to limit, and improve, or perfect them, by the Dictates of religious Wisdom: that we may in no Case, either endeavor to secure ourselves from Danger, by acting wrong, nor have any Doubt of Support in acting right. But we are too apt to look upon Religion in a very false Light, as only prescribing disagreeable and unprofitable Duties: whereas in Truth it suggests the kindest, the wisest, the most profitable, and the best Advice; and lovingly adds the most comfortable Promises. Sentiments of Virtue and Religion, are the Seeds of all true Happiness—the best Security in all Dangers—and the main Support in all Affliction.

While we rejoice in our Escape from Dangers, Admonitions for our Faults are very necessary, to excite in us due Thankfulness to God, from the Consideration that we are not punished, though we deserve Punishment from him: and Warnings of the Dangers we must be exposed to, by a Disregard of Religion, and a Contempt of our Duty, are indispensably necessary, to remind us of proving our Gratitude by that Obedience, which alone will secure to us the divine Protection. And could the People of this Land in general, be persuaded to make this profitable Use of the present Solemnity, it would be indeed a Season of Gladness—a Season for laying

ing the only sure Ground-Work of public Happiness. For as the Prophet said to the People of *Judah and Benjamin, The Lord is with you, while ye be with him; and if ye seek him, he will be found of you: but if ye forsake him, He will forsake you.*

I might indeed upon this Occasion, congratulate you with Views of our national Prosperity—of the Extensiveness of our Territory—of the various and happy Climates in it—of our rapidly growing Numbers—of the great Increase of new Settlements—of the Security we enjoy, by being so distant from powerful and corrupted Nations—of our various, great, and increasing Resources for Wealth or War—I might remind you, that the natural Means of our Subsistence are so great, that in a Measure, we are become the Granary of other Nations—that Knowledge, and all useful Arts are making great Progress among us—And I might boast of the Liberality and Prosperity of our free and happy Constitution of Government. But what are all these Things, without the divine Blessing and Protection? And what Purpose would all this Adulation serve, but, instead of promoting real Gratitude to God, rather perhaps to excite and encourage Pride; which is the great Bane of Man: and it is one great Purpose of God, in national as well as private Judgments, to *Hide Pride from Man.* I might indeed, have said little else, except what would contribute Something, to promote the Arrogance of national Prosperity. But perhaps I should have fallen under the Condemnation of the false Prophets in Judah; of whom *Jehovah of Hosts said,—They have healed the Hurt of the Daughter of my People slightly, saying, Peace, Peace, when there is no Peace.* For says the Prophet, *There is no Peace, saith my God, to the Wicked.* This last, is what innumerable Facts in every Age have proclaimed. But more especially, this holds true in free popular Governments, like our's. For there must be public Virtue, or they cannot flourish with Peace and Prosperity. There must also be private Virtue, or there will be no such Thing as public Virtue. There must be Religion, or there will be neither

er public nor private Virtue. There must be true Religion, otherwise there will generally be Abundance of false Religion. And there must be Attendance on the Worship of God, otherwise there will soon be no Religion at all.

Let us then earnestly *Pray for the Peace of Jerusalem*: but remember with all, that the surest Way of promoting *Peace within her Walls*, and of *seeking to do her Good*, is first to be ourselves at Peace with God. And at the same Time, let us acquiesce—in the *Wisdom*, Justice, *and faithful Loving-kindness* of Providence: and the more, as the severest Dispensations of it, are bringing forward continually, though by unseen Ways, that blessed State of Things, even on this Earth, of which, however else improbable in itself, the Attributes of God afford us Hope; and his Prophets, Assurance.'—Let us then, 'Govern our Lives by the Rules of the Gospel; and both awe and cheer ourselves, by continual Thoughts of that *Day, when God will judge the World in Righteousness, by that Man, whom he hath ordained*.' And if there were in general, such a dutiful Mind in us, we might, as a People, place a sure Confidence in this Promise made to it, *Thus saith the Lord thy Redeemer, the Holy One of Israel, I am the Lord thy God, who teacheth thee to profit; who leadeth thee by the Way, that thou shouldest go. O that thou wouldest hearken to my Commandments; then should thy Peace be as the River; and thy Righteousness as the Waves of the Sea.*

But we should bear it duly in Mind, that we owe very grateful Acknowledgments, * 'sincere *Praises* and hearty Thanks to the great Ruler of Nations, for the manifold and signal Mercies, which distinguish our Lot as a Nation; particularly for the Possession of Constitutions of Government which unite, and by their Union establish Liberty with Order—for the Preservation of our Peace foreign and domestic—for the seasonable Control which has been given to a Spirit of Disorder, in the Suppression of the late Insurrection—and generally, for the prosperous Course of our Affairs public and private. And at the same Time,' that we are in Duty bound, 'humbly and fervently to beseech the kind Author of these Blessings, graciously to prolong them to us—to imprint on our Hearts, a deep and solemn Sense of our Obligations to him for them—to teach us rightly to estimate their immense Value—to preserve us from the Arrogance of Prosperity, and from hazarding the Advantages we enjoy, by delusive Pursuits—to dispose us *to become meet Subjects for* the Continuance of his Favors, by not abusing them—by our Gratitude for them, and by a correspondent Conduct, as Citizens and as Men—to render this Country more and more, a safe and propitious Asylum for the Unfortunate of other Countries—to extend among us true and useful Knowledge—to diffuse and establish Habits of Sobriety, Order, Morality, and Piety; and finally, to impart all the Blessings we possess, or ask for ourselves, to the whole Family of Mankind.'

* Proclamation.

And may grateful Affections, and religious Desires, of such Kinds as these, possess our Minds, on this Occasion, instead of the delusive Pleasures of Luxury, Intemperance, idle Mirth, or noisy Riot and Folly: and instead of Short-liv'd Gaiety, and playful Diversions, may our religious Affections of Gratitude and Praise, and our humble and dutiful Requests to the Throne of Grace, all serve the noble, and only valuable Purpose, of fixing in us, correspondent Habits of Sobriety, Industry, Order, Peaceableness, Morality, christian Benevolence, and Piety; without which, no worldly Prosperity, can eventually be to us a Blessing; or any real Matter of Rejoicing: because, *The Prosperity of Fools shall destroy them.* For it is only to the People of God—to the Humble, Penitent, and Dutiful, that the Records of divine Truth, pronounce true Peace, or any other eventual Blessing. *Say ye to the Righteous, it shall be well with him—Blessed is every One that feareth the Lord: that walketh in his Ways.—For thou shalt eat the Labor of thine Hands: happy*

happy shalt thou be, and it shall be well with thee—Lord shall bless the out of Zion: and thou shall see the Good of Jerusalem, all the Days of thy Life. And that we may all reap the Benefit, and wisely profit, by these Observations, God, of his infinite Mercy, grant, through Jesus Christ.

Now therefore, to God the Father, Son, and holy Spirit, the one infinitely wise, good, and eternal God, in Jesus Christ, be rendered, as is ever due, all Honor and Glory, Thanksgiving and Praise, Might, Majesty, and Dominion, World without End.

AMEN

A

DISCOURSE

DELIVERED BEFORE

A SPECIAL CONVENTION

OF

THE CLERGY,

AND

LAY DELEGATES,

OF THE

EPISCOPAL CHURCH

IN THE

STATE OF CONNECTICUT,

IN

TRINITY CHURCH, NEW-HAVEN

ON THE FIFTH DAY OF MAY,

ONE THOUSAND SEVEN HUNDRED AND NINETY-SIX

OCCASIONED BY THE DEATH OF THE

RIGHT REVEREND SAMUEL SEABURY, D.D.

BISHOP OF CONNECTICUT AND RHODE-ISLAND.

BY ABRAHAM JARVIS, A.M.

PRESBYTER, AND RECTOR OF CHRIST'S CHURCH IN MIDDLETOWN.

NEW-HAVEN—Printed by T. & S. GREEN.

At a Convention of the Clergy and Laiety of the Proteſtant Epiſcopal Church in Connecticut, holden at New-Haven the 5th Day of May, 1796:

RESOLVED, That Rev. ASHBEL BALDWIN, Rev. PHILO SHELTON, and ELI CURTISS, Eſq. be a Committee to return the Thanks of the Convention to the Rev. Mr. JARVIS, for his Diſcourſe delivered before the Convention this Day in Trinity Church; and requeſt a Copy for the Preſs.

Signed by Order of Convention,

PHILO PERRY, Secr'y.

TO THE CLERGY, HIS ESTEEMED AND SINCERELY RESPECTED BRETHREN;

AND TO THE LAY MEMBERS OF THE CONVENTION.

THIS DISCOURSE IS RESPECTFULLY INSCRIBED,

BY THEIR AFFECTIONATE BROTHER

AND HUMBLE SERVANT,

ABRAHAM JARVIS.

HEBREWS 13 ch. 7 v.

Remember them who have the rule over you, who have ſpoken unto you the word of God: whoſe faith follow, conſidering the end of their converſation.

WHEN the Goſpel was firſt publiſhed to the world, the Jews who embraced the faith, were, above all other Chriſtians, hated and perſecuted by their unbelieving brethren. As their diſcouragements were more ſevere, and their temptations ſtronger, to renounce that holy religion, to which they had been ſo lately converted; they ſtood in need of greater aids to enable them to perſevere, and to keep them ſteadfaſt in their holy profeſſion to the end.

To theſe Hebrew converts, the Apoſtle ſends this epiſtle, wherein *he expounds unto them, in all the ſcriptures, the things concerning Chriſt*; his character and offices; what he ſhould do and ſuffer, as foretold by Moſes and the Prophets. The miniſtry of Moſes was repreſentative and prophetical, the law given by him was preparative, to endure but for a time, until, according to the wiſdom and good providence of God, every thing ſhould be prepared

for the coming of Chriſt, by whom, the religion he taught would be fulfilled and completed; who was to put an end to that law, and give a new one, which ever after ſhould be the rule for his church, and in him, the ſpirit of life and ſalvation unto men. Moſes, truly was faithful in all things unto which he was appointed, but he was a ſervant only in that houſe, of which Chriſt was the maſter and builder. Similar to Moſes and the law, was Aaron, and the prieſthood annexed to it; temporary, and figurative of the prieſthood of Chriſt, which ſhould be unchangeable and eternal, through which, not the Jews only, but all nations were to partake, in the ſovereign mercies of their almighty Creator. From thence he argues Chriſt's power and readineſs, to ſuccour and protect them in all their adverſities, and to relieve them in all their neceſſities. And to confirm them further in the faith of the goſpel, againſt every jewiſh pretention, he repreſents the great ſin and hazard of apoſtacy; neither could they expect any benefit from their paſt labours and ſufferings, without perſeverance. He therefore exhorts them to conſtancy and patience in their faith, by the examples of former ſaints, and alſo by thoſe of their own time, whoſe faith and lives were well known to them; who had kiſſed the croſs with joy, as it was a ſure paſſport to the embraces of their glorified Redeemer. Remember them who have had the rule over you; who have ſtood firm under the ſevereſt trials, and faithfully ſpoke the word of

of God; whoſe faith follow, conſidering the end of their converſation.

The full purport of which words are expreſſed in the following paraphraſe: "Set before your eyes the biſhops and governours that have been in your church, and preached the goſpel to you; obſerve their manner of living, and their perſeverance till death; and make their faith, their perſeverance, and conſtancy in the doctrine of the goſpel, the example for you to imitate and tranſcribe."*

Although we are to ſet before us, in every inſtance of duty, the perfect and divine pattern of Jeſus Chriſt, who ſuffered for us, leaving us an example, that we ſhould follow his ſteps; yet we ſee it is unauthoriſed to propoſe human, and imperfect characters, for our imitation. The hiſtory of men in every age affords ample teſtimony, how much they are influenced and led by the authority and power of example. Among the multitude, ſmall is the number of thoſe men, who are able to mark out to themſelves a rule in every part of their conduct. It requires more leiſure, and greater capacity, than moſt men either can or are willing to make uſe of for that purpoſe. To their wiſe men and induſtrious guides, the bulk of mankind are greatly indebted, for their labours, in teaching them the knowledge of ſalvation, and guiding their feet in the way of peace. The reſpect paid to ſuch labourers in word and doctrine, is no inconſiderable evidence, to what degree religion

* Hammond.

ligion actuated the minds of men, in the early days of christianity. Their pure faith and pious zeal, we have thus expressed: " We adore the Son of God, but the martyrs, we deservedly esteem for the love which they have borne to their King and Master; and desire to be their disciples and companions." That they might cherish the remembrance of their piety, and perpetuate the influence of their virtues, it soon became customary, to solemnize their memory upon the day of their death, which they considered as their birth-day to a life of happiness and immortality. Thus whilst God was honoured and glorified in his saints, who had enabled them to endure, and then rewarded them for their perseverance; the body of believers was encouraged and excited to follow their examples with firmness and constancy.

That which distinguishes a Christian, from a Jew or a Heathen, is his faith, his knowledge of Christ and the Gospel. By his faith, as it comprehends all the great motives of action, the Christian professes to live, that is, to have all his aims, desires, and actions, governed by what God has revealed. On that foundation he builds his hopes of happiness, derived from the divine promises.

In the eleventh chapter of this epistle, the apostle illustrates, with a beautiful variety of expression, the sovereign efficacy of that divine principle, in the actions and sufferings of the old patriarchs, who lived in the different ages of

of the world, before the coming of Christ; and shews how they overcame all difficulties and temptations, and proved themselves superior to all the snares and corruptions of the world, by the support of that steadfast faith and trust in God, to which all Christians are called.

In the beginning of the twelfth chapter, he applies the account he had given in the foregoing: that since Christians are called to the same faith, which actuated those eminent saints, and thereby were incompassed with such a cloud of witnesses, bearing testimony to its great power and efficacy, all might thence have the fullest assurance, of what they themselves might be able to accomplish. As a finishing support and encouragement in all the duties of their holy religion; and to complete the argument drawn from example; they should fix their minds invariably upon the holy Jesus, the auther and finisher of their faith; who for the joy that was set before him, as man, endured the pain and despised the shame of the cross, for which as a due reward, that nature is exalted to the highest dignity and glory, at the right hand of the Majesty on high.

Had no other pattern of holy living and dying been prescribed to us, but that of our divine Saviour, the infinite disproportion might have been discouraging; and the perfection of it, might have lessened the force of the example. Absolute wisdom and goodness, therefore, hath not only given for our use, a model of human virtue

virtue in perfection, that by looking at what is perfect, we might be perpetually growing in grace, until at last, in a future state, we should arrive unto the perfect man, the measure of the stature of the fulness of Christ: He hath moreover left on record, for our instruction, instances of men, having no higher privileges than ourselves, and given to them the testimony that they were approved of by him.

In such instances, raised up by the good providence of God, we are led to behold the faith and grace of the gospel, formed in visible image, to which it is highly proper to pay a well directed attention. For certainly, we cannot conceive of a method more effectual, to impress on the minds of Christians, the doctrines of the gospel, than to lay before them particular samples, of what that faith hath been able to effect, under which they profess to act. In this way, men are taught by their eyes, and all their senses; and are left without excuse. So that it must be the personal fault of every particular Christian, if his faith does not produce, under equal circumstances, the like degrees of virtue and holiness, to which others have attained under its influence.

Let it be noticed then, that the man, who confidently asserts, that he was not a whit behind the chief of the apostles; and who calls upon his brethren, to mark well, and to be followers of him, as he was of his holy and crucified Master: this first of saints, that he might

might minifter ftrength and refolution to the faith of Chriftians, of that day,—and the fame ftands to awaken, and to quicken ours ;—advifes—To remember them who have fpoken the word of God ; and to follow their faith, confidering the end of their converfation.—That being compaffed with fo great a cloud of witneffes—to lay afide every weight, and the fin which doth fo eafily befet us—and to run with patience the race that is fet before us.—" Here-
" in alluding, (to ufe the words of the elegant
" and pious bifhop Horn) to that prodigious
" affembly from all parts of the earth, convened
" at Olympia, to be fpectators of the games ;
" before whom the candidates contended, hav-
" ing in view thofe venerable perfonages from
" whofe hands they were to receive the palm,
" and who were immediate witneffes of their
" refpective conduct and merit.—Alluding to
" thefe circumftances, St. Paul places the
" Chriftian combatant in the midft of a moft
" auguit and magnincent theatre, filled with
" all the great and illuftrious characters, enu-
" merated in the preceding chapter, as having
" overcome through the power of faith, from
" the beginning of the world : whofe prefence
" fhould animate and fire him to engage in the
" conteft, with an ambition not to be repre-
" hended, and a fpirit altogether invincible."

Thefe ideas, which this beautiful and defcriptive allufion excites, prepare us to tafte, and feel, the full force and energy of every expreffion in the paffage. It is an argument that can never change,

change, or lofe its force. That affembly has been enlarging as the church on earth, has, from the days of the apoftles down to the prefent, been conftantly fending forth from her bofom, many worthy fons and daughters to add to its number. The Chriftian combatant of this day, may confider himfelf as acting upon the fame theatre, in the view and obfervation of the fame venerable perfonages, with the idea fwelled, and ftill more enlarged upon his mind. Happy would be the effects, was the idea cherifhed in its full magnitude and force. But the argument takes another turn, and ftands in a different light, when applied to thofe characters, while they were in the flefh, exemplifying the power of faith in the Chriftian warfare. Here we are to confider them as leading the way, and fhewing us how mighty is the principle of that religion, to which we, by the good providence of God, are called, to carry us through all temptations, and to keep us ftead faft under all trials. In the other ftate, we are to view them in the full poffeffion of that blifs, to which they were advanced, at the end of their earthly converfation, when their day of labour clofed, and this world vanifhed from their mortal fight ; and there contemplate them, as witneffes to us of the unfpeakable glories we fhall inherit, if we continue to ftrive and perfevere as they did, in the days of their flefh.

Men who lived in former times, we can only remember, by reading their tranfactions, and commemorating their faith and virtues. By con-

contemplating their examples, given in the faithful records of their lives, each one may become his own inftructor, and learn a leffon of more value, than all the treafures of the world. How fhould the luftre of their virtues encourage us to well-doing, and quicken us to an holy emulation ? How will they reproach us for our faults, and upbraid our dulnefs and defects ? Let experience be confulted, what we fee in others, and feel in ourfelves, and this reflection will lead us to fee the wifdom and duty of caution, in the choice of our more intimate companions and affociates, to whofe obfervation we lay ourfelves the more open, as they to ours : and whofe pious examples may be to us, a conftant and living inftruction. It will alfo direct us, frequently to call up, and contemplate the examples of thofe, who are deceafed ; who thereby continue, though dead, to fpeak and preach to us, what are that faith and life, which are fruits of the fpirit, and in the end will carry us to the realm of blifs.

The faints of God at all times inculcate one and the fame general leffon. Living by the faith of the Son of God, their holy tempers and purity of manners, defervedly enroll them among the righteous, who fhall be held in remembrance, and their patterns in like manner encourage, and engage us, in the uniform practice of virtue and religion.

It is then a tribute, proportionately due to perfons of our own age, who are eminent in learning,

learning, piety and virtue. As they wrought, with all diligence, to gain a clear and right understanding of the doctrines; to follow the faith, and be conformed to the life of those ancient ornaments of Christianity; so are they worthy of being held in remembrance; worthy of the imitation of those of their own times, and of all who shall retain any knowledge of them. "The nearer the example is to us, the more force it acquires. The distant report of confessors and martyrs, of men who died and suffered much for the sake of religion, and the good of mankind: these examples recorded in history, being remote from us, affect us not so sensibly as the instances of piety and virtue, of distinguished fortitude and constancy in our own times, and among our own acquaintances. Their lives, as well as their instructions, admonish us in a friendly and familiar manner, to walk circumspectly and honourably, to be blameless and harmless amidst a perverse generation."—This is the language of those, who rule faithfully in the church of Christ; who speak his word in truth and integrity, and lead the people in the way of holiness, by their own irreproachable life. To remember these men, and to follow their faith, is to retain a lively sense of that affection, esteem and reverence we had of them while living; to recollect their pious instructions, and every help we received from them, which gave light to our understanding of the doctrines, and duties of our holy religion. It is, to give every amiable grace and excellency

excellency apparent in them, and for which we judged they merited our esteem, such consideration, as will excite us to emulate those excellencies, which heightened their qualifications, and will advance ours, for the glories of immortality.

Let it be regarded then, as highly beneficial, to cherish the idea, and sanction a reverence for the memory of those who have excelled in virtue, and proved champions in the cause of our divine Redeemer. Let it be regarded, as a proof of God's abundant goodness, that he hath let no incentive, adapted to work upon our natures, be wanting, to render us, through his grace, fellow-helpers in the great work of our salvation.—If we nourish in our bosoms the pleasing image of what we admire and love in others, and awaken our thoughts habitually to the immense reward; it will kindle a zeal and resolution to become what we admire, that we may secure to ourselves an enjoyment with them, of what we all so ardently hope for.—Let this be done, and we shall then watch carefully over ourselves, and make it our daily employment to possess our hearts with all those good dispositions, which God requires, which promote our own inward peace, and give pleasure to others. We shall study to be in all things resigned to his will. If he grants to us the good things of this world, and blesses us with prosperity, we shall believe it is, that we may render him the glory, by doing good according to his bounty. If he sends adversity—that it is to correct and amend

amend us, to soften our hearts, and to wean us from the vanities of the world. Then shall we shew that we have faith in God; a faith that will be sufficient and effectual to correct the errors of our souls, and to adorn them with the beauties of the true child of God:—that will prove a shield to guard us against all the attacks of evil:—an anchor to keep us steady and unseduced, by the frowns or flatteries of the world.

By thus taking to us the whole armour of God, and watching with all perseverance, we shall stand, having our loins girded, and our lights burning, and be ready for our Master's coming. So shall we follow the example of those holy persons who are declared blessed for being found so doing.

So shall we hold communion with the saints on earth, by embracing the same common faith and hope of salvation, and by the common offices of piety and charity. We shall at the same time hold communion and fellowship even with the saints departed; by rejoicing at their bliss and happiness; by blessing God for the light of their example; by labouring to follow it ourselves; and by praying, that, together with them, we may at last receive the fulness of joy, and life for ever more.

Thus may we still hold communion with that blessed man, whose deeply lamented death, laid the foundation for this day's solemn assembling. As Christians we must bow with resignation and reverence to the hand of God, who

who with him, has ſtripped us of ſo valued a treaſure. His vacant ſeat among us, calls up our ſorrow afreſh; but we ſorrow moſt of all that we are to ſee his face no more. We may lament the loſs of him, becauſe we feel it; and he that hath chaſtened us by his removal, certainly wills us to feel the rod, that we may rightly regard it. But he, bleſſed ſoul, has fought a good fight, has finiſhed his courſe, has kept the faith, and is now gone to receive the crown of righteouſneſs; and to be enrobed with that white garment which is the righteouſneſs of the ſaints. He is gone to the great Shepherd and Biſhop of ſouls, who laid down his life for the ſheep, and will not fail to reward thoſe who have rightly divided the word of life, and ſpent their lives in feeding the ſheep of his paſture.

Juſt exceptions, I know, are often made againſt funeral characters, as exhibiting an aſſemblage of virtues, the portrait of partiality, and the child of fancy, but not formed from a living original. The juſtneſs of the exception is allowed—it ſhould give caution, but cannot be a reaſon for its total diſuſe. When any perſon hath been eminent in his ſtation and character, whether ſacred or civil; when he has done diſtinguiſhed ſervice in the church of God; to let ſuch drop unnoticed from the ſcene would be criminal ingratitude. God hath ſaid the memory of the juſt ſhall be bleſſed. By giving praiſe, and being thankful to God for the labours of his faithful ſervants, after they are call-

ed from their poſt, and reſt in their beds, we do his will. It is a tribute due to thoſe who are gone, and may be greatly uſeful to thoſe who are yet behind, travelling in the vale, and running with patience the race ſet before them. Behold we count them happy who endure, are the words of God's ſpirit and his church, ſpoken by St. James.

This was the voice of the primitive Chriſtians, when they aſſembled at the graves of their holy men and martyrs, and celebrated their praiſes, with hymns, thankſgivings, and funeral orations; exhorting each other to piety and virtue by their examples. For this, the words of our text might be thought an apoſtical authority.

In that important light, long, I truſt, will Biſhop SEABURY be remembered, who hath left his memorial in our hearts; long will his name live in our church, as worthy of all commendation. In the year one thouſand ſeven hundred and eighty three, as the war with Great-Britain was drawing near to a cloſe; while we were unable to confer with our brethren in the other ſtates, but anxious to take the earlieſt and moſt effectual meaſures our beſt diſcernment could ſuggeſt, to procure a valid epiſcopate, on which, under God, the continuance and enjoyment of our religious profeſſion would probably depend; the clergy of this ſtate, agreed to elect ſome perſon, to be inveſted with that important office. Two perſons occured to our minds, Doctor Leaming, and Doctor Seabury.

The former, by his amiable life among us, and excellent ſervices, merited our affections, eſteem and confidence; he had a juſt claim to our attention, and was our firſt choice. Debility, and the many bodily infirmities under which he then laboured, cauſed him to decline, as altogether unfited for an enterpriſe that required great vigour and firmneſs of mind. Theſe were conſpicuous in Doctor Seabury, who, in every other reſpect alſo, was the man to our wiſhes.. He accepted of our choice; and without delay undertook to carry our deſires into effect. To the Engliſh Biſhops, there appeared obſtacles exiſting in the Britiſh government, which, it was neceſſary to get removed, as the firſt ſtep in the proſecution of the buſineſs. Until that was done, they judged it would not be conſiſtent, either with their wiſdom, or duty, to give him conſecration. Efforts were made, but unhappily without ſucceſs; and no aſſurance could be obtained, that our application would be more fortunate at any future period. In this ſituation, what remained to be done? The alternative before him, was, either to deſert the cauſe, or to apply elſewhere. To give over the purſuit, and let the object be loſt, in his hands, was irreconcilable to his faithful and perſevering mind. Theſe circumſtances finally compelled him, as they did us to deſire him, to lay the condition and ſtate of our ſuffering church before the Biſhops in Scotland, with our requeſts to them for his conſecration. That venerable body readily accepted of the application and freely

freely conferred on him the episcopate. This event therefore, we are authorised to believe, laid the foundation for the episcopate that is now in the American States.

After two years absence, and chiefly at his own expence, he returned to us. By which auspicious event, our church was furnished with a proper priesthood ; and by his discreet management, and eminent talents we were put on a footing as encouraging as our best reason would suffer us to expect. And this day, my Brethren of the clergy, we are able, and as willing to declare one to another, and to the world, how happy we were under him, as our spiritual father, brother, companion and friend. With manners engaging, and by a method judicious and easy, he would commonly collect our opinions, and if different in any matter, bring them together, and so accommodate them to his own, as, with very few exceptions, to maintain a most pleasing harmony and union among us. His visitations to all the churches in his diocese, were frequent, more so than perhaps consisted with his health, usually preaching wherever he went. The people always received him with pleasure, and a numerous audience heard him gladly.

Thus did that excellent prelate, for near eleven years, fill his seat, and with great dignity execute his office. The whole of that time he was an admirable pattern and example, conformed to the character described in the text. He had

had the rule over us, and spoke the word of God ; so that we may confidently call upon our people to follow his faith—the faith that was once delivered to the saints.

He was born and educated in this state. To the place where he received his birth he was an honour, as he was to the school of sciences wherein he laid the foundation of his future greatness. Blessed with a clear understanding, and tenacious memory, a quick comprehension, and solid judgment ; these happy endowments enabled him, by an extensive reading, and intense thinking, to render his mind a rich repository of solid and useful learning. As his own resources became great, he was indeed conscious of them, but never dogmatical or assuming ; the only use he made of them, was to be more instructive and agreeable. His judicious arrangement of thoughts, was evident to all he conversed with, by his uncommonly clear and easy method of communicating them. This was one circumstance which made him so excellent a preacher. In his preaching he did not affect to appear learned, but his discourses always fully discovered both his natural and acquired abilities. The great and good man, ever appeared in the plain speaker.

Theological niceties, and conjectural divinity were ever his aversion, because too refined and visionary either to be felt or comprehended. His one object, and therefore his chief care was to explain the great articles of faith, and

and rules of life, what we must believe, and how we must live, that we may be eternally happy.

His own vital sense of religion infused itself into his discourses, and animated them with the same divine passion that warmed his own breast. His mind was too great to seek popular applause, he only wished to have his labours well received that he might do good ; that he might prevail upon people to seek their own spiritual welfare, that he might promote the cause of Christ's church, and advance pure and undefiled religion. Confident of the solid grounds on which his religion rested, he was, agreeable to the natural firmness of his mind, inflexible in his principles ; these he accounted sacred ; from which on no occasion would he allow himself to deviate, yet with a graceful ease he could give up any thing, but the truth ; and even that he would support, if possible without giving offence.

He deliberately entertained an high opinion of the church, whose most dignified office he sustained ; because he believed her to be built on the foundation of the apostles—Jesus Christ himself being the chief corner stone. Her interest, as a spiritual society, abstracted from worldly power and policy, he endeavoured with great integrity to maintain, as he supported her divine authority with a masterly hand.

His stability and zeal, his attachment and perseverance in the true faith, claim a more than ordinary

ordinary notice, at a time when so many sit loose to the fundamental articles of Christianity, think lightly of the great mysteries of our redemption by Christ; and if they do not openly avow infidelity, covertly sap the foundation of revealed religion, under the specious name of morality.

Against principles so repugnant to Christianity and dangerous to the souls of men, a number of those discourses he published, are an excellent guard. The whole are a set of fine sermons, well calculated for the use of families. Some, were professedly composed for their instruction in the nature and economy of Christ's church, and all are on subjects chosen to teach them, what, as members of that church, they are to believe and practise. Those who read them with attention, will ever find improvement, and all judges of sound reasoning and correct composition, in compliment to their own good judgment and taste, must admire the author.

Though in his last visitation some appearances of declining health were seen with concern; yet it pleased God without any preparatory admonition, to come suddenly in an instant, and at once open a passage for his soul into the world of spirits. He had nearly reached the years, which number the age of man, yet his naturally sound and vigorous constitution, without any apparent decay of his mental powers, gave reasonable hopes, that his useful life would be

be continued for years to come. Unerring wisdom judged otherwise. He was ready, and his Lord hath called him from his station and labours here on earth, to join his church in the world above.

As both are but one church; so we may believe, that those whom he makes rulers, to whom he commits the greatest places of power, and dignity, if they adorn their office, and faithfully discharge their trust here, he will not degrade in the other world. This we may infer from those words of Christ to his apostles: *Verily I say unto you, that ye which have followed me, in the regeneration when the Son of man shall sit in the throne of his glory, ye also shall sit upon twelve thrones, judging the twelve tribes of Israel.* That is, your reward and glory in the other world, shall answer to that place of trust and power and dignity, which you have had in the church on earth. And this promise was no more peculiar to the apostles, than their office. Now, if we seriously consider the state of the other world, that the blessed Jesus sits there, enthroned in majesty and glory, king of saints, and priest of the most high God, we may safely believe, that, however little the office of the priesthood is thought of in this world; and his servants often left to do the service of his altar on earth, in much poverty and want; a very different scene will open, when we come into that kingdom, where the king is himself an

an high priest, and will reward the labours of all those who serve him in sincerity and truth.*

This, my reverend brethren, should be our mighty consolation, under all the cares and inquietudes of our solemn employments. Let it ever dwell with us, to encourage us to diligence and faithfulness in that part of the ministry which is committed to our trust. The pious counsel of our late beloved bishop, given to us, in his admired charges, we have still in our hands: let us now often read them, that the words he hath spoken may abide with us, for the honour of our Lord and of his church. Let us remember his conversation and labours of love, and strive the more earnestly to preserve our wonted harmony and brotherly affection inviolate.

We have one Lord, who is our head, one faith, as a principle of action, one spirit to quicken and knit us together in that one faith, one hope of our calling, to animate us in our duty, one church, the body of that one Lord, in which we serve, let the servants be one in peace and love. Let us discharge our duty faithfully in that holy church, and wait patiently

* When a man is careful to say what is good, and to do what is honest, to speak well and act better, endeavouring to be what he would seem to be, avoiding all suspicions and appearances of evil, when he is zealous according to his capacity for the promoting of public good, acting sincerely, prudently and justly; endeavouring to make the times the better for him wherever he lives, this will be the most effectual means to make his name honourable and his memory precious. Bishop Wilkins.

(26)

ently a while, and the Lord will come, and his reward is with him, and bleſſed, for ever bleſſed, are thoſe ſervants, whom their Lord when he cometh, ſhall find ſo doing.

Finally, Let us ever bleſs God's holy name for all his ſervants departed this life in his faith and fear, and beſeech him to give us grace, ſo to follow their good examples, that with them we may be partakers of his heavenly kingdom.

And, with our prayers for this unſpeakable gift, let it be our inceſſant care, to make good that apoſtolic exhortation, which equally concerns, and is equally directed to all.

My beloved brethren, be ye ſteadfaſt, unmoveable, always abounding in the work of the Lord, knowing that your labour ſhall not be in vain in the Lord.

To God the Father, the Son, and the holy Ghoſt, be all honour and glory, dominion and power, now and for ever more. AMEN.

BISHOP JARVIS's

CHARGE

TO THE

Clergy of his Dioceſe.

DELIVERED

IMMEDIATELY AFTER HIS

CONSECRATION,

In Trinity Church, NEW-HAVEN,

ON THE FESTIVAL OF *ST. LUKE*, OCTOBER 18, 1797.

TOGETHER WITH THE

ADDRESS

Of the Convention of the Proteſtant Epiſcopal Church, in Connecticut, to their Biſhop.

AND THE

BISHOP's ANSWER.

PRINTED AT *NEWFIELD*,
BY LAZARUS BEACH.
1798.

Biſhop JARVIS's CHARGE.

MY REVEREND AND DEAR BRETHREN.

UNDER the good providence of God, we are aſſembled, on an occaſion both ſolemn and intereſting to us of the clergy, and to the church. The character in which I now addreſs you, is by divine permiſſion devolved upon me, through your unanimous, and in reſpect of myſelf, unmerited ſuffrage. Much are we obliged to the Biſhops* for their attention to your application; and our moſt hearty thanks are due to them, for the pains they have taken in coming here, to ratify your election, and ſupply this dioceſe with the office, made vacant by the death of our late Biſhop, of bleſſed memory. My own feelings aſſure me, that the tranſactions of this day, muſt have called up afreſh to your remembrance, former painful ſenſations on the loſs we ſuſtained, in the death of that moſt amiable and excellent prelate, who by every means endeared himſelf to us; and whom ſo many years experience taught us, moſt highly to eſteem and admire.

* Biſhop White, Biſhop Provoſt and Biſhop Baſs.

It is your unhappiness that he is succeeded by one, who thinks it no degradation, to acknowledge himself every way his unequal; and whose feelings would be gratified by never being brought into a comparison with him; Although he would esteem himself honoured, in the enjoyment of a lower seat near him.

But what is wanting in abilities on my part, I trust confidently, will be considered as an additional reason, for greater and more united exertions on yours, to make good the deficiency. Your friendship, together with your well grounded affections for the interest of religion, the good and welfare of the church, will, I cannot doubt, incline you to accept candidly, and assist with your best aids the well meant endeavours of one, who can with the utmost sincerity assure you, of his having an equal desire with you, to be useful according to his capacity; and is not less concerned for the interests of religion, and of this church. Most seriously is it to be lamented, that there is so much need of anxious concern on the subject.

The church of Christ hath always had, and always will have her enemies. The Kingdom of Christ is not of this world. To that kingdom, the children of this world will, some way or other, be opposed; either by open unbelief, or by errors in faith, or viciousness of life. The persons who belong to any of these descriptions, will be found, in different degrees, to be disaffected to religion in general; or, from various unhappy causes, to the duties it prescribes, or the life it requires. As men are well or ill affected towards religion, so are they accordingly affected towards the clergy, who are the teachers & supporters of it. Those who reverence christianity, and its sacred institutions, will reverence the priest-

hood, which is of the same divine establishment; through the ministry of which, they can only enjoy the consolations and blessings of their holy faith and religion. On the other hand, those who seek to undermine religion, and bring it into disrepute, are always adversaries to the Clergy. Active in discipling others to their own opinions, their first step commonly is, to persuade people to think meanly of, and to treat the clergy with contempt. As they succeed in this point, so they prepare them to sneer at, and ridicule religion; to neglect and slight public worship, and all public institutions. That this is an existing, and that it is a growing evil among us, we of the clergy, with deep concern, see and feel. In like manner does it affect the regular, and serious part of our people. It may however, afford some satisfaction to observe, that in general, they, who would deprive *us* of our orders and usefulness, are the very men, who would rob their Redeemer, of his eternal Godhead and Divinity.

What is personal, ought to be of the least consideration. We are to expect tribulation in this world, and are bound to bear with patience, reproaches for his sake, whose servants we are. We are bound also to take heed, not to deserve them. *The Servant is not above his Master. It is enough for the disciple, that he be as his Master, and the servant as his Lord: if they have called the Master of the house Beelzebub, how much more shall they call them of his houshold.**— None of us, even the best, are in every respect, such as we ought to be. This use therefore we may make of their censures, tho' a very different one, from what our adversaries intend, namely, to correct the

* *Matt.* 10. 25.

things, wherein we may perceive ourselves to be blameworthy, or may appear so to others: and their unfounded aspersions, may and should, excite us to take more diligent heed, that, as far as it is possible in us, our ministry be not blamed, or found upon the fullest enquiry to deserve it. So that—*In much patience—By pureness, by knowledge, by long suffering, by kindness, by the Holy Ghost, by love unfeigned—By honour and dishonour, by evil report and good report,—As poor, yet making many rich—in all things approving ourselves, as the ministers of God.**

No serious mind can be insensible, that to be God's minister must be to hold an office of high dignity: that it is an office, in its design greatly benevolent, and useful, and in its due execution, most extensively beneficial; and nothing can be more fatal in its consequences, than the neglect and abuse of it.

Let us then look up to the head, and founder of the pastoral office, the great Shepherd and Bishop of our souls; and behold him, in the depth of humility and meekness, teaching the ignorant, relieving the distressed, and labouring to save lost sinners. Let us recollect those, to whom he first committed the charge, of carrying on the same great work; and see them, through much tribulation, doing the work of their master, and from thence learn our calling: and under the darkest appearances, take courage, and be faithful to do our duty, and he will take care of the event.

To rescue fallen nature from the miseries of its Apostacy, and cleanse it of those corruptions, by

* 2 *Cor.* 6 *ch.* 4. &c

which it lay in ruins; was the design and end, for which Jesus came into the world, clothed by the Father with an everlasting priesthood. From these corruptions, sprang all that contradiction of sinners, all those sorrows and sufferings, which he endured. They have been, and still are, the source of all that opposition, which, his priests and ambassadors have met with, in his service, and of all the hardships they have undergone, in the labour of bringing men to their duty, and reconciling them to God; from the time, in which he sojourned on earth, down to this day. All this was perfectly foreseen by him, who knew all things. He accordingly, prepared his disciples for what they were to meet with; by telling them plainly before-hand, *Behold, I send you forth as Sheep in the midst of wolves: be ye therefore wise as serpents, and harmless as doves.** Certainly no office, or employment, can require greater, or more unremitting exertions; no one calls for more prudence, composure, and fortitude; accompanied with a well tempered zeal for the happiness of others, and an exemplary life, to encourage and guide them in the path of Salvation.

Of this every clergyman ought to be duly sensible, and by frequent reflections, to make it familiar to his mind, to prepare him to act with good judgment, and a religious sense of duty, under all the adverse casualties that may occur in the due execution of his office.

For the more faithful discharge of his duty, he should at no time forget, that he is the servant and minister, the steward and ambassador, of Jesus Christ. These are titles honorary indeed, but all of them expressive, of a state of dependance, and subjection; and speak the person to whom they belong, not at liberty to act his own humour:—but under the strictest obligation, to observe the commands of that heavenly Lord and Master, whose servant and minister he is. Obedience to his commands, is what all christrians are bound to pay; but the obligation is yet stronger upon the clergy; as the near relation they stand in to him, by the priesthood they bear, adds to all their engagements.—Every argument, for the performance of christian duties in common, concludes more particularly, for the faithful, and regular discharge of the duties of their sacred function; for the due execution of those great offices, and the pursuance of those ends, for which they were invested with this character.—It is the dignity of our office, to represent and display the honour of our great high priest, by whose authority we act; and to answer the exigences of his church. We must therefore sincerely endeavour to promote those purposes, or we violate the design of our ordination, and are manifestly deficient, in the duty we owe to him, as his ministers.

Permit me then, my Brethren, in this my first address, to lead your attention to some particulars, which I trust, you will consider with me, as important to the rightful discharge of our duty, and interesting to the people of our cures.

The first I will mention to you is, that, as clergymen, and Ambassadors of Christ, it is an incumbent branch of our duty, to use our best endeavours, that the people of our cure may understand well their christian profession; what are the duties they owe to God, as members of the church of christ; and, as much as possible, to attach their minds,

* *Matt.* 10. 16.

and religious affections, to the performance of them.

Now in order for this, people must understand the nature of the church: the relation they stand in to its head; what they must do, that they may be true and sound members of, and attain to the blessings, he has annexed to it. It cannot escape our notice that the people of our congregations, instead of attending to the instructions of the church, to which they belong; have from other sources, lost sight, to an unhappy degree, of the means ordained by our gracious redeemer, for our access to and communion with him: through which we are to partake of the aids of the Holy Spirit, to sanctify our hearts, and obtain the forgiveness of our sins: And in their place have substituted preaching or hearing of Sermons as the chief or only business of church assemblies. Thus, what was in its original institution and use, for the purpose of instructing men in the faith of the Gospel, and to awaken their consciences to do all that is therein commanded for Salvation, is hereby perverted, and made in itself an act of religion; and the end of meeting for a public, and religious service. So that preaching *in* the church, it is to be feared, perhaps it may be affirmed, has contributed much to cast religion *out* of it. This, as I apprehend, is a sad and dangerous departure from the genius, and spirit of the christian religion. A good knowledge of the christian church, as to its nature and design, will effectually correct so gross a mistake.

The church is not of an human, but of a divine original. In its nature it is an institution of God, a regular society, founded by divine authority. It is the church of Christ; because he purchased it

with his blood. He called it out, and separated it from the world, that it might be holy unto himself; and the school of holiness to all, who being admitted into it, would conform to its holy and divine nature. For this purpose he appointed its government, instituted its priesthood, and ordained its sacraments. He bestowed on it his holy spirit. He is the founder of its faith, and he gave to it the promise of eternal life. Could we persuade people, thus seriously to enquire into, and make themselves acquainted with the nature of the christian church; they would be convinced, that the design of its institution, is to call them from the dominion of sin; from a subjection to their fleshly lusts,—and passions, the vanities and follies of this wicked world; to an union with Christ, and with each other; by a new birth from the holy spirit, and to train them up, in virtue and holiness, to the Kingdom of Heaven.*

As they realize this to be the design of the church, and the end of its institution, they will have more correct and truer notions, of the relation they bear to christ, their redeemer and spiritual head. By faith in him their Saviour, they are his disciples: and being incorporated by his spirit, under him, they are a holy society; who, as members, form one body, united to him their head. Under this emblem, all christians should see their connection, subordination, and dependance, upon this their head. The body is a regular structure, the limbs of which, being joined together, are subordinate and subservient to one another, and are animated by the same soul or spirit. *For by one spirit we are all baptised into one body.* Being planted into Christ by the holy spirit, he, as the head, communicates nourishment to his body, and its several members, through the operations of the spirit, conveyed in the ordinances of his church. In the faithful use of these means, blessed and sanctified by him, his body is edified and built up in him, perfected in all things that pertain to life eternal.

As we succeed in bringing our people, thus to understand the nature and œconomy of the church of Christ, our labours will be productive of this good effect; they will learn to distinguish rightly, the holy offices of the church, from the discourses delivered to them from the pulpit; and to place their principal regard, upon the prayers and sacraments, as means whereby they hold communion, and have fellowship with the Father, and his son Jesus Christ. Being well grounded in these doctrins, we may then reasonably expect, that our people will come to church, under a clear and full sense of their duty; that they may perform it, in all due acts of adoration, petition and praise; and express the becoming affections of grateful hearts, for the privileges they enjoy in God's church, in the means of grace, and helps to a holy life, they there receive; and the hopes of future glory, of which they are the earnest and pledge.

Actuated by these principles, they will come to church, for the sake of the prayers, and sacraments. In these, they will enjoy the sincere delight of christian communion, in the pledges of their redeemer's munificence on the church, and happy sensations will rise in their breasts, and flow with their devotions to Jesus—who was crucified for sin—but—Being exalted to the right hand of God—"hath shed forth those streams of the water of life, which have been flowing ever since, from the

* See Bp. Seabury's *Sermon, of Christian Unity.*

throne of God and the lamb, through the appointed channels, to water every plant and flower in the Garden of God."

To honour our redeemer, in his own institutions and services, is the bounden duty of all christians. It is eminently the duty of the clergy; that they may prove themselves faithful stewards of those heavenly mysteries, with which they are intrusted: and to entitle them, with confidence, to look for his gracious protection and favour. Hence all christians, who will attend to us, and with minds open to the truth, hear from us, the things which belong to sound faith and godliness, will properly sort, and duly estimate, their respective religious duties, and will rate each, according to its importance. They will think lightly of none, but they will more highly reverence some than others; although they will conscientiously practice all. While we are diligent to press them, to be anxiously careful of their everlasting felicity; they will be steady and devout, in the public worship of God—as being called to one common duty, the duty of honoring and glorifying him, with one mouth and one voice—As children of one family, members of one body—having one hope of our calling, and being heirs of one common salvation. Their devotions will be animated with humble and hearty desires, that their wants, spiritual and temporal, may be supplied by our heavenly Father; and that by the same devotions, their hearts may be fixed, in the firmest resolutions of holy obedience. These desires and resolutions, thus kindled, will not suffer them to tarry behind, or stop with the ordinary service of the church. Delighing to tread the courts of the Lord's house, they will go forward to his altar, and in the sacred symbols there exhibited, will eat of that bread, which came down from hea-

ven; and drink of that cup which giveth life to the world.

ENLIGHTENED by the doctrins of the scriptures, faithfully stated to them by us, the worship they pay to God, will be understood, not as an arbitrary demand, merely to shew his sovereignty over us, but as a natural right, indispensibly due to him, the maker of all things: who gives us life, and continually provideth all things for us. In like manner, the positive institutions of the Gospel, will be received, as gracious appointments in the scheme of our redemption, and recovery to life and bliss in Christ. The holy eucharist will be applied, as the means of keeping up that spiritual life, the principle of which we received in our new birth, at our baptism; and of continuing that interest, in the benefits and blessings of christ's passion and death, which was made over to us, when we became members of his mystical body.

PRESUMING, according to my knowledge of your sentiments, my Brethren, that it is your desire, people should be well informed of their duty, and their lives be conformed to the precepts of the Gospel; I have mentioned these things, as essential to the character, and life of the christian. But it may be proper to add a further observation; that the means should ever be enforced, as they should always be used, with a view to the end of religion; and carefully discriminated from it.

THE end of Religion is the salvation of our souls. The Son of God came to seek and to save that which was lost. The church itself, and all its services, were erected and appointed for this purpose. Every act of which, as a part of her service, is therefore an act of religion, because it is a means to pre-

pare and fit us for the enjoyment of a happy state with God. While we are in the church in this world, we are in God's vineyard, are his husbandry. In complying with his commands, and doing his will, the outward and personal act is ours, the inward is his, in fashioning the soul, through the instrumentality of his institutions, into his own likeness and image. This is the spiritual building, formed by the hand of God, to endure forever. For the raising and finishing of this building, positive rites and ordinances, and all outward acts are but the scaffolding; when the building is completed, the scaffolds are removed and fall off, as being of no farther use.

WAS this truth attended to according to its importance, the close connection christ hath established, between the external ministrations of his church, and the internal renovation of the soul, would be more perfectly discerned, and comprehended. As christians come to think, and believe rightly concerning these things, they will see the necessity of communion in the prayers and sacraments of the church. These, accompanied with reading the holy scriptures, which, in the sense of those scriptures, is preaching, and the best of preaching; as they of right challenge, so will they not fail, to be most regarded and venerated. Sound religion, and vital active piety, will prevail, in proportion as the duties of the Gospel are thus understood, and practiced. People will then become more regular, and steady; and by the habits of stedfastness, will daily increase, and grow up in their holy faith, until they come unto God's everlasting kingdom. It will prevent them from being tossed to and fro, by every self authorized novel teacher, and carried about, by every wind of doctrin, with which the ignorant enthusiast, or the more subtle deceiver, strive to delude them.

AND here I may observe, that the christian faith and practice, understood in the light I have considered them, can hardly fail of leading people, into a due sense of the importance of the christian priesthood.

" THE regular ministers, (you have here the
" words of the archbishop Usher) are authorized to
" declare God's pleasure unto such as *believe* and
" *repent*; and in his name to certify and give full
" assurance to their consciences, that their sins are
" forgiven. For though others may indeed bring
" glad tidings of good things to the penitent sinner,
" as *truly* as they do, yet neither is it to be expect-
" ed that they *should*, or indeed that they *can* do it,
" with the some authority and power, with such
" full assurance and such entire satisfaction to the
" afflicted, broken and wounded conscience."

ST. Paul tells us that Christ *whom God had given to be head over all things to the church—gave some apostles, some pastors and teachers; for the perfecting of the saints, for the work of the ministry, for the edifying of the body of christ. Till we all come, in the unity of the faith, and of the knowledge of the Son of God, unto a perfect man, unto the measure of the stature of the fulness of Christ.*

CAN the intelligent christian do otherwise than reverence that office, by which he was regenerated, and grafted into the body of christ's church: by which, in the consecrated elements of bread and wine, he is admitted to the inestimable privilege of eating the flesh, and drinking the blood of the Son of God.—That blood which cleanseth from all sin, and whosoever doth it in true faith and penitence, his Saviour hath said, hath eternal life abiding in him?: in brief,—To his ministers. God hath given

power and commandment, to declare and pronounce to his people, being penitent, the absolution and remission of their sins: To them he hath committed the means, and ministrations of grace. By them men put on Christ, and are united to the Son of God; by whose prevalent acts, they are constituted members of his sacred polity, and communion. Christ's ministers lead in the prayers and praises of his church, and present them to him, the great high priest, which, perfumed by his own merits, he presents to the Father. Divine mercies in return, descend through this prevailing intercessor, and by his priests, regularly serving at his altar, are dispensed in the word and sacraments, and by blessing his people, in his name, and by his authority.

An office thus connected with all the parts form the system of christian faith and worship, must be held in reverend esteem by all who have any true notions of, or any real regard for them. It cannot in reason be imputed to the clergy, that they preach up themselves, when they teach the nature and duties of their office; for all are equally concerned to know, how they are to be saved by Christ. Whosoever he hath appointed must be important; and they cannot know the use and end of his servants, and their appointments, without knowing, that priests are ordained for men, in things pertaining to God; and that we are their servants for Jesus sake.

There is one point more to which I would call your attention. And if the fact be, as I conceive it is, we ought industriously to combat, what is so false in principle, and pernicious in practice.

By the language and conduct of men, we are to judge what are their religious principles. These shew but too plainly, that the gospel is considered by many, as being a mere system of opinions or doctrins, and conceive, that an assent to them, with the observation of some outward forms of general repute, and a behaviour that passes without reproach, in the vulgar eye, is all that is required, to constitute the christian character. The christian religion is indeed a system of doctrins, or truths, revealed in the gospel; for which we are bound earnestly to contend. But the mistake is, and it is a dangerous one; that the truths of the gospel, are mere speculative opinions, of which, men are at liberty to frame their own notions, as they chuse, and each one for himself. If they can flatter themselves that they are *sincere*, they may judge themselves safe, and their opinions true, for with them *sincerity* is the only thing necessary. This principle being allowed, it is equally good in every man, and proves every man's opinions equally true. Hence the unity of the church is destroyed, Prayer, public and private, are called in question, whether founded in reason, or of any utility. The necessity of the Sacraments, their use and significance, become greater or less, or nothing at all, just as mens opinions are. Men may divide and subdivide, into sects and parties, without number, and without end, and every mans conduct passes as harmless, without crime, in going where they please, in joining whom they please, and worshipping God as they please, in retired solitude, or a public assembly, in mute silence, or vocal harmony. The scriptures are to be interpreted according to every man's private judgment, whether he be learned or unlearned: and private judgment is the standard, by which, the truths or doctrins of the scriptures are to be measured; and all rest upon this foundation, that christianity is a religion of opinions. Private judgment is ever to be valued,

and ever used; its right ought never to be denied. But it should be remembered, that where there is a right, there is also a duty, and he who only attends to the former, and neglects the latter is sure to be in an error. Private judgment should also be claimed & used, as being private. And though one man may not be obtruded upon, or deprived of that right by another, yet he is accountable to God for his private judgment, and opinions, as he is, for the right use, or abuse, of all his faculties, and for all the means which God affords him, to know and do what he ought. But whatever opinions men entertain, and however corrupt & hurtful to themselves, so long as they confine, and conduct them, within their own right, they will do no injury to others, nor disturb the peace and order of society.

On the contrary, when particular opinions cause men to disregard the united Judgement, and voice of God's church, when they lead men to put forced constructions, upon the plainest things written in the word of God; when they dispose men to transgress his clear, and express commands; when they slacken, and melt down, all zeal for christ's church, as he framed and modeled it; for the faith he laid as the foundation; for the orders and institutions he hath erected, as the mounds about it; and for the commands he hath given, to govern and perfect its members: The principle, which brings forth such fruits, whose end is the dissolution of the church, as a Society; and makes every man a church to himself; is so visibly contrary to the whole scheme, and plan of the gospel; to its leading and fundamental doctrines, that it must be the duty of the clergy, to watch against, and do their utmost to correct such false and baneful tenets, wherever they meet with them; and to persuade men to think more justly, to receive those truths, and di-

rect their minds by those doctrines, which are according to the Scriptures, and more certainly accompany salvation. It is *not he that commendeth himself is approved, but whom the Lord commendeth.* He that will be saved, must be saved in the way which God hath appointed, and not in any way of his own. We shall be judged at last according to God's word, not according to any persuasions we may have taken up, through the prejudices of education, or the perverseness of our own hearts; all of which are indeed no better than dreams, having no foundation but on that loose bottom of human imagination, on which are built, all the visions of the night, and all the heresies in the world.*

THE several points to which, in the foregoing, I have led your attention, I hope, my Brethren, you will approve of. In my apprehension they are matters of weight. And though they comprehend but a part of our duty as clergymen, they may serve to shew in no small degree, how delicate and curious is the work, to frame the minds of men into right principles, solid and clear notions of the redeemer's kingdom, how noble is the employment to watch over the church, that God bought with his own blood. The Son of God is the first of our order, the founder of our Society. Now when we consider how various are the spiritual necessities of his church, the ignorance, mistakes, and negligence of the people, the arts, sophistry, and wiles of the adversary; these things carry conviction, that nothing but an inexhaustible source can supply its wants.

LET these things be duly considered by us, and

* *See Essay on the Church.*

let us thereby be engaged, to support and adorn our function, both by our lives, and doctrin. The way to do this, is to take care—

FIRST—To be orthodox in our opinions, keeping firm and steady to that form of sound words, delivered by Christ and his Apostles, and handed down to us by the church: giving no ear, much less a favourable reception, to those novel doctrines, which are only ancient heresies, newly dressed, and broached, by restless lovers of novelty, or by ambitious designing men. A general good rule in divinity is, the more ancient the better. What is new, is a good reason why it cannot be true. In theological questions, that which hath been always and every where, and by all received, is a safe and just standard. The streams of those waters of the Sanctuary, being the more pure, the nearer they are to the fountain head.

SECONDLY—Another subject, which it concerns us duly to attend to, is the observing uniformity in the government, and worship of our church. For these, the rules prescribed by the church, should be regarded with as great exactness as possible. The rubricks where they are definite, should direct us in the administration of our office, without deviation, or in any case, as little as may be. Where there is a latitude, individuals may judge of the propriety of it; in unnecessary cases, and it is not an easy matter to find any that are otherwise, they may regret, that any latitude is allowed; yet the inconveniences may in some measure be avoided, if we act up to our former resolutions, that all should observe the same method, in all parts of the service. This uniformity will continue to give, as I trust it has had, its happy effects, in the satisfaction, harmony, and unity, it contributes to establish, both

among us of the clergy, and among our people.—For as we esteem it a great excellence of our church, that with one mouth, and one voice, we worship God, in one beautiful system of sound words; so the more strictly we adhere to the same order in every part of the service, the more perfectly shall we illustrate that excellence.

A THIRD particular, we should be assiduous to cultivate and maintain, is love and unity among ourselves. Disaffection, and opposition among the clergy, lessens their influence, often compels them to submit to, and do things they ought not, and if they were unanimous, and would support each other, they need not do. It is ever a matter of triumph, as it affords great advantage to the adversaries of religion. Religion itself is injured, and its friends suffer, by having their minds perplexed about its truths, or by weakening the power of it upon their lives. From the ministers of christ, dedicated to his service, and teachers of his religion, example is very justly expected. Unfeigned love to God, and benevolence to men, is the pure spirit, to which all the doctrines of the gospel have the most powerful tendency, and do actually generate, in the hearts of all its genuine desciples. The ministers of christ should take heed to realize in themselves, the truths and spirit of that religion, they are bound to preach. The first and fair fruits, that spring from thence, will be love and unity with their Brethren, and fellow labourers. This assemblage of the amiable graces of the christiain, will dispose the conscientious clergyman, to be critical in respect of his own reputation; it will render him equally critical and tender of the reputation of his Brethren. A spot in his garment is easily contracted, but hard to wipe off; it is discerned with an eagle's eye; and the bow of

flander ftands ready bent, to pierce him through with her dart.

We can do but little by ourfelves, to defend the inclofures of the church, and train up children to our divine head. We are weak and feeble; the wickednefs of men makes us more fo; yet, if every one made his brother's reputation, dear to him as his own, we might do very much to vindicate the innocence, to extenuate the infirmities, to remove the reproaches, that the faithlefs and vicious caft upon the *order*. The weakeft things knit together make a ftrong refiftance, for tho we fight not with carnal weapons, yet thofe we make ufe of are mighty, under God, to break and fhatter the kingdom of darknefs and all its retinue.

Were this our conduct, we might, with that confidence true virtue always gives, afk the man, in whom zeal for the welfare of his fellow creatures, burns with the brighteft & moft ardent flame, what his patriotic and generous heart could wifh more, than that men might be brought to this bleffed temper of mind? Wherever it prevailed in its full extent, it would univerfally reform; and the church, bleffed with fuch faithful fons, would be, and might appear to her enemies, according to the language of Solomon, *Beautiful as Tirzah, and comely as Jerufalem, and terrible as an army of banners.*

Permit me to exercife your patience a few moments longer, while I fuggeft a reflection or two, to the lay members of the convention.

As the clergy have their duties it muft be remembered, that the laity have theirs. If it is our duty to take the overfight of the church, and family of Chrift, as being thereunto appointed; it muft

be the duty of the laity fo to account of us; and by a willing and difcreet compliance, enable us, as God's watchmen, to execute our truft, in all good confcience. It is a piece of juftice to yourfelves and to us, to lay a part all prejudice, to hear with fobriety and reafon, and confider with candour, what we fay to you on the great truths, and the general or particular duties of chriftianity; the things that make for the good and peace of the church; the beauty and perfection of her holy worfhip; and for every one, according to the influence he bears, among the people of his refpective church, to give proof of his own, by doing his beft to engage the zeal of all others, for our common religion.

A few judicious, active, and exemplary men, in a congregation, can give ftrength and energy to the inftructions, and labours of a faithful clergyman, more than any, without feeing the effects, would be apt to imagine. Why fhould not chriftians, fhew a zeal to fupport the faith and church of chrift, equal to that, which the infidel fhews to deftroy them? For, what does the infidel expect and hope? that he fhould be thus active and zealous? If he is confiftent with himfelf, Nothing—beyond this world. What does the chriftian? Every thing that can dignify and exalt the human mind. What does the infidel labour to rob and ftrip you of? Your faith and religion; and with them, every thing that affords you folid comfort in this life, or happinefs and glory in the next. And while they, who toil and drudge in that workhoufe of iniquity, are conftantly fending abroad their artful and elaborate abfurdities, to corrupt the minds of the common people, and diveft them of all principles, which gives fecurity to government, order and peace in civil fociety, and are the bafis of all morality and virtue; ought you not, in honour to God and his

chrift,—as friends to your fellow men, to civil government and public order—To private juftice, and common humanity;—ought you not to ftrive to to eftablifh, and give currency to your religion? A religion, which is fo beneficient to all orders and degrees, and adapted to make men of every difcription, happy in themfelves, and inftruments of happinefs to others. The clergy of our church, teaching her doctrins, and acting according to her rules, are minifters of peace, and fupporters of rational and good government. It muft therefore be the true intereft of government to encourage and fupport them.

" To thefe things Brethren, if we have any concern for the interefts of religion, or our own, we muft always induftrioufly attend; but efpecially in fuch times, as by no means admit of negligence or mifmanagement. Yet vain will be our beft endeavours, unlefs we conftantly add to them, our fervent prayers, that God would enable and ftrengthen both *us*, and all that ferve him in the gofpel of his Son, to perform our duty with faithfulnefs and fuccefs. For *we are not fufficient to think any thing of ourfelves: our fufficiency is of God*. What therefore we ought, every one of us, to beg of him at all times, let us all prefent, jointly addrefs him for, in the comprehenfive and expreffive words of our public fervice."*

Almighty and everlafting God, by whofe fpirit the whole body of the church is governed and fanctified; receive our fupplications and prayers, which we offer before thee, for all eftates of men in thy holy church; that every member of the fame, in his vocation and miniftry, may truly and godly ferve thee, through our Lord and Saviour Jefus chrift. Amen.

* *A. Bp. Seckers firft charge.*

ADDRESS

Of the Convention of the Proteſtant Epiſcopal Church, in the ſtate of Connecticut, to the Right Rev. Doctor Abraham Jarvis, Biſhop of the Dioceſe.

REVEREND FATHER,

WE, the Preſbyters and Lay-Repreſentatives of the Proteſtant, Epiſcopal Church, in the State of Connecticut, avail ourſelves of the earlieſt opportunity, that could have been preſented to us, to congratulate you, upon your elevation to the dignified ſtation of a Biſhop, in the Church of Chriſt. Moſt cordially, Sir, do we recognize you in that ſacred character, and moſt readily do we receive you, as our Superintendant and Guide;—promiſing with chearfulneſs and from a ſenſe of duty, to pay you all that reſpect and obedience, to which your office entitles you; and which, we are aſſured from the word of God, and the teſtimony of antiquity, was ever deemed to be due to the ſacred Character, with which you are inveſted.

JOYFUL, Sir, as is the preſent occaſion, which fills the Epiſcopal Chair, yet, the ſolemn ſcene

D

that has juſt been performed, irreſiſtibly leads back our minds, in ſad remembrance to *him*, whom, we have often ſeen, from that Altar breaking the Bread of Life, and have often heard from that Pulpit, uttering the words of Peace, But, Sir, portentous to the Church, as was the moment, when the great diſpoſer of events called to his reward, our late much revered Biſhop, yet we truſt, nay are confident, that your beſt abilities will be exerted, to mitigate the loſs of that wiſdom and zeal, for which, he was ſo highly diſtinguiſhed, Whatever depends upon us to lighten the burden, which, your office impoſes upon you, ſhall be cheartully contributed. Eſteeming your perſonal character, as we unqueſtionably ought, and revering the Authority, with which you are clothed, as we aſſuredly do, your Epiſcopate opens with a proſpect of Peace and harmony throughout your Dioceſe. This ſtate of the Church is, at all times, devoutly to be wiſhed; but perhaps, never more than at preſent, when unity is ſo neceſſary to render fruitleſs, all the attacks of infidelity and vice. May that divine ſpirit, who is the ſource of unity and love, continue to preſerve this Church, under your Epiſcopate, in the moſt perfect Concord! And may zeal for promoting virtue and religion, ever diſtinguiſh the Biſhop, the Clergy, and the Laity of the Church of Connecticut!

New-Haven, October—1797.

Biſhop Jarvis's Anſwer.

MY REVEREND BRETHREN,
Beloved in our Lord Jeſus Chriſt.

I RETURN you my ſincere thanks for your affectionate addreſs, Permit me to requeſt you and the lay Gentlemen of the convention to accept my aſſurance of the warm and grateful affections, with which I receive your declarations of perſonal regard and friendſhip.

YOUR ſentiments of the ſacred office of a Biſhop, perfectly accord with my own, and compel me to obſerve the reſtraint they lay upon me, from gratulating myſelf on being promoted to that dignified ſtation. Your united judgment of the circumſtances, and ſituation of our church; and an unequivocal aſſurance, that in your opinion, her exigencies, in a preſſing manner required it; were the prevalent reaſons that overruled me, to acquieſce in your election to the office, with which I am now inveſted.

DISTINGUISHED as our late revered Biſhop was, for his eminent abilities; and amiable for the ornaments of the chriſtian; the recent act performed in your ſight, of conſecrating a ſucceſſor to the vacant chair, could not fail to recall *him*, with vigour to your remembrance, So intereſting a life, juſtified the ſtrongeſt apprehenſions, that his death was an omen of unhappy import to our church,

Known unto God are all his works, in wisdom doth he dispose them all, and that unerring hand, which directeth the whole to his own glory, often strikes away all other props, to convince men, that in him alone is their unfailing strength.

May a wise and gracious providence so order events, as to evince the rectitude of our intentions, and that our proceedings may be for his honour, and the good of his church.

Next to the guidance and protection of our all gracious head, I do, and must, rely on your friendship and benevolence, to prevent, or remove, those difficulties and impediments, which, contemplated in prospect, filled me with diffidence, and caused a reluctance, which, even as yet, I have not been able wholly to surmount. Sensible I am that in me emphatically *this treasure* is lodged in an *eathern vessel*; from the divine aid and support, and the constant united assistance, of you my brethren, it is, that I can hope, in any measure, to do the duties of the office committed to my trust. Altho' solicitude and anxious doubts abide me, yet while strengthened by these helps, I may solace my heart, that the important interests of that part of the church of christ, over which I am appointed to preside, will not materially suffer, so long as, by divine permission, the charge shall rest on me to superintend her weighty concerns.

That the redeemer's kingdom may flourish, the spirit of the Gospel prevail, and its laws be obeyed, is ever to be the object of our desires, & the subject of our prayers. To promote so great a work, much depends on the exertions, and pious labours of the clergy. The assurance you give of these, and that you will ever study to cultivate the strictest harmo-

ny, and be ever ready with your best advice, as they are expressive of a well directed zeal, so are they satisfactory, and minister grounds of confidence, not to be drawn from any other source.

Charity is the bond of perfectness: It is the cement which knits together the church; in every member perfects the child of God, and completes the family of christ.

As this virtue is the summary, and crown of christian graces; by cherishing it in our own breasts, and exercising it amongst ourselves, we shall shew, that we are the true disciples, and faithful ministers of christ, his peace, which passeth knowledge, shall keep our hearts and minds; it will give energy to our labours, & render us examples to our flocks.

My future conduct, I trust, will manifest my real respect and sincere affections for you, and all, whom we serve in the Gospel of our Lord. In addition to your advice, and assistance, in our respective sacred labours; let our prayers be mutual for each other, that God will continue us, and his church, in his holy keeping; and enable both you and me, to fulfil our ministry; and that the people, especially committed to our charge, may be a mutual blessing, and a crown of rejoicing to us, and to each other, in the day when the Son of God shall appear in glory, to judge and to reward.

ABRAHAM, Bp. Epl. ch. Connect.

New-Haven, Oct. 18, 1797.

Extract from the Journals of the Convocation of the Protestant Episcopal Church of Connecticut.

At a Meeting of the Bishop, Presbyters and Deacons of the Protestant Episcopal Church of Connecticut in Convocation, holden at the house of Mrs. Sarah Munday, in Stamford, on the 16th day of October, 1805 :

RESOLVED, That the following communication be sent to Carey Leeds, Alexander Bishop and others, who are dissatisfied with the ecclesiastical proceedings of the Bishop and Clergy of the Diocese of Connecticut, in regard to Mr. Ammi Rogers :

THE Bishop and Clergy of the Diocese of Connecticut, sincerely desirous to promote the peace, and preserve the authority of the Church, have met at Stamford, in the hope that, by a friendly conference with you, it would be in their power to satisfy you of the propriety and duty of submitting to the sentence pronounced on Mr. Ammi Rogers. They regret that your refusal to engage in a personal conference has prevented that full discussion of the subject which in every point of view was so desirable. By persons who profess themselves Churchmen in principle and practice, they still cherish the hope that the following statement of facts from the authority of the Church will be duly regarded.

It appears from page 17 of the Journal of the House of Bishops, a copy of which we herewith transmit to you, that on Friday, Sept. 14, 1804, a memorial was laid on the table from the Rev. Ammi Rogers, accompanied with sundry documents, and a letter requesting that a day may be appointed for the consideration of the points therein stated." And it further appears that the following Monday was assigned for the purpose, and notice thereof given to Mr. Rogers. From page 19, it appears, that the House of Bishops resolved to go into an investigation of the matters which Mr. Rogers had brought before them, in presence of such members of the House of Clerical and Lay Deputies as should possess any information on the subject. From page 20, it appears, that the Clerical members from the State of Connecticut were admitted to a hearing on the subject of Mr. Rogers, *in his presence;* documents on both sides were read, and a hearing was given to the parties concerned. From pages 21 and 22, it appears, that in consequence of an application from Mr. Rogers, made in the absence of the Clergy from Connecticut, the House of Bishops resolved that nothing should be done in the business except in the *presence of both parties;* and that, on a further application of a Clerical member from Connecticut, both parties were introduced on the following day, and a further hearing was given. From page 23, it appears, that at 7 o'clock, P. M. of the same day, the House of Bishops met ; and that the Right Reverend Bishop White, the Right Rev. Bishop Moore, and the Right Reverend Bishop Parker, were present ; and that these Bishops came to a determination, from which the following is an extract :

" After *full enquiry*, and *fair examination of all the evidence* that could be procured, it appears to this House, That the said Ammi Rogers had produced to the Standing Committee of New-York (upon the strength of which he obtained holy orders) a certificate, signed with the name of the Rev. Philo Perry, which certificate was not written nor signed by him.

" That the conduct of the said Ammi Rogers in the State of Connecticut, during his residence in that State, since he left New-York, has been insulting, refractory, and schismatical in the highest degree ; and, were it tolerated, would prove subversive of all order and discipline in the Church : and that the statement which he made in justification of his conduct, was a mere tissue of equivocation and evasion, and, of course, served rather to defeat than to establish his purpose.

"*Therefore*, This House do approve of the proceedings of the Church in Connecticut, in reproving the said Ammi Rogers, and prohibiting him from the performance of any ministerial duties within that Diocese; and, moreover, are of opinion, that he deserves a severe eccelesiastical censure, that of degradation from the Ministry."

By recurring to the Journals, you will find that the above is an impartial statement of facts, and that the following particulars undeniably result from it. Mr. Ammi Rogers brought this business before the house of Bishops, and, in the words of his memorial, declared, that "he never has shunned investigation, but on the contrary has always *requested* it, and *now* prays that a candid and impartial enquiry may be made as to his conduct and character."* It appears that Mr. Rogers presented to the House his documents; that a full hearing of the case was at different times had in the presence of both parties; that Mr. Rogers confirmed the wish which he expressed for an enquiry, by always attending for the purpose: and it was not until the close of the enquiry, and until he had reason to fear the unfavorable result to himself, that he expressed to the Bishops that he did not wish them to come to any decision.

Now, as persons deeply interested for the peace of the Church and your spiritual welfare, we intreat your conscientious and serious attention to the following considerations. Can you suppose that if Mr. Rogers did not wish for any enquiry into his conduct by the House of Bishops, he would have permitted them to engage in it without entering his solemn protest against it? Can you suppose that the Right Rev. Bishop White, whose impartiality and mildness are so universally acknowledged; that Bishop Moore, who had been represented by Mr. Rogers as friendly to him; that Bishop Parker, who had just made his solemn vows at the altar, would have *forced* Mr. Rogers to an enquiry, if he had not solicited it, and would declare that they had made a *full enquiry* and *fair examination* of the subject, if such inquiry and examination had not been made? Can you suppose that these venerable Bishops of the Church would have violated every obligation of truth and justice, as well as the solemn vows of office, by condemning an innocent man? Could Mr. Rogers have had a trial before a more impartial tribunal? Or can you suppose that after the House of Bishops had made a full enquiry and pronounced their opinion, any thing else was left to the Bishop of Connecticut than to carry their decision into effect? Mr. Rogers made an appeal to the House of Bishops—they thought proper to investigate his conduct and to pronounce a decision. The Canons of the Church of Connecticut, in regard to the trial of Clergymen, could here have no operation. The Bishop of Connecticut was the agent to carry the decision of the House of Bishops into effect.

Mr. Ammi Rogers has been solemnly degraded from the Ministry, after a full investigation of hisconduct, and a decision in regard to him by the highest authority of the Church. We intreat you as friends to the peace of society and the order and harmony of the Church; we intreat you by your characters as Churchmen, by the memory of your Fathers who cherished the Church with inviolable fidelity; we intreat you by the prospect of that awful tribunal at which all mankind must be judged, to regard the Apostolic injunction, "HEAR THE CHURCH." In the language of the Apostle, we exhort you, brethren, "*Put from you that unworthy person.*" Remember the declaration of our Lord, "*If any man refuse to hear the Church, let him be unto you as a heathen man and a publican.*" In the spirit of meekness and affection we intreat you, rend not that divine body, the Church, which your Redeemer purchased with his blood. For ourselves, we most solemnly declare, that mindful of the commission given to us by our Divine Master, and relying on his promise that he will be with his Church alway, even to the end of the world, we shall esteem it our sacred duty to preserve inviolable the authority committed us.—And we trust that what is thus "done" by the lawful Governors of the Church "on earth will be ratified in Heaven."

A true Copy of Record,

ASHBEL BALDWIN, SECRETARY.

---

* The express words of the Memorial of Mr. Rogers to the House of Bishops, are—"He *now* prays that a candid and impartial enquiry may be made as to his conduct and character both as a *minister* and a *man*, giving him opportunity to hear the witness and answer for himself."

A

SERMON,

PREACHED AT WATERBURY, (SALEM PARISH)

Dec. 2. A. L. 5808,

ON THE DEATH

OF

MR. ASAHEL LEWIS.

—ALSO—

AT DANBURY, JANUARY 10, 1809,

AT THE FUNERAL OF

JAMES CLARK, ESQ.

BY THE REV. DANIEL BURHANS, A. M.
Rector of Trinity Church, Newtown.

It is appointed unto men once to die, but after this the judgment. HEB. ix. 27.

NEW-HAVEN,
PRINTED BY BR. OLIVER STEELE.
1809.

TO
THE MEMBERS
OF THE
ANCIENT AND HONORABLE SOCIETY
OF
Free and Accepted Masons,
OF
HARMONY LODGE, IN WATERBURY,
THE FOLLOWING
SERMON
IS RESPECTFULLY
INSCRIBED, BY
THE AUTHOR.

HARMONY LODGE, *Dec.* 2, 5808.

VOTED, That Brothers ISAAC BENHAM, ASAHEL CHITTENDEN, and JARED BURR, be a Committee to present the thanks of this Lodge to Brother DANIEL BURHANS, for his Sermon delivered this day, and request a copy for publication.

Copy of Record,

HARRISON, *Secretary.*

To the Reader.

....

SOON after the following Sermon was preached upon the death of Mr. LEWIS, the Author delivered it, with a few alterations, upon the death of JAMES CLARK, Esq. The paragraphs included in brackets were omitted, and the following Exordium, with the subjoined notes, were added.

By reading the Sermon without the notes, it will be as first delivered; and by omitting the included paragraphs, and reading the exordium and notes, it will be as delivered in Danbury.

The writer is induced to publish the Sermon in its present form, from the following circumstance. Soon after being delivered in Danbury, it was reported he had changed his religious sentiments, or preached contrary to the Bishop and Clergy of this Diocese. The reader is desired to compare the subject with the Articles and Rubrics of the Church of England, and those of the Protestant Episcopal Church; and it is presumed there will be found a happy uniformity, agreeable to that "faith once delivered to the saints."

A SERMON, &c.

My Christian Brethren,

I MEET you on this solemn occasion as a fellow mourner, conscious of the loss that civil society has sustained—of the breach made in this parish, the loss of their first Warden; but more effectually experienced by the family, in the loss of husband and a father. Yea, and I have lost a confidential friend, and Masonry an affectionate brother. In all these various connections and relations, I sympathize with you.

Convinced that it is not (in many cases) useless to pass some eulogiums upon such characters as the deceased supported, I might justify myself, and am sure of an applauding public.

But, to an audience sufficiently acquainted with the integrity and uprightness with which he filled his several stations—and disinclined to subjects of this nature in general, and unqualified on the present occasion, I shall excuse myself by making a single remark: From the seat of judgment, as a civil magistrate, he is gone to the impartial bar of justice and mercy—From the service of the church militant, we hope, to the enjoyment of the church triumphant. And as it is the living, who may derive benefit from funeral discourses, (and not the dead) I shall improve the few moments allotted to me, in offer-

ing the effusions of a sympathetic heart, sighing the welfare of immortal souls, in a discourse recently delivered on a similar occasion, from the following passage:

AMOS iv. 12, 13.

"*Prepare to meet thy God, O Israel. For lo, he that formeth the mountains, and createth the wind, and declareth unto man what is his thought, that maketh the morning darkness, and treadeth upon the high places of the earth, the Lord, the God of Hosts is his name.*"

[WHY this admonition? Because the *Lord God of Hosts, who maketh the morning darkness,* hath sent forth his summons, and called from his labor, a brother —a brother, whose conjugal and parental affections endeared him to his family; whose filial respects soothed an aged parent; whose industry and uprightness rendered him a useful and an exemplary member of society: and whose munificent charity endeared him to the *Lodge*, to the poor and distressed.

This has assembled us at this time; not to rend open the avenues of affliction, but to shed the tributary tear over his ashes; not to open afresh, the still blleeding wounds of the widow and friends, but to console and sympathize; and while *mourning with those who mourn, to bind up the broken hearted.* Not to pore over the mementos of mortality, with unavailing sorrow; but from the death-head and the mangled corpse of a brother pourtrayed upon the carpet, turn our eyes to the never fading *sprigs of cassia*; emblems of immortality; assurances that our brother "but sleepeth;" that after the wintry blasts of death, the resurrection morn shall usher in the spring, that shall ever bloom in a summer's glory, and afford autumal fruit without frost; the true bread, that shall nourish unto everlasting life.]

Open, my brethren, the attentive and listening ear, while we endeavor to arouse the luke-warm to a consideration of the certainty of death; to direct the enquirer *what he "should do to be saved"*—and conclude, by pressing home upon your consciences, the admonition of our elder brother, who, in this death speaks to all, and to this Lodge in particular—*be ye also ready.* Prepare to meet thy God, &c.

"Dust thou art, and unto dust shalt thou return," said the Almighty, in passing sentence upon fallen man. From Adam to Moses, from Moses to Christ, from Christ to the present, death has reigned universal conqueror. In every age we trace his fatal darts; in every country his destructive sword; yea, in almost every family, we hear lamentation and mourning.

Where are the antideluvians, who lived from three to nine hundred years? It is written, "and they died."—Where are the mighty conquerors who rose in the east, and swayed their sceptres over millions? They have gone down in the west: on the *level* they slumber with their meanest soldiers: but few of their names only live in the historic page.

Yea, where are our fathers, that rejoiced with our mothers, that a child was born? who watched over our infant days; nurtured us in childhood, and shed tears of anxiety while we were treading the dangerous and beguiling paths of youth: Almost all have paid the debt of nature—have gone to "that country, *from whose bourne*, no traveller returns." The few who are left, find their lives but labor and sorrow; and their whitened locks, striking indications of the shroud that must soon enwrap them for the coffin and the tomb.

But hark, hark, hark! Who comes? methinks I hear the sound of my master's feet behind me in the death of* [our brother LEWIS, warning the young and the middle aged, to "prepare to meet God."] Although the age of man is set at three score and ten, yet the bills of mortality point the age between 16 and 18, to be the average of human life. Go into the church-yard; read the inscriptions; take the *rule*, the *square* and the *plumbline;* measure the graves of our sleeping friends, and you will find this statement correct. Here lies the infant that only lived to cheer the countenance, and then wring the hearts of bereaved parents; nipped in the bud, like the under grass by an untimely frost. There moulders the youth, like the flower of the field, beaten down by

* JAMES CLARK, Esq. aged 65.

the violence of storms. Yonder *[sacred deposit contains the remains of one, who but a few days past had the fairest prospect of life: his countenance the picture of health; his bones moistened with marrow. His accounts are closed; the expectation of his dear companion cut off; and the dear babes, pledges of conjugal bliss, left fatherless. Ah! the aged mother has lost a son on whom she leaned for support, while tottering "the down-hill of life." Methinks I hear renewed the heartfelt groanings of an aged Jacob, saying, "if I am bereaved of my children, I am bereaved." Or in the still more bitter lamentation of David—"O! Absalom, my son, my son, would to God I had died for thee."] O! death, how dreadful, how universal are they spoils!† What then, I beseech you, my youngest, my most stout-hearted friends, is your security against the execution of this divine sentence, to which I am now endeavoring to call your most serious attention? Examine the world at large; look into your own neighborhood; pry with the most curious attention into the little circles of your families and friendships. Ask the families of the rich and honorable, with what sums, or with what titles they are able to bribe this universal ravager of our life's best felicities, whose [untimely] shafts we are now lamenting? Ask the young, the gay, the beautiful, the healthy, and the strong, by what means they are provided against his sudden, his prepared and uncertain arrows? Does he ask the anxious or the loving wife, when, or by what kind or gentle means he should deprive them of the best earthly felicity, the partner of their souls? Does he ever proclaim through the circles of gaity, or the mansions of pleasure, that on such an evening, he shall take from them such a number of their votaries, and that therefore they should consult amongst themselves whom they could best or most conveniently part with? Does he proclaim to the Tyler, or the Master in the east, that at *sun-rising*,

* Behold the yawning grave, made ready for his remains, which are placed here before the holy altar, to give vent to our sympathetic tears; then to receive its sacred deposit in fast hold, till the archangel's trump in the last day shall awake the slumbering dead.

† See Inwood's Sermons.

at *high-twelve*, or *sun-setting*, the "*scythe* shall cut some brittle thread of life?"

Surely, he asketh no such questions: riches and honors have no bribes for his insatiable desires; youth, or gaity, health or beauty, have no power to disarm his severity; parents can find no reprieve for their beloved children; the most unsullied, the most undivided affection, cannot blunt the arrows of his malignant wrath. Nor can the mansions of pleasure point out to him the objects best suited for his avaricious wishes.* No! without one single exception of another's making, he levels his unresisted arrows, and all must fall before him; the rich and the poor, the old and the young, the gay and the sorrowful: "The mountains become darkness; he treadeth upon the high places of the earth"—the feet stumble upon the dark mountains; the Lord of hosts commands." With this enemy there is no parley; with this foe there is no putting off, even till to-morrow.—"There is no discharge in this war." Prepare then, O! "dying mortals," to meet your God.

But why this preparation? Because "it is not" only "appointed unto men once to die," but, "after death the judgment." "God hath appointed a day, in which he will judge the world in righteousness;" when "every one shall receive according to that he hath done, whether it be good, or bad." We are, therefore, not only mortals, but we are sinners; and have immortal souls, that shall never die. Those who are sensible of this; who view themselves wandering in the dark, and are groping for the light, being "pricked at the heart," and ready to cry out, "what shall we do to be saved?" to such I turn, with the more important part of my subject. And, O! for the tongue of an angel to proclaim, "there is balm in Gilead;" there is a "light that shall rise to the upright in darkness." I "have found a ransom;" there is one, mighty to save: "his name is JESUS;" because, "he came to save his people from their sins." Follow this leader in the way of his appointments, and fear no danger. He was proclaimed, at his first advent, [in this joyful season] by an angel. "Fear not, for behold, I bring you glad tidings of great joy, which shall

* Even the power of earthly magistrates cannot ward off his dart.

be unto you and all people." Look then to him, "as the author and finisher of faith." Repent, and obey his gospel; then, with the "wondering shepherds," your sorrow and sighing will flee away." He will "open your lips," and your "mouth will show forth his praise," in joyful acclamations, saying, "Glory to God, in the highest, and on the earth, peace, good will towards men."—*Prepare then, to meet thy God, O! Israel.* Remember we are sinners, God is holy, and "we have erred, and strayed from his ways like lost sheep." Consider the infallible lips of Jesus have said, "except ye repent, ye shall perish."

But it is greatly to be feared, that through the multiplying divisions among professing christians, and that want of charity between the contending parties, many are "halting between two opinions;" nay, may I not add between hundreds; for the time has come when the saying of our Saviour is verified, "Lo, here is Christ, or lo, there." One cries, "he is in the secret chamber;" another, "he is in the wilderness."*

For this cause, many have fallen into a fashionable kind of religion; like the Laodiceans, are "neither cold nor hot;" and excuse themselves from this needful preparation, by saying, there are so many ways pointed out by different preachers, who all appeal to the bible, "I know not which way to go; and as men can no more think alike than they can look alike, I am determined to give myself no further trouble; for it will never be enquired at the day of judgment, to what sect I belonged." Hence that lukewarmness, so prevalent; the neglect of sacraments, of family religion, and the means of grace in general. And may I not say, thousands in this enlightened community are growing in years, unbaptized; out of covenant, and unconverted. Alas! my brethren, is this to be prepared to meet a holy God? who says, "My son, give me thine heart, and let thine eyes observe my ways." Is this to obey a merciful Saviour? who has said, "Except a man be born of water and of the spirit, he cannot enter into the kingdom of God"—"Except ye eat my flesh, and drink my blood, ye have no part in me?"

* Is not this prophecy fulfilled, in modern Class and Camp-meetings? Christ says—"Go not after them."

But I stand not here on this solemn occasion to denounce sectarians, or answer the objections of casuists in modern divinity; but, to warn you of approaching danger; by preaching the Gospel of Jesus Christ, "as once delivered to the Saints."

Nevertheless, suffer me just to remark, the Scriptures should not be read to select separate passages to prove a preconceived opinion; but with a teachable disposition, free from prejudice, to find out "the truth as it is in Jesus." Instead of bending them to our reason, (which at best is imperfect) we should submit our reason to the Scriptures. and then they will "make us wise unto salvation."

For the very reason that fallen men could never reason alike, God, in infinite mercy, gave them a rule by which their reason is to be governed. And because "it is not in man that walketh to direct his steps," God hath given him a path to walk in. This God has always done from the beginning. Hence, says our Saviour, "I am the way, and the truth and the life; no man cometh unto me but by the Father."* To direct man in this way hath been the grand object in all the dispensations of providence to sinful men, who "love darkness rather than light." For this purpose St. John was sent into the wilderness to prepare the way, and to "bear witness of that light. That was the true light, which lighteth every man that cometh into the world."† Therefore says Christ, "I am the true light of the world, he that followeth me shall not walk in darkness, but shall have the light of life."

After Christ ascended into heaven to continue the same way to the end of the world, he sent down the Holy Ghost upon his Apostles "to bring all things to their remembrance," to enable them to organize his Church, and send others as he had sent them, and by his influence to accompany the means he had instituted.

This is the "faith once delivered to the Saints"—the "ancient land-marks;" and, separated from "the doctrines and commandments of men," is plain and easy

* John xiv. 6. † John i. 9.

to be understood; consisting in "repentance towards God," and faith towards our Lord Jesus Christ, and charity towards all men.

A practical improvement of these is that preparation so necessary to obtain eternal life.

Repentance is commenced by coming to ourselves like the prodigal, and seeing our souls starving for lack of knowledge, and to see the perishing need of a Saviour. Faith points out the father's house, where "there is bread enough, and to spare." Charity draws us with the bands of love, trembling and halting, until we meet the Father: who, if he finds us duly and fitly prepared, pennyless, poor, blind and naked, will embrace us in the arms of his mercy, bid us enter, and clothe and refresh us and grant us special grace "to walk in his commandments blameless."

The necessity of this repentance arises from our sinfulness, and the sinless nature of God.

Therefore the "glad tidings" of the Gospel were ushered in by the crier in the wilderness, "Repent ye, for the kingdom of heaven is at hand." The first exhortation of our Saviour* was, "Repent, and believe the Gospel:" when he sent his disciples to preach, they went forth, "preaching that men should repent." And after his resurrection, he commanded that they should preach "repentance and remission of sins, through his name."† And thus we find St. Peter saying, "Repent, and be converted, that your sins may be blotted out."‡ For this reason the sinner is spared, "that the goodness of God may lead him to repentance."

The necessity of faith in the Lord Jesus Christ arises not only from the sinfulness of man, and his total inability to save himself out of Christ; but from the unchangeable nature of God, who said, "in the day thou eatest thereof, thou shalt die:" man broke this law, and nothing but death could fulfil it. Here, behold and wonder! The eternal Son of God assumed human nature, became our *elder brother*, and in that nature shed his blood, and made a full atonement for the sins of the whole world.§

* Mark i. 6. † Luke xxiv. 47. ‡ Acts iii. 19. § 1 John ii. 2.

God accepted this atonement, the assurance of which we have, "in his raising him from the dead." The application of Christ's merits is made to the sinner through faith and obedience; therefore said an Apostle, "Without faith, it is impossible to please him; for he that cometh to God, must believe that he is, and that he is a rewarder of them that diligently seek him."* The best deed ever performed by the best of men, must in degree be imperfect: therefore, nothing but faith which "operates by love" can render our best services acceptable in the sight of a perfect God. The only way to know whether our repentance and faith are evangelical and saving, is to examine our lives by God's holy word. By that we shall be judged at the last day, by that we should judge ourselves now. "Faith without works is dead, and works without faith are dead, being alone."

Charity consists in the love of God "shed abroad in the heart," by the influence of the holy spirit; "from whom all holy desires, all good counsels, and all just works do proceed." This charity "thinketh no evil, is not easily provoked"—it "envieth not"—it excites the heart by pure motives to pray and do good to all men, even our enemies—directs the hands to fill them with good things—directs the feet to run to the abodes of sickness and poverty—the widow and fatherless; it opens the lips to speak those kind words that doeth good like a medicine; and it distributes to their several necessities—it bridles the tongue against "lying, slandering, and evil speaking;" and closes the ear against evil reports.

Lastly, what crowns all, and without which all our pretensions to faith, repentance, charity and conversion, will be "like sounding brass and tinkling symbols,"—those who have injured us, we shall forgive; and to those we have injured, we shall not only confess our faults, but whereinsoever we have defrauded them, we shall make them restitution.

Whoever thinks he is converted and prepared for death without doing this, is in the "gall of bitterness and the bond of iniquity."—"He that confesseth and forsaketh

* Heb. xi. 6.

his sin shall find mercy." "Behold," says Zcaheus, "if I have taken any thing by false accusation, I restore him fourfold."* "Christ will require his own with usury."

To be enabled thus to prepare, we should be instant in prayer and live in the daily use of the instituted means of grace, "without which we can do nothing." "Ask, and ye shall receive," said he who alone hath any thing to give. "Watch and pray—believe and be baptized," said he who instituted his Church as a preparatory school to instruct, lecture and meet in—fit and prepare us for his triumphant Church in heaven. By baptism we are initiated into this Church, and thereby become visible members of his mystical body. Should any doubt of this, let him read the following text of St. Paul, with other corresponding passages. "For as many of you as have been baptized into Christ, have put on Christ, there is neither Jew nor Greek, there is neither bond nor free, there is neither male nor female; for ye are all one in Christ Jesus. And if ye be Christ's, then are ye Abraham's seed, and heirs according to the promise."† Being thus made members by baptismal regeneration, we may derive nourishment from the head (i. e.) Christ, who, by a beautiful illustration, inculcates this great and glorious truth: "I am the true vine, and my Father is the husbandman.—Every branch in me that beareth not fruit, he taketh away; and every branch that beareth fruit, he purgeth it, that it may bring forth more fruit."‡

In this way, through faith and repentance, we are to receive "special grace," viz. spiritual regeneration, or, as more correctly expressed in Titus iii. 5, *renewing of the Holy Ghost*. The continuance of this, or our growth in grace we are to expect in a faithful use of the other sacrament. "He that eateth my flesh and drinketh my blood, him will I raise up at the last day."

I know that this is unpopular doctrine with those who have substituted feelings for conversion, and consider the sacraments of little or no use. And it is equally so with those who place morals in the room of faith and re-

* Luke xix. 8.

† Gal. iii. 27, 28, 29. Gen. xvii. 10—12. Rom. vi. 3. John iii. 5.

‡ John xv. 1, 2.

pentance. I say morals, for I fear there are many who flatter themselves they may be saved, because they are no worse than their wicked neighbors. I recommend to the first a serious attention of the fiftieth chapter of Isaiah, particularly the last verse; and to the latter the history of Cain, who would not shed blood.

Suffer then the word of exhortation, for while standing "between the dead and the living," and warning others to prepare to meet God, knowing that soon I must give an account of my stewardship, I must not "*speak false for God*," neither do I fear to preach as my Saviour and his Apostles preached. And could I be an instrument of bringing home one wandering sheep "to the true fold," I should consider it infinitely better than the applause of millions! Turn then to the strong hold, "ye prisoners of hope;" and let the saying of Christ to Nicodemus, and his commission to his Apostles* have their desired effects upon your hearts, and you will not think any apology necessary on my part for the freedom in this discourse.

Have you then faith in the Lord Jesus Christ, or do you ask how to obtain it? The great Apostle to the Gentiles hath settled the whole controversy by saying, Rom. x. 17, "Faith cometh by hearing, and hearing by the word of God."† "Search the Scriptures"—"they are spirit of life."

Are there here any unregenerate, out of covenant, and of course unprepared to meet God? O! hear your Saviour: "He that believeth and is baptized, shall be saved; but he that believeth not, shall be damned." Hear the first sermon preached under the immediate operation of the Holy Ghost. What does Peter say to the enquiring multitude? Repent, and be baptized every one of you, in the name of Jesus Christ, for the remission of sins, and ye shall receive the gift of the Holy Ghost. For the promise is unto you, to your children, and to all that are afar off, even as many as the Lord our God shall

* John iii. 5. Matt. xxviii.

† I beg liberty to earnestly recommend an *Essay on Faith* by John Rotheram, lately re-printed in New-Haven.

call."—Acts ii. 38, 39. And who does he call? He calls all from the rising to the setting sun. "Their sound went into all the earth, and their words unto the end of the world.* He calls you, my hearers, by mercies. He calls you by judgments; yea, he calls in the awful voice of death!

And could our departed brother speak from the eternal world, would he not say to this †[Lodge,] Prepare to meet thy God? Would he not say to his beloved wife, Prepare to follow me; for I shall no more console you in afflictions, nor rejoice with you in prosperity.—[My heart will no more beat in conjugal affection, anticipating the growth and prosperity of our dear children; give up yourselves to Jesus in the way of his appointments.]

But, my dear madam, I forbear; it is not my wish to excite your passions, but enlighten your understanding. I feel for you—yea, I experimentally sympathize with you. I have drank of the same bitter cup that none can know but by experience. Our Saviour, speaking of the marriage covenant, said, "and they twain shall be one flesh." Rending the body asunder, gives but a faint idea of separating husband and wife by death.

But, remember, "it is not an enemy who has done this;" it is that merciful parent, "who does not willingly afflict or grieve the children of men;" but "pitieth us as a father pitieth his children." This consideration silenced the tongue of one, "who could speak well."—"Aaron held his peace." David says, "Be still, and know it is God." "It is the Lord," says Samuel, let him do what seemeth good." Job, whose trials were uncommonly afflictive, says, "The Lord gave, and the Lord hath taken away, and blessed be the name of the Lord." Therefore, with the weeping Mary, place yourself at the foot of the cross; lay your sorrows at the throne of grace, and look up "to Jesus, the author and finisher of faith." And, while you imitate him when weeping at the grave of a friend, imitate him when he lay in the agonizing garden—"not my will, but thine be done." Then, he who had compassion on a widow in the days of

* See Mal. ii. and Rom. x. 18. † Church.

his flesh, and restored her son to life, will have compassion on you; he will restore to your afflicted bosom, that which is better than earthly connections; "that peace of God, that passeth all understanding." He ever lives to make intercession for us. Look then beyond this cloud—he is now saying in his word, "I am the father of the fatherless, and the judge of the widow." We commend you to God's holy keeping,* [and the friendship of this Lodge, trusting you will improve this dispensation to the glory God, of and your spiritual and eternal good.

My brethren, methinks I hear our dear brother speaking to this [Lodge]† in that solemn address appointed to be used on certain occasions.‡

Here you view a striking instance of the uncertainty of life, and the vanity of all human pursuits. The last offices paid to the dead, are only useful, as they are lectures to the living "from us"—therefore you are to derive instruction, and ought to consider every solemnity of this kind, as a summons to prepare for your approaching dissolution.

Notwithstanding the mementos of mortality with which you daily meet; notwithstanding "you" are convinced that death has established his universai empire over all the ranks of nature; yet through some unaccountable infatuation, "you" are still apt to forget that "you" are born to die. "You" go on from one design

* And the patronage and filial respect of your dear children, who have reason "to rejoice," even in affliction, that they were not left fatherless in infancy; but were guarded, directed, and protected through the dangers and dependencies of childhood.

Yea, my weeping friends, I commend, under God, this your afflicted mother to your care: As Jesus said to his beloved disciples, I say unto you, "Behold your mother." Comfort her concerning her trial, and ease her down the hill of life. As your earthly father is taken from you, look up to that Father of all mercies and God of all comfort.

Your age, your experience, your good sense, and connections, prevent the necessity of any further counsel. I only add, "may these afflictions work for you, an exceeding weight of glory."

† Church.

‡ The above address is principally taken from the Masonic Funeral Service.

to another, add hope to hope, and lay out plans for the subsistence and employment of many years to come; until "you" are suddenly alarmed with the approach of death, when "you" least "expected" him, and at an hour which "you" probably "concluded" to be the meridian of "your" existence.

What are all the externals of majesty, the pride of wealth, or charms of beauty, when nature has paid her just debt? If for a moment, "you" throw "your" eyes on the last scene, and view life, stripped of its ornaments and exposed in its natural meanness, "you" will then be convinced of the futility of its empty delusions. In the grave all fallacies are detected, all ranks are levelled, and all distinctions are done away.

While "you" drop the sympathetic tear over "my grave," let charity induce "you" to throw a veil over "my" foibles, whatever they have been; and withhold not your memory from the few virtues I have "performed." Suffer the apologies of human nature to plead in my behalf. Perfection has never been attained; the wisest, as well as the best of men have erred. Therefore imitate "my" virtues, and derive instruction from "my" weakness. Let "my" death excite "your" serious attention, and strengthen "your" resolutions of amendment. As life is uncertain, and all earthly pursuits are vain, no longer postpone the important means of preparing for eternity: But "my brethren," embrace the present moment, while time and opportunity offer, to provide with care against that great change, when the pleasures of this world shall cease to delight, and the reflections of a life spent in the exercise of piety and virtue, yield the only comfort and consolation.

Thus shall "your" expectations be not frustrated, nor will "you" be hurried, unprepared, into the presence of that all-wise and powerful judge, to whom the secrets of all hearts are known, and from whose dread tribunal no culprit can escape.

Finally, "my" brethren, support with propriety the character of "your" profession on every occasion, and advert to the nature of "your" engagements, and pursue with unwearied assiduity the sacred tenets of masonry.

With becoming reverence supplicate the divine grace, that "you" may secure the favor of that eternal Being, whose goodness and power know no bounds; and prosecute "your" journey without fear or apprehension, to that far distant country from whence no traveller returns. By the light of the divine countenance, "you" will pass without trembling, through those gloomy mansions where all things are forgotten; and at that great and tremendous day, when arraigned at the bar of *Divine Justice*, judgment shall be pronounced in "your" favor, "you" will receive the reward of "your" virtue, and acquire the possession of an immortal inheritance, where joys flow in one continual stream, and no mound can check its course. [And might he not add, "remember the widow and the widow's son." My brethren, knowing you will do this, I commend the afflicted family to your patronage and friendship.

May the Lord prepare you, that when he comes in the east, to open the glory of the last day, you may rise to the life immortal—the key word being found, he who dwelt in the bush, and "opens the kingdom of heaven to all believers," receive you into the celestial *Lodge* above.]

And what is said unto you, I would say unto all, *Prepare to meet your God*, O! probationers! Hear the voice of the Son of God, and live. Shake off the deadly slumbers of carnal security. "Awake," and arise "from the dead, that Christ may give you light." God is speaking to all in this [awful] providence, reminding you of your own mortality, in the [sudden] death of one you all respected, and have reason to lament* [as a useful member of society.] He has "made the morning darkness," and calls upon all to prepare to meet the Lord God of Hosts. Yes, he calls upon the youth to be not less ready. My young friends, take my admonitions upon the means of grace as the effusions of a heart that would warn you, that without faith, repentance, baptism, and evangelical obedience, you have no promise of eternal life: Your nimble steps, may soon lead you down to the silent mansions of the dead, where your "active limbs" will moulder into dust, and your souls return to that God

* As a faithful and pious Warden in the Church, and a correct and useful magistrate.

who gave them, and who will sentence them to eternal happiness or misery, according to the preparation you shall make.

[To the middle aged, this death speaks in a language impossible of deception. Ye, whose mountain seems to stand strong, and who are blessed with a rising and promising family, look at yonder solitary tomb! reflect upon its contents! He who a few days past, in health and prosperity was enjoying the sweets of domestic happiness—what is he now? Look at that mourning circle, and tell me what assurance have you of long life. And suffer me to ask, with all the seriousness the subject requires, are you prepared? Have you devoted yourselves to God? Have you given up your children to the holy Jesus, in the way of his appointments? Do you live in the habitual exercise of prayer, and the other means of grace? Or are you going on in the way of sin and disobedience? If so eternal death is before you.—"Prepare then to meet God."]

The aged Fathers and Mothers will indulge me, before I conclude, to ask, shall the age of *[37] rush into the grave, and seventy, the age of man, bid defiance to its ravages? No, my respected friends, there is but a step between you and death. As monuments of God's sparing mercy, you are continued. Have you improved your talents? Are you prepared to meet your God? Your "morning has become darkness"—is your evening light? Have you a guide to lead you through the dark valley; a treasure "where moth and rust cannot corrupt, and where thieves cannot break through and steal." If so, like a "shock of corn fully ripe," you shall soon be gathered into the garner of God, and receive that heart-cheering welcome, "Come ye blessed children of my father, inherit the kingdom prepared for you from the foundation of the world."

May God Almighty bless you all, both brethren and strangers; may he enable you to be duly and fitly prepared, that when we quit this earthly tabernacle, we may be initiated into the GRAND LODGE of the Supreme Architect, the Lord of Hosts, to join the song of Moses and the Lamb forever and ever. AMEN.

* 67.

Prayer.

ALMIGHTY and everlasting GOD! who art always more ready to hear than we to pray, and who art accustomed to give more than either we desire or deserve; pour down upon us, at this time, the divine consolations of thy Holy Spirit; and be it also to us a spirit of wisdom and understanding. In thy hands are the spirits of all living, and in Thee alone we live, and move, and have our being. Thou givest, and Thou takest away. Thou doest what Thou pleasest in the heavens above and amongst the inhabitants of the earth. Be this our wisdom to know, that Thou art always in all Thy conduct, guided by infinite justice, wisdom and mercy. Give us therefore in all Thy judgments, the hearing ear and the understanding heart; and may it teach us the true lessons of meekness, resignation, and patience. Support the afflicted in every trial. And may the present dispensations extract the tear of friendly commiseration from every tender heart. Teach us all who survive these daily instances of mortality, the important value of being always prepared to meet our GOD. In the midst of life we are in death. Teach us, gracious Father, the uncertainty of all human dependencies; and may we spend the present moment, as if it were our last. Prepare us, O Lord, for all thy gracious intentions: if we live, may we live unto the Lord; if we die, may we fall asleep in Jesus; that whether living or dying, we may be thine forever. Sanctify this awful moment to the conversion of every heart; may the serious and important services in which we have been engaged, have a suitable impression upon every mind; may the aged read the certainty of death, and may the young read the uncertainty of life; and may we, one and all, be truly prepared to give that solemn account which we know not how soon we may be called to give. May pastors and people eagerly snatch the present

moment to work out our salvation with fear and trembling, seeing we know not how soon the night cometh, when no man can work; and prosper Thou the work of our hands upon us—O prosper Thou our handy work; that when Thou, who art the final rewarder of all them who labor in thy vineyard, shall come to render unto every man according to his labor and his work, we may be found among the happy number who shall receive that pleasing invitation of "Come, ye children of my Father, enter ye into the joy of your Lord:" we beg it for Jesus' sake, who has commanded us when we pray to say, "Our Father," &c.

REV. BELA HUBBARD, D.D.

A

SERMON,

DELIVERED AT

DANBURY AND RIDGEFIELD,

ON A

VISITATION,

BY THE

Right Reverend Abraham Jarvis,

BISHOP OF CONNECTICUT;

printed at the request of a number of the Members of those Churches.

DANBURY;
PRINTED BY JOHN C. GRAY.
DEC. 1809.

SERMON.

ROMANS viii. 15th.

THE SPIRIT ITSELF BEARETH WITNESS WITH OUR SPIRIT. THAT WE ARE THE CHILDREN OF GOD.

THE Son of God came down from heaven, dwelt among us in our flesh, and, by offering himself a sacrifice on the cross, made an atonement for the sins of human kind. After he had arisen from the dead, he again ascended up to heaven, there to appear as an Advocate for us in the presence of God. Seated in that exalted office before the throne of God, and clothed with the plenitude of power to provide for, and govern, his Church on earth, he sent the Holy Spirit to abide with his apostles, and with all who should, through their preaching, believe in him and his Gospel. By this Holy Spirit, the apostles were enabled to declare the whole will of God concerning the salvation of mankind. They who believe and are baptized, are by the Spirit made the adopted sons of God; and *if sons, then heirs of God, and joint heirs with Christ. As many as are led by the Spirit of God, they are the sons of God.* In support of this truth, and for the consolation of the faithful, the Spirit also himself beareth witness. *The Spirit itself beareth witness with our spirit, that we are the sons of God.*

The subject is solemn and interesting: It shall therefore be my endeavour to seek for a probable and fair solution of the two following inquiries:

1st. In what manner the Spirit of God beareth witness with the spirit of Christians, that they are the children of God.

2d. What is that hope or persuasion which this witness produceth in the minds of Christians.

The witness of the Holy Spirit to our condition as Christians, allows of no presumptive conceits, or working of human fancy. Here, that we may neither mock God nor deceive ourselves, we are bound to be cautious, and to think soberly as we ought to think. If we indulge our own fancies—if we divide the witnesses, and make the Spirit of God a single witness, and allege our inward sensations and feelings as proof, the spirit must be a false spirit, and the proof fallacious; because it is not the witness of which St. Paul speaks. Again; if we set up our own spirit by itself, for a distinct witness, the testimony in that case must be false, as it does not agree with the witness mentioned by the apostle. Every man who is able to read the language in which St. Paul wrote, may see that he uses a word which signifies a mutual concurrence of both witnesses, in one joint and united testimony. *The Spirit beareth witness with our spirit.* This cannot be understood of any immediate communication or act of the Holy Spirit on the human soul, whereby it becomes converted, and the man made an adopted child of God. Such an interpretation destroys the union asserted in the text, and makes the Holy Spirit cease to be a witness; and instead of a joint co-operation, one spirit is to be considered as doing an act, and the other as bearing the testimony to it: in other words, according to this construction, the soul that is converted is left to be the naked and solitary witness of its own conversion. The scripture, thus expounded, puts a matter of the highest concern upon the most slender and precarious footing. In a business of such moment, we may be allowed to recommend a due attention to those words of our blessed Saviour: "*If I bear witness of myself, my witness is not true.*" It is expedient then to inquire for that witness which is true, and on which the Spirit of God gives us full authority to rely.

From the scriptures of truth, the Christian derives the happy instruction of his filial relation to God. These scriptures teach us, that this new relation originates in us, by the operation of the Holy Spirit; the knowledge of which is not conveyed to our minds by any immediate or direct act; but we are to obtain it by a conclusion drawn from certain fruits and effects, given as infallible proofs, by which we are to know that the Holy Spirit dwelleth in us, and in this manner, as the author of all holiness,

accompanies and bears witness with our mind and conscience, that we are the sons of God.

In the 9th verse of this chapter, we read, "*If any man have not the Spirit of Christ, he is none of his:*" And in the 14th verse, "*As many as are led by the Spirit of God, they are the sons of God.*" If, in order to belong to Christ, it is necessary to have his Spirit, it is as necessary for a man to know that he has the Spirit, as it is to know that he has Christ for a Saviour. From revelation he learns the one; by the same revelation he is taught how to know the other. Now the same apostle, who tells us that we must have this Spirit, gives us the signs and marks which always accompany, and are certain proofs that we possess and are led by it. "*The fruit of the Spirit is Love, Joy, Peace, Long-Suffering, Gentleness, Goodness, Faith, Meekness, Temperance: against such there is no law.*" When, therefore, we find that these fruits do manifest themselves within us, we may draw the comfortable conclusion, that we are the sons of God; and although the conclusion is our own act, yet, as the arguments on which that conclusion is grounded, proceed from the Holy Spirit, he may with strict propriety be said to concur with our own mind and conscience, in attesting to the truth of it. In strict conformity with the rule of St. Paul, is that given us by St. John: "*Hereby we know that we dwell in him, and he in us, because he hath given us of his Spirit;*" chap. iv. 13th. In the 12th verse he says, "*If we love one another, God dwelleth in us.*" Here are two facts necessarily connected; and the truth of the former arises out of the certainty of the latter. We know that God dwelleth in us, because he hath given us of his Spirit; and we know that he hath given us the Spirit, from the love that we have one for another. Thus St. John tells you, that by the fruits, as described by St. Paul, you are to understand, or know, that you have the Spirit of Christ.

In reference to these fruits, which make men true disciples of Christ, and fit them for the kingdom of heaven, the Spirit is in scripture called God's *earnest.* "*Who hath given us the earnest of the Spirit in our hearts:*" 2 Cor. i. 22d. An earnest we all know to be a part of a promised price, and a pledge for the after payment of the whole sum. Thus, the Holy Spirit is given us as

an earnest, to assure us that in due time we shall receive from God whatsoever he hath promised; provided always, that we keep the earnest, and make a right use of it, and do not return it back to him, or provoke him to take it from us.

But the Spirit is represented not only as an earnest for further and future blessings; but also as the *seal* of God upon what hath been already granted. The expression is figurative, and alludes to the custom among men, of putting a seal upon their goods, to designate their owner, and to ascertain the property. The fruits of the Spirit, having this meaning affixed to them, become the standing evidence, whereby we are to know that we belong to, and are in favour with God. On this foundation, reason maintains its place, and its proper sphere of action. "Conscience, purged from sin through faith and the Spirit of holiness," becomes clothed with authority to declare our relation to our heavenly Father. "*My conscience*," says St. Paul, "*beareth me witness in the Holy Ghost.*" "*If*," says St. John, "*our heart condemn us not, then have we confidence towards God.*"

Let each one of us, then, in this manner, try the question for himself. Does his conscience bear him witness in the Holy Ghost, that God holds that supreme place in his heart, which he holds in creation? Does he love his neighbour in sincerity; and is he ever ready, in proportion to his ability, to do him good, and not evil? Can he forgive an enemy? Is he just and upright in all his dealings? Hath he taken up his cross, by denying the sinful lusts of the flesh? Does he not allow himself intentionally to speak what is false, or deliberately to commit any known sin? Is the religion of Christ to him an easy yoke, and a light burden? At all times, whether in prosperity or adversity, is it his delight, *by prayer and supplication, with thanksgiving, to make known his requests unto God?* And under all the events of life, does he maintain a due sense of his dependence on God, and put his trust in him for help and relief?—In fine, while he feels the rod, does he look to the hand that appoints it? and when afflictions await him, does he endeavour to bear them with that submission which he owes to the will of God? These are the tests, as well as the genuine fruits of the Spirit, "from whom all holy desires, all good counsels, and all just works, do proceed." If these fruits come

from the heart, and are manifested by the tenor of our life, then will our conscience bear us witness in the Holy Ghost, that we are the sons of God.

Every pretension of this kind, founded upon claims different from this two-fold witness, must be mere presumption. All claims to the title of a child of God, that they may appear just, must rest upon their proper proofs; but no proofs, except those which God requires, are to be so considered, or with safety to be relied on. God hath appointed an outward visible act, to seal a covenant union with Christ, and our adoption as sons. "*As many as have been baptized into Christ, have put on Christ.*" By the outward visible act of baptism, he gives us a new, internal, and invisible character. This invisible character he requires us to maintain and render effectual, by outward and visible acts. "*Not every one that saith unto me, Lord, Lord, shall enter into the kingdom of heaven; but he that doeth the will of my Father who is in heaven.*" "*If ye keep my commandments, then are ye my disciples indeed.*"

St. Paul, relating the foundation on which he built the peace, joy, and comfort of his mind, does not boast of his miraculous conversion; neither does he mention any secret instantaneous change wrought in him by the Holy Spirit. *Our rejoicing*, says he, *is this; the testimony of our conscience, that in simplicity and godly sincerity, not with fleshly wisdom, but by the grace of God, we have had our conversation in the world.* And elsewhere—*The life that I now live in the flesh, I live by the faith of the Son of God.* The testimony which his conscience bore to his integrity, and sincerity, and his manner of life, which was the fruit of the Spirit, were proofs to himself, and to others, that the Spirit dwelt in him, and that he was a good man; and thence arose the joy and peace of his mind.

The evidence he adduces, and the method he took to judge of his own condition, he recommends to every other Christian. *Let every man prove his own work, and then he shall have rejoicing in himself.* Here it is to be noted, that every man must have his *own work*; for he cannot prove what he has not got; and there must be a rule by which the work is to be proved; and that rule must be one common measure, to which every man

must bring his own work for proof. If, on trial, he finds his work agrees with the standard, then he shall have rejoicing in himself. Secret impulses, or any special transactions of the Spirit on the minds of individuals, for reasons known only to God, and for purposes discerned by infinite wisdom, even if allowed, affect not the argument; for they are the work of God, and not of man, and therefore not the work to be proved, for that is every man's *own* work. Now, if men compare their tempers and actions with the several marks and characters declared to be the fruits of the Spirit, and find them to agree, then their conscience will acquit, and give them satisfaction and consolation; and so shall every man have rejoicing, or that delight in himself, which a good conscience always affords.

On a point of such importance to the Christian professor, it may justly give confidence to the humble inquirer after divine truth, to find the voice of the Church adding a sanction to his construction of the holy scriptures. In her exhortation to the communion, evidently guided by the foregoing and other apostolic injunctions, she directs us, in order that we may come holy and clean to such a heavenly feast, in the marriage garment required by God in holy scripture, and be received as worthy partakers of that holy table; to search our consciences, and examine our lives and conversations by the rule of God's commandments. Thus does the Church, in union with the apostles, send us to the scriptures of truth, which reveal the fruits of the Spirit, that by them we may learn what manner of spirit we are of, and may try our work.

In the 7th chapter of this epistle, the apostle, speaking of men in their natural state, as sons of Adam, represents them as living captives and slaves to a law, or power, which indeed binds them over to death, but not as being totally dead; for with dead men there is an end of all law. The chapter which contains the text, begins with the declaration, that the redemption by Christ delivers us from the necessity of continuing under that captivity any longer. *The law of the Spirit of life, in Christ Jesus, hath made us free from the law of sin and death.* Through the redemption that is in Christ Jesus, we are put under the direction of the Spirit. From the power of the Spirit, we derive strength

to obey the law of God. "The consequence of our being under the power of the Spirit, is thus stated:" *that we walk not after the flesh, but after the Spirit*, ver. 4; *that we mind the things of the Spirit*, ver. 5; *that we mortify the deeds of the body*, ver. 13; *that we are the sons of God*, ver. 14; *that we cry Abba, Father*, ver. 15. The three first particulars describe the deeds of the Spirit, and comprehend the Christian life. They are therefore the sure guide to resolve the question whether we are the children of God. To do the deeds of the Spirit, as we learn from the same instructor, is to act according to our mind or reason; for he had before said, that reason approved the things of God; and the things of the Spirit are the things of God. Seeing, then, that the Spirit co-operates with our reason in the great work of religion, it follows, that religion is what the apostle declares it to be, our *reasonable service*. Allow this to be the true character of the religion of Christ, and you must conceive it to be the office and work of his Spirit, to exalt and perfect reason, so that is may subdue the sinful lusts of the flesh. What reason alone cannot do, it is qualified for by the Spirit of God, who worketh with it, and gives power to will, and to do, according to his good pleasure. Now, if ye will know of the doctrine, whether it be of God, ye must begin with an unfeigned desire to do his will. Therefore, to look aright for the witness of the Spirit, ye must look into yourselves, and there expect it from the report of your own reason and conscience. Do ye, with St. Paul, keep under your body, and bring it into subjection? Are your passions and appetites corrected and ruled by reason, enlightened by the doctrine, and sanctioned by the laws of the Gospel? Does your conscience acquit you at the bar of your own reason? Have you that sense of duty and filial affection, that meekness and humility, which disposes you to go, as a child to a tender parent, and cry Abba, Father? These are signs and evidences of the Spirit, that cannot deceive, and you need not mistake.

When God himself has given you the evidence, whereby you may know that his Spirit is in you of a truth; why should you desire, or why should you seek for any other?

"Hence it appears, that the evidence of the Spirit is not any "secret inspiration, or any assurance conveyed to the mind of

"the faithful; but it is the evidence of works, such as by the "Spirit we perform. And therefore, the only sign of sanctifica- "tion, is holiness; and the only mark of grace, is to obey from "the heart the word of God." *

Do we meet with persons who say they have received the Spirit; that they are converted, and know themselves to be the children of God? We ask for the evidence given by the Spirit himself, as the signs of his presence in the hearts of men, by which it should be known who are governed and sanctified by him. Jesus did not require that men should believe that he was the Christ, only because he said he was. "If ye believe not me, believe the works that I do; for they testify of me."— John sent his disciples to inquire, "Art thou he that should come?" Jesus replied, "Go and tell John the things that ye hear and see." The prophets had foretold what the Messiah should do when he come: To those works Jesus appeals, and leaves them to compare what they saw with prophetic description, and to draw the conclusion for themselves. The miracles that Jesus wrought were sufficient to prove him to be a Teacher come from God; but no miracles, except those the prophets had foretold, could have proved him to be the Messiah. In the instance above cited, we see our Lord answered those who came to inquire of him whether he was the Christ, by an appeal to his works; those very works the prophets had foretold the Christ, when he come, should perform. In the same manner, all who receive him as their Saviour, are to prove their relation to him, and their title to his promises. Having a true faith, that faith they must manifest by those works which Christ himself hath declared to be the genuine fruits of faith, and to proceed from his Spirit. Those works show the law of Christ to be written in the heart; they show the doer of them to be his true disciple, who with the heart believeth unto righteousness, and with the mouth maketh confession unto salvation. Placing our claims and Christian character on this footing, the evidence rises beyond any presumptive assertion of our own; and stands upon the high authority of Christ, and of the Spirit himself speaking to us in his Gospel. Guided by that authority, the more clearly

* Bishop Sherlock.

the subject is investigated, the more fully will it appear that the agency of the Holy Spirit is a joint act with human endeavours, and conducts men in the Christian life by the fixed rules of the Gospel. Viewed in this light, he is the *Spirit of Truth*; by his gentle, yet continual influences, disposing our minds and opening our hearts to attend to the word of God, as he did the heart of Lydia to attend to the words spoken of Paul. He excites us to listen to the scriptures, at first given by him, as he did Cornelius and his company, who stood before God to hear from Peter all things that are commanded of God. He is our *Comforter*, by cleansing the thoughts of our hearts, and inclining us to perform the various duties required; and strengthening us with stedfast confidence to pursue the course of life the Gospel points out. Thus, through him, we attain to that conversation which becometh the Gospel of Christ, and are finally made such as we should be in all holy conversation and godliness.

We may now inquire into the degree of hope or persuasion, which the witness of the Spirit truly produces and authorizes in the Christian, with respect to his final salvation.

On this point) an admired writer of the present day is so clear and home to my purpose, it must be for your advantage to give you his thoughts in his own words. "The Christian, who would travel surely in the road to heaven, must steer equally clear of *self-confidence* on the one hand, and of *vain dependence* on the other. From the consideration, that the Christian dispensation is a covenant of grace on the part of God, and that every covenant, from its nature, implies conditions, conditions of entering into it, and conditions of continuing in it; it necessarily follows, that the acquisition of the benefits contained under the Christian covenant, must depend on the fulfilment of the conditions which have been annexed to it. When the Christian disciple, therefore, talks of what the grace of God has done for his soul, he should at the same time examine how far that grace has produced its intended effect on his conduct, by enabling him to deny ungodliness and worldly lusts, and to live soberly, righteously, and godly, in this present world. According to his conclusion on this subject, admitting it to be justly drawn, must be his encouragement to look forward in hope to the glorious ap-

pearing of the great God and his Saviour Jesus Christ; on this most settled conviction, that the objects of Christ's coming was not only to die for sin, and thereby purchase salvation for the sinner, but also to prepare the sinner for the salvation purchased, by making him meet, through the sanctification of his Spirit, to be a partaker of the saints in light."

Such, my Brethren, is the Gospel which we preach. Examine it by your Bible, and you will find that it contains the words of truth and soberness. "*He that hath ears to hear, let him hear.*"

Every true member of the Church militant is in a state of progression towards the Church triumphant. Such as is the state of the Church in this world, such must be the state of every one who belongs to it. The militant state is a state of trial and probation; to which, humble trust, with a mixture of doubts and fears, must ever be attached. Assurance can only be the privilege of those, who, having passed their state of probation, are admitted into the Church triumphant. Whoever, therefore, asserts that he has arrived to a state of assurance, his assertion implies that he does not belong to the militant, but to that Church which is composed of the spirits of just men made perfect. When the victory is won, what remains but to enjoy the promised reward? Every person who claims this high character, to be consistent with himself and the tenet he holds, must dismiss the exhortations to *grow in grace*, and to *perfect holiness in the fear of God*, as not pertinent to him. For why should *he* seek to grow, who is already assured that he has attained his full stature? And of whom or of what can *he* be afraid, who, by the irresistible operation of the Spirit, has the decree of God irreversibly stamped upon him? At the point where assurance of a future event begins, for that event probation ends.

Arguments of this kind, I am sensible, will not be seen, nor the force of them felt, by persons who are accustomed to combine things that are opposite, and to hold themselves blind to the most glaring contradictions. The same is to be expected from those who do not and will not understand the nature of the Christian Church; who have no regular notions of the manner

in which Christ holds communion with it, and as the Head and King rules and governs it. Be it allowed, that human reasoning is fallible, and often inconclusive; but the word of Christ is spirit and truth; and where the word of a king is, there is power. Let us then have recourse to God and the word of his grace.

"Watch and pray; for ye know not the hour wherein the Son of Man cometh." The exhortation is general, and may be applied to every man; from which duty, no supposed condition can exempt him to the end of life; for that is the period to which our Lord assigns the reward. "Blessed is that servant, whom his Lord, when he cometh, shall find so doing." "To him that overcometh, will I give to eat of the tree of life in the midst of the paradise of God."

We do not find that St. Paul, notwithstanding his divine raptures and visions, speaks of them as giving him such a certainty of heaven, that he could not forfeit, or finally miss of it. On all occasions he utters a very different language. "I keep under my body, and bring it into subjection, lest, when I have preached to others, I myself should be a cast-away." "Brethren, I count not myself to have apprehended; but this one thing I do; forgetting those things which are behind, and reaching forth unto those things which are before, I press towards the mark for the prize of the high calling of God in Christ Jesus. Let us, therefore, as many as be perfect, be thus minded." Such is the account St. Paul gives of his own manner of life. To the like conduct he exhorts all Christians, even the most perfect. The prize is at the end of the race: towards that we are, like him, to press, and in no one stage of the course to boast of security, or think the victory is won, until we arrive at the mark. Faith and hope are the great springs of action in the Christian warfare. These two are the shield and the helmet with which we must fight the good fight, and lay hold on eternal life. Blessed be the God and Father of our Lord Jesus Christ, who hath begotten us again to a lively hope by the resurrection.

The relation recorded in the 27th of the Acts, of St. Paul's voyage to Rome, affords an illustration of the highest degree of assurance the word of God will warrant, under any circum-

stance, to be imagined. The apostle was forewarned of the shipwreck. "Sirs," said he to the men who were with him, "be of good cheer; for there shall be no loss of any man's life among you, but of the ship: For there stood by me, this night, an angel of the Lord, whose I am, and whom I serve, saying, Thou must be brought before Cæsar; and lo, God hath given thee all them that sail with thee.—I believe God that it shall be even as it was told me." Afterwards, in the critical hour of peril, when the shipmen were about to leave the ship, Paul said to the centurion and to the soldiers, "Except these abide in the ship, ye cannot be saved." Had the purpose of God been without conditions; had it been, according to that purpose, impossible for the men to have left the ship, St. Paul's assertion had been without meaning, or not true; his fears had been groundless, and his warning superfluous. More than an angel hath informed us of the salvation God hath appointed; and as we perform the conditions, and attain to the qualifications prescribed, the Spirit witnesseth with our conscience that we are the heirs of grace, and are in favour with God. The exceeding great and precious promises of the Gospel now stand by us as the angel did by Paul; and if we abide stedfastly within our place and station, and strive for the preservation of life, within the limits and according to the spirit of the promises, we shall be saved. Assurance relates to the promises; for they are certain.

Hope is excited by a firm faith, and belongs to us, while the great and final blessings exist in promises. Assurance, so long as we are in a state of probation, cannot transcend the nature and limits of that state; and therefore, when applied to the human mind, to express its prospect of eternal life, cannot go beyond hope, nor be divided from faith and hope, until the Christian arrives to that state, where faith and hope shall have an end. In this world, the highest attainment in the Christian life, is *the full assurance of hope;* and *a strong consolation* is the encouragement given as a reward to those *who have fled for refuge to lay hold upon the hope set before them:* "*Which hope we have as an anchor, to which our soul is fastened* in this stormy sea of life, *both strong and stedfast, because fixed into the place within the vail;* that is, into heaven, whither we shall be drawn by this anchor, as ships are drawn to the place where their anchors are fixed."

Recorded saints lived by faith, and are said to have died in faith. That faith, which is "the substance of things hoped for, and the evidence of things not seen," sustained them under every trial. Animated by a lively hope, they regarded the afflictions they endured but light and momentary, and as working out for them "a far more exceeding and eternal weight of glory." With this armour they triumphed even in death, and were crowned with glory.

The exhortation left for us, is, to be followers of them, "who through faith and patience inherit the promises." Patience in well-doing worketh experience, and experience hope; but hope gives us no absolute certainty of salvation: And therefore it is great presumption to talk of security. Certainty, in whatever degree it may be supposed, can only relate to our present condition, which is enough to keep our minds easy and contented. Other certainty than this, might make us remiss: This may encourage us *to run with patience the race that is before us, and to labour in the Lord; knowing that our labour shall not be in vain.*

The Divine Institution and Perpetuity of the Christian Priesthood.

A

SERMON,

DELIVERED BEFORE THE

CONVENTION

OF THE

CLERGY AND LAY DELEGATES

OF THE

Episcopal Church

IN THE

STATE OF CONNECTICUT,

IN

CHRIST CHURCH, STRATFORD,

ON THE SECOND DAY OF JUNE, 1813:

OCCASIONED BY THE DEATH OF THE

Right Rev. ABRAHAM JARVIS, D. D.

Bishop of Connecticut.

By TILLOTSON BRONSON,

Principal of the Episcopal Academy.

[N]EW-HAVEN:

PRINTED BY OLIVER STEELE,

1813.

AT a Convention of the Protestant Episcopal Church of Connecticut, holden at Stratford, on the first Wednesday of June, 1813:

Resolved, That the Rev. Charles Seabury, and Mr. Charles Sigourney, return the thanks of this Convention, to the Rev. Tillotson Bronson, for his Sermon, delivered before them, at the opening of the session, and request a copy of the same for publication.

A true copy of record.

ASHBEL BALDWIN, *Secretary.*

SORROW IS BUT
THE GUEST
OF A NIGHT,
AND JOY
COMES IN THE
MORNING

SERMON.

IN the course of Divine Providence, that portion of the Church here assembled in convention, has been lately deprived of its visible head. Our late venerable Diocesan has received that summons, which all must obey, and is gone from this to the world of spirits.——His sacred office is vacant. He will no more preside in this body. His seat is left to be filled by another. Under the immediate view of such an event, it becomes all seriously to reflect on the ways of God, in his government of the Church, during its continuance in this transitory state.

Especially should we, my Brethren of the Clergy, be deeply reminded of the solemn vows we made at our ordination; and resolve before God to feed the flock committed to our care, with the sincere milk of his word; and neglect not *to stir up the gift that is in us, by the laying on of hands.** This gift many of you received through the instrumentality of those hands, which have been lately consigned to the tomb, and are mouldering into dust. Though they have ceased any more to perform the sacred rite, yet should they be active through you, in the spiritual work, to which you are called, in repairing the waste places of Zion. And that we all may be excited, in our several stations, understandingly to engage in this great

* 2 Tim. i. 6.

work, I propose calling your attention to the words of Inspiration recorded in

HEBREWS VII. 15th, 16th and 17th verses.

And it is yet far more evident, for that after the similitude of Melchisedec there ariseth another Priest, who is made, not after the law of a carnal commandment, but after the power of an endless life. For he testifieth, Thou art a Priest for ever, after the order of Melchisedec.

The prominent object discernible through the whole of this epistle is, to show, that the law of Moses, and consequently the Aaronic priesthood, were types and shadows of better and more enduring things to come, and that, of course, they were to be superseded and done away, when the Messiah, to whom they pointed, should appear in the flesh. And this seventh chapter is wholly dedicated to the Priesthood: in which the Apostle argues, that as Levi, when in the loins of his progenitor Abraham, paid tythes to Melchisedec, his priesthood must have been of a subordinate grade; for, says he, *without all contradiction, the less is blessed of the better.** He then proceeds to argue, from the uniform tenor of prophecy, that our Lord was to spring from the tribe of Judah; of which tribe there is no mention made, in the law, of any to serve at the altar: Consequently, as the Messiah was to be the great High Priest over all, the law, and all its appointments, must have been intended by divine wisdom to be temporary. To which argument he subjoins the text; *And it is yet far more evident; for that*, or rather, as it should have been rendered, *if, after the similitude of Melchisedec, there ariseth another Priest, who is made, not after the law of a carnal commandment, but after the power of an endless life.* If, from the constant testimony of prophecy, there was to arise another priesthood, from a source not noticed in the law, then certain it is, that those men made priests by the law, were not to have perpetual succession: there was to be a change both of the law, and of the priesthood; since both are intimately united. And that such is the language of prophecy, in the last words of the text, he cites the 110th Psalm; *Thou art a Priest for ever, after the order of Melchisedec.**

* Heb. vii. 7.

Who this Melchisedec was, commentators have not been agreed. But when we consider, that in the patriarchal state, the priesthood descended by primogeniture from father to son, the better opinion seems to be, that he was the nearest first-born from Adam; and thus the high priest over all. Perhaps he may have been the grandson of Noah. And when he met Abraham, and received tythes of him, he transferred his office to that patriarch, for temporary purposes; in whom, and his posterity, it was to continue, until He, who was the first-born of all things, the eternal Son of God, should come in the flesh, and visibly commence his everlasting Priesthood among men.

True it is, the Apostle tells us, he was *without father, without mother, without descent; having neither beginning of days, nor end of life.*† Yet the marginal rendering has it, *without pedigree:* "*That is,* (say the translators,) "the line of his family is not mentioned, neither his birth, nor his death."

If this gloss should not be deemed satisfactory, as a type of Christ, and holding the everlasting priesthood transmitted to him, to be handed to another, and thus never to have an end; all that is said of him, in the text rendering, is true. *Priest of the Most High God,*‡ he certainly was, as we are told in Genesis: and we have the authority of the Prophets and Apostles to determine, that Christ the Lord came into the world, *a Priest for ever, after the order of Melchisidec.*

The substance of the argument in this chapter, may then be thus summed up: The everlasting priesthood of Melchisedec was transferred, temporarily,

* Psalm cx. 4.

† Heb. vii. 3.

‡ Gen. xiv. 18.

from him to Abraham; thence to Levi, to Aaron and his sons; and so on, down to the time of Messiah, in whom it was reinvested, there to continue to the end of the world. When to this we add the words of our Lord to his Apostles, *As my Father hath sent me, so send I you,** we come to this important conclusion, on which I shall first enlarge,

I. That there always was, and ever will be, a visible priesthood, a divinely instituted order of men in the Church.

II. And since mere men *cannot continue, by reason of death,*† the office must be transmitted to ages and generations, by succession; for which God in his wisdom has made provision.

I. Every organized society of men, for whatever purpose intended, requires some to preside and govern, and others to obey. That the Church is such a society, is certain. Nor is it less clear, that the authority alone which institutes, can rightfully appoint the grades of office, and the manner in which they are to execute their powers. Such is the uniform understanding of all men. If then the Church be a divine institution, the Priesthood is equally so.

Let us then inquire, from the records of inspired truth, how this matter stands. On this point, the history of God's dispensations to men, will afford us the best lights from whence to reason. To this, of course, I shall confine myself, in discoursing on this head. God, having created man, breathed into him the breath of life, endowed him with a reasonable soul, capable of knowing and worshipping him, and invested him with immortality; he placed him in the blissful garden of Eden, where he held communion and converse with his Maker, and enjoyed the fruit of the tree of life. And had man continued faithful to the divine command, we have every reason to believe the whole race, in union and fellowship, would here have continued to partake of the divine presence, vis-

* John xx. 21.

† Heb. vii. 23.

Ecclesiastical, not as since

in realities. Here would

state without schisms and

one institution, the tree of

tween man and man, and

As Jesus was formed

all other creatures on earth

reign of all; and partaking

God; it was fitting God should

kind of society he was to

which it was to be preserved

children, for out first parents

church, or spiritual commu

head and governor. What

whether any was lodged

the Church, it is idle to inquire

has left us no hint on this

was short. Man rebelled.

A mediator became necessary

for man had lost the image

incapable of enjoying that

he was formed. Still he

may be restored to commu

ship with his Maker,

the task, became

brought man back to the

new erection of a Church

ings and ordinances,

Not indeed we find power

men to govern and administer

God's ministers, in sacred things

one, when schisms had arisen

ed, the Church was confined

Noah and his family were saved

But few centuries elapsed

consequences followed.

and set apart, by the supernatural

Then, and his family

and when their posterity had

was called to be a ruler and

and Aaron in sacred.

7

ially displayed, not as since, by signs and symbols, but in reality. Here would have been a blessed Church state, without schisms and divisions. Here was a divine institution, the tree of life, as a bond of union between man and man, and between God and man.

As man was formed with faculties far superior to all other creatures on earth; to be the lord and sovereign of all; and partaking of the spiritual nature of God; it was fitting, God should specially institute the kind of society he was to enjoy, and the manner in which it was to be preserved. This we have seen he did do, for our first parents; constituting them a church or spiritual community; himself being the head and governor. What kind of visible power, or whether any, was lodged with man, in this state of the Church, it is idle to inquire, since the word of God has left us no hint on this subject. Its continuance was short. Man rebelled. A new state followed. A mediator became necessary between God and man; for man had lost the image of God, and was become incapable of enjoying that church fellowship, for which he was formed. Still he was a social being—still he might be restored to communion with God, in fellowship with his brethren. The Son of God undertook the task, became surety for the atonement, and brought man back to his God. And how? By the new erection of a Church, bound together with holy rites and ordinances, with sacrifices and offerings. Now indeed we find power lodged in the hands of men to govern and administer. The patriarchs were God's ministers, in sacred things. And in process of time, when schisms had arisen, and corruption prevailed, the Church was confined to the Ark, in which Noah and his family were saved.

But few centuries elapsed, before the same dismal consequences followed. Abraham was now called, and set apart, by the superadded rite of circumcision. To him and his posterity the Church was confined. And when that posterity had become numerous, Moses was called to be a ruler and governor in civil matters, and Aaron in sacred. The priesthood was specially

8

arranged; and all the holy offices designated. High-Priest, Priest, and Levite, had their grades of power assigned. I need not stop here to prove, that all this was done by the immediate appointment of God. It is too plain in scripture to need illustration. It is what all acknowledge, who admit divine revelation. God was, then, the founder of the ancient Church of Israel. And nothing that he established, might be altered or abolished by men.

If such was his conduct towards men, before the coming of the Messiah, we might well argue that such it would be after his advent; for he is the same yesterday, to-day, and for ever—his counsels are everlasting—his Church must be always the same thing in essence, varying only in non-essentials, in external rites, or in extent. Was he once the founder, he must ever be so; and man has no right to do less or more in these matters, to add or to retrench. The bounds are set; and we must not think to pass them, but under the penalty of rebellion, the heinous sin of Korah.

What we thus may argue from the institution of the patriarchal and Jewish Church, we find actually confirmed by what the Son of God did, when he came in the flesh. For he appointed officers of different grades under himself; with different powers and functions, answering to those under the law of Moses. He left not this to be regulated by the wisdom, or caprice of men. No: We find the Twelve Apostles with one kind of office, and the Seventy with another subordinate; emanating from the same source, his own will. We find him instituting holy rites, as a bond of union to the Church, like those under the patriarchal and Mosaical state. And finally, when about to leave the world, he gave a solemn commission to the Apostles, investing them with supreme power in ample form, *As my Father hath sent me, even so send I you—Go ye into all the world, and preach the Gospel to every creature—Whose soever sins ye remit, they are remitted; and whose soever sins ye retain,*

9

*they are retained.** In pursuance of this high authority, they went forth and preached. They appointed others, as their Master had appointed them; and thus established the Church by divine power. What they established, man has no right to alter. Thus the whole tenor of Scripture, the history of all God's dispensations from beginning to end, conspires to prove that God is the founder of the Church. And all this is in perfect conformity with the reason of man, and the nature of the case.

But the divine institution of the Priesthood rests not alone on this argument. It results from the reason of the thing itself; from the end and design of the Church; and from the duties to be discharged by the sacred office. The ministers of Christ are styled *Embassadors for Christ.*† Now none but the Sovereign, who sends, and in whose name they act, has a right to appoint embassadors. They are to publish and proclaim to sinful men, terms of peace and reconciliation with God; and therefore must have authority from him so to do. They are to apply, in his name, the seals of the covenant of grace, and therefore must be empowered by him, or their acts cannot be authentic. Without such commission, they would be forgeries of the name and authority of God. The Church is designed to promote spiritual harmony and union between man and man, and between man and his Maker—to be the means of nourishing the spiritual life of the soul, by the instrumentality of sacred rites and ordinances: And surely, none save God has a right to appoint such ordinances, and authorize those who are to administer them.

The gifts and graces of his Holy Spirit are in his own keeping, and he may dispense them as he will. Man has no choice, but to comply with the terms, and use the appointed means, in faith unfeigned: and God will own and bless his appointments, with growth in grace, and in holiness of life. In short, visible external ordinances, as means of grace, di-

* John xx. 21, 23. Mark xvi. 16.
† 2 Cor. v. 20.

B

vinely appointed, obviously imply the divine appointment of those who are to administer. Divine institutions administered by the authority of man, is an absurdity; or rather, perhaps we may say, an impossibility. So far as they are of man, they are not from God; and therefore not to be styled divine. So long as we continue in the present state, external ordinances are congenial to our nature. Consisting of soul and body, both are dependent on God for support. Both are therefore bound to express that dependence; to be employed in his service, in rendering praise to his name. This the body can do only by external acts; those acts which God has appointed under the administration of his Church, in which the Priesthood takes an essential part.

But whatever may be thought of the reason of the thing, certain it is, all states of religion, authorized by God, have contained visible ordinances. The tree of life in Paradise, sacrifice with the patriarchs and Israelites, and the eucharist under the Gospel, are so many examples of what is here advanced. Not that we are to believe divine ordinances operate any other way, than by being accompanied with faith in the receiver; but that thus God has chosen to communicate the influences of his Holy Spirit; to plant and nourish the seeds of divine grace in the heart; and to support the spiritual life of the soul. Such appears to be his will, by his having always authorized external ordinances; and with this we should be satisfied. And thus, in every view, a divinely instituted Priesthood solicits our faith.

II. We are now to show, that as mere men cannot continue, by reason of death, God, in his wisdom, has provided for the transmission of the office, by succession from generation to generation.

As, under the former head, we have argued the divine origin of the Priesthood, from that of the Church; so here, from the perpetuity of the Church, we may, with equal security, argue a succession in the ministry. Men are evanescent beings, in regard to the things of time, the present state of the Church.

They come up here for a short time, and disappear. One generation flies away, and another takes its place. If, then, God's institutions are perpetual, he must have provided for transmitting the sacred office from one to another. It is not reasonable to think, he should have left a thing of so much importance, to be ordered by the caprices of men. It has been already remarked, that the Church was always the same in substance, varying only in non-essential forms, in the manner of ordinances, and in the succession of the priesthood. It began in Paradise—was not demolished by the fall. It continued with the patriarchs—rode above the flood with Noah—Under Abraham, Moses and the law, underwent little other change, than a transfer of the Priesthood from the first-born to a succession, by immediate designation in the tribe of Levi; and for the High-Priesthood, to Aaron and his sons. And when Christ came, little more was done, than to open its doors to all nations.

Had we then no assurance that it should not fail, we well might argue it would not, but with the world itself. Having survived so many changes, well might we conclude it was founded on a rock sure and stedfast.

To this effect, the Prophets of the Old Testament are full of predictions, when they speak of the Kingship of Messiah, of the extent and duration of his kingdom. To David was the promise made, that his royal house should not fail for ever; that he *should not want a Man to sit on his throne*;* which can be understood of no other than Christ the Saviour; who, in the line of his human nature, was descended of David, and now reigns over his Church. Isaiah, in predicting his birth, says, *His name shall be called Wonderful, Counsellor, the mighty God, the everlasting Father, the Prince of Peace. Of the increase of his government and peace, there shall be no end, upon the throne of David, and upon his kingdom, to order it, and to establish it, with justice, and with judgment, from henceforth even for ever.*† And the prophet Daniel concludes the re-

* 1 Kings ix. 5.

† Isaiah ix. 6, 7.

markable vision, which he had, of the four great beasts, prefiguring all the great temporal Kingdoms of the world, with the assurance, that *the Kingdom and dominion, and the greatness of the Kingdom, under the whole heaven, shall be given to the Saints of the Most High; whose Kingdom is an everlasting Kingdom; and all dominions shall serve and obey him.** With such predictions as these before us, from the Spirit of eternal truth, well may we look forward to the universal triumph of the Gospel over the whole earth. We know, that since the gate of Zion has been set open to all nations; since the Church of God has been offered to the Gentiles, under the visible reign of Messiah, *the mountain of the Lord's house has been established in the tops of the mountains, and all nations have flowed into it.*† It has increased, it is increasing, and will continue to increase, until it embrace the whole progeny of Adam. Living in the age we do, at this distance of time from the commencement of the Church Christian; witnessing the conflicts she has had to encounter, from open foes without, and traitors within, corrupting the pure fountain of truth; yet still triumphant, and spreading wide her tent in the four quarters of the globe; offering the bread of life to perishing Heathens; we may well adopt the glowing language of an eminent Father of the Church, and triumphantly say, "Invaded by war, she conquers.—Surrounded "with treason, she extricates herself.—Corrupted, "she recovers, and shines the brighter.—Wounded, "she falls not under her wounds.—Tossed by the "waves, she sinks not.—Beaten by the storm, she suf-"fers not shipwreck.—Waxing in years, she decay-"eth not.—She wrestles, and is not vanquished."‡

In the faithful page of History, we have seen the Church survive the persecutions of Pagan Rome, extricate herself from numerous early heresies, rise in renewed splendor from the corruptions of papal Rome; and is at this hour rapidly extending herself among

* Daniel vii. 27.

† Isaiah ii. 2.

‡ St. Chrysostom.

the Heathens. Shall we the
shake off the heresies and the
be infested, and shine with
ness in the latter day glory
his word shall not fail. He
of men to praise him; and
shall serve him.* He will
promise is, On this rock
and the gates of hell shall
his promises are yea and Amen.
What he promises he is able
faileth not.

Thus to one declaration
more certainly announced
universality of the Church
wherever human nature is
time. When such glorious
the Church, they must be
founded by God, which we
cidedly divinely instituted
they rest assured, God in his
mission. And this could be
succession of miracles, to
procurement, or by an order
age, by the hand of man
it, too common, would
amount to no evidence
hand of man, so far as we
consistent with the nature
we have ample testimony
which he who remained
the world, to make pro
about returning to his Father
We have seen, As my Fa
And how did his Father
to send others, or he would
they be sent them as emb
meet unto the glad tidings

* Psalm lxxxii 15
† Isaiah xiii. 28
‡ Mat. xvi. 18

the Heathens. Shall we then doubt but that she will shake off the heresies and divisions, with which she is now infested, and shine with more than pristine brightness, in the latter day glory? God has promised, and his word shall not fail. He will cause *even the wrath of man to praise him; and the remainder thereof he will restrain.** *He will do all his pleasure.*† His promise is, *On this rock I will build my Church, and the gates of hell shall not prevail against it.*‡ All his promises are yea and Amen; for he changeth not. What he promises he is able to fulfil, and his truth faileth not.

Thus no one declaration in the word of God, is more certainly announced, than the perpetuity and universality of the Church: that it shall spread wherever human nature is found, and end only with time. When such glorious things are predicted of the Church, they must be understood of that society founded by God, which we have seen, of necessity, includes a divinely instituted Priesthood. For this we may rest assured, God, in his wisdom, has made provision. And this could be done only by a constant succession of miracles, to attest the divinity of the appointment; or by an orderly transmission from age to age, by the hand of man. But miracles, by becoming too common, would cease to be miracles, and amount to no evidence. Succession therefore by the hand of man, so far as we can see, is the only mode consistent with the nature of the case. And of this we have ample testimony in the word of God.

When he who *remaineth a Priest forever*, came into the world, to make propitiation for sin, and was about returning to his Father, he said to his Apostles, as we have seen, *As my Father hath sent me, so send I you.* And how did his Father send him? Certainly to send others, or he would not have sent them.—Certainly he sent them as embassadors in his name, to proclaim the glad tidings of the Gospel, or he would

* Psalm lxxvi. 10.

† Isaiah xliv. 28.

‡ Mat. xvi. 18.

not have said to them, *Go ye into all the world, and preach the Gospel to every creature*—Certainly to prescribe the terms of Salvation, or he would not have said to them, *He that believeth and is baptized, shall be saved, but he that believeth not, shall be damned*—Certainly, as Priests to apply the seals of the covenant of grace and pardon, or he would not have said to them, *Whosesoever sins ye remit, they are remitted, and whosesoever sins ye retain, they are retained*—Certainly to send others, and thus continue the succession, or he would not have sent them, as he was himself sent.

But here a question has been raised. Were all, whom he and the Apostles sent, of the same grade? Were all equally empowered to send others? It is readily admitted, that so far as the words of the commission go, there is no distinction. But in the subsequent history and writings of the Apostles, we find a wide distinction: we find them establishing different grades in the Priesthood. Some had power to administer the seals of the Covenant, Baptism and the Eucharist; and *to feed the flock of God,** without commission to send others: while some, as Timothy and Titus, are treated as having authority to appoint others; to ordain and govern the *Elders* of the Church. Surely the Apostles understood their own commission. What they did in this matter, they did by divine warrant; and therefore it is of equal authority, with what was done and ordered by Christ himself.

To this we may add, that all primitive Christianity, all those who had the best means of knowing what was the apostolical practice, so understood, and so practised. They, who at first were styled Apostles, and afterwards Bishops, and they only, ordained. And this continued to be the faith and practice of all, claiming to be Christians, until quite modern times. With such evidence, reasonable and well informed minds should be satisfied.

Thus does it appear, that God, in his wisdom, has made provision for the continuance of his Church, and of a divinely instituted Ministry, that *he may gather*

* 1 Peter v. 2.

*together in one, all things in Christ, both which are in heaven, and which are on earth.**—And to *purify unto himself a peculiar people, zealous of good works.*† Men may die, but the sacred office lives. *The foundation standeth sure.—The Lord knoweth them that are his.*‡ Under the protection of his Providence, and by the guidance of his Holy Spirit, operating on the hearts of men, the Church has continued, and shall continue to flourish, until it embrace all nations; until all shall be converted, not in outward profession only, but in truth and spirit; until all shall be truly united unto Christ, by the renewal of the heart, in righteousness, and holiness of life; until with all, *old things shall be done away, and all things become new*;‖ until the image of God, in which man was created, be restored in all men. Then shall commence the latter day glory, when all shall "hold the faith in unity of spirit, and in the bond of peace;" when, in the animated language of prophecy, *the wolf shall dwell with the lamb, and the leopard shall lie down with the kid.—And they shall not hurt, nor destroy, in all God's holy mountain; for the earth shall be full of the knowledge of the Lord, as the waters cover the sea.*§

To this glorious state, the transpiring events of a changing world are hastening the Church. Let no one then be shaken in his faith, but hold fast his profession unto the end. Under such a view as we have taken of the perpetuity of the Church, and its Ministry, we have abundant cause for exultation and triumph. For although our earthly head is removed from us, yet are we sure that the great Head over all, remaineth in heaven, and will do his pleasure; will take care of his flock, who put their trust in him, and remain stedfast in their faith. As men, we are, by this providence, reminded of our own mortality, and urged to prepare for our departure from this militant state, to that which is triumphant: but as members of the Church, our

* Eph. i. 10.

† Tit. ii. 14.

‡ 2 Tim. ii. 19.

‖ 2 Cor. v. 17.

§ Isaiah xi. 6, 9.

minds should be led to a wider view of God's ways, in his kingdom of grace; that we may be confirmed and built up in our holy faith; and thus bring forth its fruits, in unity and love unfeigned.

Here I might conclude, were it not that respect for the memory of our deceased Diocesan, and the office he sustained, require, on the present occasion, some notice of his personal character.

In common instances of mortality, such notices may justly be suspected of flattery to the living. But when we consider that he, who is to be our present subject, held the highest office in the Church, and was authorised, according to divine appointment, to ordain and send labourers into the Vineyard of Christ, it would betray a censurable disregard of propriety, not to commemorate his virtues. On the contrary, that, wherein he was worthy of imitation, should be noticed, in order that, being dead, he may yet speak, and instruct the flock, over which he presided.

The life of a clergyman is, ordinarily, too tranquil and uniform, to afford incidents sufficiently interesting for historical remark. But were it otherwise, want of authentic documents, relative to the Bishop's early life, preclude my undertaking the task. And during the time he held the responsible office, to which he was invited by the votes of his brethren, to much the greater part of my hearers, his history is well known. Suffice it, then, that I attempt a sketch of his character.

To those who were intimately acquainted with Bishop Jarvis, it is well known, he possessed a good share of common human science, acquired in his youth; to which he added, what was of more importance in his station, as a Minister of Christ, a copious fund of theological knowledge. Few eminent divines of the Church of England, who lived and wrote in the last and preceding centuries, escaped his reading. He read them, not as matter of amusement, but he thoroughly studied, and digested their matter. In such a school, he was deeply impressed with all the great and fundamental Doctrines of Divine Truth—

the fall and original corruption of man—his consequent need of a Saviour, and the operations of divine grace, to revive the image of God in the soul, and quicken the spiritual life, were, with him, first principles in Christian theology. To these he added a Trinity of persons in the Godhead, and the divine institution of the Church, its Ministers and Ordinances, as means of grace. These he firmly believed were the doctrines of the Bible, of primitive Christianity, and of the early reformers.

Thus settled in his faith, he listened not to novelties. He believed that whatever was new in Divinity, was, for that very reason, false. To improvements in human science, he was a friend: while he believed that God had long since revealed every thing necessary for man to know, believe, and do, in order to obtain salvation. Hence, nothing new was to be expected in theology. This rendered him an undeviating advocate for primitive usage and discipline in the Church. This he was, to such a degree, as to be thought by some, too unyielding, too little disposed to accommodate the feelings of others. But those who knew him well, were convinced, it was the pure effect of principle, and a sense of duty. He well knew the pernicious consequences of needless innovation, and the imposing air with which novelty too often captivates the unwary; and therefore wished to meet them in the threshold, and shut them out of the Church.

The truth was, he deliberated long and thoroughly, before he formed opinions; and when they were formed, they became principles of action, and were not readily changed. This is a trait of character, that is of great worth, in the present state of the world, when innovations in civil polity are attempting to make their way into the Church of God. At such a time, persevering decision of character is of eminent use, to preserve order and regularity, and hence peace on earth, and good will to men. Such, in the fullest sense of the word, was the character of Bishop Jarvis. His object, when settled, was ever in view. It was steadily pursued in his conduct. Convinced of its worth and

importance, and trusting in the wisdom of Providence, he ever went on, undismayed by difficulties and obstructions that might come in his way.

He entertained a becoming sense of the dignity of the clerical character, and studied to promote it, in his words, in his actions, and in the measures he proposed and followed. He was indignant at meanness; at any thing which might lower the sacred office, in the view of the world. As the embassadors of the most high God, it was his sentiment, that they should respect themselves; and so conduct, that they might command the respect of others.

As a man, his talents were rather solid than showy. His discourses in the pulpit were marked by good sense and sound divinity, rather than fine conceits, or tricks of rhetoric. And as was his matter, so his manner of delivery—always grave, solemn, earnest, and frequently impressive, in a high degree. In proof of this, permit me to cite his address delivered to this body, at its last meeting. "As it hath pleased God "to continue my life to a considerable length beyond "that of my predecessor, that single reflection is an "ample monitor to me, to look forward to an approach-"ing period, which, as it respects myself, to human "view, cannot be far distant. Under such impres-"sions, I must be sensible of increasing uncertainty "of meeting you hereafter, in your future conven-"tions."

The venerable appearance, the grave and solemn manner, in which these reflections were delivered, can but be remembered; and I trust, long will be remembered, by all who were present; especially our clerical brethren. They contain a specimen of that *sound speech, which cannot be condemned.** And it hath pleased God, that they should be prophetic. He has never had another opportunity of meeting the convention.

Though the Bishop, according to the direction of an Apostle, *in doctrine, showed uncorruptness, gravity,*

* Tit. ii. 8.

19

and sincerity,† both in public and private, in the Church, and in the friendly circle; yet was he affable, polite, and ready to converse on common topics, according to his company, and suited to occasions.— We, my brethren of the clergy, can witness, that he was always fond of seeing us at his house; that we were there hospitably entertained. Few men enjoyed society more than he. His hours were distributed, as we well know, between domestic concerns, conversation, study, and acts of piety. Fond of the family circle, formal visits were unfrequent. Correct in matters of economy, he was domestic in his manners. He was resigned to the will of Providence; patient under afflictions, of which he had his share in life; nor too much elated by prosperity; always preserving a well tempered equanimity. In fine, as a clergyman, he was correct in his sentiments; as a member of society, a well wisher to its order and peace. A tender husband, and an affectionate parent. Thus he lived, and at length, in a good old age, he has gone to that world, from whence none return.

May we, then, preserve his memory in our minds, cherish his virtues in our hearts, and imitate them in our lives. May the Spirit of truth, the Holy Ghost the Comforter, sanctify all our affections, preside in our councils, and, in due time, direct our choice to a suitable character, to fill the sacred office. May unanimity and harmony prevail, that this Church may be reorganized, and built up, in purity of faith, in holiness of conversation, and ever remain an ornament to the Church universal.

† Tit. ii. 7.

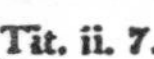

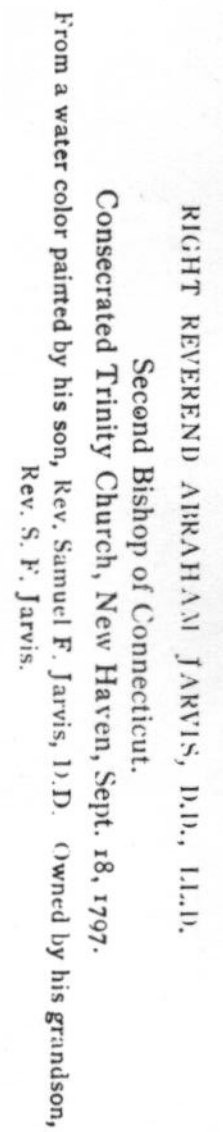

RIGHT REVEREND ABRAHAM JARVIS, D.D., LL.D.

Second Bishop of Connecticut.

Consecrated Trinity Church, New Haven, Sept. 18, 1797.

From a water color painted by his son, Rev. Samuel F. Jarvis, D.D. Owned by his grandson, Rev. S. F. Jarvis.

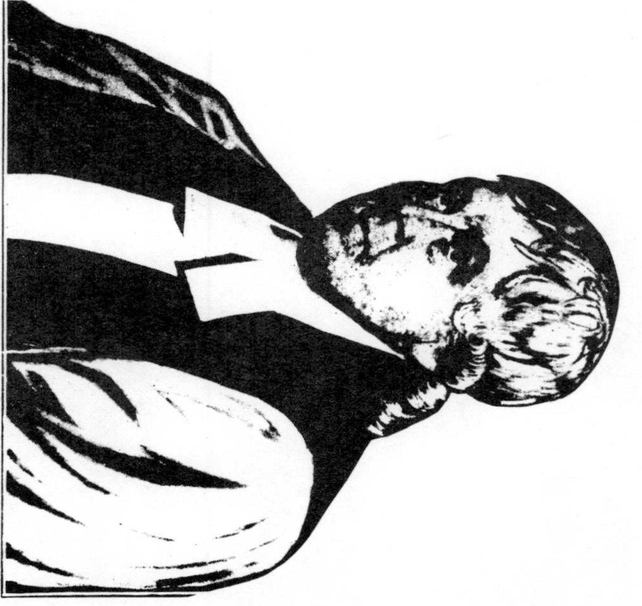

RIGHT REVEREND ABRAHAM JARVIS, D.D., LL.D.

Second Bishop of Connecticut.

Consecrated Trinity Church, New Haven, Sept. 18, 1797.

From a water color painted by his son, Rev. Samuel F. Jarvis, D.D. Owned by his grandson, Rev. S. F. Jarvis.